Privatisation Policy and Performance

International perspectives

Edited by
P. Cook and C. Kirkpatrick

PRENTICE HALL
HARVESTER WHEATSHEAF

New York · London · Toronto · Sydney · Tokyo · Singapore

First published 1995 by
Prentice Hall/Harvester Wheatsheaf
Campus 400, Maylands Avenue
Hemel Hempstead
Hertfordshire, HP2 7EZ
A division of
Simon & Schuster International Group

Typeset in 10/12 pt Times
by Vision Typesetting, Manchester

Printed and bound in Great Britain by
T.J. Press (Padstow) Ltd

Library of Congress Cataloging-in-Publication data

Privatisation policy and performance: international perspectives / edited by P. Cook and C. Kirkpatrick.
p. cm.
Includes bibliographical references and index.
ISBN 0-13-434341-7
1. Privatization–Congresses. 2. Privatization–Developing countries–Congresses. 3. Mixed economy–Congresses. I. Cook, Paul, 1944– . II. Kirkpatrick, C. H. (Colin H.), 1944– .
HD3850 P736 1995
338.9–dc20 94-32776
CIP

British Library Cataloguing in Publication Data

A catalogue record for this book is available from the British Library

ISBN 0-13-434341-7 (pbk)

2 3 4 5 99 98 97 96 95

Contents

Part III Developing countries' experience

Contributors

Colin Barnes is a business economist and Associate of Warwick Research Institute at the University of Warwick.

Dieter Bös is Professor of Economics at the Institute of Economics, University of Bonn, Germany.

Jozef M. van Brabant is Principal Economic Affairs Officer at the Department of International Economic and Social Information and Policy Analysis, Macroeconomic and Social Policy Analysis, United Nations.

Paul Cook is Senior Lecturer in Economics at the School of Economic Studies, University of Manchester.

Jean-Marc Fontaine is Maître de Conférences and Director of Centre de Recherche Économique at the Institut d'Étude du Développement Économique et Social, Université Panthéon-Sorbonne, Paris.

Vincent Geronimi is Maître de Conférences at the Université Versailles-Saint Quentin, France.

Kwame Sundaram Jomo is Professor, Faculty of Economics and Administration, at the University of Malaya, Kuala Lumpur, Malaysia.

Cevat Karatas is Associate Professor of Development Economics at Boğaziçi University, Turkey.

Gunter Kayser is Research Director at the Institut für Mittelstandsforschung (Research Institute on Small and Medium-sized Enterprises), Bonn.

Colin Kirkpatrick is Professor of Development Economics at the Development and Project Planning Centre, University of Bradford.

Sir James McKinnon is former Director of the Office of Gas Supply (OFGAS).

Frederick Nixson is a Reader in Economics at the School of Economic Studies, University of Manchester.

Tony Plumbe is a Lecturer at the Development and Project Planning Centre, University of Bradford.

David Potts is a Lecturer at the Development and Project Planning Centre, University of Bradford.

Gerd Schwartz is an economist at the Fiscal Affairs Department, International Monetary Fund.

John Weiss is a Senior Lecturer at the Development and Project Planning Centre, University of Bradford.

Michael Yaffey is a Reader at the Development and Project Planning Centre, University of Bradford.

Ralph A. Young is a Lecturer in the Department of Government, University of Manchester.

Preface

The 1980s was a decade in which privatisation became one of the most significant policy ingredients in the wave of market reforms which swept over the global economy. Few economies were left unaffected as governments around the world initiated a variety of privatisation measures. The motives for pursuing privatisation varied between countries and have altered over time. Similarly, experience has differed in the extent to which privatisation has been implemented and in performance results.

After more than a decade of privatisation, it is opportune to evaluate the outcomes and to address the lessons of experience. These are the issues addressed in this volume. Part I offers an overview of privatisation policy and experience and presents evidence of the differing approaches and results in both transitional and developing economies. The following parts provide detailed country studies. Part II focuses on transitional economies and Part III concentrates on performance in developing countries, with examples from Asia, Latin America, and sub-Saharan Africa. The majority of the chapters in this volume were originally presented and discussed at a conference on Privatisation and Performance: International Perspectives held at the Development and Project Planning Centre, University of Bradford in March 1992. The conference was a successor to an earlier conference on Privatisation in Developing Countries, held at the University of Manchester, the proceedings of which were published in P. Cook and C. Kirkpatrick (eds), *Privatisation in Less Developed Countries*, Harvester Wheatsheaf, 1988.

Financial support for the conference from which this volume has emerged was provided by the Nuffield Foundation and The British Council. The book is in turn part of the work of the Bradford and Manchester Privatisation and Enterprise Policy Research Programme which is co-ordinated by the editors.

The manuscript has been prepared at the Development and Project Planning Centre by Pearl Golden who, with her usual good humour, has overcome the many difficulties of working with two editors and multiple authors. We are grateful to her for maintaining the momentum of the project by her gentle but persistent pressure on the editors to complete the manuscript on schedule.

PART I

Overview

1

Privatisation policy and performance

Paul Cook and Colin Kirkpatrick

1.1 Introduction

Privatisation has been a key element in the ascendance of the new market orthodoxy since the 1970s, and has been at the forefront of economic policy debates in all parts of the world. The international wave of privatisation began in the United Kingdom, and thereafter rapidly spread to other industrial countries. The process of transferring public enterprises to private ownership began more slowly in the developing countries, but the pace appears to have accelerated in the later years of the decade, and has continued during the 1990s. The other group of countries that has contributed significantly to privatisation has been the previously socialist countries, now in transition, with the largest share accounted for by the Eastern European economies.

The policy objectives and motives for privatisation varied between countries and have altered with time. In the case of the industrialised countries in the early 1980s, it could be argued that the dominant motive was an ideological one, with issues of economic efficiency assuming a significantly less important role (Cook and Kirkpatrick, 1988).

For the developing countries, privatisation was linked with the macroeconomic burden of the public enterprise sector. Public enterprises were seen as an important contributory factor to mounting fiscal imbalances. Financial support for public enterprises reduced the funds available for social services, crowded out private sector borrowing and undermined the development of the private sector. In addition, the fact that by the late 1970s public enterprises accounted for one-third of all international borrowing by developing countries was a source of concern for the principal international lending agencies (World Bank, 1980). The International Monetary Fund, in particular, issued a series of research papers that examined the fiscal consequences of privatisation (Hemming and Mansoor, 1988; Mansoor, 1988). The World Bank also came to see privatisation as an important policy instrument for reducing the drag of the public enterprise sector on the fiscal budget, although the emphasis on privatisation, as distinct from public enterprise reform, only became evident in Bank lending conditionality in the later part of the 1980s.

In the ex-socialist countries privatisation has been viewed as an integral element in the process of transition from a centrally planned to a market-oriented economy, although the contribution of privatisation to the move towards a market economy has varied. In the highly centralised states in Eastern Europe and the former Soviet Union, where the state sector had accounted for between 65 and 95 per cent of gross domestic product (GDP), privatisation has been seen as a means of creating a private sector economy (Schwartz, this volume). In contrast, in many of the Asian transitional economies, where the non-state sector remained a significant component of GDP throughout the centrally planned period, privatisation has been viewed as a means of developing and strengthening the private sector (Cook and Kirkpatrick, 1994).

After more than a decade of privatisation in countries around the world, it is opportune to take stock of the experience so far. Here, we consider four questions. First, what has been happening? In 1988 we could argue that the prospects of widespread privatisation in the developing countries were limited, and the early evidence on the numbers of privatisations carried out appeared to be consistent with this view (Cook and Kirkpatrick, 1988). This is no longer the case; privatisation has become a global phenomenon, although the distribution of privatisation activity continues to be geographically uneven. Second, how is privatisation happening? Privatisation can be undertaken in a number of different ways, and the range and sophistication of the methods employed have increased steadily with the international transfer of knowledge and experience of privatisation. Third, what have been the results of privatisation? Has privatisation improved enterprise performance, and more generally, has economic welfare been increased? Finally, what policy lessons can be learned from the privatisation experience so far? These are some of the issues addressed in the rest of this chapter. The chapter is divided into five sections. The second section reviews the level and pattern of privatisation activity globally, drawing attention particularly to the differences in regional experience. The third section concentrates on the various methods of privatisation that have been used, and the sources of funding of divestiture sales. The fourth section examines the impact of privatisation in terms of various performance indicators, while the final section contains a summary and concluding comments.

1.2 The extent and pattern of privatisation

The first inventory of privatisation on a worldwide scale was published in 1988 (Candoy-Sekse and Palmer, 1988). This survey reported on the level of privatisation planning and implementation in eighty-three countries, and although the information that was collected was imperfect, it did provide the basis for drawing a number of general conclusions.

Most privatisation, in terms of number and value of sales, was taking place in the industrialised countries and a small number of developing countries. Prominent in the former category were the United Kingdom, Canada, France, Spain and Italy; in the latter group, the main countries were Chile, Jamaica, Argentina, Brazil, Malaysia, Mexico and Sri Lanka. In terms of the number as opposed to value of sales, the African economies of Côte d'Ivoire, Guinea and Togo were also actively pursuing privatisation programmes. However, for most developing countries, the plans for privatisation greatly outweighed their implementation.

Both the enthusiasm for, and ability to implement, privatisation have increased significantly over the past five years. Tables 1.1 and 1.2 show the level of privatisation transactions over the period 1988 to 1992. Industrialised country sales amounted to $36.8 billion in 1988, which represented 94 per cent of worldwide transactions. Privatisation transactions in Japan accounted for over two-thirds of industrial country sales. The share of industrialised countries in worldwide privatisations fell to 58 per cent in 1992, although the worldwide figures exclude over 11,000 privatisations which occurred in the former East Germany between 1990 and the end of 1992 (Bös and Kayser, this volume).

The proceeds from major sales of public enterprises in developing countries rose from just over $2 billion in 1988 to almost $20 billion in 1992. The developing countries' share of world privatisation sales rose steadily each year from 6 per cent in 1988 to 42 per cent in 1992, and averaged 26 per cent over 1988–92. The sharpest increase occurred in the South American economies, whose share rose from 6 per cent in 1988 to 33 per cent in 1992. In contrast, privatisation in sub-Saharan Africa has been relatively small as compared to

Table 1.1 Value of privatisation transactions (US$m.)

	1988	1989	1990	1991	1992	1988–92
Industrialised countries	36,868	20,162	19,176	32,304	26,605	135,115
of which:						
Europe	10,656	19,251	18,186	29,971	24,091	102,155
Asia/Pacific	24,250	87	–	1,620	1,297	27,254
North America	1,962	824	990	713	1,217	5,706
Developing countries	2,362	4,470	6,094	15,648	19,485	48,059
of which:						
Africa (inc. South Africa)	8	1,435	25	–	–	1,468
Asia/Pacific	–	2,550	1,430	865	4,476	9,321
South America and Caribbean	2,354	485	4,639	14,783	15,009	37,270
Worldwide (exc. Eastern Europe)	39,230	24,632	25,270	47,952	46,090	183,174
Eastern Europe	–	130	64	530	1,565	2,289

Source: Adapted from *Privatisation Yearbook* (various issues), Privatisation International Ltd, London.

Table 1.2 Percentage of privatisation by value

	1988	1989	1990	1991	1992	1988–92
Worldwide excluding Eastern Europe	100	100	100	100	100	100
Industrialised countries	94	82	76	67	58	74
of which:						
Europe	27	78	72	63	52	56
Asia/Pacific	62	1	–	3	3	15
North America	5	3	4	1	3	3
Developing countries	6	18	24	33	42	26
of which:						
Africa[a]	–	6	–	–	–	1
Asia/Pacific	–	10	6	2	9	5
South America and Caribbean	6	2	18	31	33	20

Note: [a]Includes South Africa; sales of less than 1% are not shown.

Source: Adapted from *Privatisation Yearbook* (various issues), Privatisation International Ltd, London.

South America and Asia, and is largely accounted for by transactions in South Africa in the final years of the 1980s.

Within each region, privatisation has continued to be concentrated among a few countries. Within the Western European economies, privatisation of public enterprises in the UK accounted for three-quarters of the value of transactions. Similarly, within a given year, individual country sales have often dominated the regional picture, as, for example, with Japan's single transaction of public assets which accounted for a large share of industrialised countries' privatisations in 1988.

The concentration of privatisation activity is particularly pronounced within the developing countries' regions. In Latin America, Chile, Mexico, Argentina and Brazil make up the bulk of activity (see Table 1.3). In sub-Saharan Africa, six countries – Benin, Ghana, Guinea, Mozambique, Nigeria and Senegal – account for two-thirds of the divestitures (see Table 1.4). However, the number of divestitures overstates the extent of privatisation since larger enterprises which represent the bulk of public assets have generally not been privatised.

The developing countries of Asia accounted for 5 per cent of worldwide privatisation sales during the late 1980s (see Table 1.2). In Singapore and Malaysia, Privatisation Committees were established in the mid-1980s, and there has been considerable divestiture in both countries. In Malaysia, much of the privatisation has been in the services sector (Jomo, this volume) while in Singapore, government shareholdings have been substantially reduced in a wide range of companies and statutory boards, including ship repairs, printing, banking, shipping, and airlines. Privatisation in the other ASEAN countries has been less significant in scale, although deregulation has been pursued with some vigour in certain sectors, as for example, in transport in Indonesia (Ng and Toh, 1992; Plumbe, this volume).

In South Asia, both Bangladesh and Pakistan have implemented privatisation

Table 1.3 Privatisation in selected Latin American countries during the 1980s and 1990s

Country	Number of privatised firms	Amount of sales (US$m.)	Comment
Argentina	23	3,274	Drastic and abrupt privatisation of large public firms has started from 1990 on.
Bolivia	–	–	No action. There are 67 small public manufacturing firms. Big public mining firms have political and constitutional constraints.
Brazil	20	1,470	Slow process and much rhetoric up to 1990. A big steel and an electric-mechanic company shares sold at the end of 1991.
Chile	46	3,042	Deep and abrupt privatisation implemented during 1985–89. There remains only a few public firms.
Colombia	–	–	Colombian public firms are not important in the economy; privatisation is not an issue; reprivatisation of a large bankrupt Grupo Gran Colombiano.
Mexico	615	10,000	Gradual privatisation of small and medium firms during 1982–89. Large firms privatisation from 1990 on.
Peru	5	39	Only a few cases where plants were transferred to employees. Recent legislation allows privatisation of 23 of the 186 public firms; these 23 firms represent 2% of total public firms assets.
Venezuela	–	–	No action. Reprivatisation of hotels, sugar mills, cement companies is discussed.

Source: Meller (1992).

programmes, focused mainly on industrial enterprises. In Pakistan, seventy-one industrial units and two banks have been divested and the management of a further fifty-three industrial enterprises has been transferred to the private sector. Total employment in the affected enterprises has been around 80,000 (Kemal, 1993). In Bangladesh, much denationalisation took place in the mid-1980s, as a result of which the share of the public sector in industrial fixed assets was more than halved, to below 40 per cent as compared to more than 90 per cent in 1972 (Bhaskar, 1992). A second stage of privatisation was carried out in the second half of the 1980s, which in contrast to the first was much slower and also very different in character. Between 1987 and 1989 the government sold 49 per cent of the capital in nine big manufacturing enterprises (UNIDO, 1993).

Despite the increase in both the volume and value of privatisations in the last five years, sales in most countries, particularly the developing economies, have not been significant in terms of GDP. Adam, Cavendish and Mistry (1992: 39) reported the following findings from their study of privatisation in seven Commonwealth developing countries that were actively engaged in privatisation during the 1980s: 'as a proportion of GDP, only in Jamaica and Trinidad and Tobago has the accumulated sum of privatisation proceeds reached a proportion of GDP greater than 1% ... in Malaysia, a country popularly regarded as being

Table 1.4 Divestiture of public enterprises in sub-Saharan Africa, 1986–92

Percentage of enterprises divested	Number of enterprises before divestiture			
	0–50	51–100	101–200	More than 200
0–10	The Gambia Mauritania Rwanda Sierra Leone Zimbabwe	Burkina Faso Congo Uganda Zambia	Cameroon Côte d'Ivoire[a] Malawi[b]	Kenya Tanzania
11–25	Chad	Burundi Central African Republic	Madagascar	Ghana Mozambique
26–40	Niger		Guinea Nigeria	
41–60	Guinea-Bissau	Benin Mali Senegal Togo		

Note: Divestitures include partial sales, but not management contracts or leases.
[a]Data for 1989–92. Some thirty transactions in the 1980s are excluded.
[b]Total number of enterprises includes 121 statutory bodies and 18 commercial parastatals.
Source: World Bank (1994).

in the vanguard of developing-country privatisation, the volume of privatisation revenue remained miniscule during the 1980s'. Nor does it appear that privatisation sales have made a significant contribution to improving governments' fiscal position. For sub-Saharan Africa, it was found that: 'a preliminary assessment based on scattered evidence suggests that financial flows to public enterprises remain a large drag on the government budget and financial systems' (World Bank, 1994: 106). Pinheiro and Schneider (1994) show that revenue from privatisation sales in Argentina, Brazil, Chile and Mexico, countries which were in the top five in gross proceeds from privatisation during 1980–91 (World Bank, 1992), had an insignificant impact in terms of reducing government budget deficits.

Reference to the proceeds from sales alone may obscure the significance of the changes taking place in the public sector, particularly in Eastern Europe where privatisation is a part of the process of achieving greater private ownership in the transformation of these economies. Even in these countries, however, privatisation is unlikely to be the main vehicle for private sector growth in the longer term. Since the considerable political upheavals in the late 1980s, many of the transitional European economies have begun to see significant growth in their private sectors outside of privatisation. The privatisation that has occurred has been largely in the retail trade and service sectors and in most cases has not involved a transfer of ownership rights. Instead they have often involved short-term leasing arrangements from the state (Frydman and Rapaczynski, 1993). Transformation of the larger publicly owned enterprises in Eastern Europe and the former Soviet Union has proved to be difficult (Brabant, this volume). In cases where attempts have been made to privatise large enterprises, as for example in the waves of self-privatisation in which former managers took over enterprises in Hungary and Poland after 1989 without formal authorisation, the end result was a form of asset stripping. By the end of 1993, the private sector in Poland had grown to around 45 per cent of GDP and to 40 per cent in Hungary (IMF, 1993). This shows considerable growth in comparison to the pre-reform years and although it embodies privatisation, it does point to significant independent private sector development (Hare, 1993; Schwartz and Lopes, 1993).

Privatisation has also gathered momentum in the former Soviet Union. In Russia, large numbers of small enterprises owned by local authorities were privatised after 1992. A similar process has been occurring in other parts of the old Soviet Union. In Lithuania most small local government enterprises were privatised. The pace of privatisation has been slower in the Ukraine, Kzakhstan, Turkmenistan and the Kyrgyz Republic. A summary of privatisation in Eastern Europe and the ex-Soviet Union is presented in Table 1.5.

The process of privatisation in the former East Germany has been fundamentally different to the other economies in transition to a more market-oriented economic system (Schwartz, this volume). The West German economy was able to provide considerable financial support to enable a more rapid transformation of the state sector. The mandate of the Treuhandanstalt, the trust fund agency responsible for privatising enterprises in East Germany, is to restructure and transfer most state-owned assets to the private sector by 1995. So far, marked progress towards that aim has been achieved with respect to the service and industrial sectors. More than 20,000 retail outlets, restaurants and hotels were privatised within two years of unification and around 11,000 industrial enterprises were closed and transferred to the private sector (IMF, 1993). However, as Bös and Kayser (this volume) emphasise, the longer-term viability of the privatised enterprises will depend upon their capacity to develop their management skills and market competitiveness.

Privatisation in the former socialist developing countries more closely resembles the pattern and scale observed in other developing countries (Cook and Kirkpatrick, 1994). Of the Asian economies in transition, privatisation in Myanmar, Laos and Vietnam has occurred only to a limited extent. In Myanmar, privatisation has so far been confined to returning some previously nationalised sawmills and ricemills to their previous owners. A number of joint venture arrangements have also been entered into between state corporations and foreign and domestic entrepreneurs (Cook, 1994). As in the economies of Laos and Vietnam, leasing arrangements and contracting out have also been undertaken (Nixson, this volume). Privatisation of state enterprises has been accompanied by the introduction of measures aimed at encouraging private sector development (see Table 1.6).

Table 1.5 Privatisation in Eastern Europe and the former Soviet Union

	Large scale	Small scale
Albania	None	Mainly agricultural
Armenia	None	Mainly agricultural
Azarbaijan	None (to commence 1995)	None
Belarus	Planned	Little
Bulgaria	Enterprises being prepared	Little
Croatia	Identified enterprises for privatisation only	70% of small enterprises privatised
Czech Republic	2,300 firms privatised	26,000 units sold
Estonia	Little	40% small enterprises privatised
Georgia	None	Little
Hungary	Less than 20% large firms privatised	70% small scale privatised (of those identified for privatisation)
Kzakhstan	Little	Little
Kyrgyzstan	Little	Little
Latvia	<10% eligible enterprises privatised	30% small enterprises privatised
Lithuania	Over half eligible enterprises privatised	More than 80% of small enterprises privatised
Macedonia	None	70% of small enterprises privatised
Moldova	None	Little land privatisation
Poland	Planned	Most small enterprises privatised
Romania	70% from land privatised	Planned
Russian Federation	Over 1,200 enterprises privatised. More planned	Nearly 70% small enterprises privatised
Slovak Republic	Over 700 enterprises privatised	9,000 units sold
Slovenia	Planned	Planned
Tajikistan	Planned	Planned
Turkmenistan	Some leasing	Agricultural land privatised
Ukraine	Planned	Planned
Uzbekistan	None	Some housing, trade and retail services

Source: Compiled from EBRD (1993).

1.3 How privatisation is happening

After over a decade of experience with privatisation on a worldwide scale, it is apparent that a wide variety of methods has been used to implement divestiture. This experience has also revealed interesting features about the process of privatisation that may alter earlier notions as to the most appropriate way to implement privatisation programmes.

The evidence on the experience with privatisation over the last ten or so years is derived from numerous country case and sectoral studies. In addition, there is a limited number of larger, more comprehensive surveys that have systematically provided information concerning the various methods adopted to implement privatisation and the ways in which it has been financed. An earlier survey that significantly added to our knowledge of how privatisation was being implemented, particularly in the case of the developing countries, was the seven country studies by Adam *et al.* (1992). They provided a carefully

Table 1.6 Privatisation and public sector development in Asian transitional economies

Myanmar	Vietnam	Laos
Foreign Investment Law 1988: permitted foreign investment	1982 New economic orientation shifting emphasis from heavy to light industry	Recognised role of private sector in 1979
State Owned Enterprise Law 1989: permitted private sector competition	More substantial economic reforms after 1986 (Doi Moi)	1987 Promotion of private sector
Private Industrial Enterprise Law 1990	Plans for new Foreign Investment Law and EPZs	1988 Breaking of state monopoly over certain sectors
By 1991 1,428 companies and partnerships and branches of foreign companies had registered under the Myanmar Companies Act and Partnership Act		1989 Established Foreign Investment Management Committee
		1990 Adopted privatisation degree. Leasing of public enterprises. Set up National Chamber of Commerce
Chamber of Commerce co-opted by SLORC		1991 Published policy guidelines for Foreign Investment

Source: Cook and Kirkpatrick (1994).

documented set of case studies on the volume of privatisation, the financial and institutional arrangements that were used, and the resulting change in ownership patterns. The World Bank have also continued to document the progress of public enterprise reform and privatisation in a series of documents issued between 1988 and the present (World Bank, 1989, 1991, 1992). A recent study by UNCTAD (1993) also reports the findings of a worldwide review of the experiences with privatisation in over forty-six countries.

In the industrialised countries and in the UK in particular, experience reveals that privatisation has occurred principally among two groups of activities (Vickers and Yarrow, 1988). The first has concerned the extensive privatisation of activities that have had competitive markets to fit into. In the case of the UK, these were the early privatisations and occurred predominantly in housing and the industrial sector. The second consisted of large monopoly utilities, such as gas, electricity and water, which were either privatised as complete monopolies or with limited competition. In these activities external forms of regulation were introduced to form elements of surrogate competition and protect the public interest. The regulatory bodies will also encourage greater competition in the future (McKinnon, this volume).

In developing countries, when measured on the basis of the number of transactions, most privatisation is occurring in the manufacturing and service sectors. However, the sectoral order changes when the extent of privatisation is measured by the proceeds. This difference is illustrated in Table 1.7 which shows the number of privatisations between 1980–90 in seven countries. Commerce, manufacturing and services accounted for 64 per cent of privatisations, whereas Table 1.8 indicates that transport and communications contributed 61 per cent of privatisation sales receipts.

In Eastern Europe and the old Soviet Union most privatisation has occurred in the retail trade, service sector and small-scale manufacturing. Privatisation of larger-scale enterprises is hampered by the lack of development of a secure system of property rights, complex legal arrangements concerning ownership and market entry, and ill-defined incentive systems for enterprises under newer forms of ownership that result from schemes of mass privatisation and ownership transfer (Brabant, this volume; Cook and Kirkpatrick, 1995).

The ex-socialist economies have usually proceeded with the privatisation of small enterprises. These have consisted to a large extent of shops, restaurants, hotels and other small businesses. Preparation for the sale of enterprises involves valuation, usually with reference to discounted cash flow or replacement cost methods, and a range of legal and administrative procedures. For example, in Russia privatisation plans have to be approved by local, Soviet and worker collectives with final approval required from the Property Committee (EBRD, 1993). Most former Soviet Union republics outside Russia itself have only slowly begun to implement privatisation programmes.

Transferring large enterprises into the private sector is more difficult as it involves complex procedural arrangements and politically sensitive issues such as those relating to the welfare of the workforce. With the exception of Bulgaria,

Table 1.7 Number of privatisations by method and function of enterprise in selected developing countries[a]

			Private sale			Management contract and lease		
	Total	Public sale	Domestic	Foreign	Joint	Domestic	Foreign	Joint
Commerce, manufacturing and services	63	7	26	13	4	4	1	8
Finance and banking	6	4	1	1	0	0	0	0
Transport and communications	11	3	0	5	2	1	0	0
Water and energy	0	0	0	0	0	0	0	0
Regulatory and marketing	0	0	0	0	0	0	0	0
Agricultural	18	0	9	4	0	3	1	1
Total	98	14	36	23	6	8	2	9

Note: [a] Jamaica, Kenya, Malawi, Malaysia, Papua New Guinea, Sri Lanka, Trinidad and Tobago.
Source: Adam *et al.* (1992).

Table 1.8 Privatisation proceeds by country and function of enterprise (US$m.)[a]

	Total	Commerce, manufacturing and services	Finance and banking	Transport and communications	Water and energy	Regula; tory and marketing	Agriculture
Jamaica	230.7	104.2	16.1	110.3	0.0	0.0	0.0
Kenya	9.1	0.0	9.1	0.0	0.0	0.0	0.0
Malawi	7.2	5.4	0.0	0.0	0.0	0.0	1.8
Malaysia	180.3	18.4	8.7	133.5	0.0	0.0	19.5
Papua New Guinea	4.5	0.8	0.0	1.0	0.0	0.0	2.7
Sri Lanka	10.7	10.7	0.0	0.0	0.0	0.0	0.0
Trinidad and Tobago	94.5	6.3	3.3	84.9	0.0	0.0	0.0
Total	537.0	145.8	37.2	329.7	0.0	0.0	24.1
Average value	6.8	2.6	6.2	33.0	0.0	0.0	4.0

Note: [a]Excluding management contracts, leases and closures.

Source: Adam *et al.* (1992).

all Eastern European countries began privatisation of small enterprises soon after reforms were introduced.

Privatisation of larger-scale enterprises has proceeded furthest in the Czech Republic using a wide variety of methods consisting of vouchers, public auctions, tenders, foreign investment, dircct sales and free transfers to pension funds and municipalities (EBRD, 1993). However, despite the relatively few privatisations of large-scale enterprises in Eastern Europe and the former Soviet Union, most of these countries had by 1992 opted to pursue some kind of privatisation scheme (see Table 1.5).

Privatisations in infrastructure, including transport and telecommunications account for 35 per cent of the revenue generated from privatisation in developing countries in recent years. The industrial sector accounted for 20 per cent, and denationalisation and privatisation of financial institutions a further 27 per cent (Sader, 1993).

The main difference in the sectoral composition of privatisation between developing country regions is the absence of infrastructure in privatisation in sub-Saharan Africa. In this region, industry and services between 1988–92 accounted for most asset sales. In contrast, in South America, where the sectoral distribution of privatisation is similar to the global picture, infrastructure accounts for around 35 per cent and financial services for another 30 per cent. In East Asia and the Pacific area the percentage of infrastructure privatisation is even more dominant, rising to 80 per cent. As a general rule, privatisation of manufacturing appears relatively more important within the lower income economies of sub-Saharan Africa and South Asia and accounts for between 40–50 per cent of revenue.

Foreign investment has accounted for an increasing share of privatisation sales in less developed countries (LDCs). Sader (1993) estimates that while foreign investors participated in only seven operations in 1988, they were involved in 191 separate transactions in 1992, and in a total of 375 over the period 1988–92. A total of $18 billion in foreign exchange was generated as a result, contributing on average about 30 per cent of total revenue (see Table 1.9).

Foreign direct investment (FDI) has been the most common means of foreign participation in privatisation transactions in the developing countries. Of the total foreign exchange contribution to privatisation of $18.5 billion, some $14.5 billion (78 per cent) was in the form of FDI. Direct foreign investment in privatisation accounted for about 10 per cent of all FDI flows to LDCs over the 1988–92 period (see Table 1.10). Table 1.10 also clearly shows the differences between regions. While African privatisation has been relatively insignificant in world terms, it does rely to a greater extent than other developing countries on foreign investors. In contrast, domestic investors have been much more prominent in the privatisation programme of economies in East Asia. The other form of foreign investment in privatisation has been portfolio investment. Here, direct portfolio investment in LDCs has been limited, and has instead been through the purchase of equity instruments, traded in international security markets. These instruments have been used extensively in the sale of large Latin American telecommunications companies.

The statistics on foreign investments inflows for privatisation understate the

Table 1.9 Foreign exchange as share of total privatisation revenue, 1988–92 (%)

	1988	1989	1990	1991	1992	Average
Europe and Central Asia	80.6	55.6	36.1	55.8	63.0	55.7
Latin America and Caribbean	8.2	43.9	37.8	38.4	16.7	28.8
East Asia and Pacific	0.0	0.0	0.0	19.5	13.0	8.4
South Asia	0.0	3.8	36.2	3.5	8.4	8.8
Sub-Saharan Africa	0.0	34.7	47.2	1.1	35.9	36.7
Total	9.3	20.9	33.4	40.2	24.6	30.7

Source: Sader (1993).

Table 1.10 Foreign direct investment for privatisation 1988–92

	From privatisation (US$m.)	As share of total FDI (%)
Europe and Central Asia	5.869.0	31.90
Latin America and Caribbean	8,112.0	16.40
East Asia and Pacific	376.0	0.68
South Asia	52.0	3.40
Sub-Saharan Africa	71.4	0.99
Total	14,480.4	10.98

Source: Sader (1993).

degree of foreign involvement and control in privatisation, insofar as debt–equity swap arrangements have been used. These agreements result in increased foreign ownership of the enterprise, but do not result in an inflow of foreign exchange. A number of Latin American countries has made extensive use of debt–equity swap facilities in their privatisation programmes (UN, 1992).

The involvement of foreign capital in privatisation presents the government in many developing countries with a serious dilemma, insofar as attempts to put restrictions on foreign participants for domestic distributional reasons quickly narrows the range of financing options and willingness of foreign investors to become involved in the privatisation sales.

It is impossible to assess in more than the broadest terms the extent to which developing country governments have been compelled to compromise on their ownership and distributional objectives in order to secure foreign capital inflows. But it is possible to put forward several arguments to support the general contention that governments have increasingly found it necessary actively to seek foreign participation.

Pressure to rely on foreign buyers has come from several sources. The first has been the influence of the international financial institutions through the conditionality attached to structural adjustment loans. The World Bank, and its sister organisations the International Finance Corporation (IFC) and the Multilateral Investment Guarantee Agency (MIGA), have been active in encouraging privatisation in developing countries. About 70 per cent of all structural adjustment loans and 40 per cent of sectoral adjustment loans made during the 1980s contained a privatisation component. Between 1981 and 1992 the Bank supported 182 privatisation operations in sixty-seven countries (World Bank, 1992). Typically, the Bank has encouraged foreign involvement in privatisation sales.

The reliance on foreign involvement in privatisation has also been a response to the shortage of balance of payment finance. With the dramatic decline in commercial bank lending – from 46 per cent of the LDCs' external finance in 1989 to 17 per cent in 1991 – many LDCs have adopted a more proactive policy stance to foreign investment, and FDI now accounts for a much larger share of external finance flows to developing countries (see Table 1.11). As we noted earlier, as much as 10 per cent of FDI inflows in recent years has been linked to privatisation.

There are clear links between the type of enterprise, the method of ownership transfer and the source of finance for privatisation (Adam *et al.*, 1992). Direct domestic private sector participation has been concentrated in smaller-scale activities associated with commerce, manufacturing, service and agricultural sectors. Larger sales in utilities and infrastructure depend more on direct foreign investment and public share issues. In general, the higher the value of sales, the more likely is a higher proportion of foreign investment.

The experience of the last decade or so has also revealed different approaches to the attention given to enterprises prior to selling them, and to the kind of

Table 1.11 Pattern of external finance to developing countries (%)

Types of finance	1981	1991
Official grants	7.3	14.5
Official loans	26.0	30.8
Suppliers of export credits	11.0	12.3
Commercial bank loans	46.1	17.4
Bonds	1.2	4.8
FDI	8.31	6.5
Portfolio equity	0.1	3.7
Total	100.0	100.0
Total (current US$b.)	156.9	205.3

Source: World Bank (1993).

broader policy framework that needs to be encouraged and developed. The former involves the degree to which enterprises should undergo some process of restructuring, involving either financial reconstruction or physical rehabilitation. As Heald (1992) has pointed out, there is a need here to distinguish between the performance improvements required with the existing capital stock, the rehabilitation of physical assets involving further investment, and the breaking-up of existing enterprises into several enterprises. The latter involve the degree and form of market liberalisation that is necessary to accompany privatisation, and also the extent to which regulatory mechanisms need to be established.

The trade-offs concern the fiscal gains to be made from placing sound and attractive enterprises in the marketplace against the costs involved in prior preparation for sale and the risk of the failure to improve performance once funds have been spent. The potential gains from some form of financial restructuring are obvious since, from an economy-wide point of view, little would be gained by placing loss-making enterprises into the market with high degrees of debts and correspondingly overvalued assets. Indeed, to place such loss-making enterprises in the market, the government is likely to have to pledge and deliver offsetting concessions that may in the end be quite costly to the economy. It is not easy, however, to turn a loss-making enterprise into one that operates efficiently and profitably. The exercise itself involves an admittance and recognition on the part of government and those operating the enterprise that things were very wrong in the first place.

Although some degree of financial and managerial change within the existing enterprise may be necessary prior to privatisation, there appears to be general acceptance that new investment by the public sector prior to privatisation may not be worthwhile. Besides considerations of opportunity costs in terms of other worthwhile investments and the questions of budgetary constraints, particularly for low-income countries, the issue of whether the incoming private sector operator actually wants the type of investment that has been undertaken needs to be considered. The current view, expressed by the World Bank for example, is that the private sector is better able to rehabilitate enterprises and the new owners should undertake changes to the capital stock (World Bank, 1992). Reinforcing this argument is the World Bank's finding of a positive correlation between privatisation and new investment once businesses have been transferred to the private sector. The case for physical restructuring may be stronger where enterprise break-up rather than investment is involved. The break-up of enterprises may be a necessary part of the process of creating competition within the sector being privatised, particularly in the privatisation of large utilities.

The experience with the measures taken in the pre-privatisation period in relation to the wider policy environment has also varied across countries. As Heald (1992: 253) notes:

> The Chilean utility privatisation program demonstrates how intensive efforts on pricing reform preceded divestiture. In sharp contrast, the Jamaican government did not appear to appreciate fully the implications of the extension of its divestiture policy from the competitive sector to the public utility sector. Virtually no groundwork was done, save the measures necessary to facilitate the sale of shares to the chosen partner, Cable and Wireless.

Also, corporate control is likely to be weaker in stock markets that are still in their infancy and have not become firmly established (Singh, 1992).

In particular, there has been comparatively little attention given to monopoly regulation outside the OECD countries. A feature of the recent privatisation experience has been the increase in monopoly power of privatised enterprises. This appears to be a feature of developing, rather than industrialised, countries, where there has been more divestiture in utility and other monopoly sectors and where market concentration is more prevalent (Frischtak, Hadjimichale and Zachau, 1989). As Leeds (1989) noted, nine of the initial eleven enterprises that were privatised in the 1980s in Malaysia as monopolies were established without a regulatory framework for controlling potential monopoly abuses. The importance of this point is heightened by the fact that these forms of privatisation in developing countries are also accompanied by the strong participation of foreign investors, and undertaken where, in some instances, capital markets are underdeveloped and function inefficiently and where the antitrust and restrictive business practices regulatory framework is weak (Gray, 1991). Legislative controls and the development of institutions to prevent collusion, price fixing and predatory pricing practices have long attained a degree of maturity in the OECD economies. This is in marked contrast to the situation in developing and transitional countries where, by 1992, sixteen had restrictive business practice legislation (Argentina, Brazil, Chile, Czechoslovakia, Hungary, India, Kenya, Pakistan, Peru, Poland, Republic of Korea, Russian Federation, Sri Lanka, Thailand, Tunisia and Venezuela) (Bennett, 1993). The Latin American economies in this group had established controls for market abuse much earlier in response to the concern to curtail the activities of subsidiaries of multinational corporations. The measures in this instance were less concerned with curbing the growth in the size of firms than with abuses of market power, such as tackling pricing irregularities.

The lack of development towards competition policy in developing countries can in part be explained by the high demands it places on administrative capacity that is already known to be weak and subject to manipulation by influential interest groups (Grindle and Thomas, 1991).

It is noteworthy that the IMF and the World Bank do not generally include restrictive business practices legislation in their structural adjustment conditions (Gray, 1991). Indeed, there appears to be a presumption by these agencies that competition between firms will result from various types of economic reforms, such as trade liberalisation and deregulation of markets rather than through legislative controls that prevent anti-competitive behaviour.

A similar picture of underdevelopment emerges in relation to the regulation of privatised monopoly utilities in developing countries. Even in Malaysia the issue of post-privatisation regulation came late, although five regulatory bodies, developed according to the UK model, now exist. The Malaysian Privatisation Masterplan calls for the eventual unification of the regulatory structure (Adam *et al.*, 1992).

Developing countries have found it difficult to establish procedures and institutions to regulate large utilities that would both satisfy demands to safeguard the public interest and promote private sector investment in sectors that were previously starved of state sector capital funding. This is a particularly acute problem that faces the low-income developing economies in the short term. Although public utilities may be the most viable enterprises for privatisation from the perspective of private investors in those countries, it is unlikely in the short term that institutions capable of providing credible commitments to refrain from arbitrary administrative action can be developed (Levy and Spiller, 1993). In these circumstances Levy and Spiller (1993: 37) argue that: 'plausible alternatives include using sequenced domestic reform as a substitute source of commitment, using international guarantees as substitutes, working actively to alter the "exogenous" endowments that constrain regulatory development, or simply waiting until circumstances have changed'.

Finally, regulatory reform in the transitional economies of Eastern and Central Europe, besides being in its infancy, appears to be regarded less as an instrument to promote competition and efficiency than as a means that will attract private investment by ensuring that firms under regulation make an adequate return on their capital.

1.4 Performance with privatisation

The assessment and evaluation of the effects of privatisation are difficult to accomplish, and immediately encounter several serious methodological constraints. The first difficulty relates to the measure of performance or 'success'. Ideally, performance should be assessed in terms of the objectives set for the privatisation. For some, the objective of privatisation is broadly defined in terms of expanding the share of the private sector and fostering market development. Weiss (this volume), using the example of Mexico, argues that the impact of privatisation should be assessed less in terms of its economic efficiency effects and more for its contribution to a hardening of the government budget constraint and a deregulation of the state sector in the economy in general.

An alternative approach is to assess private performance in terms of macrolevel indicators. The contribution to government revenue and the reduction in the budget deficit relate directly to one of the main objectives of privatisation. The impact of privatisation on investment – as examined by Fontaine and Geronimi (this volume) for sub-Saharan Africa – or on foreign direct investment inflows, are alternative indicators of macrolevel impact.

More commonly used yardsticks of privatisation performance are measured at the enterprise level in terms of economic efficiency or financial profitability. In both cases, a range of indicators can be calculated. Examples are found in the country studies in this volume. Karatas uses profit margins, profit–asset ratios, and labour productivity in assessing performance of privatised enterprises in Turkey. Potts uses production and exports data in his study of estate agriculture in Tanzania. Weiss's study on Mexico uses several alternative measures of sales performance.

A fourth approach to assessing the results of privatisation is to assess performance outcome in terms of social impact. Here, the most commonly used measures are employment, wage levels, and associated employment-related benefits. A closely related set of indicators assesses the impact on labour that is retrenched as a result of privatisation, and cover unemployment and redundancy payment, and related safety-net provisions.

Finally, it is possible to assess performance impact in terms of the effect on economic welfare, using a cost-benefit approach. This has the attraction of allowing different effects to be valued in terms of a common unit of measurement and aggregated to give a single, overall measure of the results of privatisation.

Irrespective of the indicator of performance that is selected, there are further difficulties in developing an appropriate methodology for impact assessment. The problem is the familiar one of establishing the counterfactual: that is, what would have happened in the absence of privatisation? If the counterfactual can be identified, it becomes possible to separate out the extent to which observed changes in the performance indicator are due to privatisation itself, and the extent to which they are due to exogenous changes in the industry of economy as a whole. Two approaches have been widely used. The first is to compare performance before and after privatisation. The second is to compare performance of privatised enterprises to that of similar enterprises that have not been privatised and to take the observed difference as evidence of the effect of privatisation. Both approaches have their drawbacks and provide only an approximation to the ideal counterfactual-based estimate.

Assessing the performance with privatisation is also made more difficult by the tendency among policy makers, particularly in the industrialised countries, not to be concerned with detailed monitoring and evaluation of enterprises that in effect become part of the private sector. This attitude might be accepted, if the private sector operated in a well-functioning competitive environment with appropriate institutions to check abuses of market power. However, these conditions often do not exist. The emerging market structures in Eastern Europe and the ex-Soviet Union have yet to develop an environment that can adequately safeguard against potential abuses of market power, and in many developing countries there is an absence of role models in the private sector for divested enterprises to pattern themselves on and to compete with (Heald, 1990).

In view of the methodological and empirical difficulties in assembling evidence on post-privatisation performance, it is hardly surprising that the available evidence is limited, making comprehensive and systematic assessment difficult.

The World Bank (1992) attempts to provide a general assessment of international privatisation. Here, it is concluded that privatisation has had a positive impact on economic performance, measured in terms of increased investment, improvements in productivity, and output growth and diversification. It is also concluded that economic welfare has improved as a result of privatisation: 'the benefits from properly executed privatisation have proved to be considerable, as revealed in cases in Latin America (Mexico, Chile, Jamaica), Africa (Niger, Swaziland), Asia (Malaysia, Korea), and developed countries (UK, France, Japan, New Zealand)' (p. 9).

The conclusions drawn in World Bank (1992) are largely based on a World Bank research study on the welfare consequences of privatisation (Galal *et al.* 1992). In this study, the cost-benefit approach is used to calculate the net economic welfare effect of divestiture, where the change in welfare is decomposed into a change in consumer surplus and enterprise profits. The summary report concludes: 'so did privatisation make the world a better place or not? Our case studies answer this question with a resounding "yes"' (p. 1). The case studies in question concern twelve firms in four countries, namely, Chile, Malaysia, Mexico and the United Kingdom. The firms consist of three telecommunications companies, four airlines, two electricity companies, one lottery business, and single companies for transport and a port. Despite the fact that this was a carefully executed and extensive investigation that examined the economic, financial and social welfare implications of privatisation using a before–after approach, it has to be admitted that the country selection and the number of enterprises used in the study make it difficult to draw global conclusions.

The World Bank's assessment of privatisation in sub-Saharan Africa is that 'such limited privatisation has had little impact on efficiency and economic growth' (World Bank, 1994: 105). Several reasons are cited. In some cases, government has continued to hold a major share – and to intervene – in partly privatised firms. In many circumstances the new owners received favourable treatment – tax benefits, duty-free imports, tariff protection and priority access to credit and other scarce inputs, that reduced the potential gains from privatisation. In some countries, corruption and cronyism were reflected in a lack of transparency, and underlined the performance benefits.

An attempt to widen the assessment of privatisation performance to cover a multinational, multi-industry sample of companies is provided in Megginson, Nash and van Randenborgh (1993) who compare the pre- and post-privatisation performance of 61 companies from 18 countries (6 developing and 12 industrialised) and 32 different industries. The evidence suggests that profitability and operating efficiency increased significantly after privatisation. The study finds no evidence that employment levels fall after privatisation. The sample of companies is limited to publicly quoted firms that were privatised through public share issues.

The social impact of privatisation has been examined mainly in terms of employment effects. The World Bank's view is that privatisation has not made workers as a whole worse off. It is argued that where sizeable reductions in employment have been incurred these have resulted either from changes introduced in enterprises while under public ownership, or because of exogenous changes in the general level of employment and demand. It is further argued that severance packages have created a social safety net, 'and dismissed workers have benefited from severance packages in excess of the benefits required by law in many countries' (World Bank, 1992: 32). In some countries, jobs have been safeguarded by contractual arrangements for the transfer of ownership.

Evidence from individual countries' studies on the effect of privatisation on employment is more mixed, and in some cases contradicts the Bank's position. Bhaskar (1992) reports that privatisation reduced employment in the jute industry in Bangladesh; Kemal (1993) estimates that some 43 per cent of workers employed in public enterprises that were privatised in Pakistan were laid off by the new owners; in Nepal it is estimated that in excess of 50 per cent of employees would become redundant if the privatisation programme is fully implemented. In Central and Eastern Europe, large-scale redundancies have occurred in the wake of privatisation and the resultant restructuring.

1.5 Concluding comments

The decade of privatisation can be seen as one in which the early expectations and policy stances of the various actors involved have been altered and redefined as experience has accumulated. For political leaders in many developing countries, the first wave of privatisation in the early 1980s brought exaggerated expectations as to the ease with which privatisation could be implemented and the size of the potential benefits that would be generated. Under a barrage of overoptimistic claims that privatisation would improve the budgetary situation and raise economic efficiency performance through the discipline of the private sector, a pattern of policy paralysis was induced, with other policy reforms being delayed or abandoned in anticipation of the benefits that would follow from privatisation (Cook and Minogue, 1990). This notion that privatisation would be a panacea for major structural imbalances and economic malaise was due, in part, to the tendency to equate privatisation with economic liberalisation, rather than as one element in a general programme of economic policy reform. The damaging effects that exaggerated expectations had in paralysing public sector reform are attested to by Heald (1992: 253–4) who refers in particular, to the experience of Pakistan and Thailand. Here:

> effective privatisation programmes are being endangered by unrealistic expectations of how much divestiture is feasible in the short and medium term. Once persuaded of the necessity or virtues of privatisation, ministers often confuse aspiration and feasibility. ... Two dangers arise from this confusion. First, the predictable failure to achieve preannounced targets is likely to create disillusion, perhaps even discredit the programme. Second, the emphasis on privatisation will divert attention from policy and institutional reforms within the public enterprise sector.

A contrary interpretation of the relationship between the emphasis on privatisation and more general policy reform is given by Adam *et al.* (1992), who argue that privatisation has had a benefit impact through its so-called threat effect. This argument is based on the premise that privatisation does not necessarily have to be carried through to implementation to have an effect. In fact, as we have seen in an earlier section, the record of implementation is a patchy one, particularly in the lower-income developing countries. The positive impact comes from the slowing down in the expansion of state sector activities resulting from the anti-state enterprise environment created by the threat of privatisation. The argument could be extended to suggest that many governments, particularly in low-income countries where progress with privatisation has been slowest, now view the idea of public enterprise reform more benevolently than they did in the 1970s.

There is a thin but growing literature that claims that privatisation has brought substantial benefits, both in economic and social terms. As we saw in the preceding section, proponents of the view – and the World Bank is the most prominent – are convinced that privatisation is the most effective means of generating performance improvements. The argument that the move towards privatisation is necessary for performance gains has strengthened the notion that 'ownership' matters, an argument consistently put forward by the property rights theorists (Commander and Killick, 1988).

This emphasis on privatisation and ownership change represents a shift in emphasis from the earlier part of the 1980s, when the conclusion that emerged from the debate on performance and ownership was that gains in efficiency performance were more likely to result from an increase in market competition than from a change in ownership. This conclusion was drawn from several arguments. First, the evidence from empirical studies that compared the performance of private firms to public enterprises on a 'like for like' basis indicated that economic efficiency could be achieved under either type of ownership (Millward, 1988). Second, there were reservations as to the applicability of theories arguing in favour of private ownership when account was taken of their stringent conditions and assumptions. As Chang and Singh (1992: 42) conclude in their recent view of the literature on the comparative performance of public and private sector enterprises:

> there exist neither compelling theoretical reasons nor unambiguous empirical evidence, for either developed or developing countries, suggesting the pervasive 'inefficiency' of public enterprises. The picture is far more complex than one of 'efficient' private enterprises versus inefficient public enterprises. Among the PEs in various developing countries, we can find anything from world-class manufacturers (e.g. Posco in the Republic of Korea), very respectable enterprises (e.g. TANESCO in the United Republic of Tanzania), to the usual distressing examples of inefficiency-laden, politically corrupt PEs.

The potential for generating performance improvement while retaining ownership in the public sector was recognised by the World Bank in the early part of the decade: 'the key factor determining the efficiency of an enterprise is not whether it is publicly or privately owned, but how it is managed' (World Bank, 1983: 50). This was reflected in the concentration of public enterprise reform, rather than privatisation, in the Bank's lending conditionality in this period (Mosley, 1988). Similarly, political obstacles were clearly recognised as a constraint to privatisation at this time, and were viewed as significant by the Bank's publication on the *Techniques of Privatization of State-Owned Enterprises*, despite the fact that only one page was devoted to their analysis (Vuylsteke, 1988: 69).

The World Bank's current views reflect the conviction that even if competition is important to generate efficiency gains, it alone is not enough and ownership therefore matters. In its latest review of the experiences with privatisation it intimates that privatisation is superior to public enterprise reform for three main reasons (World Bank, 1992). First, public enterprise reform is technically and politically more difficult to implement than privatisation. Second, undertaking a full public enterprise sector reform programme may be unworkable owing to the enormous difficulties with co-ordinating the relationships that are required between government agencies, financial institutions and the enterprises themselves. Third, previous attempts to reform public enterprises have not been entirely successful because reforms have been introduced in periods of crisis. Once the crisis has passed, the reforms have usually faltered, and performance improvement has not been sustained.

The view put forward in recent World Bank literature that ownership matters also undermines the successful enterprise reforms that have been introduced in a range of countries. These have been shown by the well-known case of enterprise reform in Korea (Song, 1993), and, more recently in the case of Kenya (Grosh, 1992). Grosh has shown that profitability and efficiency among many public enterprises in Kenya were significant and sustained for lengthy periods and that the private sector could not be considered to operate in a superior manner. Some public enterprises were holding their own against competition from domestic and foreign firms, demonstrating that it is possible to create the kinds of incentives that will contribute to efficiency under any type of ownership. Mayhew and Seabright (1993) have shown that in the case of public enterprises in the transitional economies of Europe, sizeable gains can be expected by giving explicit consideration to the development of new management forms rather than relying solely on privatisation. Similarly, Hume and Pinto (1993) show how the large state-owned industrial enterprises in Poland have responded positively to reforms affecting the market environment within which they operate.

The shift in the World Bank's thinking is encapsulated in the interpretation given to the reform process in New Zealand. Earlier, the reforms introduced in New Zealand, in the form of 'corporatisation' and the subsequent profit levels achieved by corporated businesses, were evidence that reform could work. Despite the high profit levels of corporatised public firms in New Zealand, the World Bank now argues that profitability could even be higher with privatisation. In this respect, then, corporatisation can only be viewed as a stepping stone towards eventual privatisation. The World Bank's argument is reinforced by its insistence that while corporatisation may provide short-term gains, it will encounter longer-term problems (World Bank, 1992: 5).

In this chapter we have examined three main questions concerning the worldwide shift towards privatisation that occurred in the 1980s: What has been happening? How has it been happening? What have been the results? In addressing these questions, we have revealed a complex and sometimes contradictory picture, with significant differences being observed across sectors and countries, and over time. The experience with both policy and performance has been extremely diverse, making it difficult to identify broad patterns of experience or general lessons for policy.

What is apparent, however, is that generating improvements in enterprise performance involves much more than simply a change in ownership through privatisation. As Chang and Singh (1992: 54) observe, bringing about improvements in the performance of enterprises is not just a question of economics, but also involves issues of organisation, institution-building and political economy. Equally, enterprise performance improvement needs to be viewed in the broader context, as one element in a national process of economic, social and political reform directed at creating long-run and sustainable improvements in standards of living and general welfare.

References

Adam, C., W. Cavendish and P. S. Mistry (1992), *Adjusting Privatization: Case studies from developing countries*, London: Currey.

Bennett, A. (1993), 'Regulatory framework for privatised monopolies', in *Methods and Practices of Privatisation*, UN Department for Development Support and Management Services, New York: UN.

Bhaskar, V. (1992), 'Privatization and the developing countries: the issues and the evidence', Discussion Paper No. 47, Geneva: UNCTAD.

Candoy-Sekse, R. and A. R. Palmer (1988), *Techniques of Privatization of State-owned Enterprises*, vol. 3, *Inventory of Country Experience and Reference Materials*, Technical Paper No. 90, Washington, DC: World Bank.

Chang, H-J. and A. Singh (1992), 'Public enterprises in developing countries and economic efficiency', Discussion Paper No. 48, Geneva: UNCTAD.

Commander, S. and T. Killick (1988), 'Privatisation in developing countries: a survey of the issues', in P. Cook and C. Kirkpatrick (eds), *Privatisation in Less Developed Countries*, Hemel Hempstead: Harvester Wheatsheaf.

Cook, P. (1994), 'Privatisation and private sector development: the case of Myanmar', *South East Asia Research*, **2** (2), 1–32.

Cook, P. and C. Kirkpatrick (eds) (1988), *Privatisation in Less Developed Countries*, Hemel Hempstead: Harvester Wheatsheaf.

Cook, P. and C. Kirkpatrick (1994), 'Privatisation and enterprise reform in transitional economies: a comparison of European and Asian experience', paper presented to UK Academy of International Business Annual Conference, Manchester, March.

Cook, P. and C. Kirkpatrick (1995), 'Privatisation in transition economies: East and Central European experience', in F. Burton, M. Yamin and S. Young (eds), *International Business and Europe in Transition*, London: Macmillan.

Cook, P. and M. Minogue (1990), 'Waiting for privatization in developing countries: towards the integration of economic and non-economic explanations', *Public Administration and Development*, **10** (4), 389–403.

European Bank for Reconstruction and Development (1993), *Annual Economic Outlook*, September, London: EBRD.

Frischtak, C., B. Hadjimichale and V. Zachau (1989), 'Competition policies for industrializing countries', Policy Planning and Research Paper No. 1, Washington, DC: World Bank.

Frydman, R. and A. Rapaczynski (1993), 'Privatisation in Eastern Europe: is the State withering away?', *Finance and Development*, **30** (2), 10–13.

Galal, A., L. Jones, P. Tandon and I. Vogelsang (1992), 'Welfare consequences of selling public enterprises', Country Economics Department, Washington, DC: World Bank.

Gray, C. S. (1991), 'Antitrust as a component of policy reform: what relevance for economic development?', in D. Perkins and M. Roemer (eds), *Reforming Economic Systems in Developing Countries*, Boston, Mass.: Harvard University Press.

Grindle, M. and J. Thomas (1991), *Public Choices and Policy Change: The political economy of reform in developing countries*, Baltimore: Johns Hopkins University Press.

Grosh, B. (1992), *Public Enterprises in Kenya*, London: Lynn Reinner.

Hare, P. (1993), 'Privatisation in comparative perspective: an overview of the emerging issues', paper prepared for Workshop on Economic Transformation in Central and Eastern Europe, WZB, Berlin, May.

Heald, D. (1990), 'The relevance of privatisation to developing countries', *Public Administration and Development*, **10** (1), 3–18.

Heald, D. (1992), 'How much privatisation should there be in developing countries?', *Annals of Public and Co-operative Economics*, **63** (2), 229–69.

Hemming, R. and A. Mansoor (1988), 'Privatization and public enterprises', Occasional Paper No. 56, Washington, DC: IMF.

Hume, I. and B. Pinto (1993), 'Prejudice and fact in Poland's industrial transformation', *Finance and Development*, **30** (2), 18–20.

IMF (1993), *Economic Outlook*, Washington, DC: IMF, October.

Kemal, A. R. (1993), 'Retrenchment policies and labour shedding in Pakistan', Occasional Paper No. 17, Interdepartmental Project on Structural Adjustment, Geneva: ILO.

Leeds, R. (1989), 'Malaysia: genesis of a privatisation transaction', *World Development*, **17** (5), 741–57.

Levy, B. and P. Spiller (1993), 'Regulation, institutions and commitment in telecommunications: a comparative analysis of five country studies', paper prepared for the Annual Conference on Development Economics, World Bank, Washington, DC, 3–4 May.

Mansoor, A. (1988), 'The fiscal impact of privatisation', in P. Cook and C. Kirkpatrick (eds), *Privatisation in Less Developed Countries*, Hemel Hempstead: Harvester Wheatsheaf.

Mayhew, K. and P. Seabright (1993), 'Incentives and the management of enterprises in economic transition: capital markets are not enough', *Oxford Review of Economic Policy*, **8** (1), 105–29.

Megginson, W. L., R. C. Nash and M. van Randenborgh (1993), 'The financial and operating performance of newly-privatized firms: an international empirical analysis', mimeo, University of Georgia; forthcoming, *Journal of Finance*.

Meller, P. (1992), 'Latin American adjustment and economic reforms: issues on recent experience', Discussion Paper No. 53, Geneva: UNCTAD, December.

Millward, R. (1988), 'Measured sources of inefficiency in the performance of private and public enterprises in LDCs', in P. Cook and C. Kirkpatrick (eds), *Privatisation in Less Developed Countries*, Hemel Hempstead: Harvester Wheatsheaf.

Mosley, P. (1988), 'Privatisation, policy-based lending and World Bank behaviour', in P. Cook and C. Kirkpatrick (eds), *Privatisation in Less Developed Countries*, Hemel Hempstead: Harvester Wheatsheaf.

Ng, C. Y. and K. W. Toh (1992), 'Privatization in the Asian-Pacific region', *Asian-Pacific Economic Literature*, **6** (2), 42–68.

Pinheiro, A. C. and B. R. Schneider (1994), 'The fiscal impact of privatisation in Latin America', mimeo, Federal University of Rio de Janeiro and Princeton University.

Sader, F. (1993), 'The experience of privatization in the developing world: 1988–92', International Economics Department, WPS 1202, Washington, DC: World Bank, October.

Schwartz, G. and P. Lopes (1993), 'Privatization: expectation trade offs, and results', *Finance and Development*, **30** (2), June.

Singh, A. (1992), 'The stock-market and economic development: should developing countries encourage stock markets?', Discussion Paper No. 49, Geneva: UNCTAD.

Song, D. (1993), 'Public enterprises in South Korea', paper presented to Third Asia Pacific Conference of Management, Brisbane, Australia, August.

United Nations (1992), *World Investment Report, 1992*, Transnationals and Management Division, New York: UN.

United Nations Conference on Trade and Development (UNCTAD) (1993), 'Design, implementation and results of privatization programmes: a cross-country analysis of national experiences', Trade and Development Board, September.

United Nations Industrial Development Organisation (1993), *Industry and Development Global Report, 1992-93*, Vienna: UNIDO.

Vickers, J. and G. Yarrow (1988), *Privatization: An economic analysis*, Cambridge,

Mass.: MIT Press.
Vuylsteke, C. (1988), *Techniques of Privatization of State-Owned Enterprises*, vol. 1, *Methods and Implementation*, Technical Paper No. 88, Washington, DC: World Bank.
World Bank (1980), *Borrowing in International Capital Markets, 1979*, Washington, DC: World Bank.
World Bank (1983), *World Development Report*, Washington, DC: Oxford University Press for the World Bank.
World Bank (1989), *The Reform of State Owned Enterprises: Lessons of World Bank lending*, Washington, DC: World Bank.
World Bank (1991), *Public Enterprise Reform: The lessons of experience*, EDI Development Studies, Washington, DC: World Bank.
World Bank (1992), *Privatisation: The lessons of experience*, Country Economics Department, Washington, DC: World Bank.
World Bank (1993), *Global Economic Prospects and the Developing Countries, 1993*, Washington, DC: World Bank.
World Bank (1994), *Adjustment in Africa: Reforms, results and the road ahead*, Policy Research Report, Washington, DC: World Bank.

PART II

Transitional and European countries

2

Privatisation in Eastern Europe

Experience and preliminary policy lessons

Gerd Schwartz

2.1 Introduction

Just as state-owned enterprises (SOEs) lie at the heart of planned economies, privately owned enterprises lie at the heart of market economies, and privatisation is central for the transition from plan to market. While for market economies the fundamental argument for privatisation is that it results in improvements in allocative and productive efficiency (Hemming and Miranda, 1991), for economies in transition (EITs) three other possible arguments for privatisation have been suggested: (i) creating a private economy; (ii) establishing a political system based upon private property rights and individual freedoms; and (iii) boosting state revenue (Dhanji and Milanovic, 1990). However, the outcome of privatisation policies is largely independent of these general objectives and typically may involve a combination of all three.

Given vastly overextended public sectors, both goals and methods of privatisation in EITs are fundamentally different from those in market economies. While many enterprises in EITs may remain state-owned for a while, several countries, notably some of the early reformers in Eastern Europe, have already achieved significant progress in privatising their economies. In reviewing this experience, this chapter outlines some of the fundamental problems encountered in large-scale privatisations, discusses unresolved policy choices, and draws preliminary conclusions regarding the desirable properties of privatisation schemes for EITs.

The chapter is structured as follows. The second section examines the general trade-offs encountered by all policy makers. The third section reviews the general experience with privatisation in selected Eastern European countries, concentrating on issues that affect the quality of privatisation schemes, such as the overall role of privatisation in the process of transition, the observed compartmentalisation of privatisation policies, property rights and corporate control, banking reform, and the problem of large enterprises. Based on this discussion, the final section tries to draw some preliminary general conclusions regarding the desirable properties of privatisation schemes for EITs.

2.2 Privatisation: the trade-offs

It has been argued that policy makers, faced with having to initiate large-scale privatisations, typically tend to define privatisation policy objectives rather broadly (Maurer, Sander and Schmidt, 1991), thereby running the risk of creating a set of mutually inconsistent policies. This section presents some evidence for broadly defined privatisation policy goals, and argues that broad objectives frequently tend to obscure the trade-offs all policy makers face.

In general, the definition of a 'good' privatisation scheme strongly depends on a country's specific economic and political conditions; the policy maker's objective function has to be adjusted according to the particular circumstances of each country. Privatisation schemes have been promoted in countries with extremely differently sized public sectors (see Table 2.1), and there can be no standard recipe for privatisation. As a result, the experience of one country may only be of limited use in another country with an SOE sector that is significantly different in size and scope.

Still, regardless of the particular circumstances, the policy maker's objective function may comprise a fairly large number of general policy objectives, and the declared goals of selected Eastern European privatisation schemes, shown in Table 2.2, may be considered typical in this respect. In the case of Poland, for example, following an initial criticism that the government's privatisation programme was devoid of any clearly identifiable goals (Gruszecki and Winiecki, 1991), the Ministry of Privatisation put forward eight specific privatisation objectives (see Table 2.2). A proliferation of goals naturally leads to the question of mutual compatibility.

In general, a typical set of privatisation policy objectives may include: (i) choosing the 'right' buyers; (ii) getting a 'fair' price; (iii) privatising a certain number of enterprises within a given time frame; (iv) safeguarding employment; and (v) obtaining investment guarantees. Unable simultaneously to control all five variables – ownership, price, time, employment, and new investment – trade-offs are inevitable. For example, by selecting a strict time frame for privatising the economy, the other four variables will normally have to be left more or less free of restrictions. Whilst it is possible to develop distinct privatisation goals and strategies for separate sub-groups of SOEs, it is generally implausible to pursue more than one policy objective for any given subset of SOEs.

Given multiple and not necessarily compatible goals, it comes as no surprise that actual privatisation schemes also operate with multiple privatisation tools (see Table 2.3), and the trade-offs that exist at the level of privatisation objectives

Table 2.1 Share of the state sector in selected countries

	Per cent of value added	Per cent of employment
Eastern Europe		
Czechoslovakia (1986)	97.0	–
East Germany (1982)	96.5	94.2
Soviet Union (1985)	96.0	–
Bulgaria (1990)	92.0	–
Poland (1985)	81.7	71.5
Hungary (1984)	65.2	69.9
Selected OECD economies[a]		
France (1982)	16.5	14.6
Austria (1978–79)	14.5	13.0
Italy (1982)	14.0	15.0
Turkey (1985)	11.2	20.0
West Germany (1982)	10.7	7.8
United Kingdom (1983)	10.7	7.0
Portugal (1976)	9.7	–
Denmark (1974)	6.3	5.0
Greece (1979)	6.1	–
Spain (1979)	4.1	–
Netherlands (1971–73)	3.6	8.0
United States (1983)	1.3	1.8
Sweden	–	10.6
Finland	–	10.0
Norway	–	6.0
Selected other economies		
China (1984)	73.6	–
Venezuela (1978–80)	27.5	–
Tunisia (1978–79)	25.4	–
Malawi (1979)	25.0	8.0
Malaysia (1985–88)	25.0	–
Singapore (1983)	25.0	–
Bolivia (1974–77)	21.1	–
Jamaica (1984)	21.0	11.0
Sri Lanka (1988)	20.0	40.0
Trinidad and Tobago (1985)	16.0	13.0
Kenya (1977)	15.0	15.0
India (1978)	10.3	6.0
Papua New Guinea	10.0	–
Niger (1980s)	10.0	–
South Korea (1981–83)	9.0	7.0
Pakistan (1974–75)	6.0	2.8
Paraguay (1978–80)	3.1	–

Note: [a] Excludes government services, but includes state-owned enterprises in commercial activities.

Source: Milanovic (1989); Adam, Cavendish and Mistry (1992); and data provided by the World Bank.

are closely associated with similar trade-offs that exist at the level of privatisation tools. For example, mass privatisation schemes, designed to transfer ownership rights of a large number of SOEs to the population at large, are closely associated

Table 2.2 Declared goals of selected Eastern European privatisation programmes

Czechoslovakia	The aims of the privatisation programme of the CSFR are both political and economic. Among the political aims are changes in the social structure. The economic aim of privatisation is to increase the ability of the economy to adapt to external conditions. (Ministry of Finance (CSFR), 1991)
Germany	The German privatisation programme has three primary objectives: (i) restructuring viable enterprises in order to make them competitive under market conditions; (ii) privatising enterprises; (iii) promoting demonopolisation in order to provide Eastern Germany with an efficient market structure. (Maurer *et al.*, 1991)
Hungary	The principal aim of the Hungarian privatisation scheme is to create a real market economy. It is the government's objective to reduce the share of state owned enterprises in the sphere of industry, trade, banking, and other economic activities from 90 per cent to 30–40 per cent in a few years. (State Property Agency (Hungary), 1991)
Poland	The Polish privatisation programme is based on the following objectives: (i) move the economy from a centrally planned system to a competitive market system which would encourage the creation of a profitable private sector; (ii) improve the performance of enterprises through a more efficient use of labour, capital, and management skills; (iii) prevent possible distortions of the privatisation process, such as the sale of state assets to foreign investors at unduly low prices; (iv) reduce the size of the public sector and the burden on the public budget and administration; (v) generate funds from the sale of enterprises or their shares; (vi) ensure a wide diffusion of ownership of privatised assets; (vii) provide an effective system of corporate governance; and (viii) commence the programme of exchanging the country's external debt into equity of privatised enterprises. The privatisation programme will transform Poland's ownership structure to resemble that of Western Europe within five years, with approximately half of the state-owned assets to be transferred into private hands within the first three years. (Ministry of Privatization (Poland), 1991b)

with meeting time objectives. With time being dominant, there can be little selectivity about ownership, price and employment. Similar conclusions hold for other privatisation tools: one-by-one asset auctions would be the most appropriate privatisation mechanism for policy makers wishing to maximise proceeds from sales, whereas special employee or management buy-out or leasing schemes target specific groups of potential buyers. In general, the number of privatisation tools should equal the number of privatisation goals policy makers wish to pursue.

2.3 The privatisation experience of selected Eastern European countries

Ever since the rapid demise of socialism, the new governments of Eastern Europe have been busy transforming their respective economies into market

Table 2.3 Privatisation tools adopted in selected Eastern European privatisation programmes

Bulgaria	(a) *Restitution* of agricultural land, small shops, some industrial property, and residential properties. (b) *Small enterprise privatisation* involving the auctioning of small shops and gasoline stations. (c) *One-by-one privatisation* using a multi-track approach, with details still to be defined, but which will involve direct (trade) sale and public share offerings. Shareholding schemes will include minority shareholding by employees (who will be allowed to purchase non-voting shares at a discount), and establishing of mutual funds.
Czechoslovakia	(a) *Restitution* of land and of commercial and non-commercial properties. (b) *Small enterprise privatisation* in the form of auctioning or leasing small business units with priority being given to domestic investors. (c) *Large enterprise privatisation* in the form of: • *direct* (*trade*) *sale* to foreign or domestic investors; • *mass privatisation* with no provision for minority shareholding by employees.
East Germany	(a) *Restitution* of land and of commercial and non-commercial property. (b) *One-by-one privatisation* via direct (trade) sale, in whole or in parts, to domestic and foreign buyers, but also in the form of management buy-outs (MBOs), management buy-ins (MBIs), and worker buy-outs (WBOs). Simplified privatisation rules for small enterprises.
Hungary	(a) *Restitution* of agricultural land; compensation for non-agricultural property given in the form of partial compensation via securities. (b) *Small enterprise privatisation* via the direct sale to domestic buyers of selected small commercial properties, mostly in retail trade, services, and tourism. (c) *One-by-one privatisation*, alternatively through: • *public share offering or direct* (*trade*) *sale* to domestic or foreign investors of selected medium to large enterprises; programme is initiated by the privatisation agency which brings companies to the market simultaneously in small groups of 20 to 40; • *self-privatisation* in the form of management- or worker-initiated privatisation proposals that are supervised by the privatisation agency; this may involve MBOs, MBIs, WBOs, or direct (trade) sales to foreign or domestic investors; • *investor-initiated privatisation*, supervised by the privatisation agency.
Poland	(a) *Small enterprise privatisation* involving the sale to domestic buyers of small commercial properties, mostly in retail trade, services, and tourism. (b) *Commercialisation path*; after being transformed into a joint-stock or limited liability company that is wholly owned by the state treasury, enterprises may be privatised in one of the following ways: • *one-by-one privatisation* in the form of a public share offering or a direct (trade) sale to domestic or foreign investors; • *mass privatisation* with a provision for employees to become minority shareholders; • sectoral privatisation as a way to 'package' weaker companies with stronger ones; • *privatisation-cum-restructuring* to assist small to medium-sized state-owned enterprises to prepare for eventual privatisation. (c) *Liquidation path*; after being liquidated in the legal sense, enterprises are either sold or leased to an interested buyer. This may involve: • *direct sale*, in whole or in parts, in the form of an MBO, or WBO, a purchase by a joint venture, or a direct purchase by domestic or foreign investors; • leasing, in whole or in parts, typically in the form of an instalment sale to the employees of the former SOEs, where employees pay a leasing fee until the company is paid for in full. (d) *Privatisation of state housing*; sale of state housing to tenants.
Romania	(a) *Small enterprise privatisation* via leasing, management contract offers, or sale to domestic buyers of up to 75 per cent of the total asset value of small commercial units, mostly in retail trade, services, and tourism. (b) *Early privatisation* of 30 commercial enterprises in good financial condition. (c) *Mass privatisation* with no provision for minority shareholding by employees. (d) *Privatisation of housing and land*; sale of state housing to tenants; land reform programme that is to privatise most agricultural lands.

Source: Information provided by the respective privatisation agencies.

economies. Fischer (1991) has argued that advice on how to privatise Eastern Europe has rapidly converged on a standard approach: small firms should be privatised quickly; larger firms should be corporatised fast, put under the direction of independent corporate boards, and their shares should be distributed to some combination of current workers, current management, mutual funds, holding companies, banks, insurance companies, pension funds, citizens, and the government. Still, even though the issues addressed by the various existing privatisation schemes necessarily show a number of important commonalities, privatisation policies (and successes) differ significantly across Eastern Europe. Drawing upon the privatisation experience of selected Eastern European countries, this section discusses five aspects of privatisation policies that have an important bearing on the eventual success or failure of privatisation schemes: (i) the role of privatisation in the transition process; (ii) the compartmentalisation of privatisation policies; (iii) property rights and corporate control; (iv) banking reform; and (v) the problem of large enterprises.

2.3.1 *The role of privatisation in the transition process*

Hare and Grosfeld (1991) have argued that the virtual absence of well-established and functioning financial markets, and the lack of an established and well-understood legal and regulatory framework require great care to be taken in determining the place of privatisation in the sequence of transition. By now, however, privatisation is considered a cornerstone of the transition process in all of Eastern Europe. While some countries, such as Bulgaria and Romania, are still in the process of setting up a fully defined privatisation scheme, other countries, notably Czechoslovakia, Hungary and Poland, already have their basic systems in place, even though changes, refinements, and amendments are being discussed frequently.

Initially, the discussion on the role of privatisation in the process of transition focused on the speed of privatisation, and it was far from clear whether privatisation should lead, accompany, or follow the process of transition. Proponents of slow privatisation put forward three basic arguments: (i) macroeconomic stabilisation, domestic price liberalisation, and current account convertibility have to precede privatisation because efficient decisions can only be made on the basis of correct relative prices; (ii) introduction of competition policies and current account convertibility has to precede privatisation to prevent monopoly profits; and (iii) introduction of modern tax systems and accounting procedures, and financial market and capital market reforms, have to precede privatisation to allow for proper enterprise valuation (Keating and Hoffman, 1991). Proponents of fast privatisation basically pointed toward the broader macroeconomic consequences of continuing to burden the economy with a large and inefficient state enterprise sector for decades to come (Hemming, 1992).

By now it has become widely accepted that the transition from plan to market, and the urgently needed improvements in enterprise efficiency, are unlikely to occur without extensive and rapid privatisation (Hemming, 1992). This view is reflected in the mass privatisation programmes that are discussed and set up in countries like Czechoslovakia, Romania and Poland. Poland, for example, after initially experimenting for about nine months with UK-style one-by-one privatisations, that involve valuations, prospectuses, subscriptions, underwritings, and so on, found it necessary to broaden its approach in summer 1990 after experiencing very slow progress with its original approach (Gruszecki and Winiecki, 1991).[1] With all Eastern European countries swiftly implementing macroeconomic stabilisation policies, domestic price liberalisation and current account liberalisation, arguments for delaying privatisation were significantly weakened. The rapid progress that was achieved on devising mass privatisation schemes that would allow for fast nominal divesting of state assets while delaying the question of asset valuation, further strengthened arguments in favour of fast and comprehensive privatisation.

2.3.2 *Compartmentalising privatisation policies*

The existence of trade-offs implies that policy makers have to decide what part of the privatisation process should be controlled. However, given rather broadly defined objective functions, policy makers in most countries have opted for a similarly broad range of privatisation tools to be adopted. As no single tool is best to meet all policy objectives, and given that the demand for the various parts of the existing portfolio of state assets is also highly differentiated, privatisation policies in many Eastern European countries have become compartmentalised in the sense that separate policy objectives are pursued for specific subsets of SOEs: that is, new owners are carefully selected for some SOEs, prices are maximised for others, a strict time frame is pursued for a third group, and employment guarantees are safeguarded in a fourth group, and so on. The many policy objectives, and the highly differentiated demand for the existing portfolio of state assets have brought about a whole range of privatisation tools to be adopted, which include: special programmes for small enterprise privatisation; enterprise liquidation with asset sale or auction; leasing of state assets; management/employee buy-out/buy-in; direct (trade) sale to foreign investors; restitution of previous owners; and mass privatisation. Table 2.3 provides an overview of the various privatisation tools of selected Eastern European privatisation programmes.

The case of Poland may be used as an example to illustrate the compartmentalisation of privatisation in Eastern Europe. The privatisation strategy of the Polish Ministry of Privatisation is based upon 'a multi-track approach comprising separate privatisation paths for the various categories of enterprise, often with a simultaneous use of different techniques of privatisation within a category' (Ministry of Privatization (Poland), 1991b). Enterprises are separated along the following lines: (i) size; (ii) demand; (iii) perceived economic and financial viability; (iv) level of state ownership and clarity of legal situation; and (v) quality of labour relations between management, workers, and unions within the enterprise (Ministry of Privatization (Poland), 1991b). Privatisation is then carried out as a two-step procedure. The first step is a legal one, where enterprises that have applied for privatisation are either 'commercialised' (i.e. transformed into a joint-stock or a limited liability company that is wholly owned by the State Treasury and is governed by the commercial code) or 'liquidated' in the legal sense. The second step consists of applying one of the various possible privatisation tools (see Table 2.3).

While the Polish case may be extreme in its degree of compartmentalisation of enterprises, it is not unlike the schemes operated by other countries. In fact, all Eastern European privatisation programmes have a number of important commonalities. One element common to all Eastern European privatisation programmes, for example, is special rules for the privatisation of small enterprises, such as retail stores, hotels, restaurants, gasoline stations, small service enterprises and cinemas. Private savings are generally sufficient to purchase these enterprises and accordingly, they have faced a strong domestic demand in all Eastern European countries. By the end of 1991, in Hungary, for example, close to 90 per cent of all small enterprises had either been sold or were in the process of being sold. Similarly, in East Germany by the end of February 1992, close to 80 per cent of all small commercial entities had been sold. In Czechoslovakia, where foreigners are not allowed to participate in the small enterprise privatisation programme at least during the initial round of sales, a more cautious approach to small-scale privatisation has been adopted, which involves the extensive use of leasing during the first years of transition.

Almost all Eastern European privatisation programmes contain an element of restitution. In East Germany, large parts of industrial property and land are subject to restitution claims. While restitution claims have clearly slowed down the privatisation of land, the German privatisation agency was given early permission to ignore restitution claims in case of an overriding public interest. In cases where justified restitution claims were ignored, financial compensation may be given instead. In general, Eastern European countries have decided in favour of physical restitution rather than financial compensation, but some countries did severely limit the property subject to restitution. In Czechoslovakia, for example, a strict deadline for filing claims and the decision to restrict restitution claims to property that was nationalised under Communist rule (i.e. between 1948 and 1989) effectively limit the amount of property subject to restitution. As most nationalisations of large industrial enterprises in Czechoslovakia were carried out under the democratic government between 1945 and 1948, only about 6 per cent of state assets are affected by restitution (OECD, 1992). In Hungary, physical restitution only exists for agricultural land; non-agricultural property is only compensated for by giving securities to the former owners. In Poland, restitution remains largely unresolved (Sadowski, 1991). However, an early decision was made not to return properties that were expropriated in accordance with the nationalisation laws passed under the Communist system. Hence, in practice outright return of property is limited to small, illegally seized enterprises. However, even there, no legitimate claimants exist in most cases (S. Wellisz, 1991).

There are other elements that are common to Eastern European privatisation programmes, such as the largely demand-determined early privatisations of companies in good financial condition. However, only Romania has an explicit programme for enterprises in good financial health. There are also marked differences among Eastern European countries, particularly with respect to the acceptance of mass privatisation and the acceptance of foreign investment. In general, domestic credit in Eastern Europe is severely constrained, particularly in relation to that available to potential Western buyers. Hence, in the absence of mass privatisation schemes, domestic credit constraints would make sales to foreign investors almost unavoidable. In Hungary, for example, the rejection of mass privatisation has necessarily meant a strong openness to foreign investment. Other countries, particularly those in which mass privatisation is expected to play an important role, have sometimes placed more restrictions on foreign investment. Stricter controls on foreign investments have usually been reasoned out by the need to ensure congruence of interests between enterprises and nations regarding long-term corporate strategies (Carlin and Mayer, 1992). In Poland, for example, foreign investments require special approval by the Agency of Foreign Investment if the par value of the shares bought by a foreign investor exceeds 10 per cent of the share capital of the enterprise (Ministry of Privatization (Poland), 1991a).

2.3.3 *Property rights and corporate control*

Eastern European governments have sometimes been reluctant to mandate changes in enterprise behaviour, be it through privatisation, the development of restructuring and business plans, or participation in technical assistance programmes. This behaviour has been attributed to a desire to avoid charges of centralised control over firms, which had been blamed for the economic crisis under the Communist governments (Kharas, 1991). In Poland and Hungary, for example, privatisation is largely carried out on a voluntary basis, and at least in Poland, a fundamental clarification of property rights has yet to take place.

Problems of clarifying property rights have contributed to the difficulties experienced in addressing questions of corporate control. In principle, two models of corporate control are available: the *outsider model* which is found in the United Kingdom and the United States; and the *insider model* which is found in most of Western Europe and in Japan. The outsider model is characterised by: (i) dispersed ownership, and separation of ownership and control; (ii) little incentive for outside investors to participate in corporate control, and consequently weak commitments of outside investors to long-term strategies of firms; and (iii) friendly and hostile takeovers, and frequent market entrance and exit. In contrast, the insider model is characterised by: (i) concentrated ownership, and association of ownership and control; (ii) corporate control being exercised by shareholding parties (banks, other firms, employees), with outside interventions being limited to periods of clear financial failure; and (iii) absence of takeovers, and infrequent market entrance and exit (Corbett and Mayer, 1991).

Under the outsider model, commercial banks rarely hold equity shares, and play no active role in management; enterprises rarely hold substantial equity stakes in their suppliers or customers. Instead, commercial banks hold enterprise debt, while equity shares are held by a wide range of individuals, financial, and non-financial institutions, with few stakes being large enough to ensure a controlling interest (Hare, 1991; Corbett and Mayer, 1991). In the outsider model, exit (for individual shareholders) and friendly and hostile takeovers are the main mechanisms for ensuring management discipline; if an enterprise is perceived to be poorly managed, individual investors will either sell their equity shares quickly, or put together a group that will attempt to acquire the enterprise and introduce changes and adjustment measures (Hinds, 1991; Borensztein, 1991). Under the insider model, mutual funds, commercial banks, and other interest groups make up a group of core investors that hold substantial equity, and enterprises are frequently interlinked through extensive cross-shareholding. In this model, core investors are active participants in enterprise management as it is considered the most effective way of protecting and increasing the value of their stake (equity plus debt) (Hare, 1991).

After first having given consideration to the 'British model' of privatisation via initial public offerings (Sachs, 1991), the governments of Czechoslovakia, Poland and Romania are now advancing mass privatisation schemes; in Hungary mass privatisation was never actively considered. Under mass privatisation, the core investor principle can be preserved in a number of ways; each possibility involves some type of mutual funds that act as core investors and which in turn are owned by the general public. Lipton and Sachs (1991) envision core investors to be created by the government which would also endow them with certain initial equity holdings and appoint their initial directors. In contrast, Frydman and Rapaczynski (1991) propose free entry into the mutual fund market, and competition among the mutual funds to obtain shares from the public. While Sachs (1991) argues against allowing mutual funds to gain a majority stake in individual enterprises, Frydman and Rapaczynski (1991) propose auctioning of enterprises to the different mutual funds in such a way as to ensure a few large initial shareholders. Clearly, countries that are actively considering mass privatisation with mutual funds have, implicitly or explicitly, given a large role to the insider model of corporate control. On the other hand, countries that largely rely on individual sales, notably Hungary, have not yet made a clear decision on the system of corporate control. In any case, in all countries where privatisation has been slow, there has been a continuation of a system where corporate control is largely exercised by the state. While Eastern European governments have little experience with regulating a private-sector-based economy in a non-intrusive way, the design of a simple and unambiguous system of corporate control is a priority task.

2.3.4 *Banking reform and privatisation*

This section discusses proposals to use privatisation as an instrument of banking sector reform. Hare (1991) has pointed out that, traditionally, the banks of Eastern Europe were agents of the central authorities, part of the mechanism for plan implementation. The abolishing of central plans has left the commercial banking sector of Eastern European countries in a state of disorientation that has sometimes led to virtual paralysis. While it would be difficult to make a meaningful argument for privatisation to precede banking sector reform, in reality this is just what seems to be happening in Eastern Europe.[2]

Svejnar (1991) has argued that the limited availability of commercial credit caused by Eastern Europe's underdeveloped banking sectors has been the single most important hindrance to the growth of private sector activity. Failure to undertake comprehensive banking sector reforms has implied that the role of banks in the emerging corporate structure of Eastern Europe remains yet to be defined. In addition, Carlin and Mayer (1992) have suggested that the extreme difference in the amount of credit available to foreign and domestic investors makes it far from evident that privatisation via sale of enterprises allocates ownership and control appropriately. Comprehensive banking sector reform in Eastern European countries has four main elements: (i) restructuring and possibly consolidating state-owned banks; (ii) enacting a banking law that provides for establishing new private banks; (iii) adopting and implementing modern banking supervision standards; and (iv) resolving the problem of non-performing loans in bank portfolios. Of these four elements, probably the most difficult problem to resolve concerns the non-performing bank loans to enterprises. The magnitude of the outstanding bad loans is estimated to be in the range of 15–20 per cent in Hungary and Czechoslovakia, and may reach 30 to 40 per cent in Poland and Bulgaria (Bruno, 1992). While there are different ways to address this problem, for the purpose of this chapter, proposals that link bank recapitalisation to privatisation are clearly most important.[3]

One way to address the problem of non-performing enterprise debt to banks is to provide banks with shares of newly privatised enterprises. This would address the recapitalisation needs of banks, and facilitate writing off non-performing assets in bank balance sheets. Fischer (1991) has pointed out that, since part of the non-performing bank assets are loans to the same firms that are being privatised, there is some logic in compensating the banks in advance.

This solution, however, is not without controversy. Since bank participation in privatisation also means bank participation in the exercise of corporate control over enterprises, the problems encountered in linking bank recapitalisation and privatisation take us directly back to the issue of property rights and corporate control discussed before. While providing banks with enterprise shares has been advocated, for example, by Lipton and Sachs (1991) for the case of Poland, others have strongly opposed it, arguing that it causes inequities, misallocation of resources, increased financial instability, and potential conflicts of interest. Borensztein (1991), for example, on the basis of evidence presented by Hinds (1991) and by Lipton and Sachs (1991) for the case of Chile, suggests caution in establishing close relationships between banks and their clients. Similarly, Kornai (1991) has argued that putting a sizeable proportion of industrial shares in the hands of large banks is premature in Eastern Europe, particularly when banks are still state-owned. He suggests that banks, as shareholders of large stock companies, may fail to apply regular business criteria to the stock companies in which they hold a stake, and may generally share the interest of the stock companies in being bailed out and artificially sustained. This argument is supported by Schwartz (1991) who, citing evidence from Hungary, has pointed out abuses of close bank-client relationships. The need for unambiguous incentive structures has led McKinnon (1991) to propose an extreme solution, where privatised firms are given no access to credit from the traditional banks, which implies that they would have to finance investments either from retained earnings or by raising funds in capital markets from the non-bank public.

The above discussion points to the urgency of a comprehensive reform of the banking system, and to use the specific problems related to the recapitalisation of banks. Using privatisation to recapitalise banks is considered highly controversial; it should neither be considered as a general solution nor completely ruled out from the outset. If it is decided to use privatisation in the recapitalisation of banks, mechanisms and incentive structures need to be designed with great care. One possibility, suggested by Fischer (1991), would be to hold the shares earmarked for banks in a separate general fund, which would be used at a later stage to infuse funds into banks, and to restructure bank balance sheets with safer assets. In any case, privatisation policies can only be one part in a comprehensive bank restructuring scheme, but can never be a substitute for fundamental bank restructuring.

2.3.5 *The problem of large enterprises*

The privatisation of small enterprises, mostly retail stores and enterprises in trade and services, has proceeded with rapid pace across Eastern Europe, while privatisation of large enterprises, such as mines, steel mills, shipyards, petrochemical complexes and textile mills, has been proceeding with much slower speed. This has been due to two main reasons: (i) large enterprises usually have an obsolete capital stock and employ obsolete production technologies, and may therefore be unlikely to attract interested buyers at positive prices (C. Wellisz, 1991); and (ii) large enterprises account for a big share of employment and production in the economy, and privatisation or shut-down may be politically difficult for various reasons ranging from nationalism (Applebaum, 1992) to the potentially strong adverse impact on output and employment.[4] Still, it is clear that ultimately there may only be two solutions for these enterprises: (i) shut-down and liquidation in parts; or (ii) massive investments to modernise the capital stock. Given that few local individuals have the financial resources to carry out the necessary investment, governments have three basic choices, each of which involves abdicating responsibility for problem enterprises: (i) find ways to attract foreigners on a large scale; (ii) establish diluted share ownership by local individuals via mass privatisation; (iii) break up the existing large-scale enterprises into smaller units that are privatised separately.

Given the scale of the problem, Eastern European governments have been hesitant or unable to tackle the question of large enterprises in a comprehensive fashion. Instead, they have begun to construct privatisation policies around the possibility that these enterprises remain state-owned for a while. Usually, this involves the construction of 'halfway houses'. Halfway houses come in various forms, but usually involve putting the enterprise under the control of an independent board of executive directors, and transforming it into a joint stock or limited liability company. In Hungary, for example, property rights were redefined to make the State Property Agency (SPA) the sole owner of all SOEs; the enterprises were then given a board of directors who required them to produce properly audited balance sheets, and the SOEs were supervised continuously with the help of independent contractors. In Poland, the concept of commercialisation is similar in that it legally transforms SOEs either into limited liability companies or into joint stock companies wholly owned by the state treasury. A basic difference between the Hungarian and the Polish concepts is that in Poland commercialisation is a possible outcome of a voluntary enterprise decision to be privatised. Czechoslovakia, in contrast, has adopted a more radical position, where the speedy transfer of ownership rights to the private sector was thought to alleviate the need for halfway houses. Bruno (1992) has argued that halfway houses to privatisation are generally inevitable, unless one is willing to take the line that what cannot be privatised instantaneously had better be junked immediately. While commercialisation entails a number of problems, the perceived advantage is that SOEs start being covered by normal commercial law and obtain corporate governance through a professional board of directors (Sachs, 1991).

In general, halfway houses do not solve the problems of privatising large enterprises. In particular, they fail to fully expose SOEs to a uniformly hard budget constraint that implies the risk of bankruptcy (Kopits, 1991), may induce decapitalisation by the firm's managers (Bruno, 1992), and can easily put the government in a position where it either has to provide a bail-out for the firm or let it go bankrupt. While halfway houses may allow governments some more breathing space, eventually decisions will have to be made.

2.4 Privatisation: some preliminary policy lessons

The Eastern European privatisation experience, as discussed above, would seem to lead to a number of preliminary policy 'lessons' for governments of other EITs wishing to reduce an overextended public sector. The following proposes five policy lessons around which further discussion on privatisation policies in EITs may be focused; no claim is being made that the lessons are complete or final.

(1) Privatisation is a cornerstone of the transition from plan to market. Hence, it must be accomplished in a speedy and comprehensive fashion. The rapid creation of a legal framework that defines ownership rights in clear and simple terms facilitates public understanding of privatisation, stimulates broad-based ownership, prevents abuses of power, and speeds up privatisation. Given a variety of policy objectives and a highly differentiated demand for the existing portfolio of state assets, the use of a broad set of privatisation tools helps to speed up the process. Separate privatisation programmes for small commercial units targeted at domestic buyers, and limited physical restitution should be part of any privatisation scheme. Reliance on UK-style one-by-one privatisation is time-consuming and unnecessarily slows down the process of transition. Problems of valuation of enterprises are no reason for delaying privatisation. Mass privatisation schemes and other techniques that allow the structure of property rights to change without necessarily requiring asset valuation should be given strong consideration. While broad-scale commercialisation should always be accomplished rapidly, the extensive use of mass privatisation helps to prevent these halfway houses from becoming costly semi-permanent solutions. Foreign investment should generally be considered welcome; there is little economic rationale for placing an upper limit on the share of state-owned property that foreigners may buy.

(2) People are more willing to bear an inevitable burden if they can expect tangible benefits. To be socially more acceptable, any privatisation scheme should have a distributive component. Creating broad-based ownership rights, as envisaged under the various mass privatisation programmes, facilitates income policy reform and supports efforts to reform social policy. For the same reason, management and employee buy-outs and partial employee ownership schemes should be encouraged. It is unlikely that the creation of such broad-based ownership rights would jeopardise macroeconomic stabilisation

efforts by fuelling consumption. Still, distributive questions have to be handled carefully. For example, large segments of society would be excluded from employee ownership schemes simply because they do not work for the companies that are privatised. Also, given strong quality differences in the portfolio of state assets, employee ownership schemes are highly inequitable. This can easily create new tensions in societies that are already overburdened with tensions and contradictions. Hence, while offering a minority share to workers can be very useful, overly preferential treatment, in particular with respect to purchase prices, has to be avoided.

(3) For privatisation to be successful, banking sector reform is crucial. Reasons for this include the significant investments that are required to make Eastern European industries competitive, and the problem that property rights may not be reallocated efficiently if potential buyers do not have access to credit. Credit should be given on 'hard' terms as it helps to signal from the outset that potential owners need to be willing and able to take on risks, and that privatisation does not merely involve an ownership change with the financial risk remaining with the public sector. A comprehensive reform of the banking system has four main elements: (i) restructuring and possibly consolidating state-owned banks; (ii) enacting a banking law that provides for establishing new private banks; (iii) adopting and implementing modern banking supervision standards; and (iv) resolving the problem of non-performing loans in bank portfolios.

(4) While Eastern European governments have little experience with regulating a market economy in a non-intrusive way, the design of a simple and unambiguous system of corporate control is a priority task. The two main Western systems of corporate control – that is, the insider model and the outsider model that were discussed above – both have advantages and disadvantages for EITs. For Eastern Europe, most advice has favoured the insider model, which is characterised by: (i) concentrated ownership, and association of ownership and control; (ii) corporate control being exercised by shareholding parties (banks, other firms, employees), with outside interventions being limited to periods of clear financial failure; and (iii) absence of takeovers, and infrequent market entrance and exist. While this would mean that banks and non-bank financial institutions become closely involved in the process of privatisation, using privatisation in the recapitalisation of banks is highly controversial and great care has to be taken in the design of control mechanisms and incentive structures in order to avoid abuses.

(5) Some local and national government ownership is compatible with the establishment of a market economy. Given the tremendous size of the public sector, the provision of public goods and services as well as selected activities in various sectors is likely to remain in the public domain over the medium term. Still, given the extent of investments that Eastern European economies

require to bring their domestic energy, telecommunications, and transport sectors up to modern standards, private sector solutions should be encouraged.

Notes

1. See C. Wellisz (1991) for a detailed account of the problems of enterprise valuation experienced in the case of Poland.
2. Corbett and Mayer (1991) have suggested that, in the minds of most people, capitalism is synonymous with stock markets, and that the creation of domestic stock markets epitomises the break with socialism more than anything else. This may help to explain why most Eastern European Governments first addressed the politically visible task of opening a stock market (on which there is still hardly anything to trade), but have delayed comprehensive banking sector reform.
3. See Bruno (1992) for an in-depth discussion.
4. In Poland, for example, the top 400 enterprises, ranked by sales, accounted for 36 per cent of total employment in 1990 (Lipton and Sachs, 1991).

References

Adam, C., W. Cavendish and P. S. Mistry (1992), *Adjusting Privatization: Case studies from developing countries*, London: Currey.

Applebaum, A. (1992), 'Econophobia', *The Washington Post*, Washington, DC, 16 February 1992, C1–2.

Borensztein, E. (1991), 'Comments on David Lipton and Jeffrey Sachs, "Privatization in Eastern Europe: the case of Poland", Roman Frydman and Andrzej Rapaczynski, "Markets and institutions in large-scale privatization: an approach to economic and social transformation in Eastern Europe", and Manuel Hinds, "A note on the privatization of socialized enterprises in Poland"', in V. Corbo, F. Coricelli and J. Bossek (eds), *Reforming Central and Eastern European Countries: Initial results and challenges*, Washington, DC: World Bank, 289–92.

Bruno, M. (1992), 'Stabilization and reform in Eastern Europe: a preliminary evaluation', Washington, DC: IMF, 31 January.

Carlin, W. and C. Mayer (1992), 'The Treuhandanstalt: privatization by state and market', paper presented at the NBER Conference on Transition in Eastern Europe, Cambridge, Mass. 26–29 February.

Corbett, J. and C. Mayer (1991), 'Financial reform in Eastern Europe: progress with the wrong model', *Oxford Review of Economic Policy*, **7** (4), 57–75.

Dhanji, F. and B. Milanovic (1990), 'Privatization in East and Central Europe: objectives, constraints and models of divestiture', paper presented at the Conference on Privatization and Ownership Changes in East and Central Europe, World Bank, Washington, DC, 13–14 June.

Fischer, S. (1991), 'Privatization in East European transformation', Working Paper No. 3703, Cambridge, Mass.: National Bureau of Economic Research, May.

Frydman, R. and A. Rapaczynski (1991), 'Markets and institutions in large-scale privatization: an approach to economic and social transformation in Eastern Europe', in V. Corbo, F. Coricelli and J. Bossek (eds), *Reforming Central and Eastern European Countries: Initial results and challenges*, Washington, DC: World Bank, 253–74.

Gruszecki, T. and J. Winiecki (1991), 'Privatization in East-Central Europe: a comparative perspective', *Außenwirtschaft*, **46** (1), 67–100.

Hare, P. G. (1991), 'The assessment: microeconomics of transition in Eastern Europe', *Oxford Review of Economic Policy*, **7** (4), 1–15.

Hare, P. and I. Grosfeld (1991), 'Privatization in Hungary, Poland and Czechoslovakia', Discussion Paper No. 544, London: Centre for Economic Policy Research.

Hemming, R. (1992), 'Privatization of state enterprises', in V. Tanzi (ed.), *Fiscal Policies in Economies in Transition*, Washington, DC: IMF, 80–98.

Hemming, R. and K. Miranda (1991), 'Privatization', in K. Chu and R. Hemming (eds), *Public Expenditure Handbook*, Washington, DC: IMF, 139–45.

Hinds, M. (1991), 'A note on the privatization of socialized enterprises', in V. Corbo, F. Coricelli and J. Bossek (eds), *Reforming Central and Eastern European Countries: Initial results and challenges*, Washington, DC: World Bank, 275–88.

Keating, G. and J. Hoffman (1991), 'Privatisation theory: hold back for a swift advance', *Central European*, April, 32–4.

Kharas, H. J. (1991), 'Restructuring social industry: Poland's experience in 1990', Discussion Paper No. 142, Washington, DC: World Bank, December.

Kopits, G. (1991), 'Fiscal reform in European economies in transition', Working Paper, No. WP/91/43, Washington, DC: IMF, April.

Kornai, J. (1991), 'The principles of privatization in Eastern Europe', Harvard Institute of Economic Research Discussion Paper No. 1567, Cambridge, Mass.: Harvard University, September.

Lipton, D. and J. Sachs (1991), 'Privatization in Eastern Europe: the case of Poland', in V. Corbo, F. Coricelli and J. Bossek (eds), *Reforming Central and Eastern European Countries: Initial results and challenges*, Washington, DC: World Bank, 231–52. Also published in *Brookings Papers on Economic Activity*, **2**, 293–334.

McKinnon, R. I. (1991), *The Order of Economic Liberalization*, Baltimore, Md.: Johns Hopkins University Press.

Maurer, R., B. Sander and K.-D. Schmidt (1991), 'Privatisierung in Ostdeutschland – Zur Arbeit der Treuhandanstalt', *Weltwirtschaft*, **1**, 45–66.

Milanovic, B. (1989), *Liberalization and Entrepreneurship*, New York: Sharpe.

Ministry of Finance (CSFR) (1991), *Kupónová Privatizace* (Voucher Privatization), Information Booklet, Prague: Ministry of Finance.

Ministry of Privatization (Poland) (1991a), *Guide to Foreign Investment in Poland*, Warsaw: Ministry of Privatization, September.

Ministry of Privatization (Poland) (1991b), *Guide to Foreign Investment in Poland*, Warsaw: Ministry of Privatization, December.

OECD (1992), *OECD Economic Surveys: Czech and Slovak Federal Republic, 1991*, Paris: OECD, January.

Sachs, J. (1991), 'Crossing the valley of tears in East European reform', *Challenge*, Sept.–Oct., 26–34.

Sadowski, Z. (1991), 'Privatization in Eastern Europe: goals, problems and implications', *Oxford Review of Economic Policy*, **7** (4), 46–57.

Schwartz, G. (1991), 'Privatization: possible lessons from the Hungarian case', *World Development*, **19** (12), 1731–6.

State Property Agency (Hungary) (1991), *Privatization and Foreign Investment in Hungary*, Budapest: State Property Agency, March.

Svejnar, J. (1991), 'Microeconomic issues in the transition to a market economy', *Journal of Economic Perspectives*, **5** (4), 123–38.

Wellisz, C. (1991), 'Privatization in Poland: the problem of valuation', *Journal of International Affairs*, **465** (1), 247–70.

Wellisz, S. (1991), 'Poland under "Solidarity" rule', *Journal of Economic Perspectives*, **5** (4), 211–17.

3

On the economics of property rights and privatisation in transitional economies

Jozef M. van Brabant

3.1 Introduction

To accelerate their transformation into mainstream market economies, not only do the planned economies in transition need to be thoroughly restructured and reorganised, but the very core of their socio-political and economic systems will have to be reconstructed almost from the ground up.[1] As distinct from a centrally or administratively planned economy, a planned economy in transition is characterised by pluralistic decision making and the gradual emergence of market mechanisms as the primary vehicle for co-ordinating the activities of various agents in society, especially as concerns the allocation of resources. Profound changes in ownership and property rights are at the core of this venture into the unknown. This is not a melodramatic claim. The mature market economies matured over at least two centuries. Trying to reproduce this experience in a matter of a few years is truly an adventure into the unknown.

This chapter sets out to provide a backdrop to the debate on and experience with privatisation in selected Eastern countries. The next section outlines the core of the subject matter. The third section briefly recapitulates the nature of markets, how the creation of market systems relates to ownership and property rights and why property rights reform is a necessary, if insufficient, condition for successfully moving toward market-based decision making. The key features of property rights and the contrast between what exists in centrally or administratively planned economies and what needs to emerge are examined in the fourth section. After a brief discussion on restitution and the compensation claims of former owners, the fifth section details the various objectives for privatisation in alternative socio-political systems. Elements of a competitive environment and how they relate to privatisation and property rights, as well as the various implications of alternative ownership forms, are clarified in the sixth section. The seventh section sets out the critical technical problems inherent in alternative methods of privatising state assets in centrally planned economies. The forms and experiences with privatisation form the subject of the eighth section. Conclusions regarding how privatisation fits into the transition process are drawn in the final section.

3.2 Radical restructuring and the role of the state

In late 1989 and early 1990, overly optimistic expectations were aired on how quickly the countries of Eastern Europe could be thoroughly transformed into effective pluralistic societies with functioning market economies. In the event, the radical restructuring of the East is proving to be a contentious, protracted and exceedingly painful process that will probably be stretched out over decades rather than a few years. One fundamental issue revolves around the prospective role of the state in the economy and the newly built society following the transition. Eventually, the state will become a central co-ordinator and orchestrator, rather than a detailed prescriber of production, distribution and consumption patterns. These tasks should be increasingly devolved to financially autonomous firms that operate within the guidelines set by the newly emerging institutions and by the framework of macroeconomic policies that aim at co-ordinating decisions indirectly. However, what precisely the latter entails is still the subject of, at times, acrimonious debate. This debate concerns microeconomic matters as well as the desirable shape of the democratic, market-based institutions and the most appropriate macroeconomic policies, and how the state will have to disengage itself from the legacies of over-centralised decision making and administration.[2] All of these are highly controversial issues.

The wide diversity of views and passions in the transitional economies is not surprising, especially in view of the key features of a centrally or administratively planned economy that have been jettisoned, but have not yet been fully replaced. These were societies where public ownership dominated almost completely for over 40 years.[3] From it emanated a power base in the form of an all-powerful bureaucracy, including state-owned enterprises (SOEs). Sovereignty of the individual; autonomy and private property; business, political and intellectual freedoms; the institutions of democracy; and the rule of law, were suppressed for decades. It is not surprising therefore that the recent revolutionary changes in most of the East have included an unrestrained reaffirmation of private property, and in some cases, outright opposition even to the principle of non-private ownership.

Ideological and political considerations are, thus, inextricably intermingled with the fundamental economic issues of establishing effective markets. Indeed, the 'confidence with which privatisation is favoured as a means of achieving superior results betrays the ideological content of the message' (Commander and Killick, 1988: 96). The reality of the planned economies in transition enormously complicates the task of economic policy making and calls for a good deal of improvisation, pragmatism and compromises on the economics of privatisation. Yet it is instructive to distinguish between economic rationality and the more emotional, political and ideological *obiter dicta* that are so pervasive in the literature on transition, if only to sort out the various options from among which policy makers must soon adopt workable variants.

As concerns the role of the state in the transition, the various opinions cover a broad spectrum. There is little dispute about having the government concentrate on governance. As far as economics is concerned, there is also broad consensus in the Eastern economies about having the government create and maintain a stable macroeconomic environment. There is widespread agreement too about the government promoting the institutional framework that is essential to ensure an economic order for exchange operations among economic agents which is in conformity with the broad requirements of the market economy. However, all other functions of the state in the societies under reconstruction, including proscribing environmentally unsound industrialisation strategies, regulating economic affairs and redistributing incomes, are matters of vigorous debate.

Perhaps a more fundamental point for discussion is the degree to which the state should become involved in the growth process. There is no doubt that it should set up, delineate and maintain a stable and transparent arena for economic agents to pursue their own interests at their own risk. Likewise there is agreement that the state should extricate itself from the pervasive meddling in economic affairs that occurred under central planning. To achieve a properly functioning market, central government intervention of the right kind and in the right areas is necessary (Streeten, 1991). Examples of such intervention are safeguarding a competitive framework and taking advantage of the beneficial 'crowding in' effects of infrastructural investments. But to be more concrete about what precisely the state's role should be invokes considerable controversy. What is apparent, however, is that the transition cannot be engineered simply on the advice of professional economists (Madzar, 1990: 145–6).[4]

It will help to focus the discussion if we define the property rights and privatisation concepts. For the purpose of this chapter, a property right is a socially enforceable right to select uses of scarce goods. The holder of such a right should be entitled to engage in any mutually agreed contractual arrangement, though not all such agreements need to be validated through government action. That is to say, ownership cannot be satisfactorily defined unless the right of property is the right of dealing with things in the most absolute fashion the law allows.[5] The crucial element, in Roman law, is the *ius utendi, fruendi et abutendi*, that is, the right of use (*usus*), enjoyment of the fruit (*usus fructus*) and disposal of the object of ownership (*abusus*); the latter may comprise the right to change the form and substance, or to transfer one or more of the rights specified earlier to another party (Pejovich, 1990: 28). The divisibility of property rights into logically separate components is crucial in analysing the purposes of privatisation during the East's transitions. It forms a major element of the central point developed in this paper.

Capturing what precisely is meant by privatisation is more difficult. The arguments in the debates on privatisation are extremely varied, ranging from alternative notions of freedom and democracy to divergent views on the lessons to be derived from past experiences with both public and private enterprises. However, one economic issue – namely, the question of the relationship between the efficiency of a firm and its ownership (Newbery, 1991; Tomlinson, 1986) – is of paramount importance. It can encompass a wide variety of changes in control over assets; some are concerned with alternative approaches to the supply and financing of services provided by local and central governments. As such, privatisation can be described as an umbrella term for a variety of policies that are loosely linked by the way in which they are taken to mean the strengthening of the market at the expense of the state (Vickers and Wright, 1988: 1). In this chapter, privatisation will mean the transfer from the public to the private sector of the entitlement to residual or net profits that accrue from operating an 'enterprise'. The chapter concentrates therefore, on the stock of assets and their transformation. Questions dealing with new capital formation and entrepreneurship are touched upon only marginally. Likewise, broader definitions, which include deregulation and entrepreneurship (Eliasson, 1991) or user fees for government services (Vickers and Wright, 1988: 3), are not used.

3.3 Establishing market systems, property rights and privatisation

Property rights reform has several dimensions. One includes questions revolving around the assignment of property rights associated with existing assets. Another aspect is the assignment and guarantee of property rights to assets to be created from gross public and private savings.[6] Property rights reform is indeed an integral component of the measures to sensitise these societies to market incentives. But the market system as such has little to say about the distribution and possible abuses of ownership. Among the complex conceptual issues associated with the establishment of markets, none has been more controversial than the capital market. Those organising capital markets should be concerned, at least conceptually, with four core issues: (i) to ensure the efficient allocation of the service streams coming from the existing capital stock as an essential ingredient of reaching efficient allocation of existing resources; (ii) to foster an environment in which capital assets can be traded for holdings in wealth portfolios as one element of intermediating between savers and investors; (iii) to provide incentives for the most effective creation of new capital, including the provision of liquidity and the transformation of short-term deposits into long-term lending; and (iv) to set the framework for the disposition, through exit and entry, of capital owned by the state or by the private sector and, thus, to raise capital's net worth through competition.

Under some circumstances, (ii) and (iv) could coincide, but it will prove useful to separate them during the transition process. The first is especially important, for ownership *per se* has little to do with enhancing the techniques of allocating scarce resources. What matters first and foremost is the allocation of user rights to capital through unambiguous contractual relations. This can proceed through effective capital markets, given the level of development of the country in question (see Brabant, 1989, 1991b); it could also proceed by internalising the cost of allocating these services, for example, through private ownership.

Moreover the complexity of economic activities means that ownership patterns will also be complex (Barzel, 1989). The most efficient owner of a particular attribute of an asset, say, ownership *per se*, is not necessarily the most efficient owner of the asset's other attributes (such as utilisation of the service stream or the *usufruct*). It may be advantageous, then, to split the ownership rights of an asset among several economic agents. Because the asset itself as an object of property is not physically unbundled, its owners may find it easy to consume some of each other's unpriced attributes if they are not constrained through the effective enforcement of property rights.

One of the crucial questions at this juncture facing the leaderships of the planned economies in transition is what to do with publicly owned capital now that the state has decided in principle to withdraw from exercising direct ownership functions. The most liberal reformers in the planned economies in transition advocate the widespread privatisation of state assets by selling them off quickly or giving them away, if not all at once, at least swiftly. In some cases, this may be warranted from a strictly economic point of view. If capital services can be allocated at lower cost by internalising the co-ordination of the service stream of assets rather than through a formal market process, private property would be the answer, for the ultimate owner then exercises full control. But it does not necessarily follow that divestment should always be enacted quickly or below 'fair market value' (Comisso, 1991).

The strategy of organising capital markets can best be tackled by recognising that neither private nor public ownership of assets by itself guarantees the most efficient exploitation of user rights. By disjoining, at least conceptually, ownership from ownership rights (all property rights minus final disposition or alienation of the assets, for example), one could start thinking about the proper technical issues at stake.[7] In that context, it should be recognised that in a planned economy in transition any kind of property reform may prevail. Its justification may be various, but an economic one would simply be that there will be at least one productive endeavour for which one of the possible property forms will be best suited in the sense that in this way the service stream emanating from the assets can be co-ordinated at least cost per unit of value-added generated. The potential for disassembling property rights in the case of planned economies in transition is considerable, provided the transition gets off to a robust start and technical issues are considered on their own merit. Furthermore the exchange of property rights thorough entry and exit should be ensured, including those for publicly owned funds. That can best be organised through open, competitive bidding.

If there is free exit and entry, subject to regulatory powers to correct market failures, new capital will be formed according to whatever enhances the allocation of resources. However, this cannot be anticipated for the publicly owned capital stock at the outset of the transition. The key questions of privatisation and property rights reform in the case of existing assets should, then, address the allocation of the usufruct of capital assets and how best to guarantee that assets are not misappropriated for 'private' gain. This applies with minor modifications also to the use of natural resources and intangible assets, most of which cannot be sold. There are, of course, other issues that concern entry, capital formation, innovation and expansion of existing assets.

To recapitulate, in discussing how best to allocate existing assets with a view to maximising some returns, it is useful to distinguish between ownership *per se* and the usufruct component of property rights. For all practical purposes, a substantial proportion of the entire capital stock in place in planned economies in transition will continue to belong to a society as a whole for years to come.[8] This will be more so for infrastructure, public utilities and large SOEs, and perhaps land too, than for housing, service operations, and other small productive endeavours. Moreover even divestment of the latter cannot be enacted instantaneously. Although state ownership under the typical planned economy established clear property rights, that monopoly was frequently utilised to project state power (Kanel, 1974: 828–9). Furthermore these rights were diluted by efforts to improve economic performance through the devolution of administrative responsibilities. This resulted in ill-defined property rights: enterprise or workers' councils disposed of the capital stock, but it was unclear whether they were the owners with all consequences for the disposition of final ownership of the property at stake. Re-establishing secure property rights for these assets and protecting them by orderly judicial and legislative procedures can help limit arbitrary decisions by the powerful. In this connection, whatever rights are assigned and however they can be separated, mechanisms must be put in place to ensure that the value of capital assets is not eroded at the expense of the ultimate owner. This may warrant the establishment of insurance schemes in addition to legal redress early on during the transformation.

3.4 Property rights, ownership and privatisation

Interactions among socio-economic agents are conditioned by two broad sets of constraints. One stems from the physical limits on resources, including, in many cases, the service streams emanating from reproducible assets. The other derives from various arrangements for the mobilisation of scarce resources. Rules, including property rights, define the framework within which actors formulate choices and respond to incentives. If the social limits to individual behaviour are well defined, and hence rights are enforceable, social interaction will materialise within an 'order' that reconciles on a consensual basis the conflicting interests of various agents.

There are two aspects to the key question of how property rights affect economic decisions. First, there are transaction costs to economic behaviour that, in addition to intrinsic resource scarcity, determine outcomes. Often, the magnitude of these costs can be verified only in the process of enforcing property rights and they embody, therefore, an element of uncertainty (Barzel, 1989). Second, property rights cannot always be unambiguously described and defended, and for that reason there often exists an opportunity to capture attributes of these transactions when they are not checked by the institutions in place. Alternative property rights exert different effects on the allocation of resources. That the owner of property rights should be entitled to the residual benefits of that ownership is clear: but what does ownership mean and which residual benefits are targeted?

Unambiguously demarcated property rights must be vested as much as possible in the hands of actors with purely economic responsibilities; they must be enforceable by a neutral party through an effective juridical system and modern civil and commercial codes; and policy-making authority, including the ability to prescribe what kinds of activities the bearer of property rights can engage in, must be entrusted to institutions that themselves neither exercise property rights nor enforce them – a role that normally belongs to the legislative branch of government.

Property rights are important in explaining the uses of resources in terms of both allocative and productive efficiency of firms (Vickers and Yarrow, 1988: 3) since they affect the objectives of the 'owners' of the firm and the way in which resources are utilised.[9] Public and private ownership differ in both respects (Nuti, 1991b). As a result, changes in property rights from public to private sectors necessarily alter the relationship between those responsible for the firm's decisions and the beneficiaries of its profits, thereby affecting the incentive structure of management, and managerial behaviour and company performance. For the indirect co-ordination of decentralised economic decisions about production, distribution and consumption to function well in a society where knowledge is widely diffused, economic agents must have secure, alienable property rights to assets that can be traded, possibly in unbundled form, at mutually agreed prices in reliable contractual transactions. Such contracts must be negotiable at a fairly low cost (North, 1990).

The allocative and productive efficiency implications of property assignments depend very much on the competitive and regulatory environment in which economic agents operate. This environment typically has substantially larger effects on performance than ownership *per se*.[10] Ownership, competition (hence the monitoring system) and regulation are essentially shorthand expressions for complex sets of mutually interlocking influences and the efficiency implications of a change in one or more of these elements will, as a rule, be contingent upon what happens to the other two. The effects of privatisation, therefore, cannot properly be assessed in isolation from these additional influences on incentives.

Even when an asset sale occurs, much of the impact of policy may arise from decisions about competition and regulation rather than from the mere transfer of ownership title. In the case of large assets, the immediate effect of such privatisation is to substitute shareholder for governmental monitoring and control of the SOE's management. The impact of that shift in monitoring, therefore, depends very much on the degree to which the new shareholders can motivate management to become more receptive to maximising net asset values. Matters are different with small and medium-sized firms where owners might themselves manage the assets or, when they do not, the problems of ensuring adequate monitoring are likely to be less severe.

The foregoing suggests that privatisation as an operational policy category is often ill-defined (Brabant, 1991a; Milanovic, 1991). The notion has been used to describe a whole range of activities, including all kinds of deregulation, that may be undertaken with the help of government to improve the functioning of the market economy. It could be seen as a process that takes the state (political bodies as well as government administration, including the *nomenclature*) out of the decision making over the allocation of the usufruct, and in some cases even the ownership, of state-owned assets. In that sense, privatisation should provide the overriding framework of the East's transformations.

It is important, however, to utilise one unambiguous definition. 'Privatisation' here means the transfer to other agents of the right of the state to influence directly the allocation of capital resources to non-state entities, to whom the residual or net profits of utilising assets accrue.[11] When privatisation as defined refers to enterprise reforms that alter the legal position of the enterprise from being a state agent into some joint-stock company, the term 'corporatisation' is used. With it, the state remains the owner. But the allocation of the usufruct of ownership, which is within the competence of management, will henceforth be monitored by some state asset-management agency. The latter's operations, however wide an authority may be delegated to that agency, should be subject to tight supervision by the emerging democratic process (parliament or one of its watch-dog committees).[12]

When corporatised firms in the above sense are also subject to a 'hard budget' constraint – that is, they have to be profitable or otherwise be sold or dissolved – the term 'commercialisation' is invoked. This involves the fine-tuning of managerial incentive schemes so that management seeks to maximise net asset values. The latter should be contestable so that the ultimate owner can appoint the management that best serves his or her interests.

Finally, the notion 'divestment' denotes the irrevocable release of all property rights from the state to another agent. Such transactions include outright sales, for which precisely that term will be used, through a variety of channels as well as programmes for the free distribution of the assets, often referred to as 'give-aways'.

The sale of assets in the planned economies in transition is generally separated into so-called small (or 'petty') and big (or 'real' or 'mass') privatisation. This distinction was first introduced by the reform leadership of Czechoslovakia, but it has since gained wider acceptance for two reasons. One is the goal of improving the efficiency of asset use, buttressing private ownership as a key ingredient of strengthening democracy and rewarding the population at large with new forms of assets and risks. The other is that it is now widely recognised that the speed of privatisation, especially in the case of core industry ('real' privatisation), can proceed only over a fairly protracted period of time even if policy makers are bent on divesting assets without having to worry much about proceeds and wealth distribution.

The dividing line between small and big privatisation is not set hard and fast, however. The first is essentially concerned with the sale to the public-at-large (possibly residents, nationals, expatriates and foreign private and legal persons) of assets that the state should never have arrogated to itself in the first place.[13] These are essentially capital goods (including housing, service shops, retail outlets, catering establishments, small workshops and similar productive units) for which the process of co-ordinating the service streams yielded by these capital assets can be ensured at least cost through private ownership. These should be sold quickly through fair allocation mechanisms, such as the auctions under way in Czechoslovakia.[14] On the other hand, big privatisation refers to the divestment of the vast bulk of SOEs that tend to be large, organised in conglomerates and highly monopolistic. The objectives of such divestment as well as the ways in which it could be achieved are, therefore, considerably more complex than is the case for assets that form the subject proper of small privatisation.

3.5 Restitution, compensation and objectives of privatisation

In examining privatisation in the broad sense adopted here, it is important to separate the motivations underlying this component of the transformation from the ways in which the East hopes to accomplish the change in property rights. An important aspect of the transition process is that there may be a socio-political consensus on restituting property that was earlier confiscated. This issue first emerged in Czechoslovakia as one important wrong to be righted after the 'velvet revolution'. It was an integral component of efforts to merge the Eastern parts of Germany into the institutional framework of the new Germany. The issue has subsequently also arisen in Hungary, Poland and Romania. Poland has already decided, as Czechoslovakia did, to consider restitution in some cases. Most claims of former owners will be handled through compensation bonds. In Hungary, preference is for some form of compensation, but mostly in the form of claims on shares in SOEs to be privatised. The latter has become the norm also in Czechoslovakia and the former German Democratic Republic. Elsewhere in the East, most of the issues of whether – and how – to compensate former owners have yet to be conclusively dealt with.[15] The basic problems that arise in this connection can be summarised as follows.

Restitution has been justified on moral or ethical grounds. The recommitment to democratic values and respect for the rule of law in the planned economies in transition argues in its favour. But any such commitment is bound to complicate the transformation of these societies into market entities. Even if the former owners can be clearly identified, it is by no means unambiguous whether the usufruct that has since been entrusted to or the property rights that have since been acquired by others can be revoked.[16] Matters become far more complex in the case of factories whose structure has been substantially modified during the period of central planning than, say, in the case of land on which no structures were erected during Communist rule.

The greatest problem facing any attempt to resort to restitution in any but the most narrowly defined circumstances is that the legal infrastructure of these economies, which was inadequate to start with, is likely to get hopelessly entangled in and bogged down by claims for years to come. For that reason, a commitment to compensate those whose assets were earlier confiscated is less troublesome. Of course, this too presents some complications: compensation would put pressure on government budgets (possibly in the future because of privatisation bonds or free shares in privatised SOEs), and the matter of ascertaining the propriety of property claims would have to be tackled. Any attempt to ask the new governments to compensate former owners out of state revenues is misguided, given the already exceedingly weak fiscal base of all planned economies in transition.[17] At the very least, compensation should be funded from the proceeds of asset sales, perhaps by giving away shares of SOEs to former owners or, as in Hungary, giving them chits that can be exchanged for shares in SOEs to be privatised.

Perhaps a commitment in principle to compensate former owners from the proceeds of the sale of capital assets (including the transfer of shares in SOEs, if so desired) would go a long way to complying with restitution commitments without disrupting the transition process. This is essentially the path embraced to date by Hungary, although the constitutional issue of restoring the land claims of former owners has not yet been resolved.

In the planned economies in transition there are at least four motives for privatisation that are largely absent in market economies. One is essentially political in nature, namely retribution for the long years during which private ownership was denied and the state arrogated to itself the entire capital formation and allocation process.

Related to this is the desire of the former planned economies simply to become like any other country. This is very often equated with the ambition to become a liberal market economy, the latter's prototype often being some naive proto-capitalist organisation with elementary market relations driven by owners who actually exercise full property rights over their assets.

Another motive derives from the fact that under central planning, management of SOEs was often entrusted to the Party faithful and their protégés (*nomenclature*) rather than to individuals with demonstrated abilities to operate capital assets in the state's best interests and accordingly being held responsible and accountable.

The last distinguishing motive of privatisation in the planned economies in transition is also largely political. The process of firmly rooting democracy in these societies has some way to go. To buttress it and make it irreversible, a critical minimum of mass private and other forms of non-state ownership must be established.

In discussing the objectives of privatisation, it is necessary to come to grips with the legacies of central planning and abuses of power under Communist rule. Resorting to the outright divestment of state-owned assets, to break this power structure can be crucial at a time when the move toward democracy has not yet been completed or continues to be rather weak. However, once the new political structures are firmly in place, the abuses of the *nomenclatura* in operating state-owned assets as their own fiefdom should be curtailed and altogether excised through that political process. It would not necessarily require outright divestment. In fact, 'confiscation' of the property rights vested *de facto* with the *nomenclatura* might be counterproductive from the point of view of improving allocative and productive efficiency.

Moreover, when discussing the availability of managerial talent in the planned economies in transition, two considerations are important. One is that management under central planning, irrespective of how it came to be appointed, sometimes has a claim to property rights. This was especially the case under administrative planning when management was called upon (at some risk to itself and when the state declined to monitor the performance) to allocate resources with the goal of maximising output. Taking these rights away altogether might well result in their destruction. This might even be unfair as adjudicated by the new democratic values. The *nomenclatura* has, of course, other property rights, some of which it arrogated to itself in ways that are now no longer deemed acceptable.

Also, management under administrative planning was never called upon to maximise net asset value. Instead, it was expected to execute plan targets in accordance with prevailing rules on the allocation of inputs and outputs that were largely administratively assigned. This could involve skilful bargaining with ministries over the procurement of inputs and the disposal of outputs, including through foreign trade. In other words, it is erroneous simply to label a priori the management of SOEs prior to the creation of markets as inefficient because it did not maximise net asset values.

In the matter of establishing a minimum of private and non-state ownership, an important consideration is that the ability to raise savings in these countries commensurate with the vast capital required for economic reconstruction is limited.[18] For this reason, it may be desirable to divest quickly some portion of the existing capital stock through imaginative schemes other than outright sales and to foster private-property formation from new savings as rapidly as possible. Among those schemes that are currently being considered, notably in Czechoslovakia, Poland and Romania, are the free or near-free distribution of a certain proportion of shares in SOEs to the public at large, perhaps in the form of a stake in investment or mutual funds yet to be created; allowing workers to buy a stake in their enterprises at a preferential price, something that is especially important in Poland; devolving ownership to local and municipal authorities, which in turn will utilise this stake to finance part of their own expenditure, as pursued to some degree in Hungary and Poland, (Dhanji and Milanovic, 1990).

The above discussion suggests that there is rarely a single objective to be served especially as regards the sale of state assets. The desirability of divestment, therefore, depends not only on the different possible forms of resource allocation, but also on the weights attached to the alternative objectives policy makers pursue. In other words, for each type of divestment a 'divestment function' could be specified with, as arguments, revenue generation, improvements in allocative and productive efficiency, contribution to stabilising democracy, getting even with the Party and its associated bureaucracy, breaking the back of other interest groups, disbursing wealth to society at large to foster private-property ownership and others. Although this cannot possibly be a linear function, the non-negative weights attached to each of the arguments and the revelation of other preferences must necessarily emerge through the social consensus-building process. Seen from this angle, the a priori case for quick and cost-free divestment appears to be rather weak because the weights attached to the other arguments are unlikely to be identically zero.

It is appropriate to examine the aims of privatisation in order to set forth criteria by which its success can be evaluated. Six objectives stand out: (i) buttressing democracy and personal freedom; (ii) elevating the efficiency of assets presently owned by the state through market discipline, competition and the elimination of government intervention, which in a number of cases requires outright divestment; (iii) raising revenue for the budget and reducing budgetary allocations (such as subsidies), including the administrative burden of the government's administering of state-owned assets, notably SOEs; (iv) allowing firms to raise capital in commercial markets; (v) contributing to the widening and deepening of the capital market, possibly to encourage savings (such as through workers' share-holding or stock-owning incentives); and (vi) undercutting entrenched positions of interest groups (such as trade unions, the Communist Party and the *nomenclature*). As there is a wide diversity in these pragmatic, ideological, economic and populist objectives, a range of 'successful' outcomes can justify privatisation.

As regards the role of private capital formation early on during the transition, it is especially important to encourage new agents into exerting greater domestic competition. Special measures may be required to stimulate this process, possibly by making available most of the cash flow in the state sector for the creation of small and medium-sized private enterprises.[19] The channelling of these funds through commercial banks, which are yet to be created in an effective form, perhaps at favourable, but non-discriminatory, interest rates, might impart a critical impetus to strengthening the private sector. But other preferential schemes may have to be initiated to overcome inertia and the uncertainty that prevails in the planned economies in transition. How this could best be done and what its links should be to the sale of state assets remain to be investigated.

The objectives that decision makers of the planned economy in transition may wish to pursue in the matter of privatisation determine to a large degree the methods of divestment to be employed. Thus, if budget revenues must be maximised, assets must be priced at the highest value that can be obtained from those possessing wealth. But if the prime motive is to buttress democracy or advance libertarian values associated with private property, divestment through outright sale of or through free distribution of assets should be carried out as rapidly as possible. If it is possible to reach those known to be interested in exercising property rights to achieve the maximum economic benefit, so much the better. Whether that should be done by giving each citizen an equal share in social property, as had originally been aimed at by the leadership of Czechoslovakia, or through the creation of the institutions of the emerging capital market (including pension funds, insurance companies and mutual funds as they are presently being introduced in Czechoslovakia and Poland), is something to be considered carefully. The broad free distribution of assets, whatever its justification, would result in enormous administrative costs and give rise to formidable monitoring problems, not to mention its adverse effects on capital formation. This is one of the many reasons that persuaded Czechoslovak policy makers to modify their earlier views on divestment.

There is, however, little doubt that virtually all planned economies in transition have now decided to move forward rapidly with the sale or free distribution of petty assets, while deferring consideration on large privatisation because of the many issues involved. In most cases, the drive to divest the state of small assets revolves around the organisation of competitive auctions, initially open to resident nationals. There are, however, other important policies, which sometimes act as constraints on the divestment campaign. Thus, in Poland it would have been all but impossible to initiate the broad divestment effort without the government taking into account the existing property rights of workers' councils. As a result, workers are being offered first choice in divestment efforts and some stake at a favourable price in the SOEs to be privatised. Likewise in Hungary, policy makers have encouraged 'privatisation from below', but since the installation of the democratic government this has been closely supervised by the government, to take advantage of the skills of existing management.

Until the end of 1990, the scale of divestment of petty assets, on the whole, remained very small. In 1991, however, rapid progress was made by Czechoslovakia, the former German Democratic Republic and Poland. Several other countries, including Bulgaria, Romania and possibly Albania and the Soviet Union, are also planning to move forward with it quickly. The process was well under way in Yugoslavia too, before it became the victim of ethnic strife.

3.6 Privatisation and the creation of a competitive environment

State-owned assets represent societal savings that had earlier been appropriated and disposed of in line with socialistic precepts as well as through chicanery, zealotry and overbearing bureaucratic interference. The governments of the new societies must, therefore, ensure that these resources are utilised as efficiently as possible in the new environment. This raises two broad issues, namely, the allocation process as such and how to obtain a proper value for assets to be sold.

Reform socialism entrusted assets to the enterprise collective, either in some variant of worker self-management, as in Poland and Yugoslavia, or to managers, as in Hungary, without the state ensuring effective monitoring. The highly monopolised structure of production in these economies embodied economic rents that the SOE captured for itself rather than on behalf of the state as owner. In many cases, this led to raising wages to ensure loyalty to management, which would not, of course, put at risk its entrenched position.[20] Just as markets cannot function well without competition, the same applies for the utilisation of assets. The latter cannot be fully contested unless there is economically motivated exit and entry, and some modicum of a functioning capital market. Structures must also ensure that rents accrue to those having property rights – not necessarily the ultimate owners. These latter may content themselves with a fixed rate of return or a similar compensation for their opportunity cost.

Governments keen on freeing themselves of direct involvement in SOEs, yet bent on retaining ownership, can explore at least two alternative organisational forms which do not disturb ultimate ownership structures. One is arranging leases of assets of SOEs to the highest bidder or to a party selected as the most appropriate one under the circumstances. Another option is management contracts (Vuylsteke, 1988, 1990). Following disappointing progress with privatisation, management contracts are now being looked upon more favourably in a number of countries, notably Hungary and Poland. The advantage is that the benefits of ownership are retained in the public sector, while the operations of SOEs are in effect privatised. It gives the government time to decide on divestment while helping to establish the SOE's comparative advantage and real asset value. Alternatively, the government could make a genuine declaration to the effect that, irrespective of its ownership, it undertakes not to interfere in commercial decisions of the SOEs so identified; but it would certainly have to ensure proper monitoring itself and by agents acting on its behalf.

But management contracts are not altogether without drawbacks. A key issue is the determination of the proper rental fee and the monitoring of the contract holders to ensure that assets are not stripped or otherwise alienated. One critical presumption against public ownership has been put forward by many observers: government cannot be expected to refrain from meddling in enterprise affairs even in matters that go beyond managerial efficiency. It is true that the experience with public enterprise in many countries has been rather discouraging in this respect. However, now that there are new governments in place in most of the planned economies in transition, the former umbilical cord between politics and state firms has presumably been severed. That begs the question of whether the political system will inevitably be burdened by patronage and political rents, as argued, for example, by Stanley Fischer (1991: 5). Yet it is not clear why a government that is properly monitored by a duly constituted parliament should inevitably be lured into meddling with SOEs for other than economic reasons.

These alternatives to divestment presuppose that it is possible, without disturbing ownership and management structures, to devise criteria of managerial behaviour that force the SOE to operate as if it were bound by market disciplines in all facets of decision making. Criteria would include, for example: specification of a minimum required rate of return on capital; targets of overall and perhaps of disaggregated net returns, unit costs and productivity; and the obligation to procure working capital and investment funds on commercial terms in the emerging capital markets. This leads to a paradox: although divestment may seem most appropriate for SOEs operating in competitive markets, these are precisely the firms whose performance with respect to internal efficiency can be most readily ameliorated by reforming their monitoring systems (Zeckhauser and Horn, 1989: 55–6).

Perhaps the most important obstacle to property rights reform in planned economies in transition has been the deeply engrained sentiment for income equalisation. Any incentive scheme that rewards enterprise management in accordance with its ability to maximise long-run profits, encourages innovation and risk, and penalises failure, perhaps through takeovers or outright bankruptcy, is likely to entail a considerable disparity in individual incomes. Furthermore, fostering the proper allocation of incomes between consumption and savings, even if private property is not formally envisaged, will eventually lead to unequal asset ownership and hence to disparities in inherited wealth. This dilemma between the need to foster income and wealth differentiation, yet ensure the measure of equity demanded by the socio-political consensus, can be resolved only through thorough fiscal reform.

3.7 Salient obstacles to divestment in the East

Market structures are key ingredients in arriving at any informed decision to divest for economic reasons (Fershtman, 1990; Newbery, 1991). Once taken, many practical obstacles lie ahead. Key questions are: how to evaluate the assets; how quickly the sale of assets should proceed; whether a reservation price should be established; and for what purposes the proceeds should be earmarked.

The experience with divestment in market economies is of limited value to the Eastern economies for a number of reasons. The principal ones are: the comparatively small size of the state sector in market economies; the fact that property rights are clearly defined; that functioning capital markets exist; that there is sufficient wealth to purchase SOEs; that monitoring mechanisms are available, although they are far from perfect (see Corbett and Mayer, 1991; Singh, 1990; Stiglitz, 1991); and that managerial incentive schemes can be readily enacted.

The experience in the market economies has shown that divestment has not unambiguously lowered product prices, improved allocative efficiency, ameliorated internal efficiency in privatised enterprises or generated better service. Moreover experience has shown that SOEs have more often than not been divested below their market value, as shown, for example, by the quick capital gains reaped in the British and French privatisation campaigns. Although policy makers had hoped to promote broadly based share ownership by divesting state-owned assets, most of those who acquired shares quickly cashed in on their 'capital gain' (see Vickers and Yarrow, 1988, 1991; Yarrow, 1986).

Above all, the outcome of divestment in market economies with respect to efficiency gains has underlined that the superiority of private enterprise depends critically on the degree of competition prevailing in the market, the incentives incorporated in the different organisational forms and the effectiveness of regulatory policies designed to correct market failures, rather than ownership *per se* (Yarrow, 1986: 333). Whereas there can be a presumption that private enterprise tends to be more efficient than public enterprise, there is no guarantee that the discounted additional gains over the firm's lifetime will offset the initial loss in selling assets below market value.

At the outset of the East's revolutions, the complexity of managing divestment programmes was vastly underestimated by virtually all observers, most notably the new political leaderships of the planned economies in transition and key decision makers of the international economic and other organisations called upon to ease the transition. The hurdles to be jumped have been many indeed.

A first group encompasses technical issues. Given that divestment can in principle not be enacted all at once, a detailed analysis and classification of SOEs is highly desirable. This would enable decision makers to identify: firms that can be sold immediately with success (perhaps because they had significant exports to market economies at competitive prices); those that need rehabilitation prior to divestment (for example, because their export markets in the East have been undermined or altogether lost); those that must be retained (owing to strategic or social importance); and others that must be liquidated (perhaps because their markets in the East depended critically on the existence of the now defunct transferable-rouble trade and payment regimes). At the same time, steps must be taken to corporatise and commercialise SOEs. To sell SOEs, a proper economic assessment is necessary. Furthermore, clear guidelines and administrative responsibility for programme implementation need to be adopted. In that context, a legal and institutional framework may have to be set up to resolve policy and administrative conflicts. Finally, there is a severe shortage of people with the technical expertise to prepare for and negotiate the divestments in the planned economies in transition. Relatively underdeveloped capital markets and shortages of investment bankers, enterprise valuation experts and similar personnel further compound matters.

Once the decision is made to move ahead, various other difficulties associated with divestment in the East have to be faced. First of all, the real worth of capital assets should be assessed and be turned over to society, perhaps as a means of reducing state liabilities (such as debt or social-service claims). At all cost, reformers should avoid a sell-out of existing firms at prices that deviate substantially from the intrinsic value of the assets being alienated, however approximately this can be gauged in the absence so far of functioning markets. As recent experience has amply demonstrated, the political backlash of underpricing assets can be very serious indeed.

Although free distribution of shares may, in principle, circumvent the extremely complex issue of proper pricing, this holds true only at the time of divestment. If the electorate has a longer memory, the backlash of 'give-aways' that fall short of distributing equal shares to each citizen in each SOE being privatised is bound to be considerable. It will be all the greater the more the inequality results from the 'give-away' itself, rather than from the improvements in assets generated by the emerging market economy. The likelihood of the former outcome is greatest during the initial phases of the transition, when economic activity tends to be subdued at best.

It is by no means easy to abide by the above guidelines, given the problems of establishing a market value for assets that have never been priced in a competitive environment. Adequate pricing must, in the first instance, be based on the discounted value of the expected net returns to capital over the lifetime of the assets, as calculated by prospective buyers. Unfortunately, in the planned economies in transition the latter income stream cannot even approximately be anticipated until stable markets emerge and lead to even 'moderately predictable' prices. Market valuation, hence setting a fair price, can only begin once a certain volume of shares or assets has been distributed, perhaps to the population at large.

To circumvent these problems, some planned economies in transition have unwittingly allowed one group, usually the management in place, to capture the value of part of its specialised knowledge by transforming it into a property stake. In some countries, this has resulted from explicit makeshift rules on economic decentralisation. Certainly those agents held property rights that cannot all be swept aside. Honouring legitimate rights is, however, different from allowing insider information to remove property rights that legitimately belong to others, perhaps society at large. Capturing these rights is perhaps the more egregious way in which part of society's wealth in some Eastern economies has been alienated, although not always as a result of malevolence or incompetence. The problem is most serious during the initial phases of the transition, when those still in power capitalise on their property rights and build a private stake for their survival in the new society. The process has led to numerous complaints, particularly in Hungary and Poland (see Lee and Nellis, 1990). It is still rampant in the confused circumstances of other planned economies in transition, notably the Soviet Union.

The pricing of such assets is a very difficult task, given the lack of transparency that is inherent in the planned economies in transition, and it must be accepted that determining asset values in an extremely fluctuating environment, such as that in most planned economies in transition, is a hazardous proposition.[21]

Another obstacle to divestment is that there is simply no capitalist class in the newly constituted planned economies in transition. This lacuna has several dimensions. One is that there is insufficient indigenous savings, which precludes the outright purchase by domestic agents of a sizeable portion of state-owned assets. Certainly in some of these economies there is a substantial monetary overhang that could be mobilised for the acquisition of state assets. However, these funds often stem from activities that were deemed illegal. It would be odd to legitimise them *ex post*. In most planned economies in transition, any monetary overhang that existed at the inception of the transformation has already been substantially eroded as a result of inflation. Those savings that remain could be earmarked for the purchase of housing, small plots of land, small handicraft or service firms. But it remains to be seen whether savers are interested in such purchases without there first being other substantial reforms, especially macroeconomic stabilisation, a more market-supportive fiscal system, demonopolisation and genuine wholesale trading. In some cases, however, setting up autonomous financial institutions, such as pension funds, insurance schemes and commercial banks, to whom state liabilities are 'sold', as alternatives to the institutional monopolies in place, can assist with intermediation.

Whether it would be worthwhile to sell off SOEs piecemeal and give part of the shares to workers at preferential prices is something to be carefully weighed (Newbery, 1991). Inasmuch as society's assets have been built up essentially by inhibiting individuals from accumulating real wealth, an argument can be made for an egalitarian distribution. How to do this, even if shares are given away, poses technical problems that may not be surmountable in the short run. A wide distribution of assets would avoid future resentment about 'give-aways' to a favoured class, a danger that is present in selling SOEs to their managers at 'fire-sale' prices. It would also ensure support for the temporarily painful measures needed to render those assets more productive by reforming monetary policy, freeing prices and ending subsidies. Above all, it would support democracy by greatly reducing the economic power of the *nomenclatura* and strengthening the economic power of the electorate.

However, if revenue must be raised and concerns about resource allocation, property administration and principal-agent problems loom large, auction markets that are as transparent as circumstances permit are advisable. This transparency can be enhanced by rationalising the SOEs, at least to make their books reflect real values that can be audited according to internationally accepted practices. In the absence of widespread experience with this method of divestment, however, careful experimentation appears to be warranted both in the methodology of organising markets and in the phasing in of the sale of assets.

The two countries that have been assiduously pursuing 'give-aways' – Czechoslovakia and Poland – have adopted different paths, after considerable debate. Thus, Poland is setting up about two dozen investment funds in which adult citizens will own shares that, after some time, can be openly traded. Both national and foreign experts will be invited to manage these funds, and their rewards will be directly linked to the performance of the companies in their assigned portfolio. These funds will be entrusted with monitoring firms belonging to some sectors and will engage in limited competition for shares. Czechoslovakia is hoping to create a capital market for shares that individuals have acquired through the betting of voucher points. Vouchers will be distributed to all adult citizens at a nominal fee and the points that they represent can be pledged against shares of firms to be privatised.

There is, of course, a reverse side to the absence of a capitalist class, namely, the predisposition of savers to be risk-averse and to appreciate the 'societal nature' of state assets. Apart from the uncertainty introduced in having share prices fluctuate, the population at large in the planned economies in transition used to enjoy a great deal of certainty over jobs, labour incomes and perquisites, as well as social transfers. Although they may espouse the ideals of a market economy, they may find it difficult in the short term to come to grips with bankruptcy and the attendant fluctuations in individual and collective fortunes.

All planned economies in transition have been hoping to attract foreign direct investment (FDI), by methods which include joint ventures and the outright sale of SOEs. In a number of countries, especially Hungary and Poland, this has led to concerns that society's assets might be sold to foreigners at below what is perceived as 'fair' market value. FDI would furnish badly needed capital, managerial expertise, technology, marketing skills, access to established markets and other benefits. Whether these advantages outweigh the perceived losses in revenue that result from selling at below 'fair' market value remains to be seen. Selling to foreigners does presuppose a willingness by society to accept such a dilution of its economic sovereignty. But this cannot automatically be assumed in countries whose scope for political autonomy and economic sovereignty was so narrowly circumscribed for so long. However, the question is probably less whether to sell assets to foreigners as such than in what sectors and to what degree foreign ownership will be regulated.

A further difficulty in the way of divestment is that exit and entry of firms in the erstwhile planned economy did not occur in response to the venturesomeness, thrift and acquisitiveness of some layers of society. Furthermore managers of SOEs were on the whole entrusted with priorities and guidelines that oftentimes had little to do with their ability to enhance the firm's net worth. This suggests that even if the state and its appointed officials were to withdraw quickly from microeconomic decision making, it is not clear who would take their place. Even if replacements can be found, it is not assured that they could manage successfully, or even protect, assets in the short to medium run. It would seem, then, that for quite some time to come the bulk of management will necessarily have to remain in place. To guide them into behaving more like managers of firms that are owned by others in a market environment will be a complex task that can be accomplished only over a long stretch of time. Once new transparent incentives and behavioural guidelines for management are in place, there is no reason to believe that all managers will necessarily fail to adapt themselves to market-based criteria: under central planning and under administrative planning, many managers were quite ingenious in fulfilling plan targets and maximising their own objectives. But not all of them can be expected successfully to adapt themselves to the new environment.

Another impediment to divestment is that SOEs have not kept their books according to transparent criteria and much of this accounting has in any case been shielded from public scrutiny for reasons that transcend the confidentiality which can legitimately be attached to 'commercial secrets'. Thus, the ideological phobia about interest and capital, including proper depreciation for natural resources, played an important role in the engineering-type bookkeeping that SOEs used to engage in. Accounting will have to be radically changed so that it can be audited according to standard rules of probity.

Finally, in some countries legal ownership became blurred as a result of SOE assets being simply turned over to enterprise or workers' councils (Nagy, 1991; Szalai, 1991). To remove this confusion, it would be desirable to transfer legal title to SOEs to some national trustee charged with divestment. However, whether this can be accomplished without explicit recognition of the property rights of workers, as was insisted upon in Poland and Yugoslavia, or of management, as was the case in Hungary and elsewhere, poses some thorny problems in the political debate about divestment.

The various obstacles outlined above could be reduced by privatising state assets through other means than outright divestment. Separating ultimate ownership from the appropriation of the usufruct, as argued earlier, will not, of course, eliminate all of the key obstacles to divestment discussed here. Thus leasing or contracting out operations to private entrepreneurs requires that a 'proper' rent should accrue to the state, and this, too, will have to be established in an environment that lacks stable markets. But such leasing arrangements would leave a much greater degree of freedom in deciding the ultimate disposal of state assets and, for example, there could be more resort to determining the value of capital services through auctions.

To provide some guidance to auctions, the state may start off a contracting arrangement by offering assets at a positive rent that reflects its own expected rate of return and value of assets. This may create ample opportunity for capital gains. To foster markets, letting demand and supply set the proper leasing fee would allow owners the option to transfer their lease to others willing to outbid them. At least this would mitigate the loss of revenue to the state that is bound to result from allowing sizeable capital gains to be reaped by those able and willing to acquire shares, as in the case of Czechoslovakia, where the initial offer price of shares in companies to be divested was the book value of the firm in question.

Of course, some of these assets will be taken up cheaply, while others will not find a taker. Such an investment in the creation of effective markets may yield a temporary loss in the revenue that the government might have been able to capture, but it is an investment that may well be worth the revenue foregone. Perhaps more difficult would be the enactment of insurance schemes to protect state assets against negligence or misfortune, and the passage of measures that encourage entrepreneurs to upgrade these assets.

It is often assumed that the new owners or managers of newly privatised state assets will allocate capital services more efficiently than state-appointed officials. There is no guarantee, however, that inexperienced owners or managers will automatically begin to maximise the net worth of their assets, so long as adequate competition cannot be assured. Also, few individuals in planned economies in transition have had experience with proper enterprise management and such skills cannot be quickly assimilated.

Moreover the assumption that individuals are interested in holding part of their wealth in the form of shares in enterprises and will rationally decide to exercise their ownership rights by monitoring management is hardly realistic (Grosfeld, 1991). In the former planning environment, households were not encouraged to develop the kind of mentality required for the smooth operation of a market economy. Stock-holding was particularly alien to this mentality. Giving each individual a stake in the market economy, perhaps on an equitable basis, by distributing public assets free of charge would certainly help to create such a mentality, but it would take time. Setbacks are bound to occur. Moreover, as is so well known from the experience of market economies, most households do not, and do not wish to, hold a share of their wealth in stocks. Even if individuals own shares, they rarely exercise the right to vote on management and will leave monitoring up to institutional investors. Participation costs for individuals may be very high in some cases. But apathy toward monitoring management and 'appointed' directors probably plays a much more substantial role, as does the 'satisficing' of share owners by management. Many individuals will probably quickly sell their shares, thereby depressing prices and possibly undermining the incipient capital markets.

It is sometimes assumed that the planned economies in transition will in due course bring about market competition. But substituting private for state monopolies will not necessarily enhance efficiency or increase the net worth of the firm as competitive bidding is virtually precluded in the process. Unless effective competition and regulation are introduced, divestment of firms with market power brings about private ownership in precisely the circumstances where it has least to offer (Newbery, 1991). The desire to sell off SOEs speedily, to widen share ownership quickly and to raise short-term revenue should not stand in the way of devising adequate measures of competition and regulation for many industries.

The existence of management that holds a monopoly on information, because of a wide dispersion in shareholders or of a market monopoly, leads to principal-agent problems. If the intensity with which management is monitored is low, managers will be able to pursue their own objectives rather than those of the owners. This was often the case in the administratively planned economy and is a serious problem in market economies (Stiglitz, 1991). It is bound to emerge in the planned economies in transition, regardless of divestment efforts. Monitoring, therefore, is essential in structuring incentives to induce management to behave according to the revealed interests of owners, whether private or not. It is critical to ensure that the firm's monopoly of information is broken and that the regulator has independent access to detailed information bearing on, for example, the potential for cost reduction and the relative costs of services supplied by a multiproduct firm.

Vigorous competition must apply also to the acquisition and disposal of private assets. For that, it is necessary to have in place a minimum of capital markets, including proper safeguards and regulatory mechanisms to protect against abuses of stock-exchange provisions. Such a market can function only if there is sufficient transparency in the market. This requires that firms adhere to certain supervisory and accounting rules that foster competition among economic agents on the basis of actual and expected returns to capital. Once again, this can emerge only over time. An adequate capital market, for example, cannot crystallise without there being participants. These themselves will come to the fore only over time and will have to be coached through the elementary elements of the capital market, namely, the banking system (Bohn and Levey, 1991; Corbett and Mayer, 1991; Singh, 1990).

3.8 Forms and experience of privatisation in the East

Although privatisation can take many forms, this chapter will consider only four types: (i) spontaneous privatisation; (ii) the gratis transfer of title; (iii) leasing and management contracts; and (iv) outright sale.

3.8.1 *Spontaneous privatisation*

Many planned economies in transition, as already noted, have had some experience with this form of divestment. 'Spontaneous privatisation' means that those entrusted with state assets take possession of them in one way or another. One favoured instrument has been turning the SOE into a joint stock company, whose shares can subsequently be sold to private agents, including foreigners. This was the route that Hungary initially chose to take because decision makers did not really wish – or dare – to renationalise assets. Other forms have included the incorporation of state assets with management signing away property rights to private ventures that it owned wholly. Also, in order to safeguard deals, the rights can be sold to the other owners, which essentially involves the managers trading off the loss in revenue against guarantees for their own jobs. Some of these forms of capturing property rights in assets that are ostensibly owned by the state presented an array of highly contentious issues in the German Democratic Republic and Poland until the non-Communist governments put an end to the most crass abuses.

The experience with spontaneous privatisation has not been very satisfactory financially, legally, economically or organisationally (Lee and Nellis, 1990). Financially, spontaneous privatisation allows former management, and possibly workers, to become owners without paying a fair price and thus deprives the government of revenues needed to offset its liabilities. From an economic point of view, there is no reason to believe that turning over assets to those who ran these facilities poorly when they were formally under state control will improve resource allocation. Being entrusted with assets may change the allegiance of management away from the Party to the true asset holders, but for such a change to take place on a sufficiently large scale as to make a difference in the process of resource allocation is by no means assured. Furthermore, because of its wealth effects, such a free distribution to existing management or workers may exacerbate already existing inflationary pressures (Nuti, 1991a).

Present management was frequently appointed under the *nomenklatura* rules. At the very least, conflict-of-interest laws should have been used to prevent managers from laundering state assets through dummy corporations that they created. There is also bound to be a problem of equity. Worker ownership might be fine for those employed in profitable or potentially profitable ventures, but it is not for those in persistent loss-making operations. Moreover those not employed in SOEs, who none the less involuntarily contributed to asset formation, would be excluded altogether.

Finally, there is an organisational problem with worker management in the sense that those belonging to the former managerial group, who have the experience and know-how to supervise the firms, may be eliminated from the newly formed managerial base.

3.8.2 *Gratis transfer of title*

This form of divestment of state assets has been debated at great length first in Czechoslovakia and more recently in Poland, and is now being introduced in these two countries; but giving title to assets free of charge in some other form than vouchers or shares in mutual funds has also been considered, notably in Albania and Romania.

Most common has been worker management of SOEs, which is essentially an extension of the labour-managed firm. This tends to encourage maximisation of income per worker rather than the long-run profitability of the firm (Estrin, 1991). This bias is exacerbated when there is no capital market to enable workers voluntarily to sell their rights to participate in future profit earnings at a market valuation based on the expected earnings of the enterprise. In other words, worker management is insufficient to ensure efficiency; clear ownership and a market in which such property can be traded are also required.

The second form of gratis transfer of title is distributing property to workers on the grounds that ownership in state firms should be transferred to those employed, who will be requested to ameliorate the firm's profitability. The key assumption of such transfer is that property owners automatically improve the allocation process and render the firm profitable. Such an assumption is not only fallacious but also inequitable. For one thing, the value of capital per worker in state firms varies a great deal for reasons that have nothing to do with the relative merits of the present labour force. Furthermore free distribution of assets fails to provide funding for the government to remove some liabilities. It also tends to favour reinvestment in existing activities under present management and continued employment of the present labour force.

Although the labour-managed firm appears to have several drawbacks, some form of employee share-ownership programme may be worth considering, especially if it can be coupled with undertakings to limit demands for monetary compensation, to foster productivity, to change work rules and to embrace other measures that would give workers a material stake in their enterprise. It should be noted that this can be done without outright sale of SOEs. All it requires is that the latter become a joint-stock company: the performance incentives would then include obtaining a share in the firm's capitalised value.

A third form of gratis transfer is the distribution of property to society at large either on an individual basis or to households. However, the merits of an equitable distribution on these grounds are highly debatable. This form of divestment is also advocated in view of the inadequacies of capital markets and the shortage of domestic capital in planned economies in transition (Hinds, 1990, 1991; Lipton and Sachs, 1991). It may also forestall the emergence of proxies for foreign owners.

Although free distribution of shares in SOEs is intuitively appealing, there are serious drawbacks to such divestment, apart from wealth effects (Nuti, 1991a). First, there are potential losers as well as beneficiaries. Moreover the fiscal base of centrally planned economies depends to a significant extent on corporate taxation. In the absence of a personal income tax, the already inadequate revenue-raising ability of the government would be further hampered (Borensztein and Kumar, 1991). Divestment should ideally be accompanied by the retirement of state obligations and fiscal reform centred around personal-income taxation. Clearly some assets built up over the years can be considered as collateral against the future claims of citizens on disbursements by the state. Most of these claims (such as pension rights, medical and disability benefits, rights to education and claims on protecting minimal levels of living) will not be voluntarily relinquished during the transition. It would be irresponsible policy making to encumber future generations with fiscal levies out of current incomes to meet accumulated past claims for which, at some point, adequate assets were accumulated.

An equitable distribution of shares would imply any household holding only a minuscule interest in any single firm, rendering the distinction between the pre- and post-reform situation largely nominal. Greater concentration of ownership might come about through the creation of several investment or mutual funds that would each act as core monitors for some sector, yet compete in supervisory roles with each other. Shares in these funds could be randomly allocated to households (Feige, 1990a; Lipton and Sachs, 1991). But how to ensure that each household receives portfolios of approximately equal value, given serious asset-valuation problems in the planned economy in transition, is a conundrum yet to be addressed.[22]

Unquestionably the most serious shortcoming of this approach is that divestment does not exert beneficial effects on management – normally, the principal aim of privatisation. The population at large is unlikely in the near future to consist of sophisticated investors who attend board meetings. Even mutual fund managers will not have the knowledge or incentive to assess managerial performance and promote takeovers when needed. And the question remains as to who is to monitor them (Bardhan, 1991). There is, therefore, a potentially serious principal-agent problem. Numerous alternatives have been considered by, among others, the planned economies in transition themselves.[23]

3.8.3 *Leasing and management contracts*

Taking the state out of enterprise management can be accomplished by distributing user rights, for example, through leasing and management contracts.

Custodial rights over the use of social property could in principle be traded in functioning capital markets (Vuylsteke, 1988, 1990). Theoretically, such a market for the usufruct of capital could improve the allocation of scarce resources (Brabant, 1989, 1991b). However, given the complexity of ensuring such efficient markets, even in mature market economies, it is hard to envisage how the planned economy in transition could institute fully functioning capital markets within a comparatively brief period of time and at a tolerable transaction cost. The only useful alternative is to enact far-reaching property rights reform and foster the gradual emergence of capital markets for the bulk of society's capital. Indeed, the internalisation of the co-ordination problem at the outset of the transition may proceed at a smaller cost than would be required to ensure co-ordination through fully fledged capital markets.

3.8.4 *Outright sale of state assets*

The final form of privatisation that will be considered involves the outright sale of state assets through auctions or more discretionary channels. How to set prices and for what purpose the proceeds will be earmarked remain difficult questions. Apart from the fact that auctions have to be organised, the sale of state assets runs into the obstacle of the limited volume of private domestic savings. Whether society would be prepared to put even these limited funds into company shares and at what price the auction should be reserved are problematic issues. To mitigate the effects of the lack of funds and to entice individuals into adopting a share-holding culture, one of the more attractive forms of selling off state assets is through debt-financed auctions. Such divestment would essentially consist of putting generous financial resources at the disposal of those willing to acquire state assets. In essence, the state as lender would become a *rentier* while private sectors would end up as debtors and capitalists, hopefully without differential access to foreign capital distorting the process. Of course, how best to ascertain creditworthiness and the potential for successfully managing such assets are pertinent questions that remain unanswered to date.

Setting a reasonable reservation price and ensuring that discrete sales do not infringe upon society's rights are by no means simple tasks.[24] Regarding the determination of a reservation price, some carefully conducted research by custodians of property under the supervision of the newly formed parliamentary organs should yield a plausible, if perhaps quite wide, range of asset values. The situation could be ameliorated through assistance from outside accounting firms. For most undertakings, there should be some positive price that can realistically be established with some good will on the part of all actors involved.

It is not easy to specify all of the different privatisation mechanisms pursued in the planned economies in transition or to draw a clear picture of where the entire process stands at this juncture. There is little doubt that all Eastern countries have now decided to enact far-reaching property rights reforms and to pursue some form of privatisation. New capital formation in new ventures is benefiting from unencumbered property rights, but assignment of rights to existing assets has proved to be a more cumbersome matter.

Most attention in the privatisation campaign has been devoted to bringing manufacturing and service enterprises into the private sector. The latter is the core of the 'petty' privatisation, while the bulk of the former forms the object of the 'large' privatisation. For some curious reason, the focus of virtually all observers has been on ownership reform in industrial and commercial restructuring. This is a limited perspective: parallel questions are raised in connection with agriculture, public utilities, housing, some other infrastructure and land, all of which pose difficult problems that derive in part from property rights that cannot be monetised.

There is little doubt that the debate on privatisation and the actual enactment of some forms of privatisation has proceeded farthest in Czechoslovakia, Hungary and Poland. Divestment in the former German Democratic Republic has provided a unique experience (Pohl, 1991). The implications of its transformation, in spite of the managers of the transition having to contend with few ideological, political or philosophical obstacles to divestment, offer some lessons that could usefully be heeded by other countries that still have a range of privatisation options to choose from. Its experience also suggests pitfalls that these countries may wisely attempt to avoid. Matters are much less clear in the other countries, including the Baltic republics, but some progress has been made, notably with petty privatisation, in virtually all of them. The Soviet republics arguably constitute the largest exception. The debate on what to do with state-owned assets there, including agriculture, land and housing, remains highly divisive and unsettled at this stage.

Throughout the economies in transition large privatisation has thus far remained limited. Some SOEs in Hungary and Poland have been divested through open auctions. Others have been sold to domestic managers and workers or to foreigners through more restricted channels. But the task ahead remains daunting. Poland hopes to give away a large stake in SOEs to the population at large through investment funds. Czechoslovakia was set to do likewise through the voucher system. Hungary continues to emphasise sales of SOEs at 'fair' market values, even if that slows down the privatisation process.

Although there do not appear to be many differences in the situation regarding privatisation in the other countries, this impression applies mainly to the ultimate goal envisaged. Looking at the actual state of affairs, considerable progress has been made – or promises soon to be made – in Bulgaria, Romania and Yugoslavia (prior to the current civil strife). The Baltic republics will probably move forward rapidly with privatisation in the near term. Albania may follow suit in due course, but matters there are in many respects at least as fluid as they are in the remaining Soviet republics. In some countries, the process continues to be hampered by deeply engrained ideological and political commitments to state ownership. The revamped federation and the successor republics, notably the Baltic states, will presumably set a new agenda for property rights and privatisation. In any case, because of this reality the entire range of issues pertaining to the best use of existing assets in the remaining republics of the Soviet Union is a case *sui generis*, as has been true for so many aspects of the transition there.

Much more progress has to date been made with 'petty' privatisation. This holds true especially for the three Central European countries (as well as the former German Democratic Republic). But even this process has been marred by considerable volatility. In some cases, compensation and restitution claims have been inhibiting the new owners from pursuing their long-term interests. Indeed, uncertainty appears to be one critical component that is holding back private economic activities, something that has been most pronounced in the case of capital formation. Elsewhere, progress with 'petty' privatisation has remained rather uneven.

'Petty' privatisation can be easily undertaken through outright sale. In cases where inflation has wiped out savings or available funds are otherwise inadequate, special financial incentives can be created. Thus, the government could make available generous credit to those willing and able to run the risk. In the first instance, this refers to small enterprises, chiefly in the service sector. The comparatively small industrial firms that are the objectives of 'petty' privatisation can be disposed of through sale to an individual or a group, preferably through open auctions or at least transparent dealings, or assets can be sold or leased after liquidation of the SOEs for their disposal value (as in the cases of 'privatisation through liquidation' in Poland).

It is perhaps curious that the privatisation of small firms has received much less attention than that of the core SOEs. Yet its importance should not be underestimated. For one thing, most of the assets coming under the label of 'petty' privatisation are for undertakings in which the state itself should never have become embroiled in any case. From a purely technical point of view, there was no reason to believe the state had any comparative advantage when it came to minimising the cost of co-ordinating decisions about the service streams embodied in those assets or even in identifying the potential service streams.

Future growth in the planned economies in transition is more likely to ensue from small and medium-sized firms than from the core SOEs, even if they are privatised, restructured or commercialised. The comparatively rapid pace that can be pursued with the development of firms of this size and with the privatisation of existing firms can make a 'key contribution to the development of market economies' (Fischer, 1991: 10).

When it comes to the core industrial or large commercial SOEs, however, the options are also whether first to corporatise or commercialise by setting the SOEs into a different legal framework and nominating corporate boards. The key issue here is the membership of the boards and control over these enterprises, and how the leadership can avoid reproducing the *nomenklatura* under a different guise. These firms can also be divested by distributing or selling shares. In most Eastern European economies, there is now a legal framework for turning SOEs into corporations. Progress with the commercialisation of these corporations and with putting them into a more competitive framework has been rather limited to date, however.

Finally, all planned economies in transition have recognised the need for a transparent framework that acknowledges and enforces property rights. Progress with implementing the framework, even in the case of new capital formation, has been quite slow, however. The legacies of administrative planning are formidable. The basic obstacles to taking initiative and risk in these societies stem from the numerous regulations and special exceptions applicable to privately operated ventures.

3.9 Privatisation and the transformation process

Given the many problems that planned economies in transition face in improving the allocation of capital, the question arises of when and how to privatise. A sequencing could be very useful and could encompass several stages, the time intervals for each essentially depending on concrete circumstances. Thus, when the situation in the country has deteriorated into pervasive paralysis and instability, the intervals between the initial phases would need to be very short indeed. It would probably be hopeless to try to manage an orderly privatisation campaign in a highly unbalanced socio-economic environment. It might then be better just to go ahead and do it, and hope that a solid buttress for better governance in both the enterprise and the political spheres will emerge fairly quickly.

Because of the complexity of the divestment and privatisation functions outlined earlier, implementation of privatisation programmes must remain a daunting task. Pragmatism will be the best guide in this case. At the very least, given the East's harsh realities, it needs to be emphasised that if headway is to be made with privatisation, it can only be done pragmatically. In the present economic, political and social situation, policy makers must move ahead comparatively quickly and on a broad front. From the analysis outlined in the chapter, it can be seen that privatisation, including divestment, could usefully be organised in three or four waves, with the difference between them being determined in the light of prevailing circumstances.

Very early on during the transition, the state should unambiguously determine existing property rights, without pulling the economy into the morass of restitution, though compensation may be arranged; should recognise in principle the validity of all property forms; and should begin to divest itself of assets, such as housing, restaurants and small retail outlets, that it should never have acquired at all. A neutral party, in the form of a state asset-management agency, for example, could help in organising expeditious and equitable auctions open to all. Private property in these instances is the most effective way of co-ordinating the service flows from them. It is also likely to provide a critical minimum of support for moving toward markets and buttressing democracy.

The second critical part of the transition is the disposal of the remaining assets. As concerns land, a bold move forward with *de facto* land reform would seem to commend itself. All other state assets used in the economy, especially SOEs (excepting perhaps some strategic goods and public utilities), should be turned into joint-stock companies and placed under the supervision of an impartial, professional body. Again, its main task should be to enforce commercial behaviour on the part of management in SOEs. It might also consider leases or managerial contracts. The trustee should monitor carefully such transfers.

Commercialisation of SOEs is critical because divestment of large assets by its nature will take a lot of time. If for social and political reasons (perhaps also to mitigate the impact on budget outlays) unemployment and wholesale bankruptcy of the economy must be avoided, clear-cut rules on wage subsidies must be set.[25] A credible framework for phasing them out is necessary. Management that cannot abide by such a 'transition impact' must be replaced as soon as feasible. This can be done by exploring alternatives such as leasing, management contracts, employee or management buyouts, and other avenues that can prepare the SOEs for eventual privatisation. The objective of privatisation should be to divest the state of assets and liabilities, and to ensure that private initiative aims at fostering efficiency. Certainly it will not be easy to commercialise SOEs. But to dismiss such possibilities out of hand (see Milanovic, 1991; Sachs, 1991a, b) begs the question of what to do in the interim with SOEs (and indeed with those that will remain in state hands) and how to ensure that assets which are divested will be managed more effectively.

Finally, once a sufficiently competitive and regulatory environment in a moderately stable economic arena is in place, state-owned assets should gradually be offered for sale to the public at large. Little by little, such assets should be opened up for competitive bidding for leases or management contracts, the supervisory authority being charged with maximising the return on assets, while protecting their integrity against abuses ('asset stripping' through 'insider information').

This chapter was deliberately intended to inject some element of scepticism into the undifferentiated advocacy of fast and widespread divestment of state-owned assets in the planned economies in transition. Under most conditions, there will be a better pay-off for society in focusing the government's attention first on other policies, including regaining domestic economic stability, formulating balanced macroeconomic policies, fostering domestic and foreign competition, and adequately regulating aberrations from the market environment. Perhaps most important will be focusing on the structure and governance of industry (Corbett and Mayer, 1991), something that has not received adequate attention in the debate on transition.

It has been suggested in this chapter that undertaking a massive programme of ill-prepared privatisation in a hurry for ideological, political or sentimental reasons may lead to 'casino capitalism' (Vickers and Wright, 1988: 25). This would be an unjustified way for the state to divest itself of assets that it holds in trust for the nation, however badly these resources may have been utilised in the past and even if the new state in the East aims at substantially reducing its economic role. Nor can privatisation be viewed as offering a panacea for improving economic efficiency. That depends critically on the creation of the most essential elements of a competitive environment, including effective control mechanisms, and the recognition in principle of the validity of all alternative property rights.

Being fully aware of these constraints is not the same as giving up on privatisation altogether. Headway with privatisation should be aimed at, but preferably in a structured approach within the capacity of the new state to manage the transition. But if the socio-political consensus does not exist for the government or a competent civil service to patiently guide the transition, it may well be wise to push forward with rapid divestment of some part of state assets as soon as possible after the political revolution.

Notes

1. There is presently a wide variety of names for these countries (including post-communist or post-socialist historically planned, previously centrally planned, Central and East European, newly emerging market, former Soviet and socialist economies, reforming socialist economies, as well as socialist economies in transition). The designation favoured here – planned economies in transition – arguably identifies more accurately where these Eastern countries come from, hence the obstacles that will need to be contended with during the transition and what their present status is. For a more complete justification, see Brabant (1992).
2. A market economy need not be based on some variant of pluralistic democracy. However, the mutations in the East are for now directed toward emulating the type of political democracy typical of Western Europe.
3. Ellen Comisso (1991) has made a strong case for phrasing the issues in terms of 'communal' property, rather than state or public ownership, in the erstwhile socialist economies. The suggestion is that communal property is the real culprit responsible for property rights being ill-defined, especially in the administratively planned economy. In her view, then, 'public' or 'state' ownership, now odious in the economies in transition, could be reinstated as viable forms of well-defined property rights.
4. For such a rather naive claim, see Sachs (1991a: 180). There are many other commentators who insist on keeping economic matters to technical solutions (see Calvo and Frenkel, 1991a, b; Dornbusch, 1991; Fischer, 1991).
5. There are legal differences between ownership and property rights: see Munzer (1990).
6. Proper depreciation of state assets would yield significant funds that could be appropriated for investment purposes through commercial markets (Dembinski, 1990, 1991; Hinds, 1990, 1991; Murrell, 1990). This avenue is often ignored in proposals about hastening privatisation through sales.
7. The so-called Furubotn–Pejovich effect (see Furubotn and Pejovich, 1972), which states that an individual without the right to alienate property (i.e. the right to

ultimately dispose of property through destruction, sale, give-away and the like) will have no incentive to invest, should not be exaggerated. For one thing, most investment is time-bound. If that horizon is shorter than the investor's life span, the Furubotn–Pejovich effect degenerates, for all residual profits accrue to the investor regardless of who holds the ultimate property right. Likewise, when risk can be separated from investment financing, provided private property is not explicitly prohibited by law, there is no reason for the effect to hold.

8. One major exception would be instantaneous privatisation by giving away all state assets in one quick transaction. The lack of realism of such an option has by now tempered political revendications for the more populist kinds of divestment in the East, as described in the next-to-last section.
9. The property rights school (see North, 1989, 1990) usually also specifies adaptive efficiency, which is essentially efficient allocation over time, including meeting competitive challenges through innovation.
10. Unlike many other treatments of the subject (for an example, see Blommestein and Marrese, 1991; Blommestein, Marrese and Zecchini, 1991), we argue the case for the applicability of multiple determinants of a firm's performance also to planned economies in transition.
11. This broad definition is often rejected (see Blommestein, Marrese and Zecchini, 1991; Bouin and Michalet, 1991), because it is too broad and, hence, encompasses activities that do not unambiguously place all property rights in the hands of private agents or their representatives
12. For a more detailed analysis of how such a state asset-management agency could be conceived and function, see Brabant (1992).
13. Some countries, notably Czechoslovakia and Poland, have set explicit rules for petty privatisation that initially exclude aliens or even non-resident nationals. Even more rigid rules apply to the divestment of SOEs to foreigners in some countries. In the case of Poland, for example, foreign entities are allowed to acquire not more than 10 per cent of the shares of any SOE being privatised without the explicit permission of the government.
14. This is not a patent recipe for speed. Although Czechoslovakia at first expected to complete small privatisation (which has a somewhat broader connotation than in other Eastern countries) in two years, policy makers now reckon on at least five years (Kupka, 1991). Moreover the auctions conducted thus far have been bedevilled by challenges of 'dirty' money and the absence of clear property rights to real estate because of potential restitution claims.
15. For most state-owned assets of the present Soviet Union, however, the issues concerning the compensation of former owners are less acute, given that confiscation took place about seven decades ago.
16. Petty privatisation in Czechoslovakia of assets on which there might be prior property claims has proceeded by setting 'rental charges' for two years (presently five-year leases are being considered) because of restitution claims. Likewise in Hungary, but here largely because of problems with the state divesting itself irrevocably of real-estate ownership.
17. For a claim to the contrary, see Fischer (1991). Many economists would like to entrust the state with all kinds of liabilities that may be hard to discharge under weak market arrangements, including taking over the bad assets of banks and SOEs, compensating former owners, minimising fiscal distortions and funding a broad social safety net.
18. Certainly, as already demonstrated in countries that chose to move rapidly toward economic stabilisation (as in Czechoslovakia and Poland), there is room for mobilising private savings to some degree. However, available savings are not likely

to be adequate to finance both sales of state-owned assets and the important new small and medium-sized private enterprises that will be so vital for the success of the transition to market systems.

19. The nature of this cash flow differs depending upon the structure of enterprise organisation (Dembinski, 1990, 1991). When firms are fully included in the government budget, it is simply the difference between revenues and outlays of SOEs. Otherwise it is the sum of depreciation of fixed assets and net profit transfers from SOEs.
20. This symbiosis between old-style management and workers in SOEs explains one of the paramount paradoxes of the transition: the relatively mild reduction in employment at a time of a very sharp economic recession. The transformations even in countries with a leadership strongly committed to the rapid transition to markets (including Czechoslovakia, Hungary and Poland) have all exhibited this feature. It should not, however, have been surprising. Management in place is concerned about its future and, hence, colludes with workers into the latter supporting measures that will keep management in place as a trade-off for not laying off workers.
21. This may be the case also in mature market economies, given the less than optimal functioning of financial markets (Corbett and Mayer, 1991; Singh, 1990; Stiglitz, 1991).
22. This issue is, unfortunately, ignored by those who enthusiastically advocate free distribution (Borensztein and Kumar, 1991: 305), perhaps hoping that the electorate will fail to notice the lottery character of free distribution.
23. For a survey of the alternatives, see Borensztein and Kumar (1991); Bouin and Michalet (1991); Feige (1990a, b); Hinds (1990, 1991); Lipton and Sachs (1991); Milanovic (1991).
24. Setting the reservation price at book value is likely to be highly arbitrary, given that the accounting system of SOEs under planning was designed neither to reflect true assets value nor the intrinsic profitability of SOEs.
25. For a scheme along those lines designed to remedy the calamitous situation in the Eastern part of Germany, see Akerlof *et al.* (1991). Dornbusch (1991) has criticised that as ignoring the fact that the vast majority of firms there should be liquidated in any case and that, under the circumstances, it would be better to do so immediately and earmark subsidies to encourage the creation of new firms.

References

Akerlof, G. A., A. K. Rose, J. L. Yellen and H. Hessenius (1991), 'East Germany in from the cold: the economic aftermath of currency union', *Brookings Papers on Economic Activity*, **1**, 1–87.

Bardhan, P. (1991), 'Risktaking, capital markets, and market socialism', paper presented to Conference on Perspectives on Market Socialism, University of California, Berkeley, Calif., 16–19 May.

Barzel, Y. (1989), *Economic Analysis of Property Rights*, Cambridge: Cambridge University Press.

Blommestein, H. J. and M. Marrese (1991), 'Creating conditions for the development of competitive markets in economies in transition', revised draft of the paper prepared for the Conference on the Transition to a Market Economy in Central and Eastern Europe, OECD's Centre for Co-operation with the European Economies in Transition and the World Bank, Paris, 29–30 November 1990.

Blommestein, H. J., M. Marrese and S. Zecchini (1991), 'Centrally planned economies in transition: an introductory overview of selected issues and strategies', in H.

Blommestein and M. Marrese (eds), *Transformation of Planned Economies: Property rights reform and macroeconomic stability*, Paris: OECD, 11–28.

Bohn, J. A. Jr, and D. H. Levey (1991), 'Models of capital market development', in J. C. Brada and M. P. Claudon (eds), *The Emerging Russian Bear: Integrating the Soviet Union in to the world economy*, New York: New York University Press, 87–113.

Borensztein, E. and M. S. Kumar (1991), 'Proposals for privatization in Eastern Europe', *IMF Staff Papers*, **2**, 300–26.

Bouin, O. and C.-A. Michalet (1991), *Rebalancing the Public and Private Sectors: Developing country experience*, Paris: Development Centre of the Organisation for Economic Co-operation and Development.

Brabant, J. M. van (1989), 'Economic policy aims and their implementation: summary', in *Economic Reforms in the European Centrally Planned Economies*, New York: published by Adeco, Geneva, for the United Nations, 219–25.

Brabant, J. M. van (1991a), *Integrating Eastern Europe into the International Economy: Convertibility through a payments union*, Dordrecht: Kluwer Academic Publishers.

Brabant, J. M. van (1991b), 'The role of governments in Eastern Europe: a discussion', in G. Bertsch and S. Elliot-Gower (eds), *The Impact of Governments on East–West Economic Relations*, London: Macmillan, 209–20

Brabant, J. M. van (1992), *Privatizing Eastern Europe: The role of markets and ownership during the transition*, manuscript, New York.

Calvo, G. and J. A. Frenkel (1991a), 'From centrally planned to market economy: the road from CPE to PCPE', *IMF Staff Papers*, **2**, 268–99.

Calvo, G. and J. A. Frenkel (1991b), 'Obstacles to transforming centrally-planned economies: the role of capital markets', Working Paper No. WP/91/66, Washington, DC: IMF.

Comisso, E. (1989), 'Property rights in focus', *Acta Oeconomica*, **4**, 210–16.

Comisso, E. (1991), 'Property rights, liberalism, and the transition from "actually existing" socialism', *East European Politics and Societies*, **1**, 162–88.

Commander, S. and T. Killick (1988), 'Privatisation in developing countries: a survey of the issues', in P. Cook and C. Kirkpatrick (eds), *Privatisation in Less Developed Countries*, Hemel Hempstead: Harvester Wheatsheaf, 91–124.

Corbett, J. and C. P. Mayer (1991), 'Financial reform in Eastern Europe: progress with the wrong model', *Oxford Review of Economic Policy*, **7** (4), 57–75.

Dembinski, P. H. (1990), 'Alternative financial approaches to privatisation', paper prepared for Conference on Transition in Eastern Europe, OECD, Paris, 29–30 November.

Dembinski, P. H. (1991), 'Alternative financial approaches to privatization of post-communist economies', paper prepared for Conference on Privatization in Eastern Europe, International Center for Monetary and Banking Studies, Geneva, 20–21 September.

Dhanji, F. and B. Milanovic (1990), 'Privatization in East and Central Europe', paper prepared for the Conference on the Transition to a Market Economy in Central and Eastern Europe, OECD and the World Bank, Paris, 28–30 November.

Dornbusch, R. (1991), 'Comments and discussion', *Brookings Papers on Economic Activity*, **1**, 88–92.

Eliasson, G. (1991), 'The micro frustrations of privatizing Eastern Europe', paper prepared for Conference on Privatization in Eastern Europe, International Center for Monetary and Banking Studies, Geneva, 20–21 September.

Estrin, S. (1991), 'Some reflections on self-management, social choice, and reform in Eastern Europe', *Journal of Comparative Economics*, **2**, 349–66.

Feige, E. L. (1990a), 'Perestroika and socialist privatization: what is to be done? and how?', *Comparative Economic Studies*, **3**, 1–54.

Feige, E. L. (1990b), 'Socialist privatization: response', *Comparative Economic Studies*, **3**, 71–81.
Fershtman, C. (1990), 'The interdependence between ownership and market structure: the case of privatization', *Economica*, **3**, 319–28.
Fischer, S. (1991), 'Privatization in East European transformation', Working Paper No. 3703, Cambridge, Mass.: National Bureau of Economic Research, May.
Furubotn, E. G. and S. Pejovich (1972), 'Property rights and economic theory: a survey of recent literature', *The Journal of Economic Literature*, **2**, 1137–62.
Grosfeld, I. (1991), 'Privatization of state enterprises in Eastern Europe: the search for a market environment', *East European Politics and Societies*, **2**, 142–61.
Herrmann-Pillath, C. (1991), 'Systemic transformation as an economic problem', *Außenpolitik*, **2**, 170–82.
Hinds, M. (1990), 'Issues in the introduction of market forces in Eastern European socialist economies – Annex 1: enterprise reform issues', mimeo, Washington, DC: World Bank, March.
Hinds, M. (1991), 'Issues in the introduction of market forces in Eastern European socialist economies', in S. Commander (ed), *Managing Inflation in Socialist Economies in Transition*, Washington, DC: World Bank, 121–53.
Kanel, D. (1974), 'Property and economic power as issues in institutional economics', *Journal of Economic Issues*, **4**, 827–40.
Kupka, M. (1991), 'Transformation of ownership in Czechoslovakia', paper prepared for Conference on Privatization in Eastern Europe, International Center for Monetary and Banking Studies, Geneva, 20–21 September.
Lee, B. and J. Nellis (1990), 'Enterprise reform and privatization in socialist economies', World Bank Discussion Paper 104, Washington, DC: World Bank.
Lipton, D. and J. Sachs (1991), 'Privatization in Eastern Europe: the case of Poland', *Brookings Papers on Economic Activity*, **2**, 293–334.
Madzar, L. (1990), 'The price of the turnaround', *Communist Economies* **2**, 143–56.
Milanovic, B. (1991), 'Privatisation in post-communist societies', *Communist Economies and Economic Transformation* **1**, 5–39.
Munzer, S. R. (1990), *A Theory of Property*, Cambridge: Cambridge University Press.
Murrell, P. (1990), '"Big bang" versus evolution: East European economic reforms in the light of recent economic history', PlanEcon Report, No. 26.
Nagy, A. (1991), '"Social choice" in Eastern Europe', *Journal of Comparative Economics*, **2**, 266–83.
Newbery, D. M. (1991), 'Reform in Hungary: sequencing and privatisation', *European Economic Review*, **3**, 571–80.
North, D. C. (1989), 'Comments 2', in J. E. Stiglitz *et al.* (eds), *The Economic Role of the State*, Oxford: Basil Blackwell in association with Bank Insinger de Beaufort, 107–15.
North, D. C. (1990), *Institutions, Institutional Change and Economic Performance*, Cambridge: Cambridge University Press.
Nuti, D. M. (1991a), 'Stabilization and sequencing in the reform of socialist economies', in S. Commander (ed.), *Managing Inflation in Socialist Economies in Transition*, Washington, DC: World Bank, 155–74.
Nuti, D. M. (1991b), 'Privatisation of socialist economies: general issues and the Polish case', in H. Blommestein and M. Marrese (eds), *Transformation of Planned Economies: Property rights reform and macroeconomic stability*, Paris: OECD, 51–68.
Pejovich, S. (1990), *The Economics of Property Rights: Towards a theory of comparative systems*, Dordrecht: Kluwer Academic Publishers.
Pohl, G. (1991), 'Privatization in East Germany and Eastern Europe', paper prepared for the Conference on Privatization in Eastern Europe, International Center for Monetary and Banking Studies, Geneva, 20–21 September.

Sachs, J. (1991a), 'Privatization is top priority in Eastern Europe', *IMF Survey*, 27 May, 161, 170–1.

Sachs, J. (1991b), 'Accelerating privatization in Eastern Europe', paper prepared for the World Bank Annual Conference on Development Economics 1991, World Bank, Washington, DC, 25–26 April.

Singh, A. (1990), 'The stock market in a socialist economy', in P. Nolan and D. Furen (eds), *Economic Reform in Post-Mao China*, Cambridge: Polity Press, 161–78.

Stiglitz, J. E. (1991), 'Government, financial markets, and economic development', Working Paper No. 3669, Cambridge, Mass.: National Bureau of Economic Research, April.

Streeten, P. (1991), 'Markets and states', mimeo, Boston: Boston University.

Szalai, E. (1991), 'Integration of special interests in the Hungarian economy: the struggle between large companies and the Party and state bureaucracy', *Journal of Comparative Economics*, **2**, 284–303.

Tomlinson, J. D. (1986), 'Ownership, organisation and efficiency', *The Royal Bank of Scotland Review*, **149**, 11–23.

Vickers, J. and V. Wright (1988), 'The politics of industrial privatization in Western Europe: an overview', *West European Politics*, **4**, 1–30.

Vickers, J. and G. Yarrow (1988), *Privatization: An economic analysis*, Cambridge, Mass.: MIT Press.

Vickers, J. and G. Yarrow (1991), 'Economic perspectives on privatization', *Journal of Economic Perspectives*, **2**, 111–32.

Vuylsteke, C. (1988), *Techniques of Privatization of State-Owned Enterprises*, vol. 1, *Methods and Implementation*, Technical Paper No. 88, Washington, DC: World Bank.

Vuylsteke, C. (1990), 'Privatization in emerging economies: constraints and practical responses', paper prepared for the Conference on Privatization and Ownership Changes in East and Central Europe, World Bank, Washington, DC, 13–14 June.

Yarrow, G. (1986), 'Privatisation in theory and practice', *Economic Policy*, **2**, 324–77.

Zeckhauser, R. J. and M. Horn (1989), 'The control and performance of state-owned enterprises', in P. W. MacAvoy, W. T. Stanbury, G. Yarrow and R. J. Zeckhauser (eds), *Privatization and State-owned Enterprises: Lessons from the United States, Great Britain and Canada*, Dordrecht: Kluwer Academic Publishers, 7–57.

4

The last days of the Treuhandanstalt

Dieter Bös and Gunter Kayser*

4.1 Introduction

On 1 March 1990, the government of the German Democratic Republic (GDR) decided to establish a trust for the 'fiduciary administration of the people's property' (Treuhandanstalt – THA). The trust was established as part of an intended move towards market-economic socialism; East German key-sector industries should be made somewhat more similar to Western enterprises, for instance by changing their legal form into that of a stock company or a company with limited liability. Privatisation at that time was not the primary goal. After THA's establishment all of the people's property came under THA's trusteeship. Combines, governmental institutions, and authorities of the socialist party held the shares of THA. This transaction had only the character of a cosmetic operation without curing the patient, and consequently the first democratically elected GDR government liquidated the institution and issued a new law on THA, effective from 1 July 1990 (which was also the effective date of the economic, monetary and social union between West and East Germany).

This was the birth of today's THA. Its task was precisely proscribed: the state's entrepreneurial activities should be reduced as quickly as possible. THA was instructed to reorganise the combines, to make the enterprises competitive by restructuring them, to sell as many enterprises as possible to private investors, to maintain a maximum of jobs, and to make new jobs available to those who would lose their former jobs by privatisation or restructuring. The treaty on German unification, in article 25, repeated word for word this description of THA's tasks which had already been in effect since July 1990.

* This chapter was completed on 1 November 1992.

To understand THA's transactions we have to distinguish three periods:

1. Between March 1990 and July 1990 nothing really fundamental happened. Privatisation was not the central point of THA's activities but it was possible and it happened at least as far as formerly leading managers or officials of the socialist party could acquire ownership of parts of an enterprise. This time was a 'grey zone'. It is nearly impossible to document it under the rules of statistical significance or evidence.
2. Between 1 July 1990 and 3 October 1990 (German unification), THA already had its final structure but it was run predominantly by East German officials. THA suffered from a lack of information and skills, which of course was an advantage for some pioneers who in these days created the East/West 'rope parties'. THA's activities were mainly restricted to providing the enterprises with sufficient liquidity to compensate for the effects of the monetary union with West Germany.
3. After 3 October 1990, THA came under the control of West German managers and officials: it was the beginning of the operations which have continued up to the present. Transparency has been given to THA's activities by monthly publication of statistical data. Finally, in early 1991, THA's president at that time, Detlev C. Rohwedder, formulated the institution's philosophy to 'privatise as quickly as possible, to restructure resolutely and to liquidate as carefully as possible'.

Only after a final inventory, however, did it become evident how big the task would be from a quantitative and even more from a qualitative point of view. Quantitatively, the THA's portfolio consisted of 270 combines (Kombinate). Each combine, in turn, owned between 20 and 40 separate enterprises. These enterprises were made separate economic units and, consequently, the THA had to evaluate the market-economic viability of more than 8,000 enterprises. When analysing these 8,000 enterprises, THA obtained for the first time insider information on their *qualitative* situation. Through visits, and analysis of enterprises' balances and transactions, THA was able to draw conclusions on the enterprises' viability in a market economy. The results were not encouraging and all German officials should have known by that time that restructuring and not privatisation would become the central issue.

Internally, the THA had to reorganise itself to avoid too high a degree of centralised decision making. Large enterprises, real estate, and public enterprises supplying energy and water or transportation services, remained under the authority of the THA head office in Berlin. Two central affiliates are TLG (Treuhandliegenschaftsgesellschaft), managing the privatisation of real estate, and GPH (Gesellschaft zur Privatisierung des Handels), which has been charged with the privatisation of retail trade operations, hotels and restaurants. Furthermore, THA founded 15 regional branch offices for the privatisation of small and medium-sized enterprises (SMEs), in particular service enterprises, craft establishments and small manufacturing units.

Since mid-1991, it has been hotly debated what THA's central activity should be. West Germans have focused primarily on privatisation, defined as the sale of companies to private bidders, typically other companies. East Germans have put decidedly more emphasis on the restructuring of companies. First, this is due to an increasing prejudice against Western investments which supposedly have the character of a so-called extended work bench (verlängerte Werkbank) and which in the eyes of East Germans are more suitable for job destruction than for job creation. Second, the East German population believes that a reduced speed of economic change would offer them a greater chance to adapt to a competitive situation. Third, East Germans consider the letting go of workers as a failure of market economics and therefore plead for job-maintaining methods of restructuring. Liquidations are not popular at all, neither in West Germany nor in East Germany.

All Western officials of the ruling conservative and liberal parties hope that THA's work will come to an end very soon, because they do not want a public holding which might continue to exist for quite some time. THA therefore must aim at becoming redundant within a short period of time.

4.2 Privatisation

4.2.1 *The different forms of privatisation*

At first sight, the privatisation activities of THA are impressive, at least if one only focuses on the figures. By the end of July 1992, 22,300 retail and wholesale stores and restaurants had been sold, in addition to 141 hotels, 1,618 pharmacies and 378 cinemas.[1] These results of 'small scale privatisation' have often been ignored in the public discussion, where privatisation is a synonym for THA's core activity, the sale of the key-sector enterprises. The figures for these enterprises are also impressive. By August 1992, 9,338 key-sector enterprises or parts of them had been partly or completely privatised (see Table 4.1).

The figures show that THA uses the word privatisation in three different senses:[2]

1. *Total sale of an enterprise*; here THA has given up its involvement in the enterprise.
2. *Sale of a viable part of a larger enterprise*; here other parts of the firm remain fully in THA ownership.
3. *Partial privatisation of an enterprise*, with a minority participation of THA.[3]

In any case, THA has to control whether the investors comply with their investment pledges and job guarantees. Recently THA and investors have begun in some cases to renegotiate these guarantees. Until now, however, THA has never enforced the penalties which had been stipulated for the violation of investment and job pledges.

Table 4.1 Privatisations by THA as at 31 August 1992

Mining Properties	229
Total Privatisations	4,181
Partial Privatisations (more than 50 per cent)	580
Privatisation of Parts of Enterprises	4,348
Total	9,338

Source: THA *Monthly Bulletin*, 31 August 1992.

The THA's terminology makes it difficult properly to understand its monthly published statistics. First, the THA inventory of enterprises has been rising over time. Beginning with the approximately 8,000 firms which resulted from splitting up the combines, further disentangling led to a total inventory of 12,142 enterprises at the end of August 1992. Hence in a hypothetical extreme case it could be possible that THA privatised twenty enterprises in a particular month, but, due to an increase in its inventory, at the end of that month had more 'enterprises left for privatisation' than one month previously. Even in less extreme situations, one has to be careful when dealing with the figure of 'enterprises left for privatisation'. Since an interpretation of this figure gives a good insight into THA's monthly activity profile, let us consider it in more detail (see Table 4.2).

Two things become clear when the figures in Table 4.2 are interpreted:

1. First, care has to be taken in the interpretation of any figures, given the possibility of changes in the terminology. Minus 42 cases of total privatisation seems to be a rather strange figure. Did THA start to renationalise enterprises? Of course not. It changed its terminology. The new category of privatisation of mining rights gives 229 cases of total privatisation, and hence in August 1992 we have a figure of 229 – 42 = 187 cases of total privatisation. Unfortunately, changes in the terminology happen quite frequently.
2. Second, it becomes clear from this table that the privatisation of parts of enterprises is not included in the calculation of 'enterprises left for privatisation'. In August 1992 as many as 367 parts of enterprises were privatised.[4]

The intricacies which result from THA's calculation of 'enterprises left for privatisation' may be further illustrated by way of an example. Consider a textiles manufacturing company. One bidder is only interested in that part of the enterprise which produces children's clothes. The company also produced underwear and clothes for adults, male and female.[5] After protracted negotiations THA agrees to give away the unit producing children's clothes, while the rest of the factory remains under THA's administration. Thus, next month when the new statistics are published, we can register one more sale of a part of an enterprise but the total number of enterprises left for privatisation has not

Table 4.2 THA's monthly activities

	31 July 1992	31 August 1992	Difference
THA inventory of enterprises	12,036	12,142	106
minus:			
Mergers	231	233	2
Mining rights		229	229
Full privatisations[a]	4,223	4,181	−42
Partial privatisations[b]	577	580	3
Reprivatisations[c]	907	973	66
Transfer to local communities	285	286	1
Liquidations:			
ongoing	1,682	1,821	139
finished	29	29	
Total	7,934	8,332	398
Left for privatisation	4,102	3,810	292

[a]Category (1) in the text.
[b]Category (2) in the text.
[c]These cases mostly refer to the privatisation of SMEs which were socialised in 1972.
Source: THA *Monthly Bulletins*.

changed. Let us now assume that in our example the textile manufacturing unit without the segment of children's wear is of no interest to any potential bidder. This would change if it could be offered in two parts, one of which produces underwear and the other, male and female clothes. Splitting up the rest of the factory into two enterprises, however, increases the number of enterprises left for privatisation. This leads to the seeming absurdity that despite the continuing privatisations the number of enterprises remaining in THA's hands does not decrease proportionally. It must be doubted whether that number will ever reach zero, the target figure which would mean that the task of THA had been fulfilled. In other words, there exists a conflict between the hope nourished by THA itself, that in the near future THA can be dissolved, and the procedures that obviously point to a durable institution – if not as THA, then with another name.

4.2.2 *New organisational models for non-privatised firms*

Already at the very beginning of privatisation one could often hear the objection that the most attractive enterprises or parts of them would be sold in the first weeks and that after some time THA would only own leftovers which no one would want to buy. Although this initial forecast did not prove true, the purchasing interest of potential investors has in fact been decreasing, an indication of the declining interest of THA's portfolio. This is another reason for the suspicion that THA will exist longer than was supposed at the very beginning of privatisation and one can even get the impression that THA is on its way to being transformed into a public holding which may continue to operate for a long time. The following examples illustrate in which way THA is trying to avoid such a development.

Since May 1992 there has been growing emphasis by THA on special constructions like 'as-if-privatisations' (Als-Ob-Privatisierungen) and 'management limited partnerships' (Management Kommanditgesellschaften). The two models have been favoured particularly by East German officials and East German members of parliament (not only by social democrats but also by conservatives).

'As-if-privatisation' is still a theoretical model and has not been applied in practice. The concept is straightforward. THA accepts liability for the debts of an enterprise and equips it with equity capital. The permanent THA support for the enterprise, however, comes to an end. If the enterprise intends to invest, it has to get the money from banks. If the enterprise lacks success it has to face the consequences. THA hopes that these enterprises will themselves seek investors instead of waiting until THA finds someone who is interested in a takeover. In practice, it will be very difficult for the enterprises to find an investor, in particular because of their rather small equity–capital ratio and their limited creditworthiness caused by their lack of real-estate property. Apparently banks and investors estimate the credit rating of an enterprise doing business under THA's supervision as higher than that of an enterprise which has been equipped with capital and securities but acts under its own responsibility.

These problems could, of course, be solved by THA assuming continued liability. Since this is not acceptable, another solution would be to equip these enterprises with 'sufficient' real-estate property and equity capital. However, 'as-if-privatisations' are difficult to perform, because a high level of information is required about how much capital and land is 'sufficient' to guarantee the viability of such an enterprise (this varies according to branch and size of the firm, to its export capabilities, and so on). Finally, the lack of East German entrepreneurial skills is a further obstacle to any successful continuation of 'as-if' privatised enterprises.

THA's favourite plan for ending its privatisation activities is therefore the creation of 'management limited partnerships', two of which were founded in May 1992.[6] As of March 1993 the number of 'management limited partnerships' has grown to three, comprising 32 enterprises. Two further 'management limited partnerships' comprising 21 enterprises will begin operating in May or June 1993. They have the legally acceptable but controversial form of a company where the general partner of a limited partnership is a limited liability company.[7] The managing limited liability company is typically run by a director from THA. THA, moreover, is the only limited partner of the limited partnership, and has two-thirds of the voting rights. Management limited partnerships have the character of a roof organisation which combines different enterprises: that is, it operates as a holding company. In an example given by Härtel *et al.*, (1992a) enterprises of a conglomerate structure have been bundled in two management limited partnerships, which are managed by two business experts who participate in the returns on privatisation of the enterprises belonging to the holding.

THA argues that such a procedure would give the enterprises access to management know-how. It must be doubted whether this aim will be reached. The already existing management partnerships contain, *inter alia*, an enterprise producing heavy machines, another producing printing machines, some enterprises belonging to the building and construction sector, and one enterprise belonging to the transportation sector. In other words, the holdings exhibit a completely heterogeneous pattern. However, it is one thing to run a holding as a manager and another thing to manage individually nineteen different companies. It is not too far-fetched to suppose that the only effect of management partnerships is the artificial disappearance of unsold enterprises from THA statistics. This hypothesis, at the moment, can be supported by evidence from the THA's branch offices. They are up for closure by the end of 1992, which means they will have to decide on the fate of all the remaining small and medium-sized enterprises that are still under their administration.

Consider, for example, the THA branch office in Schwerin (Mecklenburg-Vorpommern). By 31 August 1992, this branch office had officially brought its privatisation activities to an end. What precisely does that mean? It had privatised 123 enterprises, but it should have privatised 125. Two enterprises were left. In one case, THA still holds a minority participation; in the other case, a so-called Parking Ltd[8] was established (i.e. a non-viable enterprise has been 'parked' in this legal entity which resembles a management limited partnership). These two enterprises are still administered by the branch office, at least as long as they are not included in one of the holdings of THA's head office. After these organisational tricks the branch office in Schwerin could report that its privatisation activities had come to an end, enterprises left for privatisation being equal to zero.[9] At the end of 1992 six of the THA branch offices reported that their operative activities – that is, the selling of enterprises – had come to an end. It can be expected that in 1993 the same phenomena will be observed in other branch offices and in the head office in Berlin. However, the liquidation of THA branch offices and finally that of the Berlin head office does not mean the total disappearance of these institutions. They declare their core business of selling companies to be completed, but they remain to supervise the fulfilment of the agreements contracted between THA or its branch offices and the investors.

4.2.3 *East Germans versus West Germans*

East German members of parliament have increasingly been criticising the fact that most purchasers of East German enterprises are West Germans.[10] Both as-if-privatisations and management limited partnerships allow East German managers to remain in their companies. They would allow a higher East German involvement in key-sector enterprises. West Germans' objections against these two models focus exactly on this point. East German managers often lack the knowledge and skills needed to survive and to succeed in a competitive market. They are not aware of the fact that the sale of key-sector enterprises is a part of the transition to a market economy which must be given priority over regional and psychological aspects.

Any policy which unduly favours East German bidders or managers neglects that important fact. Additionally, it disregards the fact that more than two-thirds of privatisations originate from THA's regional branches, which exclusively handle sales of smaller units with a strong regional impact (e.g. craft enterprises, transportation companies, small industrial enterprises, and services). There is no evidence that the share of SMEs coming into the hands of East German bidders is significantly smaller than that going to West German investors. Moreover nearly 100 per cent of the privatised retail and wholesale stores, restaurants, pharmacies, cinemas and smaller hotels were sold to East German bidders.

East Germans are not very impressed by these figures, in particular because there is increasing evidence that many of the small units mentioned earlier are unsuccessful in competing with units run by Western managers. This clearly shows managerial deficiencies that would have made it impossible to privatise key-sector enterprises run by East German managers. At the moment East German managers in general are still unable to develop a strategic conception for the enterprise they would like to buy – with some remarkable exceptions, of course. Apart from their lack of business administration skills, because of their Eastern orientation they have only a sketchy knowledge of Western markets, although this is not a disadvantage for the time being. Nevertheless, it will be quite some time before the skills and experiences of East and West German managers are at a comparable level.

Despite these well-known facts it is to be feared that the German government will give in, if not to East German proposals, then to compensatory measures which in the end will mean that responsibilities and risks at many different companies and institutions will be government-subsidised. THA will have finished its core business with great applause ('privatisation task successfully fulfilled'), and the many companies and institutions which keep non-viable firms artificially alive will be organised in such a way that the impression of a general government holding will be avoided. This guarantees the highest possible extent of non-transparency of government policy with respect to the leftovers post-THA – and it is to be feared that German politicians want to achieve just that.

4.3 Restructuring

4.3.1 *Privatisation versus restructuring*

Exact figures about restructuring are not available. THA's monthly reports do not provide information on the number of restructured enterprises nor on the techniques used to restructure the companies in its portfolio. The THA's restructuring activities obviously are hidden in the figures of 580 privatised enterprises in which THA holds a minority partnership, in the leftovers resulting from the 4,384 privatisations of parts of companies, and in the 3,810 'enterprises left for privatisation'. In October 1992 THA published its opening DM-balance dating from 1 July 1990.[11] The balance reveals liabilities of DM 323.5bn., of which DM 121bn. result from privatising and restructuring of enterprises. These figures give at least an impression of the financial dimensions of the restructuring process (since most of these liabilities can be assumed to result from restructuring).

Restructuring of enterprises means that the firms which have not yet been sold to bidders are made more attractive. In the meantime, the enterprises' production still goes on. This often leads to competitive advantages for those enterprises which are in the process of restructuring. Their losses are covered by THA and hence they produce at subsidised costs. Therefore they are able to offer products at lower prices than competing enterprises which already produce under market conditions.

Restructuring has given rise to considerable controversy. The German Council of Economic Advisers (Sachverständigenrat) strongly opposes any transformation of THA from that of a privatising into that of a restructuring institution, knowing that pressure would then be exerted to make THA a government holding which would maintain non-viable enterprises and thus hinder the structural changes of industries and regions from differing sides.[12] We agree with these arguments. However, the pressure will come in particular from the unions and the social-democratic party. The unions and some of the state governments in East Germany are already pleading forcefully for a radical change in THA activities.[13] They would prefer to stop all activities of privatisation in favour of restructuring. They suggest as a final compromise an industrial holding which keeps alive all existing enterprises in favour of job maintenance and 'social peace'. Certainly the enterprises still belonging to THA are not happy to leave the relative security of THA's guardianship, while THA itself moves between the two poles of privatisation and restructuring without revealing its basic orientation, unless it is demonstrated by the two models we introduced in the preceding section.

4.3.2 *Restructuring: a conflict of interests*

THA decides on restructuring by asking for the opinion of external experts and for a business plan from the enterprise itself. A restructuring plan is drawn up by a professional consultant in accordance with THA and the affected enterprise. If THA is confident of an enterprise's chances for survival in a competitive situation, restructuring begins, ultimately aiming at the privatisation of that enterprise. In any particular case, restructuring can mean nearly every policy measure which might improve the enterprise's performance. Machines may be bought, a distribution system may be integrated into the company, and it may be provided with an R&D department. When restructuring is underway, the previous (East German) management of the enterprise loses its independence and acts as an agent of THA. Investment plans, activities that influence the enterprise's structure or its core business, in fact, every decision which ranks higher than the daily routine, has to be discussed with THA, which agrees to or prohibits the proposed action.

THA's attitude toward the enterprise and its management depends on whether or not there is a realistic chance of privatising the enterprise in a short time. If, for instance, a bidder appears, THA stops restructuring and begins to negotiate about privatisation. This can also lead to further THA restructuring measures: for instance, THA can agree to a bidder's proposal to buy special machines and, after this, sell the company to that bidder.

Restructuring by THA has a fundamental disadvantage. It is difficult to accept that THA has better ideas about the chances of an enterprise than a private investor. It should not be forgotten that, before restructuring begins, the enterprise had been posted for sale without success. The original announcement, or any negotiations which followed it, might have taken the wrong direction, possibly right from the beginning of the procedure. The case of the Elbo-Building Group is often cited. Politicians were ambitious enough to request the privatisation of this organisation *en bloc* as a mega group. Bidders regarded this a disadvantage and withdrew their offers. After posting the various parts of Elbo-Group for sale as individual units, they were sold.[14] If THA (influenced by some politicians) had insisted on its previous plans, the Elbo-Group would have come into the restructuring process for the sole reason that THA's original idea of the future form of this company, wherever it came from, was wrong.

If there is no potential investor at the beginning of the process, THA increases its own inputs, hoping to attract at least one or two potential bidders. If an investor finally emerges, it is a question of his or her individual skills in negotiating with THA, not a convincing business plan alone, that will determine whether THA will be willing to carry out further investments in the 'candidate for sale' before the potential purchaser finally agrees to the contract. This situation may be loaded with diverging interests as the following example shows. THA administers a steel company. Its management asks for money to buy a new furnace that would improve the company's competitiveness and hence its chances of survival. Attracted by THA's monthly catalogues, a potential investor comes forward (e.g. from West Germany) who is interested in the steel-company but intends to change it from a steel-producing company into a steel-processing company. Therefore he asks for an efficient micro processor. This would imply a change in the character of the enterprise and, moreover, would contradict one of the priorities of THA – the guarantee of retaining as many jobs as possible – because after privatisation the steel-processor, requiring fewer personnel, would have to dismiss a large part of the workforce. However, notwithstanding the micro processor requested from THA, the new company would also invest a large amount of money: to eliminate the contamination of the land on which the company is situated; to build some new production halls; and to educate technicians and engineers in the most modern R&D techniques. THA is obliged to privatise a company on condition that the most promising business concept should be realised and that as many jobs as possible should be saved. The most promising business concept in this instance consists in buying the micro processor, but more jobs are saved by providing the company with a new furnace.

It is impossible to foresee the outcome, either in our example or in any other case. However, it cannot be ruled out that the decision falls short of economic rationality. This problem is aggravated by interventions from governmental authorities (mostly represented by the regional ministries for economic affairs), from functionaries of trade unions and from the regional press. Supported by public protests and sometimes riots, prestige-reducing fundamental restructuring of a firm with regional popularity is often avoided in favour of half-hearted superficial strategies. The most famous examples can be found in the Hand shipbuilding and chemicals industries.

4.3.3 *Restructuring and the loyalty of agents*

Restructuring closely depends upon the recommendations of experts. THA actually is aware of the fact that the managerial capacities of its own members are limited and that the consultancy skills of experienced managers are badly needed to develop restructuring concepts. To reduce this knowledge gap, West German enterprises for more than one year have been sending their own managers to East German enterprises. The Western managers analyse the situation of the firms they join and develop strategic plans for increasing their competitiveness. In accordance with THA they formulate business plans and investment proposals and evaluate the pros and cons of the realisation of these plans and proposals. Such West German 'help for self-help' is highly appreciated by the public. It is impossible, however, to rule out loyalty conflicts for the Western managers. Normally the delegating West German enterprise will belong to the same sector of the economy as the supported East German enterprise. How can West German managers be motivated to support the future generation of their East German competitors? Two proposals are as follows:

1. If senior experts are hired, there are less problems of moral hazard. In fact, THA often appoints retired former managers from West German enterprises to join an East German company and to develop a tailor-made restructuring strategy. The Chambers of Industry and Commerce and the Association of German Industry (BDI) are the main sponsors in rehiring retired managers.
2. How to stimulate the loyalty of those managers who have been running the enterprise since GDR-times (in many cases the second-rank managers

who after July 1990 replaced politically discredited first-rank GDR managers)? Here incentive payments could be paid. These payments could be conditional upon the speed and volume of privatisation, where the volume should be measured by a weighted average of the investment pledge, the wages of the guaranteed jobs, and the revenue from the sale.

4.4 Liquidation

THA's monthly bulletin reports that final closure has been planned for 1,850 enterprises, with a loss of 268,899 jobs. More than one-third of these enterprises belong to the trade sector, while approximately 30 per cent of the jobs involved belong to the electrotechnical sector. As of August 1992 only twenty-nine liquidations had been completed. THA's opening balance estimates the sum that will be spent on liquidations at DM 45bn.

Liquidation is the most unsatisfactory part of THA's activities. Regularly, the closure of a firm is accompanied by demonstrations and nationwide discussions. Intervention by politicians and unions is a phenomenon which normally accompanies such a process. And it is in fact hard for East German representatives and employees to understand that an enterprise which worked well in the past (nobody asks why) can have no future. We are not imputing carelessness to THA in its decisions on the closure of enterprises. On the contrary, we think that THA too often is forced to discuss its decisions publicly and, as a result of these discussions, becomes dependent on public opinion and on short-term politically oriented interests, which typically are regionally and socially motivated. This creates a climate of uncertainty and distrust, supported last but not least by the fact that German media are apparently more interested in reporting failures than successes.

It has been argued that liquidation is a very expensive option for THA because it not only has to contribute a sort of bankruptcy payment to the employees, but also has to pay for disinvestments and for special 'qualification and employment corporations' that take over those employees who lose their jobs due to liquidation. Representatives of the East German states have argued that it would therefore be better to make a candidate for liquidation free from debt, provide it with land and equity capital, and let it seek its way in the market.[15] Low-price sales (at a symbolic –DM 1), have regularly been proposed, particularly in sales to the managers of enterprises for which liquidation has been agreed.

Such East German proposals result from misunderstandings and reveal mistakes in the THA's public relations activities, as well as a fundamental ignorance of economics. However, although none of these proposals until now has been realised in practice, the voices of East German politicians unfortunately do not go unheard. In many cases firms have been saved by abrupt political interventions despite THA resolutions of liquidation. The most recent example is the steel manufacturing company Freital in Saxonia: its liquidation was planned but was then postponed through intervention of the Prime Minister of Saxonia. The Chemical Industries of Leuna are still in operation because of a promise of the German Chancellor. Optical industries of Jena have been saved – at least for the time being – because of their good reputation and historical standing. The East German states act as sheet anchor by, for example, transforming companies into limited partnerships whose general or limited partners are the state or state-owned participation societies (Beteiligungsgesellschaften).

Sometimes liquidation can be avoided by bundling: an investor who badly wants to buy part A of some company, may also be 'convinced' to take over part B in which he is not interested *per se*. In such as case, THA may succeed in obliging the investor to keep alive part B although it is a candidate for liquidation. The best-known case is Elf Aquitaine's takeover of the Minol set of gasoline stations. In the opinion of Elf Aquitaine the chance to enter the German mineral oil market outweighed the risks of taking over parts of Leuna Industries, and therefore Elf Aquitaine agreed to the combined sale as proposed by THA.

To conclude the three sections on privatisation, restructuring and liquidation, one general conclusion can be drawn: THA has a compromise-based practical approach aimed at replacing a bureaucratic state-owned economy by a privately run competitive one, a policy that causes high private and public costs but which promises a rather quick global re-orientation and thus future profitability for the private sector. It is important that THA acts independently. The more it gives in to external influences, especially from the political side, the smaller is its chance to generate a fundamentally revitalised East German economy.

The only serious weakness of the model is a built-in discrimination against East German managers and potential entrepreneurs. This is not too embarrassing from a macroeconomic standpoint, but the social and psychological consequences have become more severe day by day. It is an illusion to think that the rationality of the THA system wins over the ordinary East German worker, manager or politician. From the social and psychological point of view it may be appropriate to return at least some of the key-sector enterprises to East German managers or would-be entrepreneurs. Accordingly, the emphasis on giving firms to East Germans by applying the method of management buy-out (MBO)[16] has been maintained not only by the THA but also by governmental officials. Although MBOs are forms of privatisations, their special importance makes it necessary to devote a special section to that topic.

4.5 Management buy-out

As of September 1992, 1,706 MBOs have been transacted in East Germany, 154 of them by THA's head office in Berlin and the rest by THA's regional branch offices.[17] This implies that a fairly high percentage of privatised enterprises have come under East German leadership. About 65 per cent of enterprises which have been privatised by MBO employ less than 50 people (40 employees on average). Many of them are very small companies.[18] In contrast, MBOs have not been very popular in West Germany, where in the last fifteen years, only 400 takeovers of enterprises by managers coming from inside or outside a company occurred. (Note that unfriendly MBOs in Germany are virtually illegal because the German law on joint-stock companies is very restrictive.)

THA's position with respect to that type of privatisation follows from its general attitudes. THA is the owner of the enterprises and first of all intends to sell them to private bidders. For as long as bidders do not show up, THA goes on restructuring. If bidders appear, negotiations begin. THA examines the plans bidders have developed and the enterprise will be sold to that bidder whose plan is most convincing. If the most convincing plan was developed by a manager who is already running the company he or she intends to buy, that company goes to him or her and an MBO is realised. In practice, however, this simple procedure happens only in exceptional cases.

More frequently there is no, or only one bidder. If the only bidder is the THA enterprise's manager, he or she claims an MBO. The THA will then have to examine the manager's plan before deciding to sell. However, why is the manager the only bidder for the enterprise? Two reasons are possible: first, the enterprise's status: if an enterprise has high debts, old equipment, no access to raw materials, and so on, it is obvious that other potential investors will be afraid of the risks and will withdraw from bidding. Second, the enterprise's size: if an enterprise operates in rather small markets – for instance, an engineering company or a small pottery or repairing station – normally it does not attract the attention of potential investors. This lack of information is therefore to the advantage of the East German managers of these enterprises.

Let us begin with some comments on the second case. To give away all of the very small enterprises to the managers, who typically are specialised professionals, seems reasonable. Such a transaction saves time and costs and makes THA free for the more complicated negotiations over larger firms.

Unfortunately, the first case is much more complicated. If no bidder wants to invest in an enterprise offered by THA, there must be something wrong with that enterprise. Potential investors are experienced enough to estimate the risks they would run by acquiring an enterprise. If they evaluate these risks as too high, then the enterprise cannot be sold as it is and must be restructured by THA. Is the manager of the enterprise able to evaluate the risks of running the company on his own account? This question can only be answered positively if the manager is very experienced. However, the lack of managerial skills, experience and know-how is one of the most difficult hurdles East German business leaders will have to face within the next years. Hence we cannot believe that the MBOs which were transacted in the last five or six months because Western bidders shunned the risk will bring about an efficient, competitive East German-owned business sector. Instead, we fear that these MBOs, though formally independent, will require support from the THA for a long time, otherwise they will go bankrupt. If it is not THA which takes care of them, then another governmental or semi-governmental institution like capital partnership associations (Kapitalbeteiligungsgesellschaften) will have to support them financially and technically.

We find it hard to believe that THA or West German officials are not aware of the risks of having to subsidise most of the East German MBOs for some time ahead. If, despite this knowledge, they continue to favour MBO transactions, they must be guided by non-economic reasons, influenced in particular by the psychological and emotional feelings of East Germans. To avoid a loss of self-respect by the East German population, THA and some ministers were quite happy to discover that MBOs can serve as an instrument to redistribute economic properties under special consideration of East Germans. Additionally, MBOs offer the chance for socio-political activities, in particular for far-reaching employee participation. They can participate as silent partners, as shareholders of a limited company, or as holders of vouchers for dividends. The employee participation makes MBOs an even higher political risk than would otherwise be the case: the probability that in the event of economic difficulties they will have to be saved by public intervention is rather high.

4.6 Final remarks

This chapter dealt with THA's difficulties in transforming socialist property into new viable enterprises under private leadership. It is evident that such a policy can only succeed in the presence of a highly developed market for firms, able managers, well-functioning institutions like banks and public administrations, and, last but not least, a high degree of public support. Hence the German way of transforming a formerly socialist system cannot be transferred to any other country.

The fast transition of the East German economy is also favoured by the high number of newly established enterprises. Start-up enthusiasm of East Germans is high, and about 310,000 newly created enterprises within the last three years indicate that a kind of entrepreneurial spirit has awakened in East Germany. The new establishment of big companies like Opel in Eisenach, BASF in Schwarzheide or Volkswagen in Zwickau contribute to East Germany's transformation into an export-oriented business location. Already, 973 former socialist enterprises have been returned to their previous owners, who have started their career as self-employed for a second time.[19] In a further three thousand cases, parts of former socialist enterprises have been reprivatised.[20]

All these positive aspects cannot compensate for two fundamental disadvantages: the lack of demand for East German products and the alarming de-industrialisation of East Germany. The lack of demand originates from a new orientation of East German consumers who exclusively prefer Western products and disdain products of former days; it also originates from the fact that East German producers have lost their traditional markets in the other countries of the former COMECON. The East German producers are still unable to cope with selling conditions in the highly competitive and well-equipped Western markets. The alarming de-industrialisation has very similar roots. East German industry is exposed to rising costs (most of all, labour costs) and declining sales. This discourages investors who would be able to create a new industrial enterprise in East Germany or to buy an enterprise from THA, and it also reduces the viability of subcontractors in East Germany, whose main buyers have been liquidated.

The consequences are continuing dismissals, decreasing value added and increasing political activities. It is to be feared that under the pressure of public opinion government officials and THA might give in and apply a policy of maintaining existing firms which should be liquidated. 'Restructuring' in such a case is a euphemism for artificially keeping alive non-viable enterprises. All kinds of subsidies, which find at least some public support, have either been granted or discussed. Already applied in East Germany have been grants and financial contributions to investment costs, credits at reduced rates of interest, short-term marginal wage subsidies,[21] public guarantees to raise an enterprise's solvency, guarantees for exports into former COMECON countries, special depreciation schemes, preferential treatment at public procurement, publicly supported partnerships, and many kinds of subsidised consultancy. In fact, the EC rules seem to be the only effective barrier against the subsidisation of East Germany.

The list of proposed subsidies is even longer than the list of those already applied: the most popular demands at the moment refer to advantages with regard to direct and indirect taxes, 'buy East' clauses, a general scheme of wage subsidies for key-sector enterprises, preferential treatment at THA sales of land, and higher public contributions to investment costs.

All of these applied and postulated instruments are capable of supporting industries for a while, but they are not able to create markets and skills. This is the crucial point in East Germany's future perspectives. Hence, at the moment two factions are debating two different ways of basic re-orientation: one places emphasis on industrial policy aiming at a highly subsidised and selective transformation of existing key-sector enterprises; the other puts emphasis on public investments in infrastructure in order to create demand and an environment favourable to enterprises' needs. We anticipate that neither of these formulas will be realised on its own but that a certain mixture of both will characterise future German policy for East Germany.

Notes

1. THA: *Treuhand-Initiative Mittelstand*, September 1992.
2. At least, all three meanings refer to sales to private purchasers; THA does not use the word privatisation for reorganisations without ownership changes. (Unfortu-

nately, this use of the word privatisation is very usual in West Germany.)

3. For the problems of THA participations in privatised firms see Sinn and Sinn (1991: 83–109), and the discussion of that proposal in Bös (1992: 18–22). For a theoretical discussion of the problem see Bös (1991: 134–48).
4. At the end of August 1992 a total of 4,348 parts of enterprises had been privatised, excluding 'reprivatisation' of parts of enterprises and transfer of parts to local communities. The respective figure at the end of July was 3,981. This gives a difference of 367.
5. It may be noted in passing that combines also produced packing material, replacement parts for machines and tools, and the tools needed for production; they owned car repairing stations, and brigades for painting, building and construction; the extent of horizontal and vertical integration of production was amazing.
6. Härtel, H. H. *et al.* (1992a).
7. GmbH & Co. KG.
8. Park-GmbH.
9. THA, branch office Schwerin: Balance of Success 1 July 1990–31 Aug. 1992.
10. Die Wirtschaft, No. 32/92.
11. THA: DM-Eroffnungsbilarz of 1 July 1990, pub. October 1992.
12. German Council of Economic Advisers, *Annual Report 1991*, TZ. 485 ff.
13. Friedrich-Ebert-Stiftung: 'Wirtschaftsförderungsprogramme und -instrumente von EG, Bund, Ländern und Kommunen. Umsetzung in den neuen Bundesländern', *Wirtschaftpolitische Diskurse*, **15**, Bonn 1991, pp. 49 ff.
14. Härtel, H. H. *et al.* (1992a).
15. As Gerhard Schulz, an East German member of parliament, mentioned in an interview, see Die Wirtschaft, No. 32/92.
16. Following THA's terminology we speak of management buy-outs only, although it is clear that THA also subsumes management buy-ins under this category.
17. THA: *Monthly Bulletin* 8/1992.
18. Kokalj and Richter (1992).
19. See Table 4.2 above.
20. THA: *Treuhand-Initiative Mittelstand*, September 1992.
21. According to the law on the promotion of the labour market (Arbeitsmarkt-förderungsgesetz): 'Marginal means that wage subsidies are only given if the entrepreneur proves (i) that he has created a new job or (ii) that the respective employee otherwise would actually be unemployed.'

References

Bös, D. (1991), *Privatisation: A theoretical treatment*, Oxford: Oxford University Press.

Bös, D. (1992), 'Privatisation in East Germany', Fiscal Affairs Department, Washington, DC: IMF.

Härtel, H. H. *et al.* (1992a), 'Unternehmenssanierung und Wettbewerb in den neuen Bundesländern', HWWA Report No. 103, Hamburg.

Härtel H. H. *et al.* (1992b), 'Der Einfluß nationaler und europäischer Institutionen auf den Wettbewerb in den neuen Bundesländern', HWWA Report No. 100, Hamburg.

Kokalj, L. and W. Richter (1992), *Mittelstand und Mittelstandspolitik in den neuen Bundesländern: Privatisierung*, Stuttgart: Schaffer-Poeschal.

Sinn, G. and H. W. Sinn (1991), *Kaltstart: Volkswirtschaftliche Aspekte der deutschen Vereinigung*, Tübingen: Mohr (Siebeck). (*Jumpstart: The economic unification of Germany*, Cambridge, Mass: MIT, 1992.)

5

Enterprise reform and economic restructuring in transitional economies

Mongolia, Vietnam and North Korea

Frederick Nixson

5.1 Introduction

The assumption is often made that there is a common path which is being followed by all (or most) centrally planned, less developed countries (LDCs) in their transition to more market-oriented structures and activities. A comparison of the processes of economic liberalisation/restructuring and political reform in Mongolia, Vietnam and North Korea, however, shows that there is no one 'model' of development or one 'transition to the market economy' that is being pursued.[1] The process of economic, political, social and institutional change that these economies are experiencing at the present time does not represent a common phenomenon and their diversity is as striking as the features that are common to all three. Differences with respect to historical background, contemporary economic and political structures, levels of development, degrees of industrialisation, and the extent and patterns of both regional and international integration are significant. There are also important differences with respect to the nature, direction and speed of the reform processes themselves (Nixson, 1992b).

With respect to political change, the diversity of experience is indeed striking. Mongolia's move to a multiparty political democracy has been rapid and largely peaceful. A general election held in mid-1990 resulted in opposition parties gaining 40 per cent of the seats in the State Small Hural (a standing legislature), with a non-Communist elected vice president and *ex officio* chairman of the Small Hural.

In Vietnam, on the other hand, political change has been minimal. At the Seventh Congress of the Vietnamese Communist Party (held in June 1991), a number of economic reformers were either appointed or promoted, but the Party leadership expressed its concern that Vietnam should not slip into 'East European-style turmoil'. In North Korea, there is no obvious process of political change occurring and indeed Kim Il Sung has recently attempted to assure the succession of his son, King Jung Il, by appointing him supreme army commander.

The pressures for reform have both external and internal origins. Economic reforms within the former USSR, followed by the dissolution of the Union, the break-up of the CMEA and the disruption of normal trade, commercial, financial, military, and other relationships have pushed even the most reluctant of reformers, North Korea, towards a limited degree of liberalisation and greater economic flexibility. In the case of Vietnam, the combined effects of two generations of military conflict plus the effective international isolation of Vietnam since its 1978 'invasion' of Cambodia, have inflicted great damage on the economy and society.

Internal pressures for reform originate in the perceived 'failure' of the attempt to implement successfully what have been called 'the received ideas of socialism' (Post and Wright, 1989: 4). We have argued elsewhere (Nixson, 1992b) that it may be misleading to characterise all three economies in this manner. To argue this is not to deny the need for reform however, and it is *not* the intention in this chapter to argue that reforms are neither necessary or inevitable. What we will try to do, nevertheless, is to look at the reform process and the problems that it has (and will give rise to) from a rather more critical perspective than the one adopted by many commentators at the present time.

5.2 The transition to the market economy

Lipton and Sachs (1990a; 1990b) have argued that the transformation of the Eastern European economies into market economies requires macroeconomic stabilisation, liberalisation of economic activity and the privatisation of state-owned enterprises. They describe each of these three actions as 'a monumental task' (1990b: 293) and go on to note that privatisation involves 'nothing less than the complete redefinition of property rights for literally thousands of enterprises' (1990b: 294). They doubt that privatisation will produce immediate, large increases in productivity or managerial efficiency but argue nevertheless that privatisation must proceed rapidly and on a comprehensive basis to create a privately owned, corporate-based economy (1990b: 295).

As is well known, Sachs is associated with the 'shock therapy' or 'big bang' approach to liberalisation and reform. He argues that both economic logic and the political situation demand 'a rapid and comprehensive process of transition' (1990a: 79) even though 'fundamental social, political and economic changes must be carried out in the context of a deep and worsening economic crisis, inexperience in managing a market economy, fragile political institutions, the residual pressures of the communist power structure throughout society, the re-emergence of historical enmities, and often very deep ethnic fissures' (1990a: 78).

The details will vary, of course, but the above quotation offers a fair description of the conditions under which reforms are implemented in other countries. The Mongolian economy, for example, has undergone a severe decline in real income in 1991, coupled with rising prices, increased unemployment and severe shortages of foodstuffs and consumer durables (Mongolian Peoples' Republic, 1991). In part this crisis has been provoked by Mongolia's changed economic relationship with the former USSR but that presumably offers only little consolation to those paying the price of 'shock therapy'.

Voices are increasingly being raised in Poland and Russia over the need for, and the appropriateness of, rapid and radical liberalisation. In Mongolia, on the other hand, as we note below, the 'shock therapists' appear to have won the argument, at least for the time being. In the remainder of this chapter, we will attempt to review briefly some of the main economic issues that arise during the process of liberalisation and reform in socialist LDCs (or those that were previously attempting to achieve socialist development objectives). We will argue that the case for the 'shock therapy' approach is by no means overwhelming and that gradualism and the proper sequencing of the liberalisation process remain issues of overwhelming importance. The importance of macroeconomic reform and stability and a significant degree of liberalisation of economic activity are taken as given, but it is argued that the case for privatisation in the context of reform is not as straightforward and as unproblematic as its advocates would wish us to believe.

5.3 Economic reform in Mongolia, Vietnam and North Korea

In this section, we give a brief overview of the characteristics of the reform process in the three countries under consideration.

5.3.1 *Mongolia*

The economic reform process began in the mid-1980s with attempts to improve economic management and reduce central control. Reforms at that time included: measures to give greater autonomy to public sector enterprises; the relaxation of controls on domestic wholesale prices; and the modification of the investment planning system. In 1987, a new strategy of economic restructuring was implemented and 1988/89 saw a further acceleration of the reform process. It was the case, however, that these were measures aimed at improving the efficiency of the command economy, not its radical restructuring or replacement (IMF, 1991: 9–10).

From March 1990 onwards, however, the Mongolian government implemented a comprehensive programme of economic transformation, aimed at the establishment of a market economy. Immediate objectives included an expanded role for the private sector, the promotion of trade with convertible currency areas, price liberalisation, the encouragement of direct foreign investment (DFI) through the promulgation of a Foreign Investment Law and the devaluation of the national currency (the tugrik) *vis-à-vis* the dollar, for commercial transactions, to increase international competitiveness.

The pace of economic reform has gathered momentum since 1990. Interest rate reforms, the creation of a two-tier banking system (with the establishment of two commercial banks at the end of 1990), further devaluations of the tugrik and the introduction of a foreign exchange auction (for further details, see IMF, 1991) have been followed by almost complete price liberalisation, the liberalisation of imports of consumer goods, tax reforms, financial sector reforms, and further tariff and exchange rate reforms. The government is committed to playing a much reduced role in the economy (the State Planning Commission has been abolished, for example) and has introduced a radical and comprehensive programme for the privatisation of state-owned enterprises.

According to a government document (Mongolian Peoples' Republic, 1991), 'The privatization program is designed to administer a rapid transfer of state sector assets into private hands' (p. 7).[2] The government has legalised the private ownership of herds and new private businesses and it claims that over the past year (presumably mid-1990 to mid-1991) 'approximately 2,000 small private businesses have begun operation, and recently over 30 small shops have been auctioned to the public' (p. 7). In May 1991, the Mongolian parliament approved a privatisation law which permitted the transfer of state and co-operative assets to private owners via the use of a voucher system (each voucher reported to be 'worth' 10,000 tugriks). The aim was to transfer all retail outlets, other small assets and assets in the agricultural sector to private owners by December 1991. Approximately 65 per cent of all other state assets were to be transferred to private owners before December 1991.

This latter process was to be completed in two stages. The first stage covered the period July–December 1991, during which 'green' vouchers that could be used to purchase 'small' state and co-operative assets were to be distributed to all Mongolian citizens. The second stage is to cover the period October 1991–December 1992. The remaining state assets to be privatised represented approximately 550 large state enterprises and these were to be converted into joint-stock companies and auctioned to the public for 'blue' vouchers. The shares of these new enterprises were to be auctioned in the new stock exchange and 'regional offices and communication systems will be created to facilitate these procedures' (p. 7).

5.3.2 *Vietnam*

In 1982, the 5th Party Congress adopted a set of 'new economic orientations' which included, *inter alia*, the transfer of resources to the agricultural sector; a shift in emphasis from heavy to light industry; a recognition of the need to promote exports; and a move towards greater enterprise autonomy. It has been argued, however (de Vylder and Fford, 1988: 67), that the fundamental problems of the Vietnamese economy were not addressed and that the 1981–85 period witnessed the 'ebb and flow' of economic reform.

1986 witnessed a radical reassessment of economic policies, and the remainder of the 1980s was characterised by the transformation of economic policy. The most significant macroeconomic policy reforms included: an effective anti-inflationary policy through extremely tight monetary and fiscal policies; interest rate reforms and a large devaluation of the national currency (the dong) *vis-à-vis* the US dollar.

At that time, the Vietnamese programme of economic reform and liberalisation (*Doi Moi*) was in many ways unique in the socialist developing world. Fford (1989) argues that by mid-1989, the allocation of resources was no longer based upon the direct administrative mechanisms of a 'Soviet-style' centrally planned model of development, although Vietnam could not be properly described as a 'market economy' as neither labour nor capital markets were fully developed.

The government of Vietnam has placed great emphasis on the export of processed and manufactured goods as part of the reform programme. Plans have been announced for the creation of a number of export processing zones (EPZs), which together with the Law on Foreign Investment, are expected to attract export-oriented DFI. With respect to the latter, the government has designated a number of sectors of the national economy as having a high priority with respect to foreign capital, including high-technology industries using skilled labour, foreign exchange-earning service sector activities, labour-intensive industries using local natural resources and raw materials and the construction of infrastructure facilities.

The development of the private sector (or in some cases, its re-emergence) is also a striking feature of the reform process. The government is committed to the creation of a stable environment for its development, in part through the establishment in early-1990 of the Council for Non-State Enterprises, to promote private sector interests (UNDP, 1990: 130). It is also recognised that the development of the private sector needs to be complemented by the establishment of legislation relating to domestic investment, commerce and industry laws (including bankruptcy laws), changes in credit, banking and financial institutions and the eventual creation of a stock exchange.

As far as it can be ascertained at the present time, the government is not contemplating the large-scale privatisation of state sector assets, and indeed, it has not yet abandoned its socialist development objectives. Enterprise reform, however, is high on the agenda, together with the possibility of new forms of ownership through the limited sale of equity in selected state enterprises.

5.3.3 *North Korea*

The government (as of late-1990) envisaged a very limited reform process only, although it was officially recognised that the economy was at a 'watershed' in its development. Limits to the 'inward-looking' growth model have in all probability been reached, and the government accepts that the economic system must be made more flexible, to provide greater choice to consumers, to improve the quality of output, to modernise industry and raise productivity and international competitiveness. The need to earn convertible currencies through increased exports is generally accepted.

The economic reforms that have been considered and which are likely to be implemented include: some degree of trade liberalisation to make foreign trade more diversified, efficient and competitive; the diversification of foreign economic relations, especially with the market economies; the establishment of joint ventures (JVs) with foreign capital and the development of EPZs, and the upgrading of enterprise management, largely with technical assistance from the UNDP.[3]

The North Koreans are reluctant reformers, deeply suspicious of the outside world but driven by necessity towards a limited reform process. Recent reports in the Western press (for example, the *Guardian*, 27 February 1991) suggest that the Korean economy is closer to a crisis point than is generally appreciated, especially with respect to the adequacy of domestic food supplies. If such reports are true, a deteriorating economic situation would give greater impetus to the reform process but it seems highly unlikely, to say the least, that the sale of state sector assets will become a possibility in the foreseeable future.

5.4 Outstanding issues of reform and liberalisation

For the sake of brevity and clarity, we will classify the issues of reform under four main headings: macro, regional, sectoral and enterprise. The issue of privatisation will be dealt with separately.

5.4.1 *Macroeconomic issues*

(1) What are the objectives of economic reform? The usual answer given to this question is the creation of a 'market economy', but this raises the further question of what is a market economy? This is by no means a trivial issue! Most economic reformers appear to have a textbook model of a market economy in their minds which is highly abstract, simplified and ideological. Reformers (at least in the socialist LDCs) rarely have detailed knowledge of the characteristics and *modus operandi* of actual market economies (and an appreciation of the significant differences between them). The crucial role that the state plays in both successful developed capitalist economies (for example, Japan) and the rapidly growing newly industrialising countries (the NICs, for example, South Korea) is rarely recognised.[4] Neither is it clear how socialist development objectives can co-exist with the market economy (as the Vietnamese government may well find out to its cost).

(2) What are the dynamics of the reform process? Can reforms be partial and constrained (as the North Koreans firmly believe) or will reforms themselves generate unexpected changes in unanticipated directions that are less easy to control?

(3) Can or will sufficient attention be paid to safe-guarding the past achievements of socio-economic development of the socialist development model?

(4) The development of the financial sector is a crucial issue, the importance of which is not always fully appreciated by economic reformers. The precondition of a successful market economy, it is argued, is a well-capitalised financial system capable of supporting investment where it pays and withdrawing support where it does not (Corbett and Mayer, 1991). This point is relevant both to the macroeconomic issues of resource mobilisation and allocation but also to the microlevel issue of enterprise reform and privatisation.

(5) The management of the balance of payments, the exchange rate mechanism selected and the maintenance of an exchange rate that is not too far from a market-determined equilibrium rate are of prime importance for sustaining macroeconomic stability. All three economies have explicitly recognised the need to earn more foreign exchange and, of necessity, diversify international trade relations. Mongolia and Vietnam have both devalued their national currencies. The promotion of a more export-oriented strategy of development and the rational allocation of foreign exchange between sectors and enterprises will remain important policy issues.

(6) Other macro issues that deserve mention include:

- the reform of the fiscal system and the development of a tax base that does not mainly depend on the appropriation of the surplus of profitable state enterprises;
- the development of appropriate monetary and fiscal policies to control inflation (Commander, 1992);
- the development of appropriate social security systems to cushion the impact of unemployment.

5.4.2 *The regional dimension*

The impact of reform and liberalisation on the spatial characteristics of the development process will clearly vary across countries and over time. Nevertheless, they should not be ignored, given the often fragile nature of the nation state and the potential for interregional conflict that exist in many transitional economies (and indeed, in other economies also).

In Vietnam, the geography of the country, poorly developed and maintained transport and communications networks and the differing economic, political and institutional development of the north and the south, all conspire to aggravate regional economic inequalities and tensions. The differences in abilities to respond to, and cope with, the demands of the 'market economy' are likely to create problems which will require active regional development programmes to overcome them (Nixson, 1992a).

5.4.3 Sectoral issues

Sectoral development issues are of fundamental importance but they are often not given the attention they deserve because of the emphasis given by reformers to macroeconomic stabilisation and enterprise reform/privatisation.

Within the agricultural sector, greater decentralisation often involves the reform of state farms and co-operatives, with household production given an important role (UNDP, 1990: ch. 6). Agrarian reform requires access to information about both existing and new techniques, the physical availability of new seeds, fertilizers and insecticides, access to water, and new institutional structures to make credit available.

The problems posed by the reform of the manufacturing sector are equally challenging. In Vietnam, the manufacturing sector was characterised by high cost and by low productivity enterprises, with limited or no access to modern technologies and producing low-quality, uncompetitive consumer goods with only limited export potential (UNDP, 1990: ch. 9; Nixson, 1992a). Foreign exchange scarcities had led to shortages of raw materials, spare parts, and so on, leading in turn to the underutilisation of installed capacity, and Vietnam faced constraints, both structural and policy-induced, which were similar to other LDCs pursuing very 'inward-looking' import-substituting strategies.

5.4.4 Industrial restructuring and enterprise reform

The restructuring of industries and the reform of enterprises are intimately connected with one another. It is difficult to envisage how state-controlled enterprises, with no history or experience of operating with any degree of autonomy, can be expected to adjust suddenly to the demands of a liberalised market. The precise sequencing of liberalisation, demonopolisation and privatisation is still a contentious issue but there is agreement that enterprises, once granted autonomy, will require access to financial resources and technical assistance on a massive scale. Unless foreign aid and/or foreign private investment becomes available (and it seems unlikely that this will happen for *all* countries currently planning large-scale privatisation initiatives), the survival of large numbers of enterprises must be in doubt.[5]

5.5 Privatisation

We noted above that Mongolia has proposed and has begun to implement the most radical privatisation measures, designed to transfer state sector assets into private hands within the broader context of the development of a market economy. The Mongolian proposals are ambitious, to say the least, and questions must be raised both with respect to their practicality and to their longer-term impact on the development process in that country.[6]

It should be noted, for example, that even the most enthusiastic advocates of privatisation (Lipton and Sachs, 1990a, b) have reservations about the use of voucher schemes of the kind proposed by the Mongolian government. The distribution of vouchers may well be a time-consuming and administratively costly process and when vouchers are freely distributed, the government (and the enterprises) forego a potentially large source of revenue. In addition, voucher schemes do not escape the complex problems of the valuation of the assets of state-owned enterprises.[7]

The issue of corporate governance has also attracted much attention. An ownership structure has to be created that effectively oversees the management of newly privatised enterprises (Lipton and Sachs, 1990b: 313). If ownership is widely dispersed, with large numbers of small shareholders, this may lead to suboptimal monitoring and control of management (Vickers and Yarrow, 1988). On the other hand, if, as Lipton and Sachs (1990b) suggest, financial intermediaries become effectively the owners and exercise control over management, the question of the control of those institutions still remains (as Summers (Lipton and Sachs, 1990b: 336) puts it, 'who watches the watchers?')

If, however, control is highly concentrated in the post-privatisation period (as may be the case, for example, if assets are sold to a foreign investor), the distribution of the 'efficiency gains' arising from privatisation still remains a key issue. Indeed, the whole question of foreign acquisition of public sector assets is hardly touched upon in a critical manner in the literature.

5.6 Concluding comments

(1) There is need for greater precision with respect to terminology. 'Privatisation' has become something of an umbrella term and is often taken to mean not only the sale of public sector assets to the private sector but also includes deregulation, liberalisation and franchising (Bishop and Kay, 1989). It is our belief that the term should be narrowly restricted to mean the sale of public sector assets.

(2) Terminological confirmation is unfortunate, because although closely related, the issues discussed in this chapter – stabilisation, liberalisation (deregulation) and enterprise restructuring and privatisation – are conceptually

separate. Greater allocative efficiency is a function of market structure rather than ownership *per se* and privatisation may not lead to, or be associated with, either deregulation or greater competition.

(3) Macroeconomic stability *and* the maintenance of economic growth must be the principal policy objectives in transitional economies. The sequencing of reform is of vital importance and there is no economic logic in according the priority to privatisation that it currently enjoys.

(4) To argue for a more cautious approach to privatisation is not to deny the extent of the problems that public sector enterprises face nor to deny the need for their reform. Privatisation, however, is not the *only* or the *best* answer to these problems (Christiansen, 1989).

(5) As Summers (in his comments on Lipton and Sachs, 1990b) argues, the whole privatisation issue is dogged by uncertainty. Little is to be gained and there is much that could be lost by the state giving up its ownership claims too quickly.

(6) Even when we focus more narrowly on the problems of decentralised decision making and greater enterprise autonomy, with enterprises remaining in the public sector, fundamental issues remain relating to the allocation of savings and investments and the development of appropriate allocative mechanisms and signalling systems (Yenal, 1990). This raises the wider questions of the role that the state should play in a reformed/liberalised economy and the need for selective and effective state intervention in the development process (Lall, 1991).

(7) Both Vietnam and Mongolia are committed to the development of the private sector. Such a course of action is not dependent on the privatisation of state assets but may well be associated with and encouraged by what Lipton and Sachs (1990b) call 'small-scale' privatisation – the sale of retail businesses, service sector activities (hairdressers, hotels, restaurants, and so forth), and perhaps small manufacturing enterprises. Undoubtedly a strong case can be made for the disposal of these assets by the state, and a pragmatic, rather than a purely ideological policy towards privatisation would appear to be most appropriate in both transitional economies and other LDCs.

(8) The final point returns to the question of development objectives. What objectives are transition economies pursuing? What objectives does privatisation serve? Is there a conflict between a transitional economy's development objectives (which, as in the case of Vietnam, remain socialist) and the consequences of liberalisation, deregulation, privatisation, the development of the private sector and the encouragement of direct foreign investment? What are the distributional implications/outcomes of liberalisation and privatisation and are they consistent with development objectives? Unless those who argue for reform are prepared to address these questions and attempt to provide

answers, it may indeed be the case that the governments of transitional economies may 'reform in haste and repent at leisure'.

Notes

1. The Mongolian People's Republic has now become Mongolia. The Socialist Republic of Vietnam and the Democratic Peoples' Republic of Korea as yet show no desire to change their names.
2. The authorship of this document is not clear, but given that the *Guardian* newspaper reported (2 September 1991) that 'Under a scheme devised by Harvard graduate students, investment bankers, and a tiny group of indigenous Mongolian yuppies, there is to be a privatisation of virtually everything in the world's second oldest command economy', responsibility for drafting the document probably lies with foreign advisers.
3. Two economic zones have been proposed so far. A conference in October 1991 on the Tumen River special zone was attended by China, the former Soviet Union and the UNDP (*Guardian*, 3 January 1991). More recently, a second zone in an area of North Hamgyong Province near the border with the former Soviet Union has been proposed in an attempt to attract Asian capital.
4. Alice Amsden's distinction between the market (the means to satisfy supply and demand) and the market mechanism (the rules for allocating resources) is important in this respect. See Amsden (1989: ch. 1).
5. It is important to remember that in the United Kingdom considerable effort and resources were put into nationalised industries in the pre-privatisation period in order to facilitate their restructuring and enhance their profitability at the time of privatisation. See Bishop and Kay (1989).
6. The problems of economic reform, liberalisation of markets and enterprise reform and privatisation were discussed extensively in Mongolia at an international symposium co-sponsored by the UNDP in 1990 (Collins *et al.*, 1991).
7. Hopper (in Collins *et al.*, 1991) argues that the valuation of assets is extremely problematical, even in developed capitalist economies (he cites examples from the coal industry in the United Kingdom). Lawrence Summers (in the Comments and Discussions of Lipton and Sachs, 1990b) also raises the question of asset valuation, and argues that if asset valuation is not fair, it will not be possible to achieve an equitable distribution of assets across different institutions. The free distribution, rather than the sale, of state sector assets does not overcome the problem of valuation.

References

Amsden, A. (1989), *Asia's Next Giant: South Korea and late industrialization*, New York: Oxford University Press.

Bishop, M. R. and J. A. Kay (1989), 'Privatisation in the United Kingdom: lessons from experience', *World Development*, **17** (5), 643–58.

Christiansen, R. E. (1989), 'Editor's introduction to "Privatisation"', special issue of *World Development*, **17** (5), 597–600.

Collins, P. and F. Nixson (with B. Evers and N.-A. Stewart) (eds) (1991), *Management Development and Economic Restructuring in the Mongolian Peoples' Republic*, Management Development Programme, New York: UNDP.

Commander, S. (1992), 'Inflation and the transition to a market economy: an overview', *The World Bank Economic Review*, **6** (1), 3–12.

Corbett, J. and C. Mayer (1991), 'Financial reform in Eastern Europe: progress with the wrong model', *Oxford Review of Economic Policy*, **7** (4), 57–75.

de Vylder, S. and A. Fford (1988), *Vietnam: An economy in transition*, Stockholm: Swedish International Development Authority.

Fford, A. (1989), 'The Socialist Republic of Vietnam since mid-1988: major policy changes and socio-economic developments', mimeo, report for SIDA, Hanoi, December.

IMF (1991), 'The Mongolian Peoples' Republic: toward a market economy', Occasional Paper No. 79, Washington, DC: IMF, April.

Lall, S. (1991), 'Explaining industrial success in the developing world', in V. N. Balasubramanyam and S. Lall (eds), *Current Issues in Development Economics*, London: Macmillan.

Lipton, D. and J. Sachs (1990a), 'Creating a market economy in Eastern Europe: the case of Poland', *Brookings Papers on Economic Activity*, **1**, 75–147.

Lipton, D. and J. Sachs (1990b), 'Privatization in Eastern Europe: The case of Poland, *Brookings Papers on Economic Activity*, **2**, 293–334.

Mongolian Peoples' Republic (1991), 'Mongolia's economic situation: the government's reform programme and the role for external aid', mimeo, Donor Consultation Meeting, Ulaanbaatar, 9–10 October.

Nixson, F. (1992a), 'Economic reform and industrialisation in the Socialist Republic of Vietnam', in R. Adhikari, C. Kirkpatrick and J. Weiss (eds), *Industrial and Trade Policy Reform in Developing Countries*, Manchester: Manchester University Press.

Nixson, F. (1992b), 'Economic reform in Asian socialist economies: a comparison of Vietnam, Mongolia and North Korea', mimeo, University of Manchester.

Post, K. and P. Wright (1989), *Socialism and Underdevelopment*, London: Routledge.

United Nations Development Programme (1990), 'Report on the economy of Vietnam', report prepared for the Socialist Republic of Vietnam, State Planning Committee, Hanoi, December.

Vickers, J. and G. Yarrow (1988), *Privatisation: An economic analysis*, Cambridge, Mass.: MIT Press.

Yenal, O. (1990), 'Chinese reforms, inflation and the allocation of investment in a socialist economy', *World Development*, **18** (5), 707–22.

6

Privatisation experience in Portugal

Colin Barnes

6.1 Introduction

Portugal is undergoing a major privatisation programme. While the experience of the United Kingdom and other case studies of privatisation are well documented (particularly, in recent times, the privatisation process in Eastern Europe), there is apparently less documentation of the process in Portugal, at least in the English language.

Portugal is a small peripheral economy with a population of around 10.6 million that lies on the western boundaries of the European Community, with cultural and economic linkages with both the Atlantic and Mediterranean basins as well as internationally through its early trading and colonial history (including with the ex-Portuguese African colonies: Cabo Verde, Guinea-Bissau, São Tome, Angola, and Mozambique as well as Brazil).

Portugal has for long in its history been a trading nation and this situation continues, with most trade since accession to the European Community being with other EC countries. The most important exports in value terms are light manufactures: textiles, clothing and footwear, followed by machinery, vehicles, food and beverages. In terms of invisibles, tourism is an important source of revenue.

Employment in Portugal is dominated by the service sector (45.9 per cent of employment), followed by industry and manufacturing (35.2 per cent) and agriculture (18.9 per cent). In comparison with many middle-income countries, the proportion of the active population employed in agriculture is large. As with other major privatisations, this raises questions of macroeconomic management and the impact of privatisation on different sectors of the economy, as well as broader issues such as the role of foreign capital and the distribution of ownership. There is also the issue of competition and the fact that the denationalisation process may pass power back to the oligopolistic interests which were protected during the pre-revolutionary Salazar regime.

The Portuguese privatisations have been concentrated mainly in the industrial, banking and service sectors, in companies that were nationalised during the zenith of the nationalisation process in 1975–76, under the socialist government of Mario Soares.

The movement from a partially centrally planned to a more market-oriented economy represents an attempt by the government to open up the economy, which could be described as a corporatist and protectionist economy ever since the 1920s under the Salazar dictatorship. There remains a debate, albeit currently rather muted, over domestic versus international control of capital, including the question of preserving the rights of the small/Portuguese investor.

Within the country there is also the potentially ironic situation that the circle of large oligopolies controlled by families and/or banks may return as previous interests attempt to buy back their shares which were nationalised during the post-revolutionary phase. This would in effect mean that there would be at least a partial return to the oligopolies which grew up under the protection of the state during the Salazar period.

At the same time, the Portuguese economy is attempting to rapidly modernise its economy towards a convergence with other EC economies and to this end benefits from a large net inflow of capital from the EC which is targeted on the structural modernisation of a large part of Portuguese industry as well as offering regional and social development fund assistance. The EC aid programme is mainly intended to finance the modernisation of various industries (the PEDIP programme), agriculture (PEDAP programme), as well as science and technology and research (Ciencia, PRODIP).

Portugal has become a much more open economy, although there remains an important public sector and there is still a debate on how to handle the process of privatisation, particularly with respect to the public utilities. The country presents an interesting case study for both newly industrialising countries and the countries of the Eastern bloc in that there has been a transition from a centrally planned to a more market-oriented economy with the concomitant development of new institutions and a debate on the level and ownership (national versus foreign) associated with the privatisation process. However, Portugal must be distinguished from the Eastern economies and many other states embarking on a privatisation programme in that since the 1920s there was already an important private sector in manufacturing, commerce and agriculture.

6.2 The economic and political background to privatisation

To understand the development of economic policy, the role of the state and the development of the private sector in Portugal, it is useful to consider some of the most significant developments in Portuguese economic and political history. As early as the sixteenth century the Portuguese state had intervened to protect the trading rights between Portuguese traders and colonial agents through the creation of a number of trading companies with a monopoly of commerce (the Casa da India) (cf. the East India Trading Company in the United Kingdom) and through the granting of certain monopoly rights over trade to certain commercial companies (Companhias Comerciais) (e.g. the port wine/wine trade and tobacco). In addition, there had been considerable intervention by the state under the Marquis de Pombal in the 1770s as a result of the very extensive damage from the Lisbon earthquake. This included much reconstruction of the city's buildings and boulevards and a large water aqueduct.

Over the period from 1930 to the present there has been a substantial restructuring of the Portuguese economy, with the move from a largely peasant-based agricultural economy, in which agriculture accounted for over 30 per cent of GNP and over 50 per cent of employment, to the situation in 1988, where the primary sector accounted for 6 per cent of GDP and 12 per cent of employment.

6.2.1 The Salazar period and the Novo Estado

The creation of the First Republic in 1928 and the eventual succession of the dirigiste regime of Salazar led to the increased intervention of the state in the form of corporatist management of the economy. One of the main features of the Salazar regime was the reduction of government debt. The government was successful in restoring a balanced budget over a number of years, in contrast to the budgetary imbalances of the First Republic. Indicative planning, a feature of other corporatist states, was formalised with the production of the First National Development Plan (Plano de Fomento 1953–58). During this period, a number of big utilities were created and the state developed protection against external competition through its tariff policy. It also had a partnership with private sector companies which were dominated by a number of families.

At the same time in the early period of the Republic, the government was providing external protection to certain Portuguese industries, while supporting the internal restructuring of these industries. Decree 19409 of 1929 was the basis for this process and a wide range of industries were included such as cork, textiles, wood, glass, paper, rubber, wood, iron and steel, hides and skins, and fermentation products (de Marques, 1981).

In many respects the close relationship between the state and the private sector in the Salazar period continued a patrimonial system already well developed by the sixteenth century. There were in this period seven oligopolistic companies which dominated certain key sectors of the economy – banking, insurance, electricity production, steel and shipbuilding, machinery, chemicals, and pulp and paper. Within these developments, the CUF Group (Companhia União Fabril) was the most important, with interests in over a hundred companies. Thus the early development of the industrial sector in Portugal took place in an environment of protection and state collusion, similar to that found in other corporatist economies. It was also during this period that there was considerable investment in infrastructure works, with the aim of modernising the Portuguese economy under the overall banner of the Novo Estado (New State). This included investments in the railways, roads and bridges, hydro-electric power and the construction of the Lisbon metro. During the 1950s and 1960s there was rapid economic growth in the economy (around 6 per cent per annum), although much of the investment tended to be concentrated in capital-intensive industry and not many new jobs were created.

6.2.2 *The revolution and restructuring of state power*

The role of the state became more important with the Armed Forces Movement (MFA) and the Revolution of 1974/1975, and the nationalisation of key sectors of the economy. These included banking, insurance, shipbuilding, chemicals, and pulp and paper. Reasons for the move towards a nationalisation programme included the aim of controlling key strategic sectors of the economy to reduce the oligopolistic powers of certain families within the economy. A legal framework was then established which defined public enterprises and regulated their operation (Decree Law No. 260/76). In fact there were a number of operations (EC, 1988). First, a number of public services and establishments were taken out of the administration and were transformed into public enterprises (empresas publicas or EPs). Second, new organisations were created to perform specific tasks (e.g. IPE the state holding company, ENATUR the tourist organisation). Finally, nationalised companies were restructured into new groups such as QUIMIGAL EP formed from the merging of three nationalised companies.

During the Soares regime there were signs of moves to reduce the role of the state and for the introduction of structural reform in the economy, including the two IMF agreements (1975 and 1978) which led to devaluation and a scaling down of price subsidies and controls over public expenditure. In 1976, however, nationalised companies still accounted for 29 per cent of gross domestic product, 54 per cent of gross capital formation, 20 per cent of employment and 42 per cent of the value of domestically produced intermediate goods.

The socialist government, as well as reaching successful negotiations with the IMF, managed to negotiate other bilateral and multilateral financial deals which helped to maintain the liquidity of the economy. An example of multilateral aid was the Industrial Development Fund for Portugal created in 1976, through which European Free Trade Area (EFTA) finance was channelled.

By 1985, non-financial public enterprises in Portugal accounted for 46.4 per cent of the national external debt, with 92.7 per cent of short-term debt being accounted for by this sector (Banco de Portugal). The state company sector in 1985 accounted for 30 per cent of national gross value added, 30.2 per cent of national gross fixed capital formation and 9.7 per cent of national employment, excluding agriculture (EC, 1988). It was therefore clear that the move towards privatisation was partially prompted by the increasing debt burden to the state.

6.2.3 *The move to the right and liberalism*

In 1987, the centre right Social Democratic Party (PSD) won the elections and it was clear that the role of the state would be reduced and that there would be a programme of public enterprise reform. This eventually led to the initiation of the privatisation programme in 1989. In 1988, the importance of the state sector in the Portuguese economy was shown by the extent of state ownership and participation. There are 77 companies legally constituted as public enterprises, of which 54 were non-financial and 23 financial (banks and insurance) companies; in addition, 160 companies had a majority state participation, including the state holding company IPE. In total there was state participation in 1,000 companies (EC, 1988).

Table 6.1 shows that over the period 1986–89, Portugal enjoyed relatively high rates of real economic growth, and low rates of unemployment; but debt management, debt service and inflation remained problems and real growth rate halved between 1989 and 1990.

6.3 The framework for privatisation in Portugal

The actual framework for privatisation is to be found in a combination of policy speeches by the ruling party (PSD) and subsequent legislation, which provides the legal instruments necessary for the privatisation of individual state companies. The constitution had to be revised to enable legislation to be introduced to privatise companies which were state-owned. This was because the 1975 Constitution had made nationalisation irrevocable (Santos, 1989). The

Table 6.1 Portugal – key macroeconomic indicators, 1986–91

	1986	1987	1988	1989	1990	1991
Gross domestic product (GDP) (%)	4.1	5.1	4.0	5.5	4.2	2.5
Public consumption (%)	7.3	4.4	5.4	3.1	3.7	3.5
Rate of inflation (annual average, %)	11.7	9.4	9.7	12.6	13.4	11.4
Gross public debt (% of GDP)	68.2	71.5	74.2	70.8	68.2	60.3
Financial requirements for public administrative sector (% of GDP)	10.3	10.1	9.3	5.9	6.1	5.7
Official unemployment (%)	8.4	7.1	5.7	5.0	4.7	4.1

Source: Banco de Portugal, *Relatório do Conselho de Administração*, Gerência de 1991.

problem of moving from a situation where the constitution prohibited the privatisation of nationalised industries stretched over the period 1975–1988 and the first decisive move was Law No. 84/88 which made it possible to privatise up to 49 per cent.

6.3.1 *Legal framework*

The aims of privatisation are contained in a number of documents, of which the principal laws are Law No. 71/88 and Law 11/90. The actual structure for the divestment of public investment contained in Decree 71/88 states that the sale of such interests may be carried out by open tender (concurso publico), stock exchange transaction (transação de bolsa) or individual negotiation (negociação particular), with scope for total or partial divestment and for phased divestment.

The different conditions for sale are developed further in Decree/Law No. 328/88; Annexes I, II and III to the same law give the framework for the sale of public sector participation, the general conditions for the sale of the public sector participation in the capital of the company and the formulas that should be observed for the calculation of the base price for privatisation. Within the above law the formula for corporate valuation prior to privatisation is estimated as the substantial value (i.e. the revaluation of liquid assets and liabilities), and the goodwill (i.e., estimates of the discounted value of exceptional future profits).

The overall framework for privatisation is contained in the 1990 Law (Lei No. 11/90, Lei Quadro das Privatizações) which applies to nationalisations carried out since 25 April 1975 and which revoked Law No. 84/88 and allowed for 100 per cent privatisation. The objectives for the privatisation are stated as follows (Article 3):

1. The modernisation of enterprises, increasing competitiveness and contributing to sectoral and corporative restructuring.
2. The strengthening of national entrepreneurial capacity.
3. The reduction of the state's stake in the economy.
4. Contributing to the development of the capital markets.
5. The widening of share ownership amongst Portuguese citizens with particular reference to workers within companies and to small shareholders (a percentage of the privatised capital will be reserved for workers in that company and for small shareholders, including workers (Article 10)).
6. The maintenance of the state's interests and value added in the national economy.
7. The reduction of the national debt burden on the economy.

The privatised companies will be converted into limited companies (sociedade anônima, Article 4). The state's receipts from the privatisation/reprivatisation programmes, either separately or in aggregate are for the following exclusive uses (Article 16): the repayment of the public debt; repayment of the corporate debt of state companies; debt service linked to the former nationalisation programme; and the redeployment of capital in the productive sector.

For those regional public companies in the autonomous regions of Madeira and the Azores (Portuguese islands in the Atlantic Ocean), the regional governor can influence the process of privatisation (Article 17). Revenue generated from these regional privatisations are to be used for repayment of the regional public debt and for redeployment in the regional productive sectors.

A Commission has been established for the privatisation process. Under Law 11/90, Article 20, a Commission is created for Accompanying Reprivatisation (Comissão de Acompanhamento das Reprivatizações), to monitor the process of capital augmentation and transfer and maintain transparency and legal compliance during the privatisation process. This Commission must have specialists in economic, financial and legal aspects nominated by the Prime Minister.

The Privatisation Commission supports and advises one of the Secretaries of State in the Ministry of Finance who has responsibility for privatisation. The Secretary and the Ministry agree on an annual basis the targets for privatisation, although meeting the targets takes a lower precedence than the careful preparation of the privatisation. The actual valuation of shares linked to privatisation within Portugal is decided on the basis of consultants' reports (often merchant bankers), the Secretary of State and the Ministry of Finance.

6.3.2 *Institutional framework*

The actual process of privatisation in Portugal is conducted by the company in collaboration with its umbrella ministry and the Ministry of Finance, the Ministry that sets targets for divestment for each year. The process usually consists of consultants (Portuguese and often external) who work with the company to be privatised in the production of a feasibility study. This includes an analysis of market prospects, an initial indication of corporate value and the production of a prospectus for the sale of shares. The consortium advising the company normally includes a commercial, investment or merchant bank, sometimes with advice on technical matters from a specialised technical consultancy, for example, in the field of industrial engineering.

There are two Stock Exchanges in Portugal, one in Lisbon and the other in Porto. The Lisbon SE was established in 1901, linked to the existing Commodities Exchange and operated without interruption until 1974, when it was closed during the Revolution. The Lisbon Exchange was opened again in 1976 for bond dealing and in 1977 for share dealing. There were 102 listed companies on the Stock Exchange in May 1992. There has, over the period 1981–91, been a considerable expansion in the value of transactions. The total value of transactions has increased from Escs 798.7 million in 1981 to Escs 35,985.5

million in 1986 with a massive expansion to Escs 1,093,954 in 1991. The Stock Exchange provides the institutional framework to facilitate the marketing of the equity of privatised companies in Portugal. However, of the total transactions, 72 per cent were accounted for by government bonds which offer attractive rates of interest and which according to some analysts are much more attractive investments than the equity market, interest on bonds varying between 13 and 19 per cent on Treasury bonds.

6.4 Progress on privatisation

The privatisation process in Portugal got under way properly in 1989. To date, the principal emphasis on privatisation has been on the banks, other financial service companies, and companies in the transport and breweries sectors. The majority of privatisation has been carried out through public share offers, while a few (PORTLINE and BFB, the bank) have been disposed of through public tenders (concurso public).

The total proceeds of the privatisation process up to mid-1992 were Escs 474.9 billion (US$3.26 billion) with the sectoral distribution being banking (64 per cent), insurance (23 per cent), brewing/soft drinks (12 per cent) and transport (1 per cent). Data from the Ministry of Finance show that foreign ownership varied between 26 per cent (CENTRALCER) down to 0 per cent, in all cases suggesting that the share of foreign acquisitions was below the theoretical limit (varying between 5 and 33 per cent of the total share allocation).

The central government continues to try and create a 'clean sheet' for public enterprises through the injection of subsidies and the writing off of debt. In fact, subsidies and capital transfers account for 4 per cent of GDP in 1990–91, one of the highest in the OECD grouping. The macroeconomic impact of privatisation in Portugal can be calculated using ratios developed by Marshall and Montt in their analysis of Chilean privatisation (Cook and Kirkpatrick, 1988). The results are shown in Table 6.2.

The ratios provided in Table 6.2 are not dissimilar to those found in Chile. They show that the contribution of direct privatisation sales to national GDP and investment in Portugal account for relatively small percentages. However,

Table 6.2 Macroeconomic impact of privatisation in Portugal, 1989–91 (%)

	1989	1990	1991
Sales/GDP (%)	0.99	1.63	1.39
Sales/investment (%)	3.55	5.70	5.10
Sales/money supply, M1 (%)	3.71	2.88	n.a.
M2/M1	163.38	176.70	154.90

Source: Banco de Portugal; *International Financial Statistics*, IMF, various issues.

a large volume of privatisation sales in the industrial and service sectors is still underway and the impact of these sales on GDP, government revenue and investment is too early to assess. In addition, the knock-on impact of privatisation restructuring on subcontracting companies and suppliers in the private sector remains to be assessed in the future.

6.4.1 *The state influence through the state holding company*

It is clear that the national policy makers in Portugal still perceive a role for the state holding company (IPE) in Portugal, in what is a staggered approach to privatisation and enterprise restructuring.

The Investimentos e Participações Empresárias S.A. (IPE), which was a state holding company but now manages state participation in a large number of companies and sectors, took over the participation that various Portuguese banks had in nationalised industries. Since its foundation in 1982, IPE has undergone a number of restructuring processes and since 1992, operates as a public limited liability company but with more commercial targets.

The statutes for IPE state its objectives as: the management of investments which have been confided in it; the promotion and development of companies; the development of entrepreneurial initiatives and the development of private/public sector partnerships for the development, modernisation and internationalisation of the Portuguese economy; and co-ordination and management of services for participating companies.

IPE is a public company (sociedade anônima) which has amongst its shareholders, the state, banking institutions, insurance companies, and industrial and service companies as well as other public sector organisations. IPE has capital participation in approximately 100 companies, of which the largest number are in the service sector. Using 1990 figures, IPE accounted for 4.1 per cent of national exports, 2.3 per cent of value added, 3.4 per cent of investment but only 0.8 per cent of employment Participation by IPE is distributed in four main sectors including: agro-industry, fisheries, wood, paper, cork and furniture (15 companies); mineral and extraction industries, chemical, metallurgical, textiles and glass industries (16 companies); metallo-mechanical and equipment industries, automobile and electronics industries (17 companies); and, civil engineering and construction, transport, trade, financial services and risk capital (52 companies).

6.5 Lessons of privatisation in Portugal

The Portuguese process of privatisation has gone fairly smoothly, and although there are analysts who consider that the process has been too rapidly implemented, this is certainly not the case when compared with what is proposed in certain other privatisation programmes (e.g. those proposed for the Czech and Slovak Republics), where capital markets and the networks associated with private sector development were absent.

One important factor in the success of the programme so far is that Portugal has, until recently, enjoyed comparatively favourable rates of economic growth coupled with relatively successful macroeconomic management. The liberalisation of the economy, and the entry of Portugal into the EC were additional factors which contributed to the success of this transitional phase in Portuguese economic history.

There seems to have been little political opposition to the privatisation process, apart from within the Communist Party which is now a minor player amongst the opposition parties. There has also been little opposition by labour in the form of the trade unions: Portugal has low unemployment, a fairly important black economy and there has been a real improvement in wages, factors which together may have diverted possible opposition to the privatisation issue.

Other issues remain, however, the principal ones being the following:

1. The ownership and concentration of ownership in privatisation transfers. A number of researchers have pointed out that although the rights of the small Portuguese investor should be protected, this has not really happened in spite of a number of organisations (including the Stock Exchange) holding promotional campaigns for the small investor. In addition there could be the resurgence of oligopolies similar to those that existed during the Salazar period.
2. The valuation of holdings which are transferred to former owners of businesses.
3. The high valuation of shares by government/privatisation advisors which has raised issues of affordability by local/small investors.
4. There also remains the issue of foreign ownership and ceilings for foreign ownership of privatised companies.

6.6 The future scope for privatisation and associated issues

The government intends to maintain its privatisation programme with those companies which have a majority state share holding. However, it is less clear what will happen to the utilities – water, gas, electricity, water treatment and sewerage – as well as other state-owned enterprises including the airline (TAP-Air Portugal), CTT (the post office), EPAL (water supply), and the radio and television services. It seems that the state will maintain its participation in a range of smaller companies but across a broad range of sectors through IPE. In addition it appears that the largest bank, Caixa Geral de Depósitos, as well as the investment bank, Banco do Fomento, will remain state-owned.

The privatisation of utilities would become a central issue if it meant substantial increases in the unit cost of energy, which in Portugal is already comparatively high, or in the price of other basic commodities such as water.

In addition, another large issue would be the question of who would bear the environmental costs attached to any restructuring of utilities. However, change is already under way, for even if the utilities were to remain in state hands, there is clear evidence that the government is aiming at the deregulation/removal of monopoly in, for example, electricity production.

Other companies that are in line for privatisation, but for which the timing and extent of state participation have not been decided, include those listed in Table 6.3.

The questions of regulation and competition have not become significant issues in the privatisation process in Portugal to date. There is a unit within the Ministry of Commerce which monitors prices but no specific regulatory body has been established as such to monitor the competitive environment. This distinguishes Portugal from other countries such as the United Kingdom and the United States where regulatory industries are well established to ensure the promotion of competition/antitrust legislation. The issue of regulation and competition is likely to remain given Portugal's increasing integration into the EC and the role of EC Directives on Competition and Regulation.

6.7 Conclusions

Portugal, according to most observers and analysts, has had a fairly successful privatisation programme to date. Indeed there is evidence that Portuguese

Table 6.3 Portugal – other possible candidates for privatisation

Company	Sector	Employees
União dos Bancos Portuguêses	Banking	3,911
Banco Pinto e Sotto Mayor	Banking	6,737
CPP	Banking	2,560
Petrogal	Petrochemicals	5,871
Quimigal	Petrochemicals/fertilisers	7,365
Siderúrgia	Steel	3,926
Cimpor	Cement	3,464
Portucel	Pulp and paper	4,600
EDP	Electricity	23,306
GDP	Gas	784
Rodoviária Nacional	Road transport	10,643
TAP	National airline	9,800
Portline	Shipping	479
Carris	Transport	n.a.
Metro	Transport	n.a.
STCP	Transport	3,888
TLP	Telecommunications	n.a.
Telecom	Telecommunications	11,304
Diário de Notícias (DN)	Press	n.a.

Source: Duns Europa 1991, London.

advisors and investors are being solicited to provide advice and funding to other countries embarking on privatisation programmes including Russia (O Público) and the Lusophone countries (the ex-Portuguese colonies of Angola, Mozambique, Guinea-Bissau and Cabo Verde).

Portuguese interest in extending its experience of privatisation would seem to be appropriate as it has experience of managing a large public sector as part of a planned economy alongside a reasonably buoyant private sector. In particular, Portuguese capital maintains a watching brief on those ex-colonies in which it has an economic interest, the examples of Mozambique and Angola being of particular interest. It is clear that Portuguese capital is interested in participating in the economic liberalisation process in its ex-colonies once this process becomes established.

Portugal is a good example of a small economy which, although it had the structure of a capital market, is still dominated by small enterprises. The opening up of the economy that started during the latter part of the Salazar period, and is increasing as the country becomes more integrated into the EC economy, is creating its own strains, including a more competitive environment.

Without greater guarantees of competition, the move to privatisation may reproduce the concentration of ownership which developed during the development of the corporatist state. The question of ownership and the concentration of ownership is likely to become more important in the absence of strong regulatory institutions, although EC legislation will become increasingly important. As has been pointed out previously in this chapter, there is a perception in Portugal that some of the former family interests nationalised during the Revolution may return as new private sector oligopolies, reminiscent of the Salazar era.

The liberalisation of capital movements may lead to renewed pressures to maintain a certain percentage of domestic ownership in the face of external/international capital. External pressures from EC competition and internationally are going to raise structural problems for many sectors of the Portuguese economy (the example of the textile industry in the Oporto/Vale de Ave region is a good example).

The Portuguese privatisation process is also raising issues of capital ownership and the effectiveness of Stock Exchange flotations *vis à vis* a privileged government bond market. To date, in terms of the volume of transactions on the Stock Exchange and the performance of newly privatised companies, this has not made large inroads on the government stock and bond markets which have shown better performance, possible bolstered by the Central Bank.

Portuguese experience of privatisation is relatively new. Having commenced in the financial services sector, privatisation is moving into other sectors including industry and transport. The position with respect to the energy and utility sectors remains unclear but could lead to a more robust debate with respect to pricing, competition and ownership.

Portugal has, in contrast with some of the East European economies, adopted a slow approach to privatisation, with a large generation of decree law to cover the framework of privatisation and the privatisation of individual enterprises. This gradualist approach has meant that some of the targets for privatisation proceeds and the lowering of the government debt/GDP ratio have not been met.

The original constraint on privatisation was the initial constitutional barrier to the privatisation of nationalised industries. Other factors have been: the low income of potential shareholders in Portugal; the comparative attraction of government bonds when compared with corporate equity; the problems of restructuring large and often diverse public enterprises (e.g. Quimigal); the control of monopolistic/oligopolistic structures; and the peripheral nature of the economy for inward investors.

References

Banco de Portugal (annual), *Relatório do Conselho de Administração*, Lisboa: Banco de Portugal.

Cook, P. and C. Kirkpatrick (1988), *Privatisation in Less Developed Countries*, Hemel Hempstead: Harvester Wheatsheaf.

de Marques, A. H. (1981), *História de Portugal*, 6th edn, Lisboa: Palas Editores.

European Communities (1988), *The Public Enterprise in Portugal and Spain*, Brussels: EC Commission.

Santos, A. (1989), 'Models of privatization and market structure', *Economia*, **13** (3), 56–81.

7

Regulation in the United Kingdom

James McKinnon

Over the last decade there has been a considerable expansion in the number of regulatory agencies which have been formed. This has been due to the privatisation of a series of nationalised industries over that period of time. It could be inferred from these statements that there is a causal relationship between privatisation and regulation, but it would be wrong to come to that conclusion. It would be more appropriate to conclude that regulation is needed in cases where there is an absence of competition in the individual market-place.

7.1 Various privatisation routes

This can be illustrated by reference to the privatisation of both British Steel and British Airways. Each of these former nationalised companies was launched into a highly competitive international market. In the initial stages following privatisation, international trading conditions were fairly reasonable and both British Steel and British Airways began to operate profitably. However, the serious global slump in the steel market and events which curtailed travel and tourism throughout the world had a deleterious impact on profitability. The key aspect in both cases was that the respective managements took action to reduce the external impacts on their financial viability.

They both reacted to the competitive pressures and restyled themselves as regards management composition and culture, and they retrained the workforce and reorganised their operational capability. Of these changes the most difficult to achieve is undoubtedly the change in corporate culture. In these examples no regulatory regime was introduced and experience has shown that it would have been unhelpful. The disciplines of the market have proved to be sufficiently powerful influences to bring about the marked improvement in efficiency which privatisation was expected to achieve.

The other privatisations which have been undertaken have been conducted in a fashion that left substantial monopolies in place, and as a result, it was considered necessary to construct fairly substantial regulatory regimes. It is extremely important to recognise that the characteristics of an industry and the dynamics of organisations operating within industry have to be taken into account when designing a regulatory regime. There may be specific objectives being sought for an industry, or indeed for a company, and these must also be catered for. In order to illustrate this point it may be worthwhile to examine the examples of large utilities currently being regulated within the UK. Let us consider the cases of telecommunications, gas, electricity and water.

The first distinction which emerges from these four examples is that in the cases of telecommunications and gas, the utilities were privatised and regulated as single entities. On the other hand, as far as electricity and water were concerned, the existing entities were restructured prior to privatisation and each of the chosen subsets was regulated on an individual basis. This distinction has had a clear impact on the speed with which competitive activity has been introduced within the electricity industry.

In all of the aforementioned situations there was a basic desire to enhance the operational efficiency within the privatised businesses. There was also the need to ensure that the newly privatised monopolies did not abuse their great power, and consequently price control – formulas were devised and specialist regulators were appointed to administer these schemes. The regulators were given powers to protect customers exposed to monopolies.

The desire to introduce competition was also strongly in evidence in the case of telecommunications and gas. This is hardly surprising given the sheer size and power of the privatised monopolies that had been created. When the time came to privatise the water and electricity industries, the method chosen reflected the slow progress and degree of difficulty experienced in gas and telecommunications in introducing competitive activity. In these latter cases the entire industries were restructured ahead of the actual privatisation. There was a separation of prime production, the distribution process and the marketing arrangements. In the case of the electricity industry this resulted in virtually instant competition and benefits from this were quickly obtained by the industrial customers. It must be said, however, that there has been some reaction from customers when the first flush of price benefits, arising from competition, were modified. Notwithstanding, a robust regime is in place which will be further reformed and developed, specifically, by the extension of consumer choice to all domestic users of electricity. Such an extension is expected to be completed by 1998.

Additionally, there appeared to be a unique objective associated with the water industry. A conscious effort was being made to provide funds to rehabilitate the infrastructure of the complete set of businesses through the pricing mechanism of the industry. The industry regulator has the task of making sure that the investment funds generated through prices are properly applied to the task of creating a modern and effective system of water supply and disposal.

7.2 The gas industry

Let me now refer to the industry for which I have a degree of responsibility, namely, the gas supply business. This industry is still dominated by a monopolist, British Gas, which controls a high proportion of all the gas under contract at this time, the entire pipeline system and has a total monopoly on all sales to customers using less than 2,500 therms per annum. The monopoly threshold has been reduced by governmental fiat from the original level of 25,000 therms. This change has enabled a substantial number of small business users to choose a competitive supplier rather than having to deal with British Gas. The continued control over the high volume of gas contracted by British Gas has restricted the gas available to competitors and hence has reduced the impact of competition. This will change with the passage of time but that is no consolation to those who wish to obtain gas to compete today. There are some seventeen million customers who are still bound to the monopolist, so it will be recognised that it represents a valuable source of profit to the monopolist British Gas and a possible area of exploitation if that monopolist is not kept under some degree of control. It is in regard to such a regulatory control mechanism that OFGAS, for which I have responsibility, is heavily engaged.

At an earlier point in this chapter I indicated that it was my view that where competition exists there is no need for regulation. It was with that concept in mind that OFGAS began to approach the question of 'surrogate competition' and followed that up by challenging the perceived wisdom on the topic of 'natural monopoly'.

There is no doubt in my mind that we have almost perfected surrogate competition and this was demonstrated from 1 April 1992 when our revised price formula came into play and provided price reductions of 5 per cent in nominal terms. Correspondingly, improved service levels have had to be provided by British Gas, and the combination of these two factors, reduced prices and improved service standards, has given British domestic gas users greatly enhanced value for money, arguably among the best in the world. In addition, we have pioneered the possibility of improving surrogate competitive arrangements and introducing the concept of an energy utility which would serve the needs of domestic customers for both gas and electricity. By means of this concept, customers would have the benefit of real competition in terms of choice of supplier and even better value for money. We have a strong belief that this will come to pass and, if it does, the long-held notion of a natural monopoly in both gas and electricity supply will pass into history. This aspect will be dealt with more fully at a later stage in this chapter.

7.3 Benefits from privatisation

When the process of privatisation is undertaken the objectives are fairly clear. The new shareholders will expect that they will obtain a satisfactory return on the funds invested and that the capital value will be enhanced. The management will assume that new responsibilities and challenges will confront it and the expectation will exist that compensation packages will be appropriate to recognise the changed circumstances. The workforce may feel less sanguine, but if economic growth can be achieved, employees should participate in the benefits through higher wages and better conditions. However, customers also have expectations in terms of lower prices and improved levels of service. This will be the case particularly in regard to the privatisation of utility companies, against which allegations of poor value seem to be made in every country throughout the world.

All these improvements will remain fond hopes unless a substantial increase in business efficiency can be generated. That is precisely what privatisation is expected to provide. Managements have to deliver, and they will say that they have been set free to do just that but are subject to the constraints posed by a regulatory regime designed to afford protection to vulnerable customers. It is important, therefore, to ensure that regulation should be kept to a minimum.

7.4 Zero-base regulation

Many will be familiar with the concept of zero-base budgets and it seems reasonable that it could be applied to the field of regulation, although it must be said that it has not happened in Britain in the gas supply case. It could be said that if there is fierce competition in a market segment there is no need to even consider the introduction of any form of regulation. At the other end of the scale, if a market is dominated in all respects by a monopolist, then a stringent regime of regulation should be developed to make sure that the monopolist does not abuse its position. In most situations neither of the extremes will apply and an intermediate case will exist. It will be a matter of judgement to establish the degree to which regulation should be introduced.

In these circumstances the zero-base concept could have validity. There seems to be merit in starting from the point that there should be no regulation unless a strong case can be made for its introduction. This procedure should ensure that all aspects of the trading activities in a newly privatised entity are examined with care. If it becomes clear on examination that a subsidiary company or a service department could be spun off into a competitive environment, that course of action should be followed. There are obvious benefits to be derived from a process which can bring about greater efficiency of management and from the simplification of any regulatory procedure. The process also has a benefit in regard to the identification of those activities which may appear to require long-term regulation and those in which there is the opportunity to make regulation a passing phase.

7.5 The rules of the game

When a project for the privatisation and regulation of an industry is being considered, great care must be taken to make sure that the rules are specific and their implications are understood by the participants. If it is the intention to expand competition, that should be understood by any monopolist; if an objective is to make sure that efficiency gains are shared between customers and supplier, then gains should be sought by the supplier and a satisfactory mechanism should be in place to share them equitably.

Taking the natural gas industry as an example, it is particularly important to allow access both to sources of supply of gas and to all pipeline systems by which it will be carried to customers. Pricing methods used by monopolists should be both transparent and non-discriminatory, as should their duties and powers. The extent of the powers of any regulatory agencies should be made clear. Furthermore the interaction between such powers and the methods by which customers can gain access to restitution in regard to alleged malpractice by a monopolist must be clearly spelt out.

One specific aspect deserves the attention of the entities to be privatised and that relates to the quality of financial data which is generated. One of the basic essentials will be the segregation of the financial results by activity. If that is absent, it will be the source of much difficulty when the entity begins to deal with the regulator and the public.

In the case of the privatisation of the British Gas Corporation, as it was known in 1986, all the above factors were clearly defined in the Gas Act 1986 and in the authorisation on trading given by the government to British Gas plc. At least the contents were plain enough to OFGAS, but it has become abundantly clear that the management of that company has chosen to rely on what it understood to be the intentions of the government. Whatever reason there may have been for misunderstanding prior to the publication of the legislation mentioned above, a reading thereof should have clarified the position for the British Gas management team.

There has been a growing divergence between OFGAS and British Gas on the intention of the Gas Act 1986. If OFGAS had been acting illegally during the period from 1986 to 1993, it would have been appropriate for British Gas to seek judicial review of the OFGAS actions. That it did not do so surely supports the view that OFGAS has been acting in accordance with the legislation.

7.6 An alternative configuration for the gas supply industry in Britain

In 1986 British Gas was privatised as a single entity. A nationalised monopoly thus became a privatised monopoly. There is validity in considering an alternative method of privatisation, one which is in tune with the privatisation method used in the electricity and water industries. There is no certainty that such an alternative would have been more successful than the route chosen in 1986 but it is one which has found favour in other countries when the gas supply industry has been privatised. Let us consider elements of an alternative approach. First, as gas deposits were almost exclusively offshore and had been developed by a series of competitors, it was not necessary to deal with this aspect. However, it could have been decided that any interests owned by British Gas offshore could have been floated under the control of a separate company. Second, as far as pipeline systems are concerned, a decision will normally depend on the configuration of the systems. If discrete systems are in existence, competition can be facilitated and this is also possible if a new addition is required to the system. In Britain there is only one system, so the optimal solution appears to be to place such a monopoly within the control of a separately owned company. This monopolist will require to be heavily regulated to ensure that the pricing system is totally transparent and that all users are treated at arm's length. In such circumstances, no producers, distributors or end users, should be permitted to have an ownership position in the pipeline operation.

Third, there is a strong case for the creation of separately owned distribution companies, whose number would depend on the circumstances obtaining. If it is possible to introduce competition among them, the degree of regulation required will not be heavy. Initially, competition may not be wholly possible and transitional regulation will therefore be needed. In all this, if any in-house services existed, consideration should be given to flotation and the possibility of buying in services as alternative strategies.

Of course, the permutations are very considerable and the local conditions and the objectives of the government will be brought into consideration before a final decision is arrived at. The chances of enhanced efficiency will be best improved if new entities are subjected to the greatest possible amount of competition which can be created by restructuring and the flotation of service and other entities. It should be noted that there appeared to be no support within the ranks of British Gas's management for a method which interfered with the shape of the entity in 1986, and that position has not changed to this day.

7.7 Management attitudes

When the status of a publicly owned utility changes to a privately owned one, the top management immediately becomes responsible for the creation and implementation of the future business strategy. This may not appear to present a serious problem to the members of the management team and this is normally because they believe that they can proceed along the same lines as in the past. To believe that could be fraught with danger. There is a world of difference between simply carrying out government orders and creating policy and implementing it. This world of difference is called a culture change. When one considers that many managers in public utilities have spent all or a large part of their business lives operating under the policy initiatives of government in Western countries, the difficulty emerges with great clarity. These managers will require to be reoriented so that they in turn can redirect their own colleagues in a set of new skills. This is an area of fundamental importance which has been ignored all too frequently. Plans and recommendations can be prepared by sophisticated consultants. These will undoubtedly be of a high standard and, on the face of it, will be readily absorbed by the top management team. It is when it is time to make decisions that the crunch will come. The vital question is whether the top managers, and by extension their colleagues, know how to make these new types of decisions. Some people can do this naturally, but they are in a small minority. Most people need help, but a high proportion refuse to admit it. There are all too few firms who can help in such situations and even they are not called upon at an early stage. All too often crucial errors have to occur before specialist help is called in.

The lesson is that management culture is notoriously difficult to change. It often requires a change in personnel, but if the existing personnel remain in office, they should be required to undergo a period of intensive counselling to enable them to meet the new challenges they face. If neither of these events takes place, the anticipated upsurge in efficiency and improved profitability will not happen.

7.8 Surrogate competition

In many restructuring cases involving the privatisation of public utilities, following the completion of a process of zero-based regulation design it will emerge that there will be at least one monopoly contained within the reconfigured sector. That will call for strong regulation, albeit only for the monopolist. In such a case it is recommended that a system of surrogate competition should be introduced as the preferred regulatory mechanism. Even if such a course has to be followed, hope should not be abandoned that at some future time it might be possible to replace surrogate competition with the real thing.

The basis of the approach is for the regulator to regard him- or herself as being the competitor to the monopolist, with the obvious limitation that derives from being a 'not for profit' organisation. Although it cannot be emphasised too often that the individual circumstances must be addressed, it may be helpful to outline the way in which this matter was approached in Britain by OFGAS.

No guidelines had been prepared by the promoters of the scheme of privatisation as to how a surrogate competitor would operate; in fact the concept was taken forward by OFGAS as it began to operate the provisions of the Gas Act 1986. It became clear from the first days of OFGAS that no progress could be made in respect of surrogate competition, third-party access or any objective revision of the tariff market price formula, unless the financial affairs of British Gas were segmented. The suggestion by OFGAS that such a process should be undertaken was resisted by British Gas but ultimately it was persuaded to co-operate in segmenting the financial results of its gas supply business. The key feature was the insistence of OFGAS that the gas supply business should be set within the context of the published annual accounts of the whole company. By this means nothing was omitted and nothing was counted twice. It also meant that third-party access and pricing discussions could be based on a set of data which were arranged by a mutually acceptable allocation and apportionment methodology. There was no way in which the total data package could be disputed, as it was attested to by the external auditor.

The necessity of having reliable financial data is of paramount importance. However, the regulator will be unable to operate as a surrogate competitor if he or she does not base his or her approach on marketing principles. It was to the dynamics of the market place which OFGAS turned in the first instance, to examine the volumes in each market segment, the distribution of the customer base, the geography of the various areas and the uses to which natural gas was being put – in fact a total overview of the market for natural gas. The material collected at the outset formed the basis of a model which has been kept up to date. The market study included a review of the supply and demand position, which allowed an identification of those suppliers who could become competitors in the industrial segment of the market.

A review of the needs and desires of the users of natural gas has been consistently tested by means of an outreach programme carried out by specialist staff at OFGAS. Quarterly visits to each region are designed to bring together customers and consumer representatives. It has been possible to monitor the impact of a series of changes in service standards accepted by British Gas on the initiative of OFGAS. This amounts to a top-down, bottom-up approach to policy change, such as is carried out by successful marketing companies. This was one of the first manifestations of surrogate competition, but it appeared that British Gas was unaware of the significance of this change of emphasis.

OFGAS began to monitor the risks associated with the tariff segment of the market and paid regular visits to operations in other parts of the world with characteristics similar to British Gas. Levels and standards of service were studied in a variety of situations and emerging management techniques monitored and evaluated. Rates of return were placed under scrutiny on a wide basis and a means of comparing these rates has been formulated.

In short, OFGAS has been building towards a model of a gas supply company which can offer a high level of value for money to its customers and still make a consistently good level of profitability. If it were to be made possible that OFGAS could enter the gas supply market on the basis of its model, it is confidently predicted that it would take market share away from the existing monopolist.

Furthermore it became possible in 1990, when OFGAS began to review the tariff segment price control mechanism, to develop a set of regional analyses whereby it was possible to identify potential efficiency improvements for future periods of time. By a process of synthesis a picture of costs associated with varying levels of standards of service was built up. When the above aspects had been dealt with, a package emerged, comprising service standards at selling prices. This would provide a rate of return which would be satisfactory given the level of risk being undertaken. This package would have been a platform on which a competitor to British Gas could have rolled out a successful attack on the tariff segment of the gas market. It is estimated that it would have been successful on the basis of value for money to the user of the product and satisfactory profitability for the supplier.

7.9 Real competition in the tariff market segment

Surrogate competition in the tariff or domestic market segment has achieved a great deal, but there is an air of unreality when a regulator is acting as a competitor. As such it is a second-best solution, since there is no choice of supplier available to the customer and, as a consequence, this excludes the most important aspect of the market place experience. In Britain, however, it appears that the real thing could be on its way as far as competition is concerned.

Two elements have combined to give hope that customers in the tariff market may be provided with a choice of supplier. The British government significantly lowered the fiscal barrier to competition in the tariff market in 1992 and signalled a further review of the position in 1993. The barrier was originally set at a usage of 25,000 therms per annum but was subsequently reduced to 2,500 therms subject to a further review. This opened the way for competitors to supply small businesses such as local bakeries, restaurants and launderettes, and such activity started on a modest scale.

The second aspect relates to the way in which the privatisation of the electricity industry in Britain has been carried out. As part of that process, twelve regional distribution companies were created and these have the administrative capability to serve the customers presently making up the domestic market for natural gas. Since it is feasible for these new companies to buy gas from a North Sea producer, to obtain access to the British Gas pipeline system to make deliveries to customers, and easily to make contact with their existing electricity customers, it will be readily seen that customers could be supplied with both electricity and gas by a single energy company. Almost all of the regional electricity companies have started along the competitive path. Regional electricity companies have created gas supply subsidiaries and through these have purchased gas from the North Sea. Such purchases have been supervised by the Office of Fair Trading (OFT). In terms of a gas release programme, OFT has agreed with British Gas whereby British Gas sells gas to competitors using existing British Gas contracts with producers in the North Sea. These subsidiaries have gained access to British Gas pipelines under the rules laid down by OFGAS and have thereby started to supply the categories of customer who would never have expected to be given a choice of supplier. Lower prices and more flexible contracts have been obtained by these relatively small users. All it needs now is for the government to remove the barrier of 2,500 therms usage per year and real competition can begin for domestic customers. A timetable has been laid down for the removal of competitive barriers in electricity supply by 1998. As gas supply is less complex there seems to be no reason that 1998 cannot be a target for gas users in the domestic segment. When one of the regional electricity companies makes its first delivery to a domestic user of gas, real competition will have arrived in Britain.

7.10 A final thought

A motto for a regulator could be 'Freedom for the maximum number and protection for the remainder'. Clearly that has been the approach adopted by OFGAS. It has appeared that several countries in Eastern Europe have displayed a healthier appetite for freedom of choice and a move towards free and competitive markets than some of the monopolists in the energy markets in the so-called innovative market-driven countries of the West. It is time they got the message.

PART III

Developing countries' experience

8

Private investment and privatisation in sub-Saharan Africa

J.-M. Fontaine and V. Geronimi

8.1 Introduction

Privatisation in sub-Saharan Africa (SSA) has not resulted from pressure from below. There has been very little societal demand, business circles have not been pressing for a retreat of the state, and the initiative has come from both above and outside. From above, since, in effect, states have been the initiators and proponents of privatisation. And from outside, since they responded to initiatives of foreign donors and international organisations, mainly the World Bank and the IMF, with little apparent enthusiasm. Describing the attitudes which pushed leading African officials to privatisation, a perceptive observer, John Nellis (1986), used the word 'desperation'.

Even within the Bretton Woods philosophy, the position towards public enterprises at large, and privatisation proper, appears unclear. It is a blend of concerns over budget deficits, drain on shrinking foreign exchange resources, debt, and internal mismanagement. These are basically negative arguments: public enterprises cost too much, and should be trimmed down. Notions as to how this ought to be done have evolved over time, with arguments based on efficiency considerations appearing quite late with a slight flavour of *ex post* rhetoric. The World Bank's approach to public enterprises in Senegal, for instance, started in 1978 from a project approach with technical assistance to specific public enterprises, then gradually moved into public-sector specific projects, then into institutional reform proposals, and ended up in 1982 with a general programme stressing the need for extensive privatisation (Alexander, 1986).

Even so, privatisation does not appear as an aim in itself, but rather as an instrumental move within a more general strategy. The overall attitude to public enterprise reform is summarised by the World Bank as follows: 'Reforms are conceived generically in response to two types of problems and aim to support adjustment efforts by reducing fiscal imbalances, and promote growth by improving productivity of investment' (Swanson and Wolde-Semait, 1989). Reform consequently consists of:

1. Macroeconomic policy reforms, aimed at providing a more appropriate policy framework through liberalisation of prices, elimination of protective trade policies

and state monopolies, revision of tariff structures and so on, designed to improve the competitive environment;

2. Divestiture programmes aimed at rationalising the public enterprise sector through liquidation, privatisation or management contracts;
3. Rehabilitation of viable PEs, both physical and financial;
4. Management reforms;
5. Legal and institutional reforms, including performance contracts. (Ibid. 23).

From the onset, nothing like a 'strategy' appears behind the proposals for privatisation. This leads to two remarks. The first is that the effects of privatisation cannot be judged independently of the overall adjustment strategy: privatisation is not an aim *per se*, but rather an instrumental move within the broader context of adjustment. The second is that, since privatisations did not respond to pressures from below – that is, since public capital was not displaced by a push of private investment – consideration of private investment reactions to privatisations assumes a rather paradoxical character. Privatisations come first – both logically and chronologically, in terms of adjustment sequence – and private investment second, being expected to react *ex post* both to the overall transformation of macroeconomic environment and to privatisation, which are part of the transformation process.

The remainder of this chapter is therefore organised in three main sections. The second section examines the impact of structural adjustment policies at large on the behaviour of aggregate and private investment, both at world level, and more specifically in the sub-Saharan African context. The third section focuses on the impact of privatisations proper on private investment and reviews theoretical expectations. The fourth section presents empirical material, while the final section presents brief conclusions.

8.2 Aggregate and private investment behaviour under structural adjustment

Although theoretical expectations concerning the reaction of aggregate or private investment to structural adjustment packages are a priori contradictory, there seems now to be a consensus that adjustment exerts, on the whole, no discernible positive effects on the overall rate of growth, and clearly negative effects on investment.

8.2.1 *Overall view*

One must of course distinguish between the impact of stabilisation and that of adjustment on investment behaviour. The first phase of adjustment, macroeconomic stabilisation, is designed to induce domestic contraction. Overall policies are deflationary, with tight fiscal and monetary policies. Domestic absorption – of which investment is an important component – is to be reduced in order to restore or improve external accounts. Furthermore real interest rates are targeted to increase with a view to reversing previous overcapitalistic practices and lowering the capital-output ratio, which results in a direct hindrance to capital accumulation and investment. More generally, as noted by Mitra (1986), investment will react more markedly to consumption than contraction .

Although the second phase, structural adjustment proper, is expected to be more expansionary, it is now widely accepted that stabilisation constraints will go on during this second phase: Corbo, Fischer and Webb (1992: 7), for example, describe adjustment as a 'long-term macroeconomic stabilisation', coupled with 'structural transformation of the economy'. Which means that the tight policies implemented during the stabilisation phase will be maintained during the period of 'structural reform' and that the depressing influence of stabilisation will extend over the whole time span of adjustment.

The number of factors to which investment can respond positively are then reduced. With a continually depressed home market, investment can be driven by an expansion of exports, or by prospects of 'efficient import substitution', or by 'rationalisation investments' in domestic sectors (i.e. positive reaction of investors to the increased efficiency brought about by structural reforms). But none of these motives appears to be very potent.

Investment prospects of the 'rationalising' kind cannot be expected to be very bright since economic rationalisation normally entails a decrease in capital output-ratios. Prospects for efficient import substitution will crucially depend on the nature of the foreign-trade reforms (see Geourjon, 1992, for an account of Senegal's experience, or Fanelli, Frenkel and Rozenwurcel, 1992 for a Latin American view). If import liberalisation prevails, the impact on manufacturing activity and investment will most probably turn out globally negative until the manufacturing structure has fully adapted to the change – which can take years. Finally, exports will depend on uncertain international prospects, and the size of investment required or warranted by export expansion will crucially depend on the structure of exports. If agricultural products dominate, as they do in most SSA countries, the corresponding amount of investment might turn out to be quite small.

These rather intuitive results were actually confirmed in a recent modelling exercise by Benjamin (1992). The only case where investment increased following adjustment was where exports of manufactured goods – which she questionably described as 'highly tradable' – reacted strongly to the currency depreciation induced by a cut in government spending, on the additional condition that domestic real rates of interest would fall. All other simulation exercises yielded a decline in investment – or, at best, a compensation between an increase in public investment and a decrease in private investment.

Theoretical expectations are, then, that structural adjustment packages (SAPs) will exert a negative impact on investment. This is actually confirmed by empirical findings, as shown in Table 8.1.

Table 8.1 Impact of structural adjustment programmes on selected macroeconomic indicators

Performance indicator	Mosley, Harrigan and Toye (1991)			World Bank (1988, 1990, 1992)	
	Comparison	Regression	Simulation	1988	1990 and 1992
GDP growth rate	0/+	0/+	n.a.	0	+
Exports	+	+	0/+	+	+
Investment	–	–	n.a.	–	–
Balance of payments	–	+	–	+	+
External finance	n.a.	0	n.a.	n.a.	+
Domestic savings	–	n.a.	n.a.	n.a.	+
Public deficit	n.a.	n.a.	0/–	–	–

Note: 0 indicates neutral; 0/+ indicates neutral or weak positive effect; + indicates increase; – indicates decrease; n.a. indicates not available.

Table 8.2 Impact of structural adjustment programmes on selected macroeconomic indicators in sub-Saharan Africa

Performance indicators	Leenhardt and L'Hériteau (1991)	Elbadawi (1992); Elbadawi *et al.* (1992)
GDP growth	+[a] –[b]	–
Domestic savings	n.a.	–
Investment	n.a.	–
Current account	0	n.a.
Exports	n.a.	+
Budget	0/+	n.a.
Inflation	n.a.	+

Notes: [a]After 3 years of adjustment.
[b]After 1 or 2 years of adjustment.
0 indicates no effect; + or – indicate increases or decreases in the performance indicator; 0/+ or 0/– indicate small or negligible effect.

8.2.2 African context

The results summarised in Table 8.1 were established from a sample of countries representing adjustment experiences throughout the world. Although very few global evaluations were conducted specifically for SSA countries, those which exist confirm this tendency (see Table 8.2).

The reasons for this decline in investment are not spelled out in detail, but comments by various authors give a general idea. Guillaumont, Guillaumont and Plane (1991) relate it to the contraction of national savings, the increase in the price of imported capital goods following devaluation, and the increase in real rates of interest, while Leenhardt and L'Hériteau (1991) stress the depressing impact of fiscal policies. Commenting on his own results, Elbadawi (1992: 39) writes:

> The combination of the above results on investment and ... on economic growth [implies] that the perceived increase in efficiency of investment supposed to be generated by the program has not been sufficient to counterbalance the ensuing decline in investment and hence to restore economic growth.

This means that none of the possible mechanisms which we listed earlier, by which adjustment could increase investment, actually operated in SSA. In fact, whatever improvements were obtained, for example in exports, seem to have been counterbalanced by the negative response of investment and its impact on growth rates.

Beyond the general reasons why adjustment should depress investment, one should note two distinctive features of African adjustments. First, in no African country, except in Mauritius, has adjustment been successfully discontinued. All other countries which severed links with the IMF and Bank did so either because they could not meet performance criteria or repayments, as Congo since 1988 or Côte d'Ivoire in 1987 and 1988, or because of domestic political problems or pressures, like Zambia in 1986, or Kenya in March 1993. Some countries tried to discontinue adjustment, as Senegal did in 1984 or Mali in 1986 and 1987, but growth came to an immediate halt, and programmes and financial assistance had to be quickly restored.[1] The high frequency of SAPs in SSA thus indicates that these countries are locked into adjustment policies and have not devised ways of restoring effective self-sustainable growth or development.

The other distinctive feature is the specific structure of African conditionality. The analysis presented by the World Bank's Reviews of Structural Adjustment in 1988 and 1990 suggests that there is an 'African specificity' of conditionality, with four items particularly stressed – budget and public expenditure reduction, public enterprise reforms, industrial policy and agricultural policy – with all four areas being significantly more frequent in SSA countries than in highly indebted countries (HICs) or other non-African adjustment experiences (see Table 8.3).

Budget reductions are clearly stabilisation measures which normally depress investment, either directly through public investment, or indirectly, through demand contractionary effects. And the emphasis on sectoral policies directly reflects the priority to agriculture which carries a clear, albeit implicit, anti-industrial bias. With low capital output ratios in African agriculture, this sectoral shift will normally lead to a drop in aggregate (public and private) investment. However, one specific feature, public enterprise reform, does not exert any a priori discernible impact on investment. We now turn to examine this point.

Table 8.3 Structure of conditionality: distribution of loan agreement conditions by policy area and country type – SSA, HICs and other developing countries (%)

Item	SSA	HIC	Other countries
Exchange rate	4.2	1.9	0.0
Trade policies	25.0	32.0	24.8
Fiscal policy	8.3	10.8	15.2
Budget/public expenditure	11.8	8.9	9.7
Public enterprises	19.4	16.6	11.5
Financial sector	3.5	13.1	13.3
Industrial policy	6.9	2.3	1.8
Energy policy	1.4	3.1	14.5
Agricultural policy	17.4	10.0	7.2
Other	2.1	1.3	2.0
Total	100.0	100.0	100.0

Source: World Bank, (1988), Table 4.1.

8.3 Expected influences of public enterprise reform and privatisation upon private investment

All that has been said up to now concerns aggregate, that is, public and private investment. One important measure, that of public enterprise reform and privatisation, has not been examined yet. It is an important point, since replacement of public by private initiative is one primary aim of adjustment policies.

8.3.1. *Background of privatisation strategy*

On paper, we face a neat and clear argument. In an ideal Hayekian world, private and public investment are complementary, with the state investing in infrastructure and the private sector in directly productive activities.

Previous conceptions of development strategies, however, inspired different options, and motives for public intervention were numerous: in an 'unbalanced growth' approach, leading sectors have to be developed ahead of demand, which precludes private initiative; lack of national bourgeoisies and of entrepreneurial classes shed the responsibility of industrial development upon the state's shoulders; 'learning by doing' and infant industry arguments require state intervention of some sort, either indirect, of the 'protective' kind, or direct, with the state assuming costs and initiatives and investing in production; and the need for diversification of productive activities warranted control upon strategic resources, especially export proceeds, leading to the emergence of state monopolies in banking, agriculture, mining, forestry and so on. Public and private investment then display some form of substitutability, since public undertakings compensated for the lack of private initiative.

Changes in perceptions of strategies as well as mounting public deficits have deeply modified the general attitude towards direct state intervention (Killick, 1989; Singer and Roy, 1993). With government perceived as an inefficient predator and – because it escapes market sanctions – an irresponsible agent, any shift from public to private control is to be welcome *per se* (Fontaine, 1993). New conceptions of 'market friendly' development strategy (Fanelli, Frenkel and Taylor, 1992) reinforce the case for retrenchment. Globally, by shifting capital from public to private hands, one will avoid past mistakes, increase the general level of efficiency and, consequently, the level of output and income.

Abstracting from the broader strategic question of the relative merits of a market-driven, efficiency-based, outward-oriented strategy, one important point is to know how this shift from public to private investment will come about. This point is especially important in the present context since retrenchment of state activities could open up new opportunities for private investment – even though aggregate investment might be contracting.

8.3.2 *Public–private investment relationships*

One simple story tells how private and public investment interact. On the real – or demand – side, the retreat – or the mere lifting of monopoly – of state enterprises from specific sectors will allow private entrepreneurs to move in, which implies that the previous substitution of public for private investment operates symmetrically. Where public investment substituted for the lack of private initiative in the state-driven phase of development, private investment would now substitute for public, with retrenchment stimulating private initiative.

This implies two things. The first is that private investors are actually present, and prepared to move into previously publicly organised sectors, which means that the social structure has somehow matured and that the traditional deficiency of domestic entrepreneurial classes has come to an end. The second is that the sectors offered for privatisation are actually attractive – a point to which we shall return in the next section.

On the financial – or supply – side, curtailment of public spending, and especially of public investment, will ease the credit situation, pushing rates of interest down – or bringing an end to credit rationing – thus allowing the resumption of private investment in the usual 'crowding-out' fashion.

This story is too simple by far. Although there has been little research on the actual behaviour of private investment in less developed countries – and close to nil concerning SSA countries – a number of complications to this simple scheme have nonetheless been identified.

On the supply side – or financial links between public and private investment – two completely differing approaches coexist. According to the standard neoclassical argument, a decrease in the rate of interest will lower the cost of investment, pushing capital formation up. Alternatively, in a McKinnon–Shaw fashion, a fall in the rate of interest, by depleting money balances and loanable funds, will induce a fall in investment. The financial side of the crowding-out argument is therefore ambiguous. One might reconcile both arguments by noting the existence of a chronological asymmetry between these two mechanisms. The cost impact of movements in the rate of interest on capital formation is felt in the short term – that is, an increase in the rate of interest, by increasing costs, will immediately bring investment down – while the increase of loanable funds following an increase in the rate of interest operates in a slower fashion. Investment behaviour in the medium or long run would then be positively affected by increases in the rate of interest, after a first negative reaction.

But even assuming neoclassical financial 'crowding-out' to predominate, the architecture of stabilisation and/or adjustment would not allow it to operate. Tight monetary policies accommodate, or overaccommodate to reduced government spendings, so that real rates of interest do not fall but, on the contrary, increase. This is one of the stabilisation/adjustment packages' targets which has been quite consistently achieved: while none of the 24 SSA countries for which information was available for 1975–79 displayed positive real rates of interest, 6 out of 28 showed positive real rates of interest in 1980–85, and 14 out of 30 in 1986–88. If, then, we are right in assuming that the depressing influence of an increase of the rate of interest is felt immediately, while the 'McKinnon' positive impact on investment through increases in money balances and loanable funds takes time to materialise, one would expect private investment to fall, at least in the short term, rather than the opposite. Whatever 'investment pull' element is at work in privatisations will then be contained by the evolution of the rate of interest.

Concerning demand-related or real factors, the physical relation between public and private investment is known to be more complex than simple substitution. Public investment in infrastructure is in essence complementary to private capital and obviously crowds in private capital through forward linkages. Backward linkages also operate in a crowding-in fashion: large public-owned enterprises typically create physical opportunities for private investment. Public investment might equally increase the expected profitability on private capital by stimulating aggregate demand, reducing production costs following improvements in infrastructure, by improving prospects in manufacturing activities, and so on. Finally, if transfer pricing is the prevailing philosophy in the public sector, public enterprises will supply intermediate goods and inputs below cost, thus increasing again private profitability.

To complicate matters a bit more, crowding-in and out factors can coexist. Blejer and Khan (1984) identified a positive link between private and public investment long-term trends, but an inverse relation between deviations from the trend. This would indicate that there is long-term complementarity – that is, crowding-in, presumably because of public provision of infrastructure – but short-term substitutability and crowding-out – perhaps due to sensitivity to the rate of interest.[2] In fact, as will be seen later, the econometric evidence itself appears to yield contradictory results.

We can so far only conclude that the public–private investment behaviour is a complicated one, and that theoretical expectations are a priori undetermined. On this agnostic note, we now turn to the examination of whatever empirical material is available.

8.4 Privatisation and post-privatisation experiences: an evaluation

The first paradox is that the empirical material is dramatically poor. While the World Bank produced an impressive number of documents in the early 1980s, it seems now to have lost its interest for privatisation in SSA.

The subject is hardly mentioned in the 1989 'long-term perspective' on sub-Saharan Africa (World Bank, 1989), and no background papers were prepared on that topic. The 1991 collection of papers on *Economic Reform in Sub-Saharan Africa* (Chhibber and Fisher, 1991) does not mention the issue, nor does the 1992 symposium on adjustment lending (Corbo, Fischer and Webb, 1992), while, in his assessments of effectiveness of Bank-supported programmes, Elbadawi (1992) does not even acknowledge the existence of a privatisation policy. Galal's (1991) paper on public enterprise reform presents no figures – except for a few tables copied out from the *African Development Indicators* – or analysis and, in essence, reproduces general arguments and recommendations which could already be found in a disappointing paper by Shirley (1989). The last full and informative reports on privatisation were published by the Bank in 1988 (Berg and Shirley; Vuylsteke; Candoy-Sekse and Palmer) and 1989 (Swanson and Wolde-Semait). Our impression, confirmed by informal talks with World Bank representatives, is that there is a great deal of (concealed) disappointment on this issue.

8.4.1 *Privatisations in SSA: an overall view*

Nevertheless, by putting together whatever empirical material exists, one can give a general view of the outcome of privatisation experiences.

Table 8.4 presents an update of figures presented by Candoy-Sekse and Palmer (1988) and Swanson and Wolde-Semait (1989) based upon data published in the 1992 edition of *African Development Indicators* (World Bank, 1993).

By 1990, almost 100 privatisations were completed.[3] Is this a good or bad result? As compared to planned privatisations, it is probably low. In a study by Candoy-Sekse (Candoy-Sekse and Palmer, 1988) – which most

Table 8.4 Summary of key reforms implemented, 1983–90

Country	Privatisation		Liquidation		Rehabilitation		Management contracts
	Completed	Underway	Completed	Underway	Completed	Underway	
Benin (1985)	8	6	15				2
Burundi (1986)				5		5	5
Cameroon (1985; 1987)	1		5		1		3
CAR (1985)		4	1	3	1		1
Congo (1986)					7		
Ivory Coast (1986)	14		24				5
Gabon							
Gambia (1983; 1986)	1	3	1		1		1
Kenya (1985)		1			2		2
Madagascar (1981; 1985)	34	37	12				
Malawi (1983; 1985)	1				2		1
Mali (1986)	2		7		3		2
Mauritius							
Niger (1986)	12	6	4		7		3
Senegal (1983; 1985–87)	4	18	18	5	3		2
Togo (?)	6		12	7			
Uganda (?)	7	5	1				
Zambia (?)	1						6
Zaire (1984)	1		3		2		8

Note: The years in brackets following a country name are representing the beginning of the implementation of public sector reforms.

Source: World Bank 1993 *African Development Indicators*, 1992 issue.

probably grossly overestimated the number of actual privatisations[4] – less than one out of three planned privatisations was effectively completed.[5] One will also note that liquidations outweigh privatisations proper as well as rehabilitation.

Even this relatively poor record probably overestimates the reality. A number of privatisations were really reprivatisations, with assets handed back to previous owners dispossessed in earlier nationalisation drives. This was, for instance, the case in four out of the five privatisations announced in Ghana in June 1990 – where Ghanaian citizens, formerly associated with 'Syrian' partners, were handed back assets confiscated in 1979 in a move against 'foreign speculators' – or in Uganda – where six out of the seven privatisations announced were reprivatisations either to Asian groups (Mehta, Mahdvani) or to multinationals (Lonrho, British American Tobacco, Mitchell Cotts, Bata), and the seventh 'privatisation' was a liquidation.

Furthermore successful privatisations seem to have occurred only for small enterprises. This impression, conveyed by Nellis (1986), is corroborated by the few cases where evidence on size is available (evidence from Candoy-Sekse and Palmer, 1988). In Mali, average size for all planned privatisations, as measured by total amount of yearly sales, was 6.3bn CFA Francs (FCFA), while average size of enterprises privatised was about one-fifth of this figure (1.33bn FCFA, approximately). If, however, one excludes Air-Mali (3.5bn FCFA) – which was actually leased, not sold – the average size of privatised companies falls to 256m. FCFA, that is, 25 times smaller. In Niger, net yearly income for all planned companies where information is available averaged 23.6bn FCFA, but only 8bn FCFA for companies actually privatised. In Togo, although the average size of enterprises planned for privatisations is not known, fragmentary evidence puts the average yearly revenues of effectively privatised enterprises just above 3.6bn FCFA. If, however, one excludes the STH (Togo Oil refinery), the average falls to around 400m. FCFA, which is a very small figure.

The sectoral record of divestiture (see Table 8.5) shows that the main sector concerned was the manufacturing industry. In all ten countries where sectoral composition is known, privatisation or liquidation occurred in the manufacturing sector which accounted for roughly 75 per cent of liquidations and almost 50 per cent of privatisations. The next sector was services (17 liquidations and 3 sales) followed by agriculture, which was concerned in only five countries. Given the poor record of manufacturing activity in SSA countries during the 1980s (for a detailed and informed account of this evolution see Riddell, 1990), one can surmise that the main motive for divestiture was to alleviate the budgetary burden, by disposing of subsidy consumers, rather than to attract private investment. Or, to quote Swanson and Wolde-Semait (1989) again, more to 'support adjustment efforts by reducing fiscal imbalances' than to 'promote growth by improving productivity of investment'.

So, all in all, privatisation in SSA countries displays a poor record, both at aggregate and sectoral level, with liquidations and closures predominating in the divestiture strategy.

Table 8.5 Divestiture by sectors in selected African countries

	Liquidations and closures				Sales				
		Sector					Sector		
Country	Total	Manufacturing	Agriculture	Services	Target	Actual	Manufacturing	Agriculture	Services
Cameroon	5	5			12				
Guinea	16	16			43				
Côte d'Ivoire	10		3	7	20	4	2	2	
Kenya	5	3		2					
Liberia					7				
Madagascar	5				15				
Mali	9	4	2	3	11	2	1		1
Mauritania	4	3		1	10	1			
Niger	3	1	1	1	24				
Senegal	25	24		1	10	5	3		2
Sierra Leone	1			1	10				
Sudan	10	8	1	1	n.a.	7	7		
Togo	9	9			40				
Uganda					67				
Zaire	3				37	11		11	
Total	105	73	7	17	306	30	13	13	3

Source: Berg and Shirley (1988).

The impact of these privatisations and divestitures on private investment will of course depend on the context in which they occurred – that is on the predominance of crowding-in or crowding-out behaviours – to which we now turn.

8.4.2 *'Crowding': in, out or nil?*

There is now a widespread consensus concerning the predominance of crowding-in over crowding-out effects in LDCs. This shows up in Taylor's (1988) studies and has been widely documented by Landau (1983), Blejer and Khan (1984), Okokonko (1986), and confirmed by recent analyses of private investment behaviour in less developed countries (Greene and Villanueva, 1991; Serven and Solimano, 1992; Oshikoya, 1992).

Regarding SSA countries, crowding-in does appears to be the general case. Ndulu (1991) quotes evidence of crowding-in effects[6] and Kouassy (1992) found a positive – although not statistically significant – relationship between public and private investment in Nigeria and Côte d'Ivoire.

Since the recent analyses by Serven and Solimano (1992) and Greene and Villanueva (1991) only marginally concern SSA countries (both are cross-section analyses run on respectively fifteen and twenty-three countries, but only two very untypical SSA countries, Kenya and Zimbabwe, are included), we tried to run an econometric test following the Greene and Villanueva specification on a sample of eight SSA countries[7] for which data were available in *African Development Indicators* (World Bank, 1993), extending the period of analysis to 1990. The results are presented in Table 8.6.

Serven and Solimano (1992) found a positive relationship between private and public investment, which should indicate crowding-in effect, but they did not include the real rate of interest in their analysis. Greene and Villanueva (1991) also found a positive link between private and public investment – that is, crowding-in – but this coexists with a negative impact of real rate of interest on private investment – which corresponds to crowding-out effects. In other words, there is a potential contradiction in their results: public investment crowds in private investment through 'demand factors', while financial factors crowd it out.

Our results, however, show a positive and significant impact of real rates of interest – which would plead for crowding-in – but also a negative impact of public investment on private capital formation, indicating crowding-out.

Looking for an explanation for these contradictory results, we came to the conclusion that the whole exercise was of limited value because of what appears to be an essential short-coming of the procedure. All three analyses rely upon cross-section pooled-data econometric analysis.[8] This procedure yields excellent R^2s and highly significant t-values, giving the impression of highly significant results. But when we ran the test with no explanatory variables at all, including

Table 8.6 Comparison of results of the regression for private investment rates

	Ir	TCY*t*1	Ipub	CPI	YT1	XGS1	DTOT1	Number of obser-vations	R^2	SEE
Greene and Villanueva										
1975–87	−0.083*** (−3.06)	0.249*** (6.5)	0.08*** (2.03)	−0.004*** (−4.02)	0.084 (0.32)	−0.031*** (−2.55)	−0.033*** (−2.99)	294	0.81	2.38
1982–87	−0.019 (−1.03)	0.209*** (5.67)	0.0621*** (2.05)	−0.001*** (−3.02)	−1.56*** (−2.87)	−0.003 (−0.21)	−0.052 (2.82)	138	0.92	1.56
Seven SSA countries										
1980–90	0.121** (2.18)	0.049 (0.93)	−0.296* (−1.81)	−0.108*** (−2.75)	0.004** (2.62)	−0.212*** (−3.92)	−0.0001 (−0.81)	77	0.85	2.46

Note: The dependent variable is the ratio of private investment to GDP. Ir is the real rate of interest (nominal rate corrected by GDP deflator, TCY*t*1 is per capita income growth rate; Ipub is the ratio of public investment to GDP; CPI is the rate of increase of the consumer price index; YT1 is the level of per capita income lagged one year; XGS is debt-service to export ratio lagged one year; and DTOT1 is total debt to GDP lagged one year. Figures in brackets are *t*-statistics. $\bar{R}^2$ is the adjusted R^2. SEE is the standard error of the estimate. One asterisk indicates statistical significance at the 1 per cent level, two asterisks 5 per cent and three asterisks 10 per cent level of significance. The coefficients of the countries dummy variables, which are all significant at the 1 per cent level, have been omitted from the table.

Sources: Greene and Villanueva (1991), and World Bank (1993) for estimates on the seven SSA countries.

only the country dummies, this yielded a R^2 coefficient as high as 0.77! Intercountry differences, then, probably obscure all other influences.

We turned therefore to time-series analysis on a country-by-country basis, which obliged us to reduce the number of explanatory variables since data are available for only eleven years. The new specification was Ipriv = f (Ipub, Ir,C) – where Ipriv is private investment, Ipub public investment, Ir real rate of interest, and C is a constant. This was tested in linear and log-linear forms and the results are shown in Table 8.7.

Out of eight countries (see Table 8.7), only Côte d'Ivoire presented no important first-order autocorrelation of residuals, and we applied the Cochran–Orcutt method to the remaining seven. After correction, six countries yield significant results: Burundi, Côte d'Ivoire, Gabon, Gambia, Kenya and Mauritius Senegal has no explanatory power, and autocorrelation remains strong in the case of Malawi.

This yields a more complicated image, and all theoretical possibilities actually materialised. 'Direct' crowding-out (a negative sign attached to Ipub in the regression) operates in three countries: Kenya, Gambia and Malawi. Crowding-in appears in three countries: Burundi, Côte d'Ivoire and Gabon, while two countries, Mauritius and Senegal, show undetermined or 'crowding-nil' profiles. Furthermore the direct (Ipriv/Ipub) and financial effects (Ipriv/Ir) contradict each other in three of the six cases where crowding-in or out was established: Kenya displays 'direct' crowding-out but positive reaction of private investment to real rates of interest, while Burundi and Côte d'Ivoire display direct crowding-in but negative reactions to increases in the real rate of interest. All in all, our sample falls almost equally in the three categories: crowding-out, or in, or nil; and 'exceptions' – where direct and financial effects operate in opposite direction – occur in half of the countries analysed (see summary of results in Table 8.8). As indicated in the last column of Table 8.7, the amount of private direct foreign investment is very low, except in Gambia. This means that, although foreign direct investment behaves in a rather complicated manner (Geronimi, Quiers Vallette and Saint-Alary, 1993), its influence on the overall rate of capital formation is in any case minute. 'Caution' is then the only practical advice one ought to formulate for policy makers relying on crowding-in or out behaviours.

8.4.3 *Private investment reactions to privatisation in crowding-in or out contexts*

Tables 8.6 and 8.7, however, do yield some useful information: some countries have been stronger 'privatisers' than others, and some seem consistently in-crowders, while others appear as out-crowders. Putting this information together, we attempted to contrast the behaviour of private investment between these groups, by plotting the private investment/GDP ratios as reported in

Table 8.7 Regressions by SSA countries

	AR(1)	Ipub	Ir	C	R^2	D.W.	f	Average Ipriv	average Ir	Average DFI % GDP 1981–90
Senegal	0.075	−1.44	0.043	13.94	−0.03	1.66	0.89	8.52	9.4	
corrected	(0.69)	(−0.9)	(1.36)	(2.23)					(1986–89)	−0.24
uncorrected		0.686	0.026	5.57	0.39	1.11	4.22		−0.4	
	(2.78)	(1.12)	(5.32)						(1980–85)	
Malawi	0.21	−1.18	0.01	15.65	0.54	0.69	4.53	5.71	−6	
corrected	(1.37)	(−3.62)	(0.13)	(5.66)					(1986–89)	0.1
Semi-Log	0.36	−1.68	0.003	5.22	0.34	1.45	2.54		−2.1	
	(1.18)	(−2.88)								
Mauritius	0.95	0.069	−0.068	26.94	0.7	1.21	8.258	14.54	3.5	
corrected	(3.76)	(0.32)	(−1.09)	(0.332)					(1986–90)	0.74
Semi-Log	0.95	0.076	−0.005	3.23	0.7	1.4	8.03		−1.9	
	(3.68)	(0.59)	(−1.24)	(0.73)					(1980–85)	
Kenya	0.64	−0.5	0.312	13.07	0.71	2.03	8.66	11.14	7.1	
corrected	(5.17)	(−2.44)	(3.85)	(5.71)					(1986–90)	0.26
Semi-Log	0.628	−0.506	0.03	3.26	0.67	2.33	7.068		−0.7	
	(4.507)	(−2.48)	(3.35)	(6.8)					(1980–85)	
Gambia	0.599	−0.677	−0.057	15.14	0.40	1.57	3.07	7.26	−3.2	
corrected	(2.25)	(−1.5)	(−0.47)	(2.79)					(1986–89)	2.72
Semi-Log	0.62	−1.84	−0.015	6.35	0.58	1.31	5.24		−1.8	
	(3.13)	(−2.66)	(−1.04)	(3.78)					(1980–85)	
Gabon	0.4	0.37	0.41	20.32	0.43	2.07	3.3	23.57	8.6	
corrected	(0.99)	(1.1)	(2.66)	(6.35)					(1986–89)	1.45
Semi-Log	0.49	0.134	0.0178	2.88	0.51	2.02	4.23		−1.4	
	(1.2)	(1.86)	(2.91)	(13.36)					(1980–85)	
Ivory Coast		1.55	−0.168	2.63	0.89	1.96	44.75	9.93	3.8	
uncorrected		(8.09)	(−1.26)	(2.08)					(1986–88)	
									3.6	0.48
Burundi	0.53	0.28	−0.068	−1.38	0.2	1.88	1.76	2.45	1.77	
corrected	(1.536)	(2.14)	(−1.25)	(−0.71)					(1986–88)	0.09
Semi-Log	0.55	1.21	−0.03	−2.29	0.23	2.00	1.94		−0.6	
	(1.77)	(1.72)	(−1.54)	(−1.23)					(1980–85)	

Note: AR is the corrective variable for first order auto-correlation following Cochran–Orcutt technique; Ipub is the ratio of public investment to GDP; Ir the real exchange rate as defined in the text; C is the constant, R^2 the adjusted R^2, Ipriv is the dependent variable; DFI is the ratio of net Direct Foreign Investment to GDP for the 1981–90 period.

Source: All results have been computed from *African Development Indicators*, 1992 issue, in World Bank (1993).

African Development Indicators, 1992 (World Bank, 1993). (see Figures 8.1, 8.2 and 8.3).

Looking first at countries with limited or no privatisation (see Figure 8.1), we find no clear pattern of private investment. There were no privatisations in Gabon, Kenya and Mauritius which are the best performers in terms of private investment to GDP. This seems logical, and one can argue that they did not need it, but private investment performance improved regularly in only one country, Mauritius. And there were no successful privatisations in Burundi,

Table 8.8 Crowding-in or out in eight SSA countries: summary of results

Country	Direct effects	Financial impact	Comments
Senegal (P)	n.s.	n.s.	'crowding nil'
Mauritius (NP)	+/n.s.	−	'crowding nil'
Malawi (LP)	−	+/n.s.	Crowding out, opposite effects?
Kenya (NP)	−	+	Crowding out opposite effects
Gambia (LP)	−	−/n.s.	Crowding out
Burundi (NP)	+	−	Crowding in opposite effects
Côte d'Ivoire (P)	+	−	Crowding in opposite effects
Gabon (NP)	+	+	Crowding in

Notes: 'Direct effects' indicate the impact of public on private investment, 'Financial impact' indicates the sign of the influence of the real rate of interest on private investment; /n.s. after a sign means that the coefficient is not statistically significant; 'opposite effects' means that financial effects and direct effects oppose each other; P, NP and LP after a country name means 'privatiser', 'non-privatiser' or 'low-privatiser'.

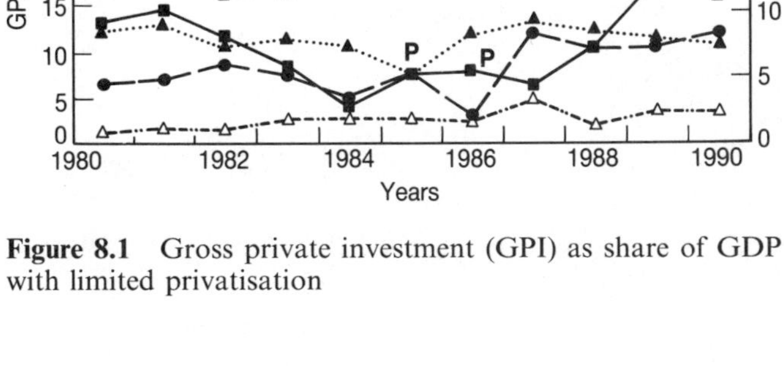

Figure 8.1 Gross private investment (GPI) as share of GDP (%): countries with limited privatisation

which is the worst performer, although a public enterprise reform programme was launched in 1986.

Gambia underwent public enterprise reforms in 1983 and 1986, and Malawi in 1983 and 1985. In both these cases, the private investment to GDP ratio increased after 1985–86. Within the sample of 'limited privatisers', the private investment to GDP ratio would seem to improve with privatisation, although one ought to be prudent here: for both these countries, only one privatisation was recorded.

Turning now to the two 'strong privatisers' of our sample (see Figure 8.2), the results confirm the crowding-in argument. Privatisations occurred in two phases – 1983 and 1985 – in Senegal. The 1983 privatisations passed unnoticed, while the second just maintained private investment around the trend, with a marginal increase from 1988 onward. In Côte d'Ivoire the bulk of privatisation occurred in 1986 but they did not reverse the falling trend of private investment; on the contrary, it appears to have aggravated it in a 'crowding-in' fashion.

If we now include Ghana within the sample of strong privatisers, we finally find one case where privatisation was associated with a rising rate of private investment. Although we have no econometric evidence regarding the dominance of crowding-in or out effects, the chronology of improvements in private investment suggests that they did not fit into a crowding-out story (see Figure 8.3).[9] Public investment was the first to increase and time profiles presented in Figure 8.3 suggest that private investment was 'pulled' – or crowded in – by public investment. Furthermore a large proportion of private investment is explained by past depreciation: Chavagneux and Grégoire (1992) estimated that only 40 per cent of gross private investment represented net investment in 1988 and 1989, and only 55 per cent in 1990.[10] This means that private investment started increasing after the level of capacity utilisation had been restored, suggesting that capital formation reacted more to 'demand-pull' factors than to privatisations (Fontaine, 1992). This is confirmed by the timing of privatisations,

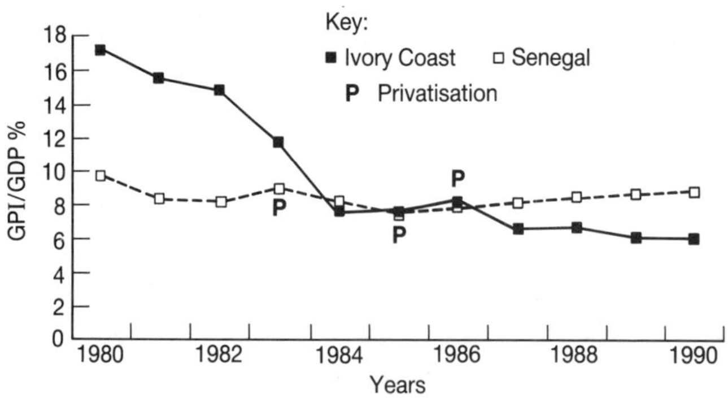

Figure 8.2 Gross private investment (GPI) as share of GDP (%): countries with strong privatisation

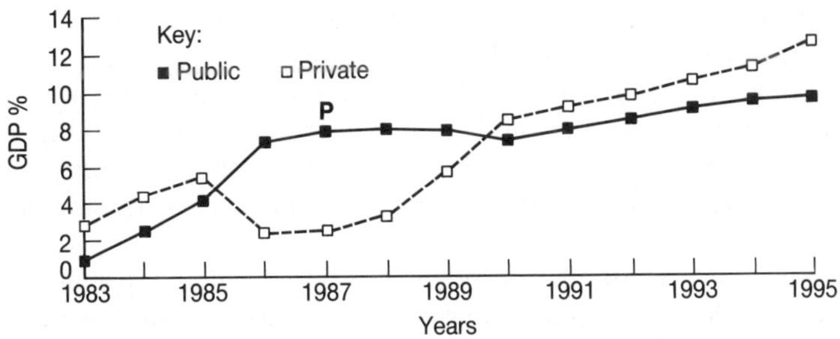

Figure 8.3 Ghana – public and private investment, actual and projected, 1983–95 (%GDP). Source: 1983–86 IMF (1991); 1987–95: World Bank (1991); 1989: provisional; 1990: preliminary; after 1990: projected

which were launched in 1987, and were effective only from 1989–90 onward, after the level of domestic activity had picked up.

This sequence of events was brought about by a specific brand of adjustment policies, somewhat unusual in the SSA context. Demand deficiency was pointed out as one important cause of economic stagnation and wages were increased throughout the economy – including those in the public sector – as was public investment, amounting to a 'rehabilitation of demand' – to quote a UNIDO (1986) report. On the supply side, one of the first major measures adopted was the restoration of import capacity through a sizeable increase in foreign financing, thereby lifting the weight of import compression on the manufacturing sector.[11]

The stabilisation episode thus incorporated strong Keynesian and structuralist elements into what turned out to be an unusual blend of Bretton Woods policy. This, together with favourable developments of exogenous factors – weather and terms of trade improvements – sparked off a domestic upward spiral, so that 'necessary policy reforms have been floated up by a rising tide of non-policy developments' (Toye, 1991: 168). When it actually came to adjustment proper, the 'market friendly' policies (Fanelli, Frenkel and Taylor, 1992) were prudently enforced (Toye, 1991), with due respect paid to 'political economy' considerations (Chavagneux, forthcoming).

8.5 Concluding remarks

Aggregate investment has fallen in SSA countries during the 1980s, reaching its lowest point in 1984–85. Private investment did not behave differently from aggregate investment.[12] Although many reasons account for this behaviour of investment, most observers now agree that structural adjustment aggravated this negative feature.

But, within the adjustment framework, did privatisation exert a positive influence on private investment? It is possible – although certainly not systematic. The evidence presented earlier indicates that private investment increased after public sector reforms in two small 'crowding-out' countries, Malawi and Gambia, which resorted to limited privatisations, but that it decreased in Côte d'Ivoire, a large country presenting crowding-in features and a strong privatiser.

If, however, one recalls the experience of Ghana, where private investment followed the resumption of public investment, and privatisations were introduced later in the reform process, one gets the impression that the restoration of overall favourable perspectives is what mattered. Thus one should not expect privatisation to trigger off private investment, but rather conclude that privatisation should follow the restoration of private investment.

This is an argument about the sequencing and timing of reforms, a plea for what could be called a 'phased crowding-in' strategy. The implications of this argument are important: the sensible sequence followed in Ghana incorporated many unusual, and even unorthodox, features. It is always hazardous to wonder whether one experience could be replicated and generalised to other African countries: political considerations were predominant, and the Ghanaian authorities were able to negotiate a better package than others. But we can nonetheless stress one feature of this gradual strategy: the restoration of demand and the relaxation of import strangulation in the manufacturing sector relied heavily on foreign financial transfers. This means that the generalisation of any form of 'Ghanaian strategy' will depend on the willingness and capacity of the international community to guarantee appropriate financing to sub-Saharan countries.

Notes

1. Leenhardt and L'Hériteau (1991) actually discovered that 'between adjustments' performances were the worst of all performances.
2. Which of these effects will prevail in the short run will depend both on the previous situation of public investment, and on the sectors in which privatisation occurs. If public investment has been run down to the point where infrastructure was not decently maintained any more, a fall in public investment will globally reduce the prospects for private investment: past depletion actualises the long-term complementary relationship found by Blejer and Khan (1984). But if the reduction of public investment is targeted through privatisation proposals, in which case it would not concern infrastructure, then substitution should occur, with private investment moving into the privatised sectors.
3. We disregard the second column as too heterogeneous since we found out that in actual practice privatisations 'underway' can mean anything from checking the accounts to discussions with a potential buyer.
4. Candoy-Sekse (1988) counted sales of assets after liquidation as privatisations, and a comparison of his figures with those available in the 1992 edition of *African*

Development Indicators (World Bank, 1993) shows a decrease in the number of recorded privatisations between 1987 and 1990 for the vast majority of countries: 36 against 14 for Côte d'Ivoire, 4 against 1 in Cameroon, 6 against 1 in Gambia, 14 against 12 in Niger, 10 to 1 in Zaire, 6 to 1 in Zambia. Ghana and Benin are the only exceptions, with respectively 6 privatisations and 0 recorded in the 1988 document against 15 and 8 in ADI 1992.

5. Note that this privatisation record rests upon the accuracy of the number of planned privatisations which were probably underreported. An extreme example is given by Côte d'Ivoire, with a 100 per cent success rate, but no listing of enterprises to be privatised issued beforehand: enterprises and candidates for privatisation or management contracts were chosen after informal contacts, and the 'programme' was announced only after it had been effectively completed. Although this phenomenon did not probably assume the same proportions elsewhere, one can imagine that there has been a significant amount of underreporting of planned privatisations.
6. The papers Ndulu refers to are working papers presented in a WIDER project concerning Tanzania, Zimbabwe, Ghana, Nigeria, Uganda, Zambia, and Senegal.
7. Burundi, Côte d'Ivoire, Gabon, Gambia, Kenya, Mauritius, Malawi and Senegal. We could not include Ghana in the sample because data are not available in ADI.
8. This means that time-series data for various countries are pooled together – so that, in part, the analysis is a time-series analysis – and each country is identified by a specific dummy, which allows for cross-section comparison.
9. Ghana was not included in the previous sample because data do not extend sufficiently far back to allow econometric analysis.
10. Only 28 per cent went into machinery and equipment, most of it in the mining sector, and more than 50 per cent in construction.
11. Comparing Ghana's adjustment programme to the neighbouring Franc Zone African countries, Leenhardt and L'Hériteau (1989) noted that the net external transfer to Ghana (with a population of 13 millions) equalled those received by Benin, Mali, Burkina, Niger, and Togo (totalling a population of 28 millions) between 1983 and 1987. IMF transfers alone represented 26 per cent of total, against an average of 6 per cent for SSA.
12. Calculations on figures presented by Pfefferman and Madarassy (1993) show that the share of private investment to GDP fell from 12.7 per cent in 1980 to 8.8 per cent in 1990 (i.e. dropped by 31 per cent) while the share of aggregate investment fell from 25.1 per cent to 17.2 per cent (i.e. dropped by 31.5 per cent).

References

Alexander, M. (1986), 'L'Appui de la Banque Mondiale à la réforme des entreprises publiques en Afrique de l'Ouest', mimeo, World Bank.

Benjamin, N. C. (1992), 'What happens to investment under structural adjustment: results from a simulation model', *World Development,* **20** (9), 1335–44.

Berg, E. and M. M. Shirley (1988), 'Divestiture in developing countries', Discussion Paper No. 11, Washington, DC: World Bank.

Blejer, M. and M. Khan (1984), 'Government policy and private investment in developing countries', *IMF Staff Papers*, **31** (2), 379–403.

Candoy-Sekse, R. and A. R. Palmer (1988), *Techniques of Privatisation of State-Owned*

Enterprises, vol. 3, *Inventory of Country Experience and Reference Materials*, Technical Paper No. 90, Washington, DC: World Bank.
Chavagneux, C. (forthcoming), *Ghana, une révolution de bon sens, ou l'Afro-optimisme en marche*, Paris.
Chavagneux, C. and L. J. Grégoire (1992), 'Ghana: a promising future', *African Markets*, January, translated from *Marchés Tropicaux et Méditerranéens*, No. 2406, December, 1991.
Chhibber, A. and S. Fischer (eds) (1991), *Economic Reform in Sub-Saharan Africa: A World Bank symposium*, Washington, DC: World Bank.
Corbo, V., S. Fischer and S. Webb (eds) (1992), *Adjustment Lending Revisited: Policies to restore growth*, Washington, DC: World Bank.
Elbadawi, I. (1992), 'Have World-Bank-supported adjustment programs improved economic performance in sub-Saharan Africa?', Policy Research Working Paper No. WPS 1001, Washington, DC: World Bank, October.
Elbadawi, I., D. Ghura and G. Uwujaren (1992), 'World Bank adjustment lending and economic performance in sub-Saharan Africa in the 1980s', Policy Research Working Paper No. WPS 1000, Washington, DC: World Bank, October.
Fanelli, J. M., R. Frenkel and G. Rozenwurcel (1992), 'Trade reform and growth resumption in Latin America', in J. M. Fontaine (ed.), *Foreign Trade Reforms and Development Strategy*, London: Routledge.
Fanelli, J. M., R. Frenkel and L. Taylor (1992), 'The World Development Report 1991: a critical assessment', in, *International Monetary and Financial Issues in the 90s*, vol. 1, Geneva: UNCTAD.
Fontaine, J. M. (1992), 'Bias overkill? Removal of anti-export bias and manufacturing investment: Ghana 1983–89', in R. Adhikari, C. Kirkpatrick and J. Weiss (eds), *Industrial and Trade Policy Reforms in Developing Countries*, Manchester: Manchester University Press.
Fontaine, J. M. (1993), 'Reforming public enterprises and the public sector in sub-Saharan Africa', Discussion Paper No. 60, Geneva: UNCTAD.
Galal, A. (1991), 'Public enterprise reform', Discussion Paper No. 1119, Washington, DC: World Bank.
Geourjon, A. M. (1992), 'Import liberalisation and the new industrial policy in Senegal', in J. M. Fontaine (ed.), *Foreign Trade Reform and Development Strategy*, London: Routledge.
Geronimi, V., S. Quiers Valette and E. Saint-Alary (1993), 'Les Investissements directs étrangers en Afrique sub-Saharienne: du risque à l'incertitude', LAREA/CERED Working Paper, Nanterre Paris X University; forthcoming in P. Hugon, G. Pourcet and S. Quiers Valette (eds), *L'Afrique des Incertitudes*, Paris.
Greene, J. and D. Villanueva (1991), 'Private investment in development countries: an empirical analysis', *IMF Staff Papers*, **38** (1), 35–58.
Guillaumont, P., S. Guillaumont and P. Plane (1991), 'Comparison de l'efficacité des politiques d'ajustement structurel en Afrique, zone-franc et hors-zone franc', Notes et Etudes No. 41, Paris: Caisse Centrale de Coopération Économique.
IMF (1991), 'Ghana: adjustment and growth', mimeo, September.
Killick, T. (1989), *A Reaction Too Far: Economic theory and the role of the state in developing countries*, London: ODI.
Kouassy, O. (1992), 'Etat et accumulation du capital en Afrique: les conséquences de la réforme du secteur public', unpublished Ph.D. thesis, Université Paris X, Nanterre.
Landau, D. (1983), 'Government expenditure and economic growth: a cross-section study', *Southern Economic Journal*, **49** (3).
Leenhardt, B. and M. F. L'Hériteau (1989), 'Situation macro économique et monétaire du Ghana', Notes et Etudes No. 39, Paris: Caisse Centrale de Coopération Économique.

Leenhardt, B. and M. F. L'Hériteau (1991), 'Une décennie d'ajustement en Afrique: performances comparées de 28 pays africains, 1980–89', Notes et Etudes No. 41, Paris: Caisse Centrale de Coopération Économique.

Mitra, P. (1986), 'Adjustments to external shocks in selected semi-industrial countries', in G. Szego (ed.), *Studies in Banking and Finance*, Amsterdam: North Holland.

Mosley, P., J. Harrigan and J. Toye (1991), *Aid and Power*, 2 vols, London: Routledge.

Ndulu, B. (1991), 'Growth and adjustment in sub-Saharan Africa', in A. Chhibber and S. Fischer (eds), *Economic Reform in Sub-Saharan Africa: A World Bank symposium*, Washington, DC: World Bank.

Nellis, J. (1986), 'Public enterprises in sub-Saharan Africa', Discussion Paper No. 1, Washington, DC: World Bank.

Okokonko, I. C. (1986), 'Public vs. private investment in a mixed economy: an empirical investigation with Nigerian data', *Public Enterprise*, **7** (1).

Oshikoya, T. W. (1992), 'Macroeconomic adjustment, uncertainty and private investment in Africa', Economic Research Paper No. 16, Abidjan: African Development Bank.

Pfeffermann, G. P. and A. Madarassy (1993), 'Trends in private investment in developing countries, 1992 edition', International Finance Corporation, Discussion Paper No. 14, Washington, DC: World Bank.

Riddell, R. (ed.) (1990), *Manufacturing Africa: Performance and prospects of seven countries in sub-Saharan Africa*, London: Currey and Heinemann.

Serven, L. and A. Solimano (1992), 'Economic adjustment and investment performnce in developing countries: the experience of the 1980s', in V. Corbo, S. Fischer and S. Webb (eds), *Adjustment Lending Revisited: Policies to restore growth*, Washington, DC: World Bank.

Shirley, M. (1989), *The Reform of State-Owned Enterprises*, Policy & Research Series, Washington, DC: World Bank.

Singer, H. W. and S. Roy (1993), *Economic Progress and Prospects in the Third World: Lessons of development experiences since 1945*, London: Edward Elgar.

Swanson, D. and T. Wolde-Semait (1989), 'Africa's public enterprise sector and evidence of reforms', Technical Paper No. 95, Washington, DC: World Bank.

Taylor, L. (1988), *Varieties of Stabilization Experiences: Towards sensible macroeconomics in the Third World*, Oxford: Clarendon Press.

Toye, J. (1991), 'Ghana', in P. Mosley *et al.*, *Aid and Power*, vol. 2, ch. 14.

UNIDO (1986), 'Industry and external debt in Africa: a preliminary analysis', *Industry and Development*, **17**.

Vuylsteke, C. (1988), *Techniques of Privatization of State-Owned Enterprises*, vol. 1, *Methods and Implementation*, Technical Paper No. 88, Washington, DC: World Bank.

World Bank (1988), *Adjustment Lending: An evaluation of ten years of experience*, Policy & Research Series, No. 1, Washington, DC: World Bank.

World Bank (1989), *Sub-Saharan Africa from Crisis to Sustainable Growth*, Washington, DC: World Bank.

World Bank (1990), *Adjustment Lending: Policies for sustainable growth*, Policy & Research Series, No. 14, Washington, DC: World Bank.

World Bank (1991), 'Ghana: progress on adjustment', mimeo, April 16, Washington, DC: World Bank.

World Bank (1992), *Adjustment Lending and Mobilisation of Public and Private Resources for Growth*, Country and Economics Department, Washington, DC: World Bank.

World Bank (1993), *African Development Indicators*, 1992 issue, Washington, DC: World Bank.

9

Privatisation: African perspectives

Ralph A. Young

Africa's experience of privatisation has considerable pedigree, and can be traced back over three decades. Since the early 1980s, however, privatisation has acquired a greatly increased importance on African policy agendas, and has done so within the context of a more broadly focused movement towards public sector restructuring and economic liberalisation that has marked out the potential for a substantial recasting of the state's role in the economic sphere – whether as the directive instrument for a strategy of socialist transformation or as the organising agency sustaining a process of private capital accumulation. In contrast to the reform processes currently underway in Eastern Europe, the divestiture of public enterprises in the African case has not commonly figured among the most central of the 'reform' options associated with this process of policy change. Yet nonetheless privatisation may prove a significant marker as to the extent to which it will lead to substantial alterations in the boundaries between states and markets in Africa.

Privatisation can be variously defined. Conceived in narrow terms, it entails a shift of productive activities or services being undertaken by the public sector to private ownership or control. Such transfers can be brought about in a number of ways, among these the direct sale of assets or the sale of part or all of the equity, leasing, management contracts, or the contracting out of functions (Hemming and Mansoor, 1988b). But privatisation can also be understood in broader terms – as referring to a process by which the state's role within the economy is circumscribed while at the same time the scope for the operation of private capital is deliberately extended. Such a shift in the balance between the state and capital might be effected, for example, through the relaxation of state monopolies where these exist, through reducing the impact of governmental regulations upon the operation of the market economy, or through the requirement that public enterprises perform according to private sector criteria of efficiency and profitability.

In the case of less developed countries, the available literature on privatisation has tended to address this question primarily in terms of the narrower formulation. And despite the widespread interest shown by LDC governments in the privatisation of public enterprises, many analysts, observing privatisation on the ground in Third World settings through the mid-1980s, were able to suggest that in practice the impact of privatisation efforts was likely to remain fairly limited.[1] Thus a 1987 World Bank study could identify only twenty-six LDCs which had by the mid-1980s placed privatisation on their public agendas (Berg and Shirley, 1987). Only seventeen, however, had undertaken actual transfers of equity in public enterprises by that stage, and with the exception of Chile and Bangladesh, the impact of privatisation programmes had been modest both in numbers of enterprises and the value of assets involved. The reasons for this limited impact could be readily traced to the role of factors such as: the technically difficult nature of the divestiture process; the unfavourable economic setting in many LDCs (and not least the underdeveloped nature of capital markets); the fact that the economic objectives of public enterprises are often mixed with non-economic (or equity) purposes which private enterprises would be unlikely to assume; the opposition of powerful vested interests; and the difficulties in any case of realising actual economic or budgetary gains from privatisation commitments.

While this stress on the narrower conception of privatisation is one that will be reflected in the following examination of the sub-Saharan African case, it is also evident that the broader conception may be important for marking out the context in which state enterprise divestiture has been occurring. Certainly this has been so for Africa. Economic adversity and escalating debt problems since the latter 1970s have exposed many governments to pressures from both multilateral financial institutions and Western bilateral aid agencies to initiate a substantial redefinition of the state's role within the economy. Against such a background (though not only for such reasons), divestiture activity in Africa has become widespread over the decade, and especially during the second half. Whereas the World Bank report cited above identified fourteen African states which had placed privatisation on their public agendas by 1985, the number which had either already engaged in such activity or made a formal public commitment to divestiture climbed to forty-three by 1992, or over 90 per cent of the total.[2]

In noting this development, however, three cautionary points should be added. First, the attempt to determine the parameters of privatisation in the African context is hampered by the fact that the dividing line between public and private sectors – far from distinct in developed economies – may be quite blurred among the less developed economies. Management contracts and joint ventures, prominent instrumentalities in the contemporary privatisation armoury, have in fact been long-established methods of incorporating especially foreign private capital into development activities over which African governments have wished to retain ultimate control. Moreover, when viewed in the context of the current 'privatisation' debate, it should also be pointed out that the African setting produces a small but significant assembly of anomalies – as where divestiture leaves government with majority control (Equatorial Guinea) or in *de facto* minority control (certain of the recent Nigerian privatisations), or where part or all of the equity is transferred to other state agencies (Nigeria again) or to external public or quasi-public bodies (Swaziland and Malawi). Lastly, whatever the increase in its geographical spread, it remains clear that the setting for privatisation in many African states is far from propitious, its execution on the ground has been cautious and selective, and its longer-term prospects as a mechanism for state restructuring appear difficult to gauge.

Africa's experience of public enterprise divestiture is of long standing, and, though prior to the 1980s the examples are not numerous, they can nonetheless be drawn from a diverse range of regimes. The best documented case, and the one which in many respects offers the closest parallels with the processes of state reform evident in the 1980s, occurred in Ghana after 1966, when the military rulers who had displaced the Nkrumah regime resolved, with subsequent (and cautious) encouragement from the World Bank, to privatise a considerable number of the enterprises created earlier that decade to assist Ghana's state-guided drive to industrialisation; this divestiture programme was to occasion a public controversy in 1967 the effects of which were still detectable in official sensitivity over the privatisation issue a generation later.[3]

Yet the significance of this and other early divestiture initiatives in the setting of the 1980s was to prove for the most part limited. And when the socialist regime in Tanzania, for example, followed its 1977 decision to reprivatise the butchery trade in Dar es Salaam by divesting several sisal plantations in 1985 because of their unsatisfactory performance under state control, the array of pressures which the Tanzanian state now faced made comparison of the two cases difficult. One component in this altered context was external to Africa. The problems of economic adjustment experienced by Western economies after the first oil shock in 1973–74 had provided impetus to a continuing debate about the appropriate balance to be sought in advanced industrial economies between the state and market forces. The debate in turn was to help shape the agendas of conservative regimes capturing office at the end of the decade in key Western states like the United States and Britain. In the American case, the divesting of public enterprises or services to the private sector was not to have the pivotal emphasis domestically that it was under the Thatcher government in Britain. But the Reagan administration's determination to utilise American foreign aid to bolster the role of the private sector in LDCs was underlined as early as the Cancun Conference in 1981.

The debate over the state's role within the advanced economies was to be paralleled by a separate (though related) debate concerning the role of the Third

World state, and especially those in sub-Saharan Africa. In the 1960s and 1970s, the first generation of independence for most African countries, a considerable expansion occurred in the size and scale of many African states – an expansion due to both political and economic priorities, and reflecting widespread assumptions regarding the centrality of the state's role in engineering economic development in the face of weakly developed indigenous private sectors and an often substantial foreign economic presence. For this expansion, the domestic political climate was generally favourable. By the later 1950s and early 1960s, Western aid agencies had accommodated themselves to this expanded role, including its encouragement of economic planning and the use of public enterprises for a variety of purposes. Though significant public sectors had frequently been handed down as one of the legacies of the colonial era, public sectors now came to embrace an expansive range of productive and commercial activities.[4] They accounted for shares of gross domestic product and of formal sector employment often substantially above the average for other regions. Though total numbers remain uncertain, one recent survey identified 2,959 public enterprises among thirty African states. Roughly half this number had been created between 1967 and 1980; over half were accounted for by an ideologically diverse cluster consisting of Ethiopia, Ivory Coast, Kenya, Malagasy, Senegal, Sudan, Tanzania and Zaire.[5]

By the end of the 1970s experience was serving to undermine earlier expectations regarding the state's developmental potential. African public enterprise sectors in particular were producing a seemingly forbidding catalogue of shortcomings. Some observers cautioned against passing judgement on this performance in isolation from the complex political settings in which public enterprises were forced to operate: 'Even though state-owned enterprises have been dismal economic failures, they have often been considerable political successes. They have provided resources, support, and legitimacy to the complicated factional disputes within . . . African regimes, and have performed important welfare functions' (Callaghy and Wilson, 1988: 1979–80).[6] Yet significant numbers of enterprises were showing a tendency to become habitual loss-makers surviving on government subsidies. Inadequate preparatory studies frequently saddled them with excess capacity. Managerial and technical manpower was commonly insufficient, while problems of overmanning existed at lower grades. The monopoly position they often occupied encouraged inefficiency; multiple and conflicting goals posed obstacles to effective performance; while the pursuit of equity or distributional objectives tended to have disappointing results. Though nominally autonomous, public enterprises were sometimes heavily encumbered by bureaucratic controls. Their proneness to political interference extended from the regulation of prices, the siting of facilities, the award of contracts, and staff management, to even routine operational decisions. Their financial operations proved hard to monitor, among other problems facilitating corruption. The fact that public enterprises were frequently undercapitalised and the difficulties encountered in financing operations from their own resources fostered a propensity to borrow, adding to domestic inflationary pressures, external debt, and balance-of-payments problems.[7]

Recognition of the failings of public enterprise sectors was widespread within Africa itself.[8] Public sector reform, however, acquired priority in the context of the mounting difficulties facing African economies after the mid-1970s. The oil shocks of 1973–74 and 1979–80 sharply boosted energy costs while depressing Western demand for Africa's raw materials. The debt burden accumulating during the 1970s rapidly assumed critical proportions when external interest rates climbed in the early 1980s, and in turn magnified the shortcomings of the import-substitution strategies being followed by many African states (because of their heavy import dependence on spare parts and raw materials). Declining agricultural exports and rising food imports underlined the disincentive role of official policies that maintained overvalued exchange rates or squeezed surplus capital from agriculture to support other economic sectors. Given the centrality of the African state's role, a crisis of largely economic dimensions necessarily became a crisis of the state itself – a circumstance which received recognition by several regimes: for example, in the Ivory Coast after 1977, Senegal after 1978, Kenya and Togo from 1979, Nigeria by 1983 and South Africa by 1985. Although the reform options for the public sector which took shape in these cases differed in their exact origins and outcomes, and in the Senegalese and Nigerian cases were quickly to become subsumed within aid packages being negotiated externally with multilateral financial institutions, they all included the possibility (and sometimes the priority) of public enterprise divestiture.[9]

The state's role as development manager was also undergoing reassessment externally. That the views of the World Bank, long a principal supplier of development capital and technical expertise to African states and hence an underwriter of public sector expansion, were shifting from established development paradigms was underscored by the publication in 1981 of the Berg Report and the 1983 edition of its annual *World Development Report* (IBRD, 1983). These documents argued that inappropriate policies and overextended state structures had distorted development performance in many LDCs (particularly in Africa); ways of scaling back the state's role had to be identified to promote macroeconomic efficiency – not least to create space for the market forces essential to sustain this efficiency. Though such ideas had found periodic expression in Bank reports despite its extensive involvement in state-led development efforts after the later 1950s, a range of new factors now shaped the Bank's posture, including pressures from ideologically conservative Western governments, the accelerating debt crisis, and the cumulative effects of its own experience in the development field. With the World Bank and the International Monetary Fund both seeking innovative mechanisms for channelling finance to LDC debtor countries, the former developed new 'structural' and 'sectoral' adjustment facilities between 1979 and 1983 in order to assist recipient economies to undergo restructuring to stimulate those economic sectors with growth potential while reducing sources of macroeconomic inefficiency elsewhere; the Bank also extended its existing conditionality provisions for project loans to make capital available only if recipient governments agreed to undertake specified policy reforms, and, along with the IMF, sought to persuade bilateral aid agencies to make their own funds contingent on compliance with these reform programmes. The Bank's policy-based (as opposed to project-based) lending increased from 6 per cent to around 20 per cent of funding disbursed between 1979 and 1986; by 1988, this proportion within the Bank's African lending stood at 40 per cent (Mosley, 1988; Jaycox, 1989).

Given the troubled economic circumstances of many African states and their intensified aid dependence, the role of external agencies in promoting privatisation has been considerable. World Bank reports and staff papers, despite the disillusionment they register concerning the role of LDC public enterprises, insist that Bank recommendations to particular countries have treated privatisation pragmatically as a component of broader parastatal reform programmes to stimulate efficiency or curb public deficits, and that divestiture is neither a panacea nor an easy alternative.[10] Recent analyses of Bank SALs between 1980 and 1986 conclude that while public enterprise reform commonly figured among loan conditionalities, divestiture itself was relatively uncommon (Mosley, 1988). Yet even then African states were being more frequently targeted for divestitures than those elsewhere. This pattern has since intensified, especially if consideration is taken not just of loan conditionality measures but of the promotional effects of funds and technical assistance made available to encourage adoption of privatisation programmes. Thus between 1980 and 1989, the World Bank made 143 loans to LDCs that included public sector reform measures, and of these some seventy-four (or 51.7 per cent) contained a privatisation component; of the seventy-nine loans within this total made to African states, forty-five (or 57 per cent) involved a privatisation component (Adam, Cavendish and Mistry, 1992: 25). By the latter 1980s, a majority of the roughly thirty LDC governments which had received Bank assistance over privatisation programmes were African; of eighteen francophone African recipients of Bank structural adjustment assistance, more than two-thirds had public enterprise programmes in place or in preparation, all containing a privatisation component. The IMF, while sharing the Bank's views regarding the shortcomings of LDC public sectors, has remained primarily concerned with their impact on governmental budgetary deficits, external indebtedness, and balance of payments problems; because the actual budgetary benefits of divestiture might prove elusive, it has tended to favour liquidations over privatisations and, until recently, over public enterprise reform (Babai, 1988).

Though having fewer resources to deploy on the ground, the United States Agency for International Development proved noticeably more evangelical over the privatisation issue than either the Bank or the IMF. In early 1985, an official telegram from Secretary of State George Schultz instructed all USAID missions abroad to give priority to privatisation in discussions with host governments.

In February 1986, USAID sponsored a major international conference on privatisation, with many of the several hundred in attendance coming from LDCs. USAID's African missions received a further instruction in June 1986 requiring each by the end of fiscal year 1987 to be involved 'in an average of at least two privatisation activities'.[11] A report published by the Adam Smith Institute in December 1988 was able to note that:

> USAID ... [had] concluded that the primary centre for privatisation expertise [was] the United Kingdom, and consequently it [was] seeking to have a closer collaboration with the UK aid programme in support of the general privatisation objectives of developing countries ... obviously USAID would like to see a greater commitment from the official British aid programme itself. (Young, 1988: 10)

In fact before this report appeared, the British Overseas Development Administration had already commenced a joint programme with the United States to provide assistance for the privatisation of public enterprises in LDCs; British missions in the Third World had been directed towards the end of 1988 to 'canvass the market' for privatisation opportunities (*Guardian*, 3 January 1989).[12]

Certainly by the later 1980s Africa was proving a seemingly fertile field for divestiture activities. Of the 1,343 privatisations worldwide of which the World Bank had record by 1988 – planned, underway or completed – African states accounted for around 35 per cent.[13] On the other hand, within Africa divestiture activity has been unevenly spread. By early 1988 four states – Guinea, the Ivory Coast, Niger and Uganda – accounted for well over half the divestitures either completed or underway; three-quarters of those still at the planning stage were in Ghana, Nigeria, Senegal and Togo. As of the end of the decade, West African states had registered the largest incidence of privatisation programmes, and so had the francophone states as a group. Though the impact of the divestiture question has transcended ideological boundaries between capitalist and socialist states, yet differences remain discernible in the degree of willingness evident among the latter to accept the privatisation option. Existing privatisation programmes differ greatly in focus and scale. Some have been limited in scope or centred on particular public enterprises (as in Malawi, Rwanda, Somalia and Swaziland). By contrast in Nigeria, the military regime of General Ibrahim Babangida, having ordered the liquidation of all agricultural commodity marketing boards in April 1986, launched an ambitious scheme to restructure Nigeria's public enterprise sector in January 1988 involving the divesting of 110 federal and state enterprises and the full or partial commercialisation of more than three dozen others; by the spring of 1993, some fifty-five state firms had been disposed of. In the South African case, the significance of the privatisation programme that took shape after 1985 derived particularly from the size and strategic importance of the enterprises involved; with the oil-from-coal producer SASOL I privatised earlier in the decade, the corporations now targeted for privatisation included those responsible for iron and steel production, electricity supply, posts and telecommunications, and South Africa's transport infrastructure. For over a third of the sub-Saharan African states, divestiture commitments appear potentially considerable, if fully pursued and especially if linked to macroeconomic shifts towards greater liberalisation.[14]

Establishing an effective administrative machinery to manage divestiture programmes has proved difficult. Rather than being delegated to sector ministries, privatisation activities have frequently been made the responsibility of separate administrative units – sometimes with ministerial status but often headed by senior civil servants (and occasionally, as in Kenya or South Africa, by figures recruited from the private sector);[15] in settings like the Ivory Coast and Malagasy, however, presidential patronage interests have clearly outweighed more technocratic concerns.[16] Divestiture programmes often require comprehensive and lengthy reviews of existing public sectors to establish regime priorities. In the Ivory Coast instance, however, although a master plan was formulated in the latter 1970s, in practice privatisation activity was subsequently guided by private approaches to government by local or foreign entrepreneurs; the government itself never formally advertised its intentions (Callaghy and Wilson, 1988). In Togo the government's attempt to 'jump start' its privatisation programme through initial deals negotiated within a loosely defined policy framework produced sufficiently generous terms for foreign and local investors as to provoke World Bank concern (Djondo, 1988).

The sectoral impact of privatisation has been varied. World Bank figures for a sample of twenty-six African states as of early 1988 show that for 465 divestitures (planned, underway or completed) those in general manufacturing dominated the field (about 30 per cent of the total); less expected was the secondary significance of commercial and service enterprises (around 10 per cent) (Candoy-Sekse and Palmer, 1988). The impact that privatisation programmes have been making on the institutional fabric linking the African state with the rural sector – in direct production, marketing and agro-industrial roles – is worth underlining; this broadly defined category constituted a quarter of total divestiture activity. The remaining seven sectors divided into three bands. Enterprises engaged in tourism, banking or financial services, or food or refreshment supply all fell in the 7–9 per cent range; those involved in transport or communications or in the refining or distribution of oil and gas supplies represented 3–5 per cent of the total, while utilities and mining enterprises each constituted less than 2 per cent. Data on the value of assets disposed of through privatisation has proved difficult to assemble. There is some evidence to suggest generally modest cash returns to African states from individual divestitures occurring thus far; in Guinea, for example, the amount received from sales of fourteen public enterprises to the private sector averaged around $770,000 – a figure unlikely to reflect closely the original value of the assets involved (Candoy-Sekse and Palmer, 1988). Gaps in the available data also make difficult any precise calculation of the role of foreign capital in African privatisations; clearly it has been substantial, though more so in francophone than in anglophone states.

In terms of the techniques utilised in completed divestitures among the same group of states, some four-fifths of the 234 cases of which the World Bank had record were accounted for by private sales, management contracts, and the sale of assets; for purposes of comparison, figures on Asia and Latin America are included in Table 9.1.

On the other hand, data from other sources would suggest considerably more numerous formal and informal liquidations than recorded in the World Bank's own records.[17] These figures also fail to provide full coverage for the relaxation of state monopolies and the contracting out of services; of these two, the former has been the more significant, especially in the sphere of agricultural marketing (as in Cameroon, for example, and Malagasy, Mali, Nigeria and Sierra Leone) and the distribution or retailing of food and domestic goods (as in Benin, Guinea-Bissau, Mali and Mauritania). With the commencement of the Nigerian divestiture programme in January 1989, the figure for public flotations emerging from this data – 2.5 per cent – has been rendered obsolete, though it underscores the manner in which the menu of available divestiture options has been shaped not just by the varying technical difficulty of the techniques themselves but by the underdeveloped nature of African capital markets. By the middle 1980s, established stock exchanges existed in Abidjan (Ivory Coast), Lagos (Nigeria), Nairobi (Kenya), Harare (Zimbabwe) and Johannesburg (South Africa). Since the later 1980s, stock markets have either opened or are planned in St Louis (Mauritius), Gabarone (Botswana) and Accra (Ghana), Windhoek (Namibia), Kampala (Uganda) and Lusaka (Zambia). The Lagos exchange played a vital part in the initial phase of Nigeria's privatisation programme, while the Johannesburg exchange has been expected to be the primary vehicle for divesting South Africa's public corporations (if this latter programme is sustained). Yet the other established exchanges have had marginal roles in this sphere – in Kenya and Zimbabwe because of the resistance to privatisation their governments have maintained till recently, and in the Ivory Coast because of the close personal control President Felix Houphouet-Boigny has exercised over the divestiture programme.

Table 9.1 Divestiture in Africa, Asia, and Latin America and the Caribbean, by technique (%)

	Africa	Asia	Latin America and the Caribbean
Private sales	42.0	33.3	65.9
Sale of assets	17.5	2.1	7.6
Management contracts	20.5	16.1	1.4
Leasing	9.4	8.6	7.1
Number of cases	(234)	(93)	(211)

Note: The figures in the table do not add up to 100 per cent because of the omission from the analysis here of certain privatisation techniques that are more secondary in the African case.

Source: Vuylsteke (1988: 167–72) and Ramamurti (1991:9).

While the privatisation phenomenon in Africa has already had significant impact, this impact has nonetheless remained uneven, the obstacles formidable, the levels of domestic support limited, and the future prospects uncertain. In contrast to the experience of developed countries, where the wave of privatisation activities in the 1980s occurred under relatively propitious economic circumstances, privatisation has entered African political agendas under widely generalised recessionary conditions that have inevitably had a dampening effect on domestic and external confidence. The structural constraints present in many African economies tending to inhibit an expanded private sector role also point to potential difficulties in encouraging the element of market competition essential for 'capturing' macroeconomic efficiency gains where privatisation occurs. Moreover divestiture programmes have typically been introduced into public enterprise sectors in a financially unhealthy condition, with individual enterprises losing money, heavily indebted, operating with inadequate records or accounts, or substantially overmanned. Where enterprises are profitable, there is understandable reluctance to privatise. Given the problems of the parastatal sector and unfavourable prospects within the larger economy, governments may find themselves facing the pressures of a buyer's market; the head of a substantial delegation of French businessmen officially invited to visit Malagasy in 1986 to explore investment possibilities told the press on their arrival: 'You must be asking yourselves why we don't leave straightaway? The first reply is that there is no plane this evening ... secondly perhaps the moment has come where a change that we could encourage could take place in this country.'[18] Where African governments are forced to offer tax, monopoly status or asset valuation concessions to attract private sector interest in state enterprises (as, for example, in Togo), the likelihood not just of long-term macroeconomic benefits to the economy but of short-term financial gains to the treasury may be considerably diminished.

Divestiture is a technically demanding exercise even in advanced economies. In the African case, existing legal frameworks or investment codes may prove unfavourable. Moreover, with the necessary skilled personnel unavailable locally, divestiture programmes have been commonly dependent on technical assistance or financial aid provided by external agencies (notably the World Bank or USAID, in turn sometimes utilising staff provided by Western merchant banks or consultancy firms). The timetables to which governments find themselves committed may be unrealistic; in the Ghana case a World Bank requirement that eighteen of the thirty-two public enterprises originally listed for privatisation (in June 1988) be divested by the end of 1989 meant that the government had to target twelve for liquidation because investor interest had failed to materialise.

However formidable the constraints on privatisation arising from the economic setting, from the difficulties of the public enterprise sector or from a state's administrative capacity, it is political concerns which frequently have overriding significance; for privatisation in practice involves a reorganisation of resources within society and hence is inherently political in the manner in which it impinges upon the existing structure of social and political interests. As a privatisation consultant working in Malawi noted: 'It was nowhere near as easy as we thought. . . . We've realised privatisation is more a political exercise than a financial one. It's basically about re-allocating power – and that's tricky' (*The Financial Times*, 30 August 1989). Even within governments showing strong pro-market inclinations, there is likely to be opposition to privatisation from vested interests with a stake in a large state sector – ministries unwilling to surrender their parastatal empires, enterprise managers with emoluments and prerogatives to protect, or business interests dependent on public sector contracts (Cook and Minogue, 1990). But public enterprises also offer strategic bases for the extraction of 'bureaucratic rents,' and often function within networks of political patronage linked to a regime's very core.

Hardly less potent are the redistributive issues which arise with regard to society at large. Though the political leverage of African trade union movements is generally not high, regimes have frequently been required to remain attentive to union objections over job losses associated with privatisation, given the volatility of urban constituencies at a time of increasing unemployment and rising pressures on lower-class living standards; as a senior figure within the former Traore regime in Mali remarked when complaining of the 'draconian' programme of state restructuring imposed by the multilateral financial institutions, 'there is an enormous social component in these measures which makes us cautious (*African Research Bulletin*, 25 April 1988). Other criticisms which unions have articulated – that privatisation might concentrate domestic economic power or transfer important sectors to foreign control – have also found echo along middle-class opinion networks. Measures that might open host economies to foreign 'recolonisation' may be a sensitive issue for indigenous entrepreneurs (especially when themselves facing severe domestic credit restraints imposed under an IMF stabilisation programme) as well as among university-trained professionals and the radical intelligentsia.

In Nigeria the decision by General Babangida's government to place privatisation on its priority agenda in 1986 provoked concerns of this nature while also rekindling deep-seated regional and class divisions over the likely distribution of benefits between the well-entrenched southern entrepreneurial elite and business interests in the less developed northern states; the privatisation strategy the government resolved upon – an emphasis on stock market flotations with limits on individual share purchases and a vigorous campaign to spread share-buying throughout the federation – appeared initially at least to have largely defused these issues.[19] The Kenya government, having launched preparations for a divestiture programme in 1983, had let momentum ebb by 1985, as it became clear that privatisation was likely to concentrate gains on the economically powerful but politically sensitive Kikuyu and Asian communities (Callaghy and Wilson, 1988). In South Africa the ISCOR flotation aroused black opinion over the privatisation issue, which was seen as an attempt by the white political establishment to protect bastions of white job privilege from the reach of a future black-dominated government; Nelson Mandela and other senior African National Congress leaders have strongly opposed privatisation on these grounds (*Guardian*, 10 May 1990).

As a mechanism for state 'reform,' privatisation has entered African policy discourse in a manner unimaginable in the early 1980s. The recency of Africa's privatisation experience, however, makes its significance not easy to assess. Moreover, though some patterning in the occurrence of divestiture programmes is discernible among regions, between francophone and anglophone states, and between clusters of regimes adhering either to capitalist or socialist development models, the impact of privatisation activity has been variable across all these categories, complicating the identification of explanatory factors. What is clear is that the privatisation phenomenon did not have its origins in any basic shifts over the past decade in the nature of African regimes or the social forces on which they are based, but rather derived its initial impetus from the increasingly adverse economic circumstances which beset most African states after the mid-1970s, from a significant policy reorientation regarding the economic role of the state occurring in the case of influential Western powers, and from shifts in the priorities guiding substantial Western aid and multilateral financial institutions; additionally Africa's socialist states faced narrowing space for manoeuvre due to the declining involvement by Russia and other external socialist states in continental affairs after the mid-1980s, and also (in cases like Ethiopia, Angola and Mozambique) due to the impact of civil conflict and external destabilisation. Developments over the decade have brought a marked shift in the political centre of gravity. Whatever the limitations on the actual implementation of divestiture programmes, the formal commitment to these indicates a changing balance of power between governments and private sectors. Though Africa offers few ideologically infused cases comparable with the Chilean divestiture programme launched in 1973, public comments by African leaders suggest that altered attitudes towards the state's role are widespread. The earlier impetus for public sector expansion has been eroded; few significant political movements remain committed to extending the state's economic power. Under the impact of unfavourable circumstances, socialist programmes have everywhere undergone considerable retrenchment; some have been effectively abandoned. At the same time there has been a measurable opening of space for capitalist development – perhaps more so, as Sklar (1988) suggests, than at any time since the pre-independence period.

On the other hand, it is evident that the main privatisation programmes in Africa have been thus far concentrated in perhaps a third of the states, and that current divestiture efforts are likely to leave substantial public sectors in place nearly everywhere; those divestitures of which the World Bank had record in early 1988 might well account for little more than 10 per cent of Africa's public enterprises. Moreover the 'external' pressures to which African states have been subjected have been only one strand in a complex setting within which African states themselves have remained central actors; though the shortcomings of their public enterprise sectors have been widely recognised, domestic political dynamics and the economic circumstances of individual countries have ensured that factors like 'political will' and 'political capacity' have remained key variables in the divestiture calculus, as the differing effectiveness in practice of World Bank conditionality measures would testify. A firm commitment to privatisation has sometimes crystallised following a change in a regime's top leadership (Nigeria after 1985, for example) or a shift in its composition (Ivory Coast); the fact that in a significant number of cases a policy shift of this nature has emerged against a backdrop of regime continuity would caution against assumptions that many fundamental conversions have occurred on the road to a 'free market' Damascus. Nor, as some analysts have recognised, will such a 'reform' process be necessarily irreversible should there be marked improvement in Africa's economic prospects – or a severe economic downturn. Again, should the economic requirements of Eastern Europe seriously reduce the aid or foreign investment available to sustain the process of economic adaptation in Africa, or should structural adjustment efforts fail to produce beneficial results (or simply prove too costly in terms of their impact on regime support), the political backwash could lead to renewed pressures for state intervention in the economic sphere.

The recent emergence of democratic reform movements in Africa – triggered by events in Eastern Europe and by sympathetic signals from several Western powers – is unlikely to lead to enhanced political resolve to pursue economic reforms designed to curtail the state's capacity to control and distribute benefits within society; indeed a 'democratic opening' in Africa, however long overdue, faces an uncertain future, presupposing as it does a capacity to respond to public demands for material improvement which, after years of economic adversity, most African regimes lack the resources to respond to.

Notes

1. See, for example, Cook and Kirkpatrick (1988: 31–3); Hemming and Mansoor (1988b: 32–3); Killick and Commander (1988: 1473–5); Wilson III (1988: 24).
2. In only two cases – Burkina Faso and Djibouti – could no evidence of privatisation since 1980 be located; in two others – Lesotho and Namibia (before independence) – the evidence was suggestive but not sufficiently detailed to allow inclusion.
3. The proposed disposal of a pharmaceutical factory to an American firm, Abbott Laboratories, via a joint venture arrangement, provoked a heated public debate over the agreement's terms and the involvement of a foreign company; Abbott eventually withdrew from the deal. Similar concerns over another proposed lease caused sharp disagreements behind the scenes among the regime's domestic civilian advisers; its foreign consultants were themselves divided over the advisability of any substantial reliance on external capital to sustain the divestiture programme. Eventually, of fifty-two state industries, four were sold outright to Ghanaian entrepreneurs and five were placed under joint venture arrangements with foreign

firms (as were two unfinished industrial projects); two leading Accra hotels were leased. But following the Abbott controversy, the momentum behind the privatisation programme appeared to ebb. See Killick (1978: 313–22); Hutchful (ed.) (1987: 143–216); Esseks (1971: 24–5); First (1970: 393–7).

4. See Kagwe (1987), Wilson III (1984); Nellis (1986).
5. Nellis (1986). The figure given in this source marginally overstates the total for the countries surveyed, since the 'base point' year selected in several cases would ignore subsequent divestitures. On the other hand, the overall African total for public enterprises must be considerably higher; among countries for which adequate data was not available were several known to have extensive public sectors.
6. See also Sandbrook (1988). It is worth underlining that the criticisms of African public enterprise were by this stage being echoed by analysts writing on public enterprises in other Third World regions.
7. See Nellis (1986); Shirley (1983); Haile-Mariam and Mengistu (1988); Nellis and Kikeri (1989).
8. And certainly so at official level: Wilson (1986: 93).
9. On the Ivory Coast and Kenya, see Callaghy and Wilson (1988); on Kenya, Adams *et al.* (1992); for Nigeria, Falola and Ihonubere (1985); Senegal, Lewis (1987); South Africa, Young (1989).
10. See, for example, Shirley (1988); Alexander (1989); Nellis and Kikeri (1989).
11. The key papers presented to the 1986 USAID conference were published in Hanke (ed.) (1987).
12. How much impact such official encouragement from the centre may have had on the ground is uncertain. As Young (1988: 14) noted of the USAID initiative, 'some (US) missions are more enthusiastic about privatisation than others. This enthusiasm is of course partially governed by the receptivity of the host government to the issue.'
13. Calculated from Vuylsteke (1988: 177–80).
14. Besides the Nigerian and South African cases, the list would include Benin, Cameroon, Cape Verde, Ethiopia, Gambia, Ghana, Guinea, Guinea-Bissau, Ivory Coast, Mali, Niger, Senegal, Togo, Uganda and Zambia.
15. Noting the vested interests potentially threatened by parastatal reform or privatisation, Mosley (1988: 135) observes: 'It has been the (World Bank's) hope that there would exist technocrats within the government with whom it deals who would be persuaded by the offer of concessional finance to confront those ... interests.'
16. The Ivory Coast is analysed in this regard in Callaghy and Wilson (1988); on Malagasy, see Baum (1989).
17. If informal closures of enterprises are added to the instances of formal liquidation, the total would certainly exceed that for private sales.
18. *African Research Bulletin*, **23** (10), 8438–9. On the problem of investor confidence in Ghana, see Tangri (1991) and Tanoh (1993).
19. Yet already by early 1990 there was concern that continued heavy reliance on the Lagos Stock Exchange might prove unfeasible because of the risk of 'crowding out' private share sales. (*The Financial Times*, 19 March 1990).

References

Adam, C., W. Cavendish and P. S. Mistry (1992), *Adjusting Privatization: Case studies from developing countries*, London: Currey.

Alexander, M. (1989), 'Privatisation in Africa', in V. V. Ramanadham (ed.), *Privatisation in Developing Countries*, London: Routledge.

Babai, D. (1988), 'The World Bank and the IMF: rolling back the state or backing its

role', in R. Vernon (ed.) *The Promise of Privatization: A challenge for US policy*, New York: Council on Foreign Relations.
Baum, D. (1989), 'The wayward siblings', *Africa Report*, 34, Jan.–Feb.
Berg, E. and M. M. Shirley (1987), 'Divestiture in developing countries', Discussion Paper No. 11, Washington, DC: World Bank.
Callaghy, T. M. and E. J. Wilson III (1988), 'Africa: policy, reality or ritual?', in R. Vernon (ed.), *The Promise of Privatization: A challenge for US policy*, New York: Council on Foreign Relations.
Candoy-Sekse, R. and A. R. Palmer (1988), *Techniques of Privatization of State-Owned Enterprises*, vol. 3, *Inventory of Country Experience and Reference Materials*, Technical Paper No. 90, Washington, DC: World Bank.
Cook, P. and C. Kirkpatrick (1988), 'Privatisation in less developed countries: an overview', in P. Cook and C. Kirkpatrick (eds), *Privatisation in Less Developed Countries*, Hemel Hempstead: Harvester Wheatsheaf.
Cook, P. and M. Minogue (1990), 'Waiting for privatization in developing countries: towards the integration of economic and non-economic explanations', *Public Administration and Development*, **10** (4), 389–403.
Djondo, K. (1988), 'Anatomy of a privatisation scheme: the Togo example', *African Business*, **114**, February.
Esseks, J. D. (1971), 'Government and indigenous private enterprise in Ghana', *Journal of Modern African Studies*, **9**, March, 24–5.
Falola, T. and J. Ihonubere (1985), *The Rise and Fall of Nigeria's Second Republic*, London: Zed Press.
First, R. (1970), *The Barrel of a Gun: Political power in Africa and the coup d'état*, Harmondsworth: Penguin.
Haile-Mariam, Y. and B. Mengistu (1988), 'Public enterprises and the privatisation thesis in the Third World', *Third World Quarterly*, **10**, October.
Hanke, S. (ed.) (1987), *Privatization and Development*, San Francisco: Institute for Contemporary Studies.
Hemming, R. and A. M. Mansoor (1988a), 'Is privatization the answer?', *Finance and Development*, **25**, September, 31–3.
Hemming, R. and A. M. Mansoor (1988b), 'Privatization and public enterprises', Occasional Paper No. 56, Washington, DC: IMF.
Hutchful, E. (ed.) (1987), *The IMF and Ghana: The confidential record*, London: Zed Press.
IBRD (1983), *World Development Report 1983*, Washington, DC: World Bank.
Jaycox, E. V. K. (1989), 'Structural adjustment in sub-Saharan Africa: the World Bank's perspective', *Issue*, **18** (1).
Kagwe, S. (1987), 'Some organisational factors affecting the performance of public enterprises in Africa', in African Association for Public Administration and Management, *Public Enterprises Performance and the Privatization Debate: A review of options for Africa*, New Delhi: Vikas.
Killick, T. (1978), *Development Economics in Action: A study of economic policies in Ghana*, New York: St Martin's Press.
Killick, T. and S. Commander (1988), 'State divestiture as a policy instrument in developing countries', *World Development*, **16** (12), 1645–79.
Lewis, J. P. (1987), 'Aid, structural adjustment, and Senegalese agriculture', in M. Gersovitz and J. Waterbury (eds), *The Political Economy of Risk and Choice in Senegal*, London: Frank Cass.
Mosley, P. (1988), 'Privatisation, policy-based lending and World Bank behaviour', in P. Cook and C. Kirkpatrick (eds), *Privatisation in Less Developed Countries*, Hemel Hempstead: Harvester Wheatsheaf.
Nellis, J. R. (1986), 'Public enterprises in sub-Saharan Africa', Discussion Paper No.

1, Washington, DC: World Bank.
Nellis, J. and S. Kikeri (1989), 'Public enterprise reform: privatization and the World Bank', *World Development*, **17**, May.
Ramamurti, R. (1991), 'The search for remedies', in R. Ramamurti and R. Vernon (eds), *Privatisation and Control of State-owned Enterprises*, Washington, DC: World Bank.
Sandbrook, R. (1988), 'Patrimonialism and the failing of parastatals: Africa in comparative perspective', in P. Cook and C. Kirkpatrick (eds), *Privatisation in Less Developed Countries*, Hemel Hempstead: Harvester Wheatsheaf.
Shirley, M. (1983), *Managing State-Owned Enterprises*, Washington, DC: IBRD.
Shirley, M. (1988), The experience with privatization', *Finance and Development*, **25**, 34–5.
Sklar, R. L. (1988), 'Beyond capitalism and socialism in Africa', *Journal of Modern African Studies*, **26**, March.
Tangri, R. (1991), 'The politics of state divestiture in Ghana', *African Affairs*, **90**, October.
Tanoh, F. N. (1993), 'Structural adjustment in Africa: Ghana's experience in the 1980s', unpublished PhD thesis, University of Manchester.
Vuylsteke, C. (1988), *Techniques of Privatization of State-Owned Enterprises*, vol. 1, *Methods and Implementation*, Technical Paper No. 88, Washington, DC: World Bank.
Wilson III, E. J. (1984), 'Contested terrrain: a comparative and theoretical reassessment of state-owned enterprise in Africa', *Journal of Commonwealth and Comparative Politics*, **22**, March.
Wilson III, E. J. (1986), 'The public–private debate', *Africa Report*, **31**, July–Aug.
Wilson III, E. J. (1988), 'Privatization in Africa: domestic origins, current status and future scenarios', *Issue*, **16** (2).
Young, P. (1988), *The Enterprise Imperative: Promoting growth in developing countries*, London: Adam Smith Institute.
Young, T. (1989), 'Restructuring the state in South Africa: new strategies of incorporation and control', *Political Studies*, **37**, March.

10

Nationalisation and denationalisation of estate agriculture in Tanzania, 1967–90

David Potts

10.1 Introduction

This chapter investigates the comparative production performance of public sector and private sector estates with particular reference to the tea and sisal industries in Tanzania both during the period of nationalisation and during the more recent period when denationalisation of some estates has taken place. Reasons for differences in performance are identified and related to the wider issues relating to ownership and autonomy.[1]

A priori arguments as to how denationalisation might lead to improvement are outlined and related to the production record of estates where denationalisation has taken place. Possible differences in perspective on what constitutes an improvement are considered.

Different approaches to denationalisation are discussed and related to the original purposes of nationalisation and the stated objectives of the Tanzanian government. It is argued that, while large-scale denationalisation may be necessary for the resolution of the financial constraints on rehabilitation, in the longer term it is likely to conflict with government objectives unless there is a change in the nature of either private sector investment or of the government objectives themselves.

10.2 The estate sector in Tanzania before nationalisation

The policies affecting the estate sector since independence in Tanzania were strongly influenced by the situation that the new government inherited. Tanganyika was made a League of Nations (and subsequently UN) mandated territory after the First World War defeat of Germany, the previous colonial power. This status acted as a deterrent to large-scale European settlement and, by comparison with neighbouring Kenya, relatively little investment was undertaken to develop the country.

The agricultural sector was divided between large-scale farms, owned almost entirely by non-Africans, and small-scale agriculture which was the occupation of the vast majority of the indigenous population. The division of the sector by scale and ownership was reflected in the types of crop grown. Sisal and tea were almost entirely estate crops while the production of most other crops was dominated by smallholders. Only in the case of coffee, cattle and cereals was there a significant mixture of different scales.

In 1958 75 per cent of the land under crops in the estate economy was under sisal and another 5 per cent under tea and coffee. The relative importance of tea and coffee is understated because of the high value per hectare of the crops, but the statistics do give an indication of the overwhelming importance of sisal in the estate economy. 61 per cent of the estate area was owned by British (including South Africans), 14 per cent by Greeks and 14 per cent by Asians. Less than 1 per cent was owned by people of African origin (Ruthenberg, 1964: 14–15).

In many cases, the estates were unable to recruit labour locally because the local people had alternative occupations as small farmers which yielded either higher incomes or a more acceptable standard of life than that which could be obtained by working on the estates, where wages were low and conditions were harsh. As a result, labour was recruited from the less developed regions of the country, some of which were deliberately treated as 'a backward labour reserve for the plantation sector' (Raikes, 1986: 107). Labourers were also recruited from other countries where land was more scarce or income-earning opportunities were less readily available.

The nature of the ownership of the estates and the origin and conditions of the labour force had significant implications for the circumstances and rationale for nationalisation and the choice of private sector estates excluded from the nationalisation of the sisal industry. The extent to which Tanzanians benefited from the existence of the estates was open to question and this was a serious issue where estates occupied land in areas with increasing population pressure on land availability.

The initial economic strategy of the Tanzanian government on achieving independence was similar to that of most other newly independent African states. Foreign private investment was welcomed and perceived as the main source of investment in the productive sectors. The first Five Year Plan (1964–9) reflected this outlook, although the National Development Corporation (NDC) was established in 1965 to manage government investments in joint ventures. These included a 50 per cent share in Ralli Estates Ltd, an Isaac Wolfson subsidiary. By 1965 doubts were already being raised about the effectiveness of a strategy based on foreign private investment. In his speech dissolving the Independence Parliament, President Nyerere stated:

> The amount of private investment which has taken place over the past year is, quite frankly, a disappointment to us. We have special tax concessions to encourage new investment; we have investment guarantees for bringing capital into the country; and we have many other arrangements designed to encourage private enterprise of a character which will serve our nation. Yet the level of private investment does not appear to be as great as that provided for in the Plan. (Nyerere, 1968: 41)

In the estate sector, lack of investment could be explained by the departure of some of the settlers and by a serious fall in the price of sisal following the price boom of 1963. Tanzania was also too poor and too underdeveloped to be attractive to foreign investors. Disappointment in the response of the private sector and political disagreements with some of the principal aid donor countries undoubtedly influenced the dramatic policy changes announced in the Arusha Declaration in 1967.

10.3 The Arusha Declaration and nationalisation of estates

In 1967 the National Executive of TANU, the ruling party in mainland Tanzania, published the Arusha Declaration committing Tanzania to a policy of 'Socialism and Self Reliance'. Under this policy the 'major means of production and exchange' were to be 'under the control of the peasants and workers'. The major means of production and exchange included 'large plantations, and especially those which provide raw materials essential to important industries' (Nyerere, 1968: 233–4). Within weeks the government had announced that it would take a controlling share in the sisal industry.

The nationalisation move was prompted by economic nationalism reflecting the powerlessness of a government dependent on a combination of foreign aid and foreign investment for its development. The indigenous capitalist class was too small to be the primary source of growth:

> I do not think there is any free state in Africa where there is sufficient local capital, or a sufficient number of local entrepreneurs, for locally based capital to dominate the economy. Private investment in Africa means overwhelming foreign private investment. A capitalistic economy means a foreign dominated economy. (Nyerere, 1968: 264)

In 1967 the Tanzanian government nationalised fifty-three sisal estates and took a 60 per cent share in thirty-three others. These estates formed the basis of the Tanzania Sisal Corporation (TSC), which also held the government shares in Ralli Estates. More estates were nationalised in 1973 under the newly formed Tanzania Sisal Authority (TSA), but some of the less viable original estates had been denationalised in 1969. In 1973 the Tanzanian government controlled just under 50 per cent of total sisal production through TSA and TSC (see Table 10.1). TSA also took over the marketing activities of the

Table 10.1 Tanzanian sisal planting and production 1971–90 ('000 tons, all grades)

Year	1971	1972	1973	1974	1975	1976	1977	1978	1979	1980	1981	1982	1983	1984	1985	1986	1987	1988	1989	1990
Planting (hectares)	10,548	8,693	10,956	14,048	15,126	13,662	9,818	6,023	3,627	6,443	2,257	2,399	3,612	2,902	3,172	4,968	6,678	7,066	4,942	3,325
TSA estates	7,246	5,950	6,202	7,849	7,534	8,340	5,306	4,066	2,224	4,730	1,785	1,492	2,035	1,475	1,695	3,276	3,657	3,801	2,116	1,336
Amboni estates	1,410	1,448	2,094	2,232	2,346	1,887	1,651	1,438	1,060	922	388	559	1,347	1,127	1,198	1,358	1,520	1,500	1,350	958
Ralli estates	877	345	1,222	1,252	1,982	1,394	1,470	219		275		164				204	922	1,065	533	877
Other producers	1,016	950	1,438	2,715	3,264	2,041	1,391	300	343	516	84	182	230	300	279	130	579	700	943	154
Production (all grades)	181.1	156.9	155.4	143.4	127.8	119.1	105.0	91.9	81.4	85.0	76.8	60.6	46.2	38.3	32.3	30.2	33.2	33.3	32.3	33.7
TSA estates	88.0	76.3	75.6	67.7	64.5	62.5	53.6	45.3	38.4	40.7	36.7	27.7	18.3	14.4	12.2	10.5	13.0	11.7	10.9	12.4
Amboni estates	30.4	28.4	30.2	27.5	24.1	25.2	24.9	21.8	23.1	23.4	19.2	20.1	18.5	16.5	14.2	12.2	11.7	12.3	12.0	12.1
Ralli estates	22.0	17.7	17.7	13.2	10.3	11.8	12.5	11.4	9.6	9.8	8.1	5.3	2.9	2.1	2.5	3.0	3.0	3.1	3.3	2.9
Other producers	40.7	34.4	31.9	35.1	29.0	19.5	14.0	13.5	10.3	12.1	9.8	7.6	6.4	5.3	3.4	4.4	5.4	6.2	6.1	6.4

Source: TSA.

previously independent Tanzania Sisal Marketing Association (TASMA), and the representational and supervisory functions of Tanzania Sisal Marketing Board (TSMB). In 1976 legislation was passed introducing single channel marketing through TSA who were given sole rights to market sisal on behalf of all growers, both private and public. In 1977 TSA took over the activities of TSC which was dissolved.

Four important sisal estate companies were not nationalised. Ralli Estates was already 50 per cent owned by the government and there was no attempt to make this a majority share. The other three large private sector growers were allowed to survive because they were perceived to be relatively progressive.

The Amboni Group, owned partly by Wigglesworth and Co., a London-based sisal merchant, and partly by Swiss interests, was the largest private sector grower not to be nationalised. Amboni had a 'history of sensitive and pragmatic response to the political climate in Tanzania' (Bolton, 1985: 90). Shortly after independence they were involved in a joint venture with the government to establish a smallholder settlement scheme at Kabuku in conjunction with the Kwaruguru sisal estate. The Amboni Group also had a record of progressive attitudes to labour relations and a willingness to reinvest profits in new activities. Similar considerations affected Lugongo Estate, a very large Dutch-owned estate where a sisal spinning mill had been established in 1966. The last large private sector grower was Karimjee Jivanjee, who also owned a tea estate. This was a company owned by a Tanzanian Asian family with a record of consistent support for the independence movement and investments in sisal spinning.

The tea industry did not experience the same nationalisation measures as the sisal industry. Some tea estates were nationalised, but these were estates owned by companies with significant interests in other areas who happened also to own tea estates. They included Kwamkoro Estate which was owned by Bird and Co., a company with substantial interests in sisal that was affected by the sisal nationalisation. This led to a situation where one of the nationalised tea estates was owned by TSA rather than the Tanzania Tea Authority (TTA), established in 1968 with primary responsibility for the development of factories to support smallholder tea growers.

The majority of private sector producers were unaffected by the establishment of TTA and the tea industry maintained its own independent growers association, TTGA, in which TTA participated. Initially the only involvement of TTA in estate tea was in some very small nucleus estates around the smallholder factories and in Bulwa Estate, which was passed to TTA after the nationalisation of its parent company. Subsequently a subsidiary company was established to look after Stone Valley Estate when all Lonrho activities were nationalised following political disagreement in the mid-1970s.

It can be seen that political factors had a very significant role in the nationalisation of estates. Growers with a record for good labour relations and reinvestment of profits were not generally affected. The sisal industry had a history of conflict and poor wages and living conditions. Many of the estates that were nationalised were those whose owners were perceived to be antagonistic to the objectives of the Tanzanian government.

Economic factors were also important. In 1967 the sisal industry was still one of the most important sources of Tanzanian export earnings and the largest single formal sector employer. Tanzania was still the largest sisal producer in the world in a situation where market prospects did not seem to be encouraging. Extensive government intervention was justified by the need to control production and marketing for price stabilisation purposes.

10.4 Comparative performance 1967–85

Tanzania experienced rapid economic growth during the first Five Year Plan period mainly due to the performance of peasant agriculture. Annual growth rates in excess of 9 per cent were recorded in the production of the main smallholder export crops of coffee, cotton, cashew nuts and tobacco (Coulson, 1982: 145). Smallholder tea production was also increasing rapidly. Economic growth continued into the second Five Year Plan period (1969–74), but problems were beginning to appear in the agricultural sector and the decade of the 1970s was one of incipient economic crisis and growing foreign exchange shortage. The war with Uganda in 1978–9 brought the crisis to a head, but the underlying problems were already apparent. Exceptionally favourable prices for sisal in 1973–5 and for coffee in 1977–8 helped to offset the impact of the rise in oil prices and to delay the impact of an export production performance that was at best stagnant and in some cases declining.

The sisal industry experienced an annual trend rate of decline in production between 1971 and 1986 of 11.3 per cent. The decline cannot be ascribed to low world prices. There was a price boom in 1973–5 and the average level of world prices for sisal in the 1970s was slightly above the average for the 1960s in real terms. Prices did decline in real terms in the 1980s but the decline in production was well under way by then.

The decline in production is also not explained by the effect of an overvalued exchange rate on export crop profitability. The rate of inflation in Tanzania during the 1970s was not significantly different from the international rate, and the problem of failure to adjust the exchange rate only became serious from 1980 onwards. Poor world prices and an overvalued exchange rate contributed in a marked way to the continued decline in the first half of the 1980s, but it is necessary to look elsewhere for the reason for the initial decline.

The nationalisation measures of 1967 and 1973 created an environment of uncertainty for the remaining private sector growers and this affected their willingness to invest in replanting and replacement of equipment. When single-channel marketing was introduced the sisal growers had to pay the cost of TSA marketing expenses and so, with a declining level of production, unit costs to the growers tended to increase.[2] Sisal growers were also unable to benefit fully from the years of high sisal prices because of the imposition of an export tax, with tax rates related to the level of sisal prices. In 1974 this tax took 36 per cent of the FOB price and even in years of normal prices it was over 10 per cent (United Republic of Tanzania, 1979: 29a). The export tax was finally abolished in 1981 but, by this time, the problems of an overvalued exchange rate combined with low world prices had taken over.

The market prospects for sisal also appeared to be uncertain. Synthetic twines were increasingly penetrating the European market and the overall market for agricultural twines was believed to be stagnant. This led the larger producers to concentrate investment into sisal spinning and diversification schemes at the expense of sisal planting and the replacement and maintenance of field and processing equipment. In retrospect it is possible to attribute a large part of the financial problems faced by TSA to misplaced investment priorities.

A further factor of importance in the decline of sisal production was a problem of persistent labour shortage. Wages of production workers were increased substantially in 1972 and 1974, but thereafter real wages declined consistently for over a decade. This occurred at a time when people in the areas from which migrant workers were traditionally recruited were encouraged to develop their own villages. The supply of migrant workers from Mozambique stopped after independence, and resettlement of Burundian refugees also affected the supply of field labour. Deteriorating housing conditions and lack of food security became problems during the late 1970s and early 1980s. The wages and conditions for field labourers in the sisal industry became increasingly unattractive and when this was combined with the traditional low status attached to estate labour it is hardly surprising that more and more sisal leaf was being left uncut.

Recruitment and motivation of skilled labour for the estates were also a problem, particularly for the nationalised estates where salary levels were determined by standard parastatal rates. Skilled managers and engineers were reluctant to move to the estates when jobs were available in more attractive conditions in the urban areas. The main training and research station for sisal at Mlingano became a more general research centre and a general agricultural training institute and this reduced the flow of new skilled workers into the industry.

For the sisal industry a picture of cumulative causation emerges to explain the persistent decline over a period of nearly twenty years. Within that decline, however, there is an interesting exception. While the production on the nationalised estates declined at 13.1 per cent per annum between 1971 and 1986 – a rate more or less identical to that of the partially nationalised Ralli Estates (13.6 per cent) and rather less than the rest of the private sector (15.1 per cent) – production of the largest single private sector grower, the Amboni Group, only declined at a rate of 5.1 per cent (see Table 10.1 and Figure 10.1).

The relatively good performance of the Amboni Group can be explained in various ways. Amboni have always been at the forefront of the industry technically and were the first producers to introduce the improved Hybrid 11648

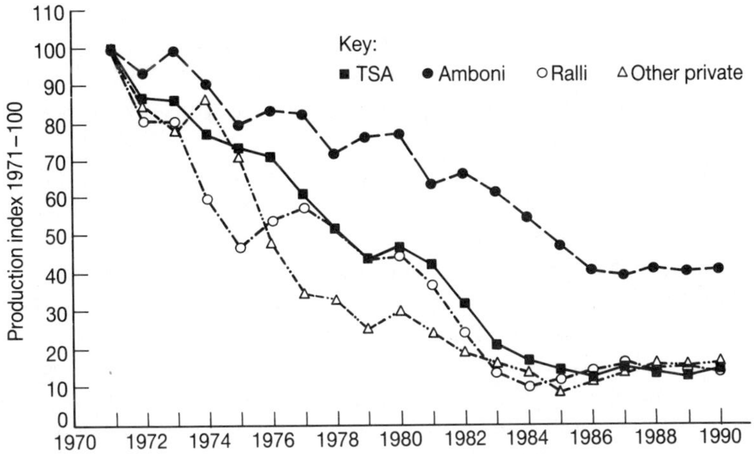

Figure 10.1 Tanzanian sisal production: indices by producer

on a large scale. They also followed a consistent policy of promoting productivity improvement rather than cost cutting as the means to maintaining profitability. They introduced a productivity-based incentive scheme for their workers a long time before any other producers. Maintenance standards and rotational replanting were kept up wherever possible. Amboni also kept up a consistent flow of information on requirements for the items that were becoming scarce in the increasingly difficult economic circumstances of the early 1980s and they were the first sisal producers to put together a project for rehabilitation of their estates.[3]

Obviously one of the reasons for Amboni's relative success can be described as 'good management'. This is not in itself a sufficient explanation because it does not explain the conditions under which it was possible to recruit good managers and allow them to perform. In this respect ability to pay good salaries and provide fringe benefits is very important. This was easier for foreign-based companies because the taxation rules facing expatriates were not the same as those facing Tanzanian nationals. Most of the top management of Amboni and nearly all of the estate engineers were recruited from Switzerland. The estate managers were nearly all Tanzanian, but the company made every effort to ensure that their terms and conditions were competitive and they were certainly not constrained by parastatal salary scales.

None of this is possible without resources. For most of the estates in Tanzania resources were always inadequate, particularly after 1979. The nationalised estates received some support from the government on a more or less *ad hoc* basis for rotational replanting and the purchase of some field equipment when it was available. It was never enough and never put together in an integrated way and so there were always bottlenecks somewhere in the process. The private sector estates, including Ralli Estates, had no backing at all for many years, although eventually some producers were able to obtain some import support funding and to join in a World Food Programme funded scheme for improving estate workers' housing. For most of the period most of the producers were operating at a loss and so naturally their assets started to deteriorate and their managers were unable to function properly.

Amboni was a larger company with a more diversified set of activities, interests in other countries, and foreign shareholders who included the main sisal merchants in London. Obviously these shareholders had some interest in ensuring that sisal was produced and marketed even if production was sometimes undertaken at a loss. Foreign investors have more resources and therefore a greater ability to survive in an adverse economic environment.

The tea industry experience shows both similarities and differences (see Table 10.2 and Figure 10.2). While the tea industry did not start to experience production decline until after 1977/8, there is a similar differentiation between the performance of the large companies backed by foreign investors and the small producers backed by local investors or owners from other developing countries.

Brooke Bond were the most successful producers, recording a trend rate of growth in production of 3.5 per cent between 1976/7 and 1986/7. George Williamson (T) was the next most successful private sector producer. Their production fluctuated, with a downward trend of 2.7 per cent becoming apparent in the 1980s but not of great statistical significance. All the other private sector estates were relatively small and they recorded fairly drastic declines in output with an average annual trend rate of decline of 9.3 per cent per annum. The worst performers were the two public sector estates in Northern Tanzania, one owned by TSA and one by TTA. These estates recorded a trend rate of decline of 13.4 per cent per annum.

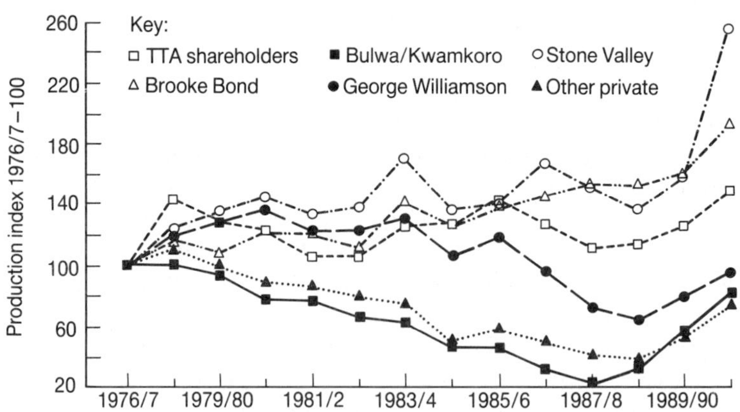

Figure 10.2 Tanzanian tea production: indices by producer

Table 10.2 Tanzanian-made tea production by producer, 1976/7 to 1989/90 (metric tons)

Year	1976/7	1977/8	1978/9	1979/80	1980/1	1981/2	1982/3	1983/4	1984/5	1985/6	1986/7	1987/8	1988/9	1989/90
TTA smallholder factories	3,293	4,733	4,237	4,064	3,469	3,485	4,137	4,181	4,688	4,149	3,648	3,717	4,103	4,877
Public sector estates – CDC	1,740	1,757	1,630	1,360	1,352	1,155	1,102	823	815	536	366	562	973	1,405
Stone Valley – Lonrho	821	1,019	1,112	1,182	1,091	1,130	1,394	1,110	1,151	1,365	1,234	1,118	1,286	2,085
Luponde – Lonrho	518	534	448	406	410	393	361	128	169	255	278	205	293	392
Dindira – Chillington	412	405	389	349	449	439	402	242	238	167	145	152	339	560
Balangai – Chillington	282	331	334	271	245	223	261	207	237	180	105	145	185	250
Brooke Bond	3,695	4,427	3,984	4,489	4,424	4,127	5,213	4,668	5,069	5,352	5,635	5,576	5,871	7,081
George Williamson	2,829	3,280	3,589	3,834	3,419	3,453	3,650	3,006	3,331	2,700	2,040	1,810	2,224	2,669
Bombay Burma	521	736	623	611	431	404	389	314	393	324	219	221	247	246
Karimi	1,110	1,150	988	884	903	786	708	518	586	470	394	327	422	624
Total	15,221	18,372	17,334	17,450	16,193	15,595	17,617	15,197	16,677	15,498	14,064	13,833	15,944	20,190

Source: TTA.

The performance of the public sector was not all bad. The ex-Lonrho Stone Valley estate had a production record after nationalisation that was not much worse than the nearby Brooke Bond estates in the Southern Highlands. The TTA smallholder factories had a mixed record with no overall trend. Some of these factories benefited from World Bank assistance and the smallholder pricing system combined with some government subsidies meant that they were not facing the same conditions as the estate-based factories.

The good performance of Brooke Bond can be explained in the same terms as that of Amboni in the sisal industry. Brooke Bond were the most innovative producers, being early investors in irrigation and experimenting with different schemes for tea pluckers. They made efforts to ensure that all essentials were available both for operating the factories and estates and for maintenance of the labour force. They had the external backing of a large multinational and expatriates in top management positions.

The good performance of the Stone Valley estate (which became Mufindi Tea Company) requires explanation. The management was entirely Tanzanian and there was no external funding, although shortly before the estate was handed back to Lonrho it had been receiving government funds for implementation of a tea planting and irrigation project. Three factors are important. First, the estate is in one of the best potential tea-growing areas in Tanzania, close to the Brooke Bond estates. These areas have a positive advantage in recruiting labour in that rainfall is reliable and this means that yields are good and food supplies do not present any problem. Secondly, the estate was established as a subsidiary company and operated with a considerable degree of autonomy. This helped the final factor which was the presence of a manager with long experience of the tea industry able to manage without undue interference from the centre.

The analysis of the relative performance of different producers in the tea industry indicates some important factors that could be overlooked. One is the location factor. All the estates in the Usambara Mountains in Northern Tanzania performed relatively badly, whether public or private (see Table 10.3 and Figure 10.3). Rainfall in the Usambaras is less reliable, the topography is less suitable for irrigation and there is greater population pressure on land resources. This leads to greater food security problems and lower yields leading to lower incomes for pluckers. All the estates in the Usambaras experienced serious labour shortage problems. The factories in the Usambaras were also older and smaller and produced lower-quality tea. They were therefore less profitable.

A second factor is the degree of autonomy of management. This is related to the resources available to managers since, without resources, autonomy cannot work. The management of Ralli Estates had a considerable degree of autonomy but no resources to work with since neither shareholder put any resources into the company. A worse situation faced the managers of the nationalised sisal estate subsidiary companies when they were set up in 1981.

Table 10.3 Tanzanian-made tea production by area, 1976/7 to 1989/90 (metric tons)

Year	1976/7	1977/8	1978/9	1979/80	1980/1	1981/2	1982/3	1983/4	1984/5	1985/6	1986/7	1987/8	1988/9	1989/90
Southern Highlands	9,409	11,541	10,909	11,640	11,072	10,792	12,797	11,357	12,142	11,827	11,383	11,060	12,010	15,075
Usambaras	5,341	6,219	5,808	5,358	4,815	4,421	4,499	3,640	4,236	3,425	2,468	2,533	3,591	4,612
Kagera	471	612	617	452	306	382	321	200	299	246	213	240	344	503
Total	15,221	18,372	17,334	17,450	16,193	15,595	17,617	15,197	16,677	15,498	14,064	13,833	15,944	20,190

Source: TTA.

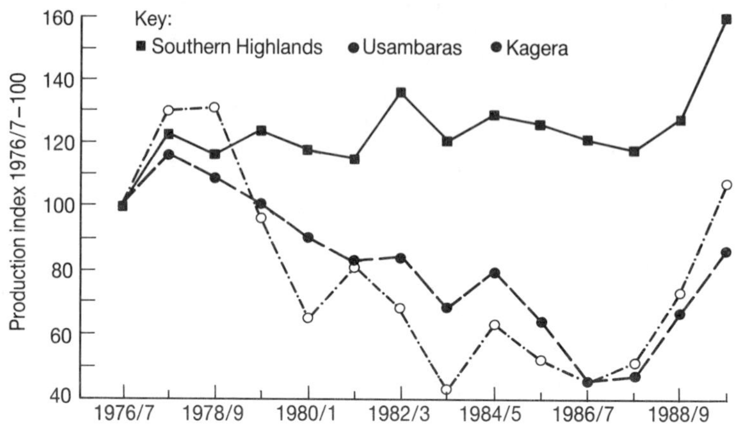

Figure 10.3 Tanzanian tea production: indices by region

No resources or even titles to assets were transferred to the managers when they took over the companies and the companies were eventually dissolved and put under centralised management. The managers of the large foreign-owned estate companies had both autonomy and the backing of the resources of a large company. The manager of Mufindi Tea Company had a relatively high degree of autonomy and the resources of a profitable estate.

10.5 The beginnings of change – government policy 1981–5

The Tanzanian economy experienced increasing problems from 1981 onwards. Partly this was due to 'external shocks', particularly the exhaustion of foreign exchange reserves through the Uganda War and the very low commodity prices facing important export crops in the early 1980s. Policies towards the agricultural sector also contributed. A large-scale indigenous private sector was actively discouraged. The rates of taxes on personal incomes, company profits and imports combined with inadequate allocations of foreign exchange, delays in remittances and difficulties in labour recruitment discouraged foreign investment. Villagisation caused widespread disruption to smallholder farmers, and producer pricing policy combined with institutional changes in marketing adversely affected incentives.[4] The parastatal enterprises were affected by rapid institutional change, inadequate funding and insufficient autonomy to provide adequate work incentives.

From 1979 onwards Tanzanian inflation rates started to diverge significantly from international rates. There was a strong reluctance to devalue and, as a consequence, the profitability of export agriculture declined drastically. Devaluations of 10 per cent, 20 per cent and 26 per cent did take place in 1982, 1983 and 1984, but these were too little and too late and did not convince the international donor agencies. A Structural Adjustment Programme (1982–4) was announced (United Republic of Tanzania, 1982) in which the importance of reviving the production of traditional export crops was emphasised, but resources were not forthcoming for this actually to take place.

Policies towards the private sector began to change and these were reflected in the Agricultural Policy of Tanzania (United Republic of Tanzania, 1983) which defined land tenure rights and recognised the role of large-scale private sector agriculture. Export Crop Packages were drawn up (United Republic of Tanzania, 1984) defining strategies and requirements for the primary export crops and a commitment was made to sell off some of the worst performing nationalised sisal estates. The government gave strong support to the Amboni rehabilitation project and, in the process, single-channel marketing of sisal was gradually eroded by individual agreements for producers to undertake independent marketing. Separate negotiations took place for Lonrho to regain majority ownership of the Stone Valley tea estate and also to take over a run-down private sector estate. This was perceived as a significant indication of a change in attitude to the private sector.

A movement towards reform was apparent, but more rapid reform was required before the necessary funding would be forthcoming for the rehabilitation of many of the run-down assets. This took place following agreement with the IMF in 1986 on a substantial and continuing devaluation. As usual the agreement had strict conditions which would not allow for the substantial investment required for the rehabilitation of all the public sector estates from government sources. Parastatals were forced both by circumstances and changing government policy to look for possible joint venture partners if investment plans were to be realised.

10.6 Denationalisation 1986–90

In this chapter the term denationalisation is used to describe the variety of measures by which ownership and control of some of the nationalised estates were divested in the second half of the 1980s. A diversity of approaches was used and divestiture occurred more due to force of circumstances and external pressure than to any internal ideological pressure. Despite a number of major policy changes there was no official change in the overall government objective of ‘socialism and self reliance’. However, significant changes in emphasis took place and it became apparent that proposals for joint ventures and other private sector investment would now be welcomed. Tenders were invited for a number of TSA sisal estates that were to be sold off.

Denationalisation is usually justified on the basis of economic efficiency or financial profitability, the assumption being that the private sector is likely to be more efficient than the public sector because of a need for greater financial discipline. In the Tanzanian case the main justifications were the inability of the parastatals to secure funds for rehabilitation and a view that at least part of the problems of the public sector estates were due to mismanagement. Assessment of denationalisation might then be seen in terms of the extent to which it led to the generation of extra funds that would not otherwise have been available and the extent to which improvement in management led to increases in the value of production.

It is too early to make any definitive conclusions about the experience of denationalisation, but some observations can be made on the production performance of some of the estates where ownership changes have occurred and it is also possible to make some observations on some of the implications of these experiences.

The production performance of enterprises where a form of privatisation has taken place can be seen from Tables 10.1 and 10.2. In the sisal industry the aggregated statistics available on the industry do not allow ready identification of the estates transferred from TSA to the private sector since 1986 although the production statistics do give an indication of the relative size of the transfer, and the planting statistics give an indication of the level of investment in the privatised estates. It is also possible to make some qualitative observations on the apparent impact of denationalisation.

Separate statistics are shown for Ralli Estates where a UK-based company took over the privately owned shares and the management and started to implement a programme of rehabilitation. The same company also took over management of Dindira Tea Estate and ownership of the nearby privately owned Balangai Estate. A different sort of private sector involvement took place after lengthy negotiations for a German aid funded rehabilitation project for the estates previously under one of the nationalised sisal estate companies. In this case a condition of the aid was the appointment of an external management company with autonomy to implement the project. The objective of the project was to bring the estates back to a sufficiently high production level within five years to allow self-sustained development from then onwards.

In the tea industry there were three important ownership changes. The Lonrho joint venture and Dindira/Balangai are mentioned above. The third change involved the two public sector estates in the Usambaras, Bulwa and Kwamkoro, which were combined in a joint venture between TTA and the Commonwealth Development Corporation (CDC) with majority ownership and management vested in CDC.

Production performance since the ownership changes has been mixed. It is easier to make judgements on the tea sector than sisal because tea bushes have a longer life cycle than sisal plants and so it can be assumed that the tea bushes required to bring production back to previous levels are already there, even if infilling and reclamation of overgrown bushes are required. Even so it takes time for infilled bushes to grow and for reclaimed bushes to recover. In the case of sisal, a ten- to twelve-year life cycle with a three-year immature period means that production is largely constrained by planting that took place prior to transfer of ownership. A further complication is that, with the exception of Stone Valley, the processing and transport facilities on all the estates where ownership changes have taken place were extremely run down. Under these circumstances it is very difficult to have an immediate impact on production.

Bearing in mind the above reservations, it is clear that the performances of the CDC tea estates and the Ralli sisal estates have been remarkably good. In both cases an almost immediate improvement in performance can be observed. The speed of the improvement can only be attributed to effective and innovative management because it would have been impossible to renovate all the facilities and to replant in that timescale. The extent of the achievement of Ralli Estates is not obvious until the replanting record in the previous ten years is considered. Production should have been going steadily downwards not upwards.

Most of the other estates seem to have experienced further decline for two or three years before recovery. This may be a reflection of failure to mobilise adequate resources in time, or it may indicate management problems during the transfer. There is no doubt that the management styles of expatriates working for foreign companies are very different from those adopted by Tanzanian parastatals and that this is a source of potential conflict. The assumption that expatriate private sector management is inherently better than that of local public sector managers is not necessarily valid. Expatriate managers may have problems adapting to local conditions and attitudes.

Private sector investors will also appoint the management that best serves their own interests, which may not always correspond with those of the labour force or with national economic objectives. For example, cost reduction measures may receive higher priority than increased production if this is the quickest way to improve profits, even though cost reduction may lead initially to reductions in both employment and production and hence reduced income to workers and reduced foreign exchange earnings.

The replanting record of the privatised sisal estates (other than Ralli Estates) does not seem to have been very impressive in the initial years but the statistics may not be very complete. Estate rehabilitation seems to have relied on the use of local funds generated from blocked remittances and, in most cases, independent investment of foreign exchange has not been forthcoming. Investors have relied on World Bank export rehabilitation loans to secure their foreign exchange requirements and this is inevitably a slower process. Relatively little new private investment has flowed into the economy and so the gain to the national economy depends on improvements in production performance and the extent to which release of blocked funds improves access to external loans.

There may be a difference in operational practice between foreign private investment and the use of foreign management for nationally owned assets. The German-aided sisal rehabilitation project has objectives established in terms of a production target over a defined period of time. Profitability might be considered as a constraint defined by the need for sustainability rather than as an immediate objective. With such an objective the relative priority of production targets and cost reduction is altered and a faster recovery in production might be expected.

It appears that, with a lag of up to three or four years, most privatised estates eventually show an improved production performance. However, despite the poor world prices for both sisal and tea in recent years, the overall conditions facing producers in the late 1980s were much more favourable than they had been for a decade. The rapid devaluation of the Tanzanian Shilling, the removal of export taxes and the reform of sisal marketing considerably improved the prospects of profitable production.[5] The estates were also no longer faced with shortages of food for workers and foreign exchange for equipment. Under these circumstances it is therefore legitimate to ask whether privatisation itself contributed to improved performance or whether a similar improvement could have been achieved with adequate funding and proper management autonomy for the public sector estates. This is certainly the view taken by some parastatal managers when considering the resources available to their expatriate counterparts engaged in the implementation of foreign-funded rehabilitation projects.

A further question that arises is the extent to which denationalisation of some estates undermines the operation of those estates that remain under the public sector. Where there exists a large parastatal head office with associated overhead costs, the more operational units that are removed the fewer there are left to cover the overheads and the greater the proportional burden for the remaining estates. This is a particular problem for TSA where many attempts to reduce head office costs have been made but they have always been undermined by the declining production base.

10.7 Conclusions: denationalisation and the rehabilitation of Tanzanian estate agriculture

A limited degree of denationalisation has taken place in the context of the rehabilitation of Tanzanian estate agriculture. Denationalisation has occurred on a more or less *ad hoc* basis reflecting the limited opportunities for funding the state sector, but it seems likely that further denationalisation of estates will take place, possibly associated with joint ventures in which the existing assets will be the government equity.

There is no conclusive empirical evidence to suggest that the economic performance of the public sector estates in Tanzania has been worse than that of the private sector in general. However, there is evidence to suggest that lack of financial and managerial autonomy has contributed to poor performance and that, in the sisal industry, the level of TSA head office costs had an adverse effect on both public and private sector estates. There is also evidence to suggest that the *ad hoc* method of funding replanting costs and occasional purchases of vehicles adopted in the public sector was an inefficient way of tackling investment requirements.

The record of Tanzanian estate agriculture indicates that the production performance of estates whether public or private deteriorated significantly in the period 1970 to 1985. Private sector estates owned by large foreign companies fared significantly better than other estates in this period, but there was no significant difference between the public sector and locally owned private sector estates. The experience of Mufindi Tea Company suggests that, given adequate resources, favourable conditions and financial and managerial autonomy, public sector estates can perform as well as any private sector estate.

The chief causes of the decline of estate agriculture lay outside the control of the estates. They were particularly related to institutional changes, access to foreign exchange and exchange rate and taxation policy. This is consistent with the view that changes in the general economic environment are more important than ownership *per se*. Although TSA accumulated a substantial debt over the years and received some development budget support, the combined effects of export taxation and an overvalued exchange rate removed far more resources than were received.

Following more than a decade of decline, the resources needed for the rehabilitation of the public sector estates were beyond the financial resources of the government. Rehabilitation was not possible without substantial foreign funding which, in the circumstances of the 'new orthodoxy' associated with the international lending agencies' conditionality, was unlikely to be available to the public sector. Furthermore the record of the parastatals, particularly TSA, on financial and managerial autonomy was not encouraging. It may therefore be concluded that, while it may not be strictly necessary, in practice, rehabilitation could not be achieved without some degree of denationalisation.

The evidence from Tanzania shows a strong positive relationship between the level of external resources introduced and the production response. This suggests that rehabilitation is far more likely to succeed if it has the backing of the resources of a foreign investor. Simply privatising without injecting new resources does not necessarily solve anything. With foreign investment the response is also quicker. Rehabilitation based on local sources of funds takes longer because local financial institutions are slower to respond and have limited resources and because local investors do not have the resources to secure substantial foreign loans.

Management flexibility is important. The evidence of both the tea and sisal industries suggests that innovative management in the fields of organisation of work and incentives and an emphasis on improving productivity through technical change are likely to be more successful than reliance on traditional hierarchical estate management approaches. Where there is a change of ownership the motivation of the existing workforce is critical. In most cases they will have been demoralised by years of underinvestment and inadequate resources and, if the estate has been in decline, they will feel threatened by the possibility that new management will hold them responsible for the decline. A positive and innovative approach is therefore needed to secure their commitment.

A basic reason for nationalising the sisal estates was the belief that estate agriculture yielded few benefits to Tanzanians, either working on the estates or elsewhere, and that foreign ownership of important export industries threatened economic independence. Denationalisation hands back ownership and control to foreign-based companies and those few local companies with the resources to undertake the large investment required for estate rehabilitation. These companies are generally owned by ethnic minorities rather than indigenous Tanzanians. The indigenous capitalist class in Tanzania is still very weak, partly because of a conscious attempt in the past by the government to prevent its development. In this respect the quotation from Nyerere on lack of locally based capital is as true in 1992 as it was in the 1960s.

The rehabilitation of estates by private foreign capital will improve export earnings and contribute to the availability of foreign exchange to the economy. It is also likely that a prosperous estate sector will be able to provide better wages and conditions of work than those previously prevailing. Where there is a joint venture the government will also benefit from any profits earned as well as from company taxes.

Nevertheless it is difficult to escape the conclusion that the industry will have gone through a full circle and that once more Tanzanian large-scale agriculture will be dominated by foreign interests. The extent to which this will be consistent with government objectives depends in part on the extent to which those objectives themselves change and in part on the relative importance of large-scale agriculture within the economy. Large-scale agriculture is certainly less important to the economy than it was twenty years ago and it may be that it is no longer regarded as strategic. It may also be that there is no realistic alternative to a return to majority foreign ownership under the current economic circumstances.

It is for this reason that innovative approaches to the management of the estates are required in which participation by the workers and the surrounding community in the ownership and operation of the enterprise is encouraged. Without this involvement the perception of the foreign-owned estate as an externally imposed and alien institution will be a continued source of antagonism and conflict. It is important not to forget the initial reasons for nationalisation if a mutually beneficial relationship is to be developed between foreign investors and local interests.

Notes

1. In this chapter production performance has been used as a proxy measure for the contribution of the estates to the national economy. This measure suffers from the obvious defect that it does not consider the cost of production or the value of the output. While differences in cost of production and quality of output undoubtedly did exist, they tend to reinforce the conclusions. Higher production levels tended to lead to lower unit costs and were also associated with higher quality of output. Profitability might provide an alternative measure but information is not readily

available and may also be misleading because poor profitability of all producers was heavily influenced by the level of commodity prices and the exchange rate and because private and national economic profitability diverged substantially for much of the period under consideration.

2. Complaints from private sector growers about the increased unit costs of TSA became a serious issue in 1980. In previous years arguments were more concerned with the marketing strategy adopted and how that affected the level of prices achieved.
3. The project was funded by the IFC, the private sector affiliate of the World Bank. Unforeseen problems were experienced in implementation because of the accidental planting of a rogue hybrid known as 'Kaptura'. The impact of Kaptura could be attributed at least in part to the collapse of sisal research at Mlingano.
4. Villagisation was the largely forced movement of the rural population from scattered settlements into villages from 1973 to 1975. The planning of the villages was based more on the economics of social service provision than on agricultural considerations and caused serious problems in some areas. The experience is described in Coulson (1982, 235–62).
5. An indication of the effect of the initial devaluation on the real shilling value of tea and sisal export prices is given in Potts (1991: 186).

References

Bolton, D. (1985), *Nationalisation: A road to socialism?*, London: Zed Press.

Coulson, A. (1982), *Tanzania: A political economy*, London: Oxford University Press.

Nyerere, J. K. (1968), *Freedom and Socialism*, London: Oxford University Press.

Potts, D. J. (1991), 'Rehabilitation of export oriented estate agriculture in Tanzania', in C. Kirkpatrick (ed.), *Project Rehabilitation in Developing Countries*, London: Routledge.

Raikes, P. (1986), 'Eating the carrot and wielding the stick: the agricultural sector in Tanzania', in J. Boesen and K. J. Havnevik (eds), *Tanzania: Crisis and struggle for survival*, Uppsala: Scandinavian Institute of African Studies.

Ruthenberg, H. (1964), 'Agricultural Development in Tanganyika', *IFO Afrika Studien* No. 2, Munich: Springer Verlag.

United Republic of Tanzania (1979), 'Annual review of the Tanzania sisal industry 1978', Dar es Salaam: Ministry of Agriculture, Marketing Development Bureau

United Republic of Tanzania (1982), 'Structural adjustment programme', Dar es Salaam: Ministry of Economic Affairs and Planning.

United Republic of Tanzania (1983), 'Agricultural policy of Tanzania', Dar es Salaam: Ministry of Agriculture and Livestock Development

United Republic of Tanzania (1984), 'Export crop packages: a framework for action', Dar es Salaam: Ministry of Agriculture and Livestock Development, Project Preparation and Monitoring Bureau

11

Privatisation policy: The lessons of nationalisation in East Africa

Michael Yaffey

11.1 Competing paradigms

Hartley and Ott (1991: 1) identify privatisation as one of a series of fashions in economic policy, following after *laissez-faire*, Keynesianism, monetarism, nationalisation and supply-side economics. Like other fashions, privatisation carries the clear danger of persuasion by force of majority instead of by evidence.

But these items are, of course, more than mere fashions. They are paradigms, in the sense described by Routh (1989: 26, 316) and one's personal inclination to espouse one or other depends on one's view of the world outside the sphere of mere economics. Such paradigms tend to coexist and compete because of the variety of extradisciplinary world views.

It cannot escape notice, however, that privatisation and nationalisation are diametrical opposites, and legitimate coexistence is impossible. The debate ought properly to involve recognition by each side that the other paradigm has been constructed, and must be critically deconstructed if the contrary case is to be fully made out. It is important to do this: no paradigm and no policy which is the diametrical opposite of another ought to be accepted as correct without consideration being given to the other, and the differences reconciled or resolved. Attention to empirical data alone is not enough even if it seems to be fairly strong. In this case it is not strong: 'At present, divestiture can only be supported or opposed on the basis of ideology, theory or politics, since there is only the most limited empirical support for either position' (Jones, Tandon and Vogelsang, 1991: 68).

Critical deconstruction of the opposing theoretical analysis is therefore necessary. But with this particular pair, each side appears to proceed quite improperly without reference to the constructs of the other. Adherents of privatisation in the 1980s and early 1990s have not, in their literature thus far, dismantled the constructs of their opponents. It is as though the pro-nationalisation literature of the previous half-century did not exist at all. Equally those who support non-private ownership have not, in the academic literature of economics at least, produced a critique of the theory of the new doctrine; nor have they confessed any error in the older logic.

Perhaps this lacuna exists because no serious empirical evidence has been available until very recently which might throw light on which particular parts of a paradigm are in error. It is only now becoming possible to test the theories of privatisation and nationalisation against the results of both, and so to bring together and integrate the two paradigms. Perhaps the sheer pace of privatisation in the 1980s ran ahead of the publication of serious critical review which did not appear until the 1990s, a delay which did not occur with nationalisation in the 1960s and early 1970s. Perhaps also the lacuna exists because economic paradigm-believers do not care to resolve extradisciplinary world views, and no professional forum of enquiry has attempted to subsume the political philosophy of recent forceful nationalisers (e.g. Nasser, Nkrumah, Nyerere and Allende) together with that of recent forceful privatisers (Thatcher and Reagan, World Bank and IMF conditionalities) into a single theory of the effects of ownership reform. There are, of course, studies which look at both private and public enterprises within the theory of a single paradigm – for example, neoclassical liberal welfare economics – which, because they take that as a point of departure, cannot be convincing to the other camp.

Some steps towards a unified theory of privatisation have been taken, such as the cost-benefit methodology of Jones, Tandon and Vogelsang (1990). This is, however, still essentially one-sided and therefore incomplete.[1]

11.2 Developing country experience of privatisation

In recent years there have been both external and internal pressures on LDC governments to privatise. The main internal pressure has been the ubiquitous budget deficit. This budgetary crisis has inserted into the public policy debate one strong reason to turn off the tap of public subsidies to loss-making state enterprises by divestiture, plus another strong reason to realise the disposal proceeds of unsaleable enterprises by liquidation, plus a third demand to capitalise on profitable enterprises by divestiture.

It may be that bad management of parastatals has contributed to the budget deficit problem, but the latter certainly has other causes, and has operated also in countries where the state sector is not particularly large (as in the UK at the present time). Whether the enterprises are profitable or not affects the manner of their privatisation, but is not a fundamental cause of it. Indeed, it is often argued that some state enterprises can and should be commercialised and their profitability improved prior to privatisation. As Bouin (Bouin and Michalet, 1991: 181) says: 'The impact of privatisation on the public finances [in LDCs] seems relatively marginal, because privatisation is not a solution for public firms with very heavy deficits.'

This essentially Treasury perspective has led several analysts to propose an approach as follows:

1. Enumerate all the public sector activities which can be privatised.
2. Divide them into profitable and unprofitable categories.
3. Sell the profitable ones.
4. Divide the unprofitable ones into those which can be reformed and those which cannot.
5. Sell the assets of the unreformable activities at break-up value.
6. Reform the remainder, using if necessary some capital proceeds from earlier disposals, until they are attractive enough to sell as going concerns.

The effect of this is to create three lists, which if reforms are successful become only two lists – profitable going concerns and break-ups – and ultimately to clear them both. The public sector shrinks to one which is regarded as irreducible for reasons of national security or other special reasons. We might for convenience label this the *modalities* technique.

It is not the only approach. In countries where new private capital is in general hard to attract, and it may be expected that all disposals whether of assets or of going concerns will fetch impermissibly low prices, and of course the state sector provides certain confidential privileges which are not captured in its fiscal results, then the reform list may be maximised, and the divestiture category reduced to a gesture regarded as essential for reasons of diplomacy, or to meet an IMF condition, or for other special reasons. Meanwhile, the Treasury approach and the modalities technique may be ostensibly adopted.

Yet another approach is to view privatisation as one of a triplet of techniques, the others being commercialisation and regulation. The entire triplet may be called restructuring or rebalancing. This is different in an important respect from the Treasury approach in which commercialisation and regulation are necessary adjuncts to privatisation in certain categories. Putting the change of ownership at the head of the agenda has quite different political implications.

All reports show that privatisation, by any approach, has proved difficult to implement, arouses fierce opposition, and has proceeded at a pace at which its advocates are impatient and disappointed, in developing countries as well as in Eastern Europe. In an extreme case such as Kenya, for example, Adam (Adam, Cavendish and Mistry, 1992: 323) says that 'To all intents and purposes there has been no privatization to speak of.'

The difficulties have been encountered at several stages:

1. *Establishing a theoretical framework* The approaches and techniques summarised above were not developed before the decision to privatise, but

during and after the implementation. For many officials concerned with implementation, this meant delay and frustration.

2. *Collecting data* There have been preliminary difficulties in enumerating the set of state-owned enterprises. This might be expected in newly independent states such as ex-Soviet states, or in countries where the public–private boundary is diffuse, such as Kenya, Thailand, or very recently China. In some other cases the state–co-operative boundary was unclear.
3. *Establishing categories* There have been enormous problems in classification. Given the background of the structural adjustment debate, the devaluation debate, and the corruption debate, which have raged in many countries, it is very problematical to say that a particular enterprise is or is not inherently profitable and will or will not be a going concern in the new liberalised environment which is to be introduced at some vague date in the medium term.
4. *Planning in haste* If there is a political imperative to meet a completion date, so that reforms and disposals must proceed simultaneously rather than in sequence, and the expertise available to carry out sound reforms simultaneously is too limited, analysis and classification at the enterprise level must be indeterminate. In several well-known cases, such as Russia, Bulgaria, Zambia, and South Africa, the political situation has been fluid, and governments have felt that they had but a short time to make irreversible ownership changes while they could be confident of remaining in office.
5. *Implementation in haste* Where there is a time limit on planning there is also pressure for rapid implementation. This may be because effective implementation is expected to produce efficiency gains which will improve political stability and so buy more time. It may be because the transfer of ownership carries with it a change in power relationships which is needed for stability. It may be because the proceeds of some disposals are needed to pay for the reforms of others. Whatever the reason for the haste, rapidly putting dozens (in large ex-Communist countries, thousands) of enterprises through a process comparable to administrative receivership creates a tremendous bottleneck if the process is to be done in a careful professional manner; we should remember that the Thatcher model has privatised less than a dozen enterprises each year, and that at significant administrative cost (fees of underwriters and professional advisers) which poorer countries cannot be expected to imitate.

11.3 History repeats itself

If one views ownership reform as including both nationalisation and privatisation, it is remarkable how the approaches and difficulties associated with privatisation describe the earlier experience.

The nationalisers had difficulty in establishing a theoretical framework; one need only recall the circumstances of the National Coal Board (UK, 1947), the

Suez Canal (Egypt, 1956), and the State Trading Corporation (Tanzania, 1967) to perceive that there was no pre-eminent model, no single motive, and no long-term strategy here. Nor can one say that in any of these leading cases, the rationale was grounded in economics.[2]

Collecting the data had been a problem for nationalisers too. The Coal Board was established without any valuation for individual collieries. The State Trading Corporation was set up by nationalising an incomplete set of import–export houses (and a few other items) compiled from the telephone directory.

Establishing categories of reformable and unreformable entities has also been problematical. In Tanzania, and coastal ex-colonies generally, the close links between export (produce) companies, import companies, and shipping agencies made it extremely difficult to segregate a group for public ownership without being dragged into associated areas in which the rationale for nationalisation was weak and the cost of acquisition high.

Planning in haste has often been a feature of nationalisation in LDCs. President Nyerere's announcement of bank nationalisation in 1967 was made unexpectedly, in banking hours, a dangerous situation which was resolved by the intervention of a team of academics who adopted three banks each. The Allende experience in Chile was criticised on similar grounds. Elsewhere it has not always been so. The Suez Canal by contrast was well planned under President Nasser, though that was even more dramatic. The impatience and frustration of the political constituency demanding ownership reform were irresistible in all these cases.

Implementation in haste is another ghost of the past. Newly independent countries such as Egypt in 1956 and Tanzania in 1967 had but few skilled managers. The pressure of work was intense. For example, the Board of the State Trading Corporation in Tanzania closed down the Tanganyika Wattle Extract Company in Arusha because it could not devote more than two and a half days to considering the company's long-term future and, indeed, did not begin to understand what wattle extract is.[3]

11.4 Rationales and expectations

Some twenty-five years ago, the case for nationalisation was argued, though with certain caveats (Yaffey: 1969). The context was East Africa and, in particular, Tanzania, which had carried out several nationalisations. This chapter attempts to examine recent privatisations in terms of the issues and concepts of the earlier paper, and vice versa.

The first point, then, was that given certain preconditions, nationalisation of enterprises belonging to a wealthy upper class should reduce the share of profits being consumed, and increase the share of profits reinvested in productive assets, thus increasing the rate of growth of GDP:

> The requisite circumstances are, first, that the élite formerly enjoyed relatively high incomes; second, that they enjoyed a high average propensity to consume; and third, that the new system can make effective use of the funds diverted into national development budgets. (Yaffey: 1969)

11.4.1 *Condition one: the initial owners have high personal incomes*

With regard to the first precondition, those who were expropriated by the nationalisations in East Africa certainly were receiving high incomes relative to the average income. This was perceived as important in that the transfer of this income to the development budget would provide a significantly large flow of investment funds. Without assuming any change in profitabilities, it was argued that the transfer of a profit stream, from private owners who would have consumed a substantial part of it to a government which would consume none of it, would have a crucial effect on the rate of growth.

The ownership reform (nationalisation) conducted in the 1960s by the Tanganyika African National Union and by comparable political parties in other countries, and that concern of economic advisers for growth through investment, occurred at a time when prevailing academic perceptions of economic growth and development were of a Harrod–Domar model, or a Rostow model, of a country in the very early stages of take-off (shortly after national independence). Significant additional investment funds were wanted in order to move the economy from stagnation on to a growth path.

Of course, this expected profit-growth-development effect cannot be a consideration of such urgency for the UK, the US or other taken-off economies. The Republican and Conservative Parties and their economic advisers have been under no comparable pressure to adopt draconian means to rake together the seed corn. But there seems no reason to retreat from the position that the flow of profits which are available for switching under a major ownership reform programme, in either direction, is indeed potentially big enough to have a very important effect on the growth of the economy, by altering the proportion taken for current consumption.

11.4.2 *Condition two: the new owners have a higher savings propensity*

So a large profit flow was removed from private hands in the 1960s. But whether those individuals actually consumed more than the directors and managers of the state enterprises who followed them is another question, one which in its converse form has attracted much more attention in the modern post-privatisation experience.

The expectation that ownership reform would reduce consumption was an unproven but plausible supposition in the conditions of the time, rather than a statement about necessary precautions which would need to be embedded in future policy, and so this precondition was not accompanied by a sufficiently explicit policy warning. In hindsight that was an error.

Looking at the academic literature on this point, it is interesting that economists normally do still choose to assume that no part of government income is consumed. Some British economists (for example, for the Overseas Development Administration (ODA) in MacArthur, 1988: 58) treat all government income as going into public sector investments. Squire and van der Tak (1975: 67) point out that marginal public revenue is used for several purposes including consumption *subsidies*; but they do not argue that expenditures on administration, defence and so forth include elements of consumption by government officers.

If we accept this assumption that government never consumes, other than by subsidising the consumption of others, it is valid to expect an improvement in the saved-profit effect to result from nationalising a private income stream. Conversely, following privatisations, it is to be expected that private recipients of dividends will divert part of them into personal consumption, whereas the state shareholder would not. But is this assumption about government behaviour correct?

An underlying assumption which needs to be challenged is that the official activities of government personnel are productive. Mainstream national income theory assumes that any income from state employment, like income from private ownership, is a legitimate payment for a factor of *production*. If, however, some of the persons are wholly or partly unproductive (let us call them 'parasites', an inexact term for ease of reference), their emoluments are to that extent unrequited transfers rather than factor payments given in exchange for a contribution to production. Being unrequited, the amount of these transfers is not determined by any market valuation of services rendered, but simply by the availability of funds for them. If this happens in the public sector, any increase in government income can be expected to increase these transfer payments and so increase personal consumption.

An increased flow of income going to non-productive persons will have a favourable impact on the growth rate only if the propensity to save of the 'parasites' exceeds that of the persons from whom ownership has been removed, by an amount which more than offsets the difference in the respective productive efforts of the two groups. Therefore, in such situations it is not safe to assume that switching income by ownership reform will produce an increase in the savings ratio.

Let us suppose that, if the facts were known, we would find that the public sector people, whether in the course of their duties or otherwise, have been consuming an increased part of the nationalised activity revenues since the 1960s in Tanzania, and not a reduced part as was anticipated, how should we interpret this? In the old paradigm it would be perceived as a surprising failure of public policy, creating conditions for a leakage of precious investible funds, and so acting as an unfortunate handicap to the growth of state enterprise activities; yet a failure capable of rectification, not an inevitable phenomenon, and therefore not a strong reason for forgoing the potential gains of nationalisation. By the same token, in Zaire, Uganda and Kenya, for the past three decades, high private incomes based on corruption of the private sector by some leading office-holders have been widely criticised and in the old paradigm these too should logically be perceived as a failure of public policy, this time acting as a handicap to private as well as public enterprise, though not in themselves inevitable. Also in the UK, and in Japan, so-called boardroom excesses and scandals in the private or recently privatised sector, and very many private financial institutions in the USA, have likewise been heavily criticised, and these too would have been perceived as policy failures, requiring rectification.

By contrast, the new paradigm perceives the high incomes drawn by office-bearers from African parastatals as symptomatic, not of poor public policy decisions capable of rectification, but of the relative inefficiency inherent in the nature of state enterprise itself.[4] If for many years a public organisation is badly governed, it must be badly ungovernable, presumably because it is public. Logically following this spurious argument in the new paradigm, the scandalous leakages by private enterprises in Uganda, Kenya, Nigeria, Japan, UK and USA ought to be perceived as symptomatic of the inefficiency inherent in private enterprise. Yet in practice that problem is agreed to be a failure of leading politicians and of the supervisory and regulatory agencies – that is, a failure of government policy – and however long-standing is the corruption, government should persevere with attempts at reform without changing the mode of ownership.

With hindsight it seems quite plausible that the greedy maximising of private income, which has been advancing in the cultural skirmishes of the post-war decades, is at the root of the malpractices in both sectors. If so, the leakages which the excesses tend to produce are inherent in both sectors, and the corruption of office-bearers and regulators must also be a powerful and tenacious tendency, as was noticed by Myrdal (1972: ch. 3). In that case, it seems that both paradigms are in error: one falls into the trap of supposing ingenuously that the official owners will be less prone to leakage than the private, of failing to ask questions about the nature of the corrupt and venal state, and the other makes the mistake of blaming the form of ownership for the inefficiency of state enterprises, while blaming state regulators for the inefficiencies of private enterprises. One view has misplaced confidence in the state, the other has misplaced confidence in the market.

Whether we are concerned with improving the flow of profit into new dynamic investment, or with 'efficiency' which in the new paradigm includes the static concept of labour productivity, any organisation which pays salaries and allowances in a totally undisciplined and unprincipled way must be inefficient, whether it is in the public or the private sector.

11.4.3 *Condition three: effective use of diverted savings*

The third precondition was that the public sector could translate its nationalised profits into growth by effective deployment of these funds. More precisely, the condition is that the aggregate IRR of investments financed by the new owners should be no worse than before the change. The statement of this condition was accompanied by a warning that if the then current policies persisted, this would not be the case. The public sector in Tanzania in 1969 was described as being constrained by wage controls and (less importantly) by costly training schemes. Neither of these requirements was imposed upon competitors in the private sector or overseas. It was forecast that this would deprive any organisation in the public sector of most of its most competent personnel and would transform it into a dull 'routinized unit, capable only of replication'. That warning, like the first, was not heeded in Tanzania. Indeed, this came sadly true in many countries. According to the recent initiative on African Capacity Building:

> Fiscal austerity has led not only to a decline in public sector real wages, but also to a narrowing of the already small differentials between management levels and lower-skill groups. Under these circumstances, many of the best public sector personnel have chosen either to devote less time to their official capacities, or to leave public service altogether. Over 10,000 trained Nigerians are reportedly now working in the United States. (World Bank 1991: 12)

It is interesting that the early warnings, and the recent criticisms, are of parastatal salaries that were controlled and set *too low*; this seems to contradict the second precondition, which was concerned with the savings ratio and suggested that they might be too high, causing a financial leakage. This seeming contradiction caused confusion at the time, not altogether dispelled today in discussions of the remuneration of public and private sector top officials.

The exclusive choice of the public sector rather than the private sector as a vehicle for wage restraint and other economic policies was an imitation of postwar British economic conduct, based on a 'commanding heights' concept. Although it was pointed out that if businesses are nationalised and then mandated to conduct their affairs with bland reference to the 'best commercial traditions' and in accordance with current wage-control legislation, there was no necessity to buy them in order to impose this mandate, but there was never any initiative taken to survey the full possibilities of modifying commercial behaviour within the private sector. The creation of ever more parastatals reflected the post-independence aspirations which had their own imperative, and in the 1980s this was allowed to go to absurd lengths. By 1989 employment in the Tanzanian public sector was triple what it had been in 1969, and effective performance by management had become extremely difficult.

The problem of handicapping the public sector by using it differentially as a means of implementing socio-economic aims can be interpreted as a problem of relations between public and private sectors. The handicapped sector loses out in the competition and its performance is inhibited. Asymmetrically, it is always the public sector which is chosen for this role. Attempts may be made to compensate for this competitive handicap by adjusting regulated prices, but for the national economy as a whole this does nothing to mitigate the effects of induced inefficiency.

11.5 The external policy effect: trade related services

East Africa in the mid-1960s still had hard currency reserves inherited from the colonial Currency Board, but as development took off, it was foreseeable that the external balance of payments would become a constraint. Agreements for the payment of compensation for nationalisation added to this problem, and attention turned to ways in which businesses which were taken into the state sector could assist in improving the balance of payments, by purposefully modifying their commercial practices. This was called the external-policy effect of nationalisation, but at the microlevel, it was a matter of commercial policy.

It was suspected, and later established by an extensive survey (Yaffey, 1975: ch. 3) that private sector importers exercised remarkably little commercial power when negotiating the prices which Tanzania paid for imported goods. They tended to act as mere agents, often contractually bound to accept unilaterally set prices, prevented from selling competing items, and lacking in price-comparison information. Asymmetrically on the export side, the typical exporter of primary produce was by and large a price-taker, with prices fixed mostly in London. The main import–export traders were subsidiaries of foreign companies with expatriate managers. There had been a deterioration in the commodity terms of trade since the Korean War, and the slump of the 1930s had demonstrated that a deterioration in the terms of trade could potentially go much further. It was reasonable to expect that purposeful price negotiation in the Tanzanian interest could only be undertaken by nationalised, entrepreneurial, restructured enterprises. The attention of the newly nationalised boards was drawn to these circumstances. In the State Trading Corporation and elsewhere, diligent efforts were made in the direction of achieving a positive external-policy effect.

Opportunities for commercial policy reform were particularly evident in banking, insurance, import–export trade, and shipping agencies, which were largely nationalised. These companies had been almost entirely in expatriate hands, aiming at the remittance of profits. Changes in the direction of trade aimed at reducing the dominant position of the former imperial power were discussed and some were implemented. Changes in banking practices, concerning the disposition of overseas reserves, were mapped out and implemented. Shipping was dominated by a cartel, the East African Shipping Conference, which set prices for the routes to Europe, circumnavigating Africa via Suez and via South Africa; the marginal cost for ships to call at Tanzanian ports on their way to Durban or Mombasa was small compared to full average cost, and prices therefore depended very much on the pre-nationalised power relationships. Efforts were made (unsuccessful as it turned out) to shift the outcome in Tanzania's interest while providing more equitable (and therefore more attractive) transit routes for landlocked Zambia and Burundi. For these specific reasons the services sector had special opportunities of contributing to the external-policy effect.

The trade-related services sector also acquired a crucial role with respect to the profit effect because in the case of banks and shipping agencies the earning powers were relatively large while the net capital employed (on which compensation for nationalisation came to depend) was characteristically very small.

These external-policy opportunities, not readily available under private ownership, are aspects of the old paradigm which were valid and are neither deconstructed or referred to by the new paradigm.

This suggests that, when developing countries embark on a privatisation programme, they will be more reluctant than developed countries to include parastatals engaged in services related to trade; and such statistical evidence as is available indicates that this is indeed the case, which supports the above analysis. Candoy-Sekse (Candoy-Sekse and Palmer, 1988) lists 1,492 privatisation measures adopted in eighty-four countries, whether completed, in progress, or planned at the time of compilation. The USA and a few other countries have to be excluded for lack of data. Of the remainder, the percentage in which the activity to be privatised was a service related to trade was 23 per cent, but within this, the figure for developing countries was considerably lower (see Table 11.1).

While this supports the hypothesis that developing countries are aware of the benefits of retaining this type of activity in the public sector, it does not signify that the costs and benefits have been established in full detail. The full exploration of the potential benefits of ownership change requires the development of new corporate strategic plans. That is an indication of the size of the task.

The calculation of compensation to the former private owners is a part of this. Either there is no compensation, or it is unknown until it is negotiated; the cost of reaching the settlement is chiefly consultants' fees which can be paid

Table 11.1 Classification of privatisation measures

	All countries (excluding USA)	Advanced countries (excluding USA)	Developing countries
Number of countries	83	18	65
Privatisations	1,492	317	1,175
Trade-related services	338	87 (27%)	251 (21%)
of which:			
Transport	122	31	91
Finance/insurance	101	30	71

out of overseas aid funds. Either way it does not in practice delay the decision making, although in principle the settlement figure (with its foreign element) might give a negative net benefit from the entire nationalisation programme. By contrast, estimation of the cost of settling with former public owners is relatively complex. Vuylsteke (1988: 139) reports the transaction cost of privatisation as including advisers' fees, underwriting and brokerage commissions, debt write-offs and conversions, tax arrear write-offs, pre-sale recapitalisations, severance pay, plant maintenance and occasionally rehabilitation, pension plan funding and sometimes retraining expenses. Discounts in offer prices are also regarded as transaction costs. This too does not in practice delay the decision making, although as before, in principle the settlement figure (with its foreign element) might give rise to negative net benefit from the entire privatisation programme.

Refusal to look at ownership reform in terms of the specifics of activities and in the light of the institutional factors, and with regard to the cost of compensation including transaction costs, is therefore indefensible in terms of logical economic analysis. It may be due to political expediency:

> Tomas Jezek, the minister for privatisation in the Czech republic, is a worried man ... Mr Jezek is responsible for processing more than 2,000 projects ... According to the original privatisation schedule, agreed a year ago, he had a month to consider proposals and counter-proposals – about four minutes per project. When the scale of the problem became apparent, he asked the federal finance minister Vaclav Klaus for more time. He was refused ... Mr Klaus, whose right-wing Civic Democratic Party is leading opinion polls in Prague has now denounced his former ally ... accusing him of a 'lack of loyalty' ... Mr Klaus said the timetable had to be followed for political reasons. (Greenberg, 1991)

The political demand for a rapid pace of ownership change without time for detailed planning or careful implementation is no doubt, in many cases, the result of external pressure. The World Bank is reported to have exerted such pressure:

> The strongest political asset of new teams and governments is often people's dissatisfaction with previous policies and their willingness to try something fresh – the honeymoon effect ... Thc key political task is to produce economic results before the honeymoon is over ... When the government moves quickly, it also reduces the opportunity for opposition to coalesce and helps increase the credibility of the reform. (World Bank, 1991: 58)

and 'although the Bank must rigorously avoid interfering in politics' (ibid.: 58) it may be found that: 'It has sometimes been politically useful to establish economic organisations of reform beneficiaries ... which also function as focal points for political support' (ibid.: 59). In Eastern Europe, Judit Kiss finds that: 'Instead of radical economic restructuring, including efficient privatisation, the new governments opt for quite counterproductive reprivatisation and restitution schemes' (Kiss, 1992: 21).

The bundle of nationalisations announced without proper preparation in the 1967 Arusha Declaration and its aftermath was strongly criticised in very similar terms at the time. Details of the package are in Kahama, Maliyamkono and Wells (1986: 31–2) and in Nyerere (1968: 231–56). The announcement of nationalisation of the commercial banks, made public on a weekday during banking hours and without prior technical preparation, was rumoured to have evoked a protest by the Minister of Finance. Nyerere himself wrote that: 'It was obvious to the Government that immediate action was required to bring uncertainty to an end, so that both private investors and the public at large knew exactly where they stood' (ibid.: 252), and privately said that very rapid action was needed to galvanise the Party and the people.

Thus ownership reform *in both directions* without detailed preparation has been justified on the grounds that it was politically necessary to move fast and dramatically. Considering the relative sizes of the Czech and Tanzanian economies, the Czech case seems far worse in terms of lost preparation time and the potential for local damage seems far greater in that there is no longer an important subsistence sector on which to fall back if the monetised economy is disrupted. Poland has taken a similar course.

It would be possible to provide an economic justification for this reckless lack of attention to specific situations if one made a Paretian assumption of perfect markets and perfect competition. If neither public nor private enterprises create quasi-rents affecting the external balance of payments, the external-policy effect will be negligible, and a broadbrush approach can then be justified. In the post-colonial dependency relationships of the 1960s no-one supposed that perfect competition, let alone perfect markets existed; the post-colonial distortions were acknowledged, and it was argued that ownership reform (nationalisation) would provide an opportunity for clawing back some of the external losses, as described above. In terms of the new paradigm, the aim is that ownership reform (privatisation) will provide an opportunity to improve competition and so diminish internal (and in the EC, regional) distortions in a Paretian sense.

To justify this latter policy it is not necessary to assume that perfect competition will result from privatisation. In terms of the neoclassical view of the world the minimum necessary assumption must be merely that there will be some net increase of welfare, in a Pareto-type closed economy. In terms of the 1960s thinking, by contrast, the minimum requirement is that, taking compensation and commercial restructuring into account, whatever shifts occur in the non-Pareto real world are likely to be positive in their net effect on the balance of external payments and on the internal rate of savings. Either of these conditions would justify an ownership change, if these two conditions were mutually exclusive, but clearly they are not.

The first of these, based on subjective welfare, is not intrinsically measurable and is therefore in a Popperian sense not a scientific hypothesis at all. But whether or not our analysis depends upon the expected consequences for the unmeasurable welfare, the proposition that ownership change (privatisation or nationalisation) will diminish price distortions by virtue of changes in market structures does require looking carefully into the specifics of price determination, before and after the change, both to achieve the practical implementation and for testing the theoretical hypothesis. The 'reform first, think second, fix it third' approach must be wrong.

Notes

1. Here we have statements of the form 'if $a > b$, government should sell' (Jones *et al.*, 1990: 16–17). There is no condition given under which government should buy. The implication is that if $b > a$, government should simply preserve the status quo. A more balanced approach would be to define a set of conditions under which government should privatise, another under which it should nationalise, and an intermediate range in which because of transaction costs it should do neither. The authors go on (*ibid.*: 17) to claim: 'If the nation is economically better off with the enterprise in private hands, then the government should be willing to pay something to accomplish this improvement. If it is neutral between funds in private and public hands, then it should be willing to pay anything, because the payment is in this case only a transfer and is welfare neutral.'
2. The author's own experience as a director of the State Trading Corporation after the Arusha Declaration in Tanzania (1967) bears this out.
3. One notes a contemporary parallel process of enterprise closures in Eastern Europe.
4. The paradigm referred to does not include the position, which, however, others take, that the state itself is the source of the problem. Evidently one cannot form a view on this without having some theory of the state.

References

Adam, C., W. Cavendish and P. S. Mistry (1992), *Adjusting Privatization: Case studies from developing countries*, London: Currey.

Bouin, O. and C.-A. Michalet (1991), *Rebalancing the Public and Private Sectors: Developing country experience*, Paris: OECD.

Candoy-Sekse, R. and A. R. Palmer (1988), *Techniques of Privatization of State-Owned Enterprises*, vol. 3, *Inventory of Country Experience and Reference Materials*, Technical Paper No. 90, Washington, DC, World Bank.

Greenberg, S. (1991), 'Prague ministers are at odds over privatisation pace', *Guardian*, 16 November, p. 8.

Hartley, K. and A. F. Ott (eds) (1991), *Privatization and Economic Efficiency*, Aldershot: Edward Elgar.

Jones, L. P., P. Tandon and I. Vogelsang (1990), *Selling Public Enterprises*, Cambridge, Mass.: MIT Press.

Jones, L. P., P. Tandon and I. Vogelsang (1991), 'Net benefits from privatization of public enterprises', in K. Hartley and A. F. Ott (eds), *Privatization and Economic Efficiency*, Aldershot: Edward Elgar.

Kahama, G., T. L. Maliyamkono and G. Wells (1986), *The Challenge for Tanzania's Economy*, London: Currey and Heinemann.

Kiss, J. (1992), 'All slaves to the past', *Guardian*, 21 February.

MacArthur, J. D. (1988), *Appraisal of Projects in Developing Countries*, for H.M. Government, Overseas Development Administration, London: HMSO.
Myrdal, G (1972), *Asian Drama*, London: Penguin Books (also Pelican edn 1977).
Nyerere, J. (1968), *Freedom and Socialism*, London: Oxford University Press.
Routh, G. (1989), *The Origin of Economic Ideas*, 2nd edn, London: Macmillan.
Squire, L. and H. L. van der Tak (1975), *The Economic Analysis of Projects*, Washington, DC: Johns Hopkins for the World Bank.
Vuylsteke, C. (1988), *Techniques of Privatization of State-Owned Enterprises*, vol. 1, *Methods and Implementation*, Technical Paper No. 88, Washington, DC: World Bank.
World Bank (1991), *African Capacity Building Initiative*, Washington, DC: World Bank.
Yaffey, M. (1969), 'The effect of nationalisation on current external payments', ERB Paper No. 69.2, Economics Research Bureau, Dar es Salaam: University College.
Yaffey, M. (1975), 'Aspects of trade theory, with reference to Tanzanian experience', unpublished dissertation, University of Sussex.

12

Mexico: Comparative performance of state and private industrial corporations

John Weiss

12.1 Introduction

During the 1980s the government of Mexico introduced major economic reforms aimed at stimulating greater efficiency, particularly in the industrial sector. A central part of this programme was based on the assumption that the ownership structure of industry was an important determinant of performance. This chapter attempts to test this by examining data on the 500 largest enterprises in the country over the period 1985–90. The next section considers government policy on ownership, and specifically the policies of privatisation and encouragement of private foreign investment. The third section considers alternative determinants of performance apart from ownership. The fourth section describes the methodology used to test for the significance of ownership, whilst the fifth section gives the results. The final section contains the conclusions.

12.2 Mexican government policy in the 1980s

A central premise of policy during much of the 1980s has been that ownership has had a significant impact on enterprise performance. This can be seen most directly in privatisation policy. Since the start of the de la Madrid administration at the end of 1982 there has been a move to reduce the size of the public sector. This policy accelerated after 1988 under the Salinas administration. In 1982, for example, there were 1,155 public enterprises under budgetary control and in total their operating financial deficit was 2.1 per cent of GDP. By 1989 there were only 379 public enterprises and by 1993 the figure had fallen to a little over 200. The financial position of these remaining enterprises turned from a deficit to a surplus in 1987, although in 1989 the state oil corporation (PEMEX), the largest single enterprise in the economy, was again in deficit.[1]

The dramatic reduction in the number of public enterprises was achieved through a combination of privatisation (direct sale to the private sector), mergers, liquidations, and transfers from central to local government. Table 12.1 shows the number of enterprises affected by these different mechanisms during the period 1988–90. The enterprises involved include airlines, the national telephone company and banks, and within manufacturing, chemical plants, truck producers, sugar factories and a steel company.

Official statements rationalise policy towards public enterprises in terms of strengthening public finances through the elimination of loss-making enterprises and the revenue raised by their sale. However, improvements in efficiency arising from a transfer to private ownership are also stressed (Hacienda, 1991).

Another aspect of ownership policy relates to the new position on private foreign investment. Mexican industry has been characterised by a relatively high foreign ownership for several decades (Jenkins, 1984). However, prior to the late 1980s, legislation imposed relatively strict controls on the extent of foreign ownership, with foreign equity holdings restricted to a minority share in much of the industrial sector. Since the late 1980s the official position has been far more welcoming than in earlier years. After legislation in May 1989 100 per cent foreign ownership is now allowed in all but selected reserved areas which total no more than 20 per cent of economic activity.[2] Although the Ministry of Foreign Trade retains a nominal control over foreign investment, investment up to US$100 million is approved automatically provided certain limited criteria are met, chiefly that foreign exchange inflows balance outflows over the first three years of operation. Projects above US$100 million or in restricted areas of activity require formal approval; however, in an attempt to speed up the process this will be automatic if a formal response is not received from the Ministry within 45 working days (Banco de Mexico, 1990). Motives behind this shift in policy are not always articulated explicitly, but in addition to a desire to attract foreign finance and technology there is also likely to be the view that foreign ownership will create improvements in economic performance, due, for example, to superior management techniques.

Table 12.1 Removal of state enterprises, 1988–90

	1988	1989	1990
Liquidation	117	103	76
Merger	10	10	5
Transfer[a]	5	3	3
Sale	72	54	54

Note: [a]To state government.

Source: Reported in *El Mercado de Valores*, no. 11, 2 June 1991.

12.3 Other influences on performance

Performance at the level of the firm can be measured in various ways and there is a considerable literature on the link between ownership and performance. Nonetheless, empirical studies have not by any means demonstrated conclusively that, for comparable sets of enterprises, private enterprises outperform state enterprises, or foreign outperform national. Other influences on performance that must be allowed for in any comparison include economies of scale, the structure of the market in which enterprises operate, and industry-specific technological trends.

The influence of economies of scale in lowering unit costs will vary between industries, but where they are significant within an industry one would expect performance to be superior for larger firms. There is a very considerable literature on the effect of market structure on firm behaviour and performance (Devine, Lee, Jones and Tyson, 1986). The hypothesis of this literature is that the degree of competition in the market will have a direct effect on performance, so that, in general, the more competitive is the market, the superior will be performance. Finally, individual firm performance is also likely to be influenced by general trends in the industry in which it is located, arising particularly from industry-specific technological innovation or demand shifts.

For Mexico the question of market structure has been examined in detail using data from the 1980 industry census (Casar *et al.*, 1990). As in many developing countries, manufacturing has a dual structure with relatively small-scale, low-technology producers coexisting with larger, high-technology, oligopolistic firms. Casar *et al.* (1990) identify what are termed 'competitive' branches, which are dominated by small-scale production and have low concentration ratios. Competitive industries account for around 25 per cent of manufacturing value added, with the remainder contributed by branches described as various forms of oligopoly. Table 12.2 gives a disaggregation of manufacturing by the categories used in the study, whilst Table 12.3 gives the formal definitions of these categories; for example, competitive industries have a four-firm concentration ratio of 27 per cent or below, more than 50 per cent of production from small-scale enterprises, and less than 2 per cent of total costs composed of advertising expenditure.

Concentration is a common measure of oligopoly and there is evidence that levels of concentration are higher in developing economies as compared with developed economies (Kirkpatrick, Lee and Nixson, 1984). For example, the four-firm concentration ratio for total manufacturing and for many branches is higher for Mexico than for the USA. However, Mexico's level of concentration in manufacturing is not particularly high by the standards of other Latin American economies (see Table 12.4).

Foreign firms are not distributed evenly within manufacturing, tending to be concentrated in oligopolistic activities, particularly involving differentiated products (as defined by the importance of advertising expenditure in total costs).

Table 12.2 Structure of the manufacturing sector, 1980

	Share of value (added %)	Average 4-firm concentration ratio (%)	Average number of workers[a]	Share of foreign firms in value (added %)
Concentrated[b] oligopoly	18.8	75.2	125	33.5
Concentrated and differentiated oligopoly	14.5	83.7	264	67.8
Differentiated oligopoly	11.5	38.7	75	34.6
Competitive oligopoly	30.4	41.3	52	24.0
Competitive industries	24.8	13.7	20	4.6
Total manufacturing	100.0	48.6	91	28.5

Notes: [a]Average per establishment.
[b]See Table 12.3 for formal definition of these categories.

Source: Casar *et al.* (1990), Tables 7.4 and 7.1.

Table 12.3 Criteria for classification of branches by competitive structure

	Concentration ratio[a]	Share of small enterprises[b]	Advertising expenditure[c]
Concentrated oligopoly (i)	>75%	0	<2%
or (ii)	>50%	<20%	<2%
Concentrated and differentiated oligopoly (i)	>75%	0	>2%
or (ii)	>50%	<20%	>2%
Differentiated oligopoly (i)	>50% <75%	>20%	>2%
or (ii)	>27% < 50%	0	>2%
or (iii)	<27%	<50%	>2%
Competitive oligopoly (i)	>50%	>20%	<2%
or (ii)	<75% >27%	0	<2%
or (iii)	<50% < 27%	<50%	<2%
Competitive industries	<27%	>50%	<2%

Note: [a]4-firm concentration ratio for production.
[b]Share of small enterprises (100 workers or less) in production.
[c]Share of advertising expenditure in total costs.

Source: Casar *et al.* (1990), Table 7.A.2.

This is illustrated in the last column of Table 12.2, which shows that nearly 70 per cent of production from the category 'Concentrated and differentiated oligopoly' comes from foreign firms. Furthermore, in the 1970s at least, foreign firms accounted for a disproportionately large share of manufactured exports, taking an estimated 50 per cent in 1974 (Jenkins, 1984: 115).

In relation to manufacturing performance various studies have attempted to explain the degree of competition (as proxied by concentration ratios) and

Table 12.4 Comparisons of concentration in manufacturing

	4-firm concentration ratio (%)	Year
Mexico	48	1980
Chile	50	1979
Colombia	62	1984
Argentina	43	1984
Brazil	51	1980
USA	43	1977

Source: Mexico and USA – Casar *et al.* (1990); Chile, Colombia, Argentina and Brazil – Frischtak (1989).

rate of profit in Mexican manufacturing. For example, for 1980, Casar *et al.* (1990) use OLS cross-sectional regressions to explain branch-level concentration ratios. They find conventional explanatory variables that capture barriers to entry to an industry to be significant: for example, various indicators of economies of scale, and capital costs for plants of minimum efficient size. Advertising costs, as a measure of product differentiation, and market size, are also significant. Less conventional variables relate to ownership; there is a significant positive relation between the degree of concentration and the share of foreign firms in a branch. The degree of concentration in the same branch in the country of origin of the foreign firms (proxied by US concentration) is also included and proves to be significant. Further, the share of public sector firms is also significantly and positively related to concentration. Thus for a given set of industry barriers to entry, concentration should be higher where there is a higher foreign and public sector presence.

A common finding in studies of the relation between market structure and performance in developed economies is that profit margins over operating costs, *ceteris paribus*, tend to be higher in more concentrated and, by assumption, less competitive branches. Application of a simultaneous equation pricing model to Mexican data for 1980 confirms a statistically significant positive relation between level of concentration in manufacturing branches and level of price–cost margin.[3]

Competition has an external as well as an internal dimension and in Mexico competition from imports is likely to have increased significantly after 1985 with the introduction of a far-reaching programme of trade reform. This involved lowering rates of tariffs on imports and a substantial reduction in the import licensing system, so that a significantly smaller proportion of locally produced goods was granted protection by licence restrictions on competing imports. To illustrate the degree of reform the trade-weighted average nominal tariff fell from 13 per cent in 1985 to 10 per cent in 1989, and the share of domestic production subject to licences on competing imports from 92 per cent in 1985 to around 20 per cent in 1990 (Weiss, 1992). At the level of manufacturing branches there is evidence that the actual or potential threat of import competition stimulated some modest gains in efficiency, particularly productivity growth, after 1985 (Weiss, 1992).

12.4 Methodology

In this study the model used to test for the influence of ownership on performance involves cross-sectional regression analysis of firm data. Changes in several indicators of performance are explained by a model including independent variables to capture the effects of scale, market structure and industry trends, as well as dummy variables to reflect the separate influence of ownership. The analysis is broadly similar to that of Boardman and Vining (1989) and Picot and Kaufman (1989), although these studies are across a range of countries and use slightly different variables. The hypothesis tested here is that ownership has a significant independent influence on performance.

The data used come from the magazine *Expansion* which publishes information on the 500 largest firms in Mexico on an annual basis. Data are given on sales, employment, assets and equity ownership. For this study only firms in the industrial sector (including mining) are examined. Unfortunately, not all firms appear in each consecutive year so that over the period 1985–90 full information is available on only around 100 industrial enterprises. Nonetheless their total activity is substantial, with sales in 1985 covering around 27 per cent of total industrial production.

Enterprise performance can be measured in a variety of ways. For example, using data at the 2-digit branch level to assess the impact of trade reform on performance, Weiss (1991) uses growth in labour productivity, total factor productivity and price–cost margins as indicators of performance. From the *Expansion* data on individual firms no information is available on operating profits per firm, so that it is not possible to calculate either profits, value added, or total factor productivity. For this reasons only three simple indicators are used here:

1. Sales at constant prices (SA).
2. Sales per worker at constant prices (SA/L).
3. Sales per unit of total assets at constant prices (SA/TA).

Logarithmic growth rates of these indicators are estimated with improved performance being a rise in each indicator. Although they are only approximate, one would expect that changes in these measures would be correlated with changes in more sophisticated indicators of performance. For example, if the share of value added in output is constant, changes in the approximate indicator sales per worker will equal those in the more appropriate measure value added per worker; similarly with constant technology, where the shares of labour capital and materials all remain constant, changes in sales per unit of capital will equal changes in total factor productivity.

The variables used to explain changes in performance are based on the four possible influences noted above: size; market structure; industry trends; and ownership.

For size, two alternative measures are used: total number of workers (*L*); and total assets (*TA*). Where the performance indicator is sales per worker (*SA*/*L*), *TA* is used to reflect size, and similarly where the indicator for performance is sales per unit of total assets (*SA*/*TA*), *L* is used for size. Both are tried alternatively with the indicator sales (*SA*). The expectation is that the size variables will be positively related to performance.

Industrial structure is reflected by two variables: four-firm concentration ratio (*CR*); and changes in nominal protection (*NRP*). These variables are available only at the level of 2-digit branches, so that each firm must be allocated to a particular branch for it to be linked with values of these variables.[4] The concentration ratio data refer to a single year 1980; however, the nominal protection estimates are available annually to allow changes over 1985–90 to be calculated.[5] Since high concentration is often linked with low levels of competition the expectation is that *CR* will be negatively associated with the performance indicators. Nominal protection estimates are used as a measure of trade liberalisation and exposure to foreign competition. Falling nominal protection implies increased foreign competition, so the expectation is that changes in *NRP* will be negatively associated with performance.

Since performance of individual firms may be influenced by industry-specific trends, for each firm the average performance for all firms in the 2-digit branch in which it is located is included as an explanatory variable (*AVSA*, *AVSA*/*L*, *AVSA*/*TA*). One would expect that the direction of change would be the same for the firm and branch-average indicators, and therefore that there would be a positive association.

Finally to test for the independent influence of ownership, two dummy variables are included separately. For firms where there is any government equity the dummy (*DVS*) takes a value of 1.0 (most state firms in the sample are wholly state-owned). For foreign firms the dummy (*DVF*) takes a value of 1.0, if the foreign-equity share is more than 25 per cent. If, as is implied by government policy statements, state ownership has an independent negative influence on performance, the coefficient on *DVS* will be negative and significant, whilst if foreign ownership has a separate positive influence the coefficient on *DVF* will be positive and significant.

The regression model can be summarised as

$$CHSA = f\,(L \text{ or } TA,\ CR,\ CHNRP,\ CHAVSA,\ DVS \text{ or } DVF)$$

$$CHSA/L = f\,(TA,\ CR,\ CHNRP,\ CHAVSA/L,\ DVS \text{ or } DVF)$$

$$CHSA/TA = f\,(L,\ CR,\ CHNRP,\ CHAVSA/TA,\ DVS \text{ or } DVF).$$

where *CH* refers to rate of change; *AV* refers to branch average; and all values

Table 12.5 Simple correlation coefficients

	TA	*L*	*CHNRP*	*CR*	*DVF*	*DVS*	*CHAVSA*	*CHAVSA/L*	*CHAVSA/TA*
TA	1.00								
L	0.47	1.00							
CHNRP	0.02	−0.17	1.00						
CR	0.26	0.16	−0.34	1.00					
DVF	−0.02	0.18	−0.06	0.01	1.00				
DVS	−0.03	0.04	0.07	0.09	−0.13	1.00			
CHAVSA	−0.20	−0.02	−0.47	0.02	0.21	−0.08	1.00		
CHAVSA/L	0.13	−0.21	0.13	0.22	0.09	0.12	0.27	1.00	
CHAVSA/TA	0.17	−0.05	−0.09	0.31	0.10	0.16	−0.01	0.40	1.00

are in natural logarithms. Table 12.5 gives simple correlation coefficients between the independent variables.

12.5 The results

The analysis is run over the period 1985–90, taking averages of 1985–6 and 1989–90 for the beginning and ending years. Table 12.6 reports the results.

In terms of growth of sales, as expected there is a positive, strongly significant, association between growth for a particular firm and the average growth for firms in the branch in which it is located. This significant branch-specific trend is found also for the other two performance indicators. Also, as expected there is a significant negative relation between growth of sales and changes in nominal protection, so that the faster-growing firms are in branches with greater than average exposure to foreign competition. Neither the size nor the concentration variables are significant, and both the alternative size variables have unexpected negative signs. For the two ownership dummies, that for state firms has a negative sign, but is not significant. The foreign dummy has a positive sign and is weakly significant at the 10 per cent level.

For the indicator growth of sales per worker, the branch-average variable is again strongly significant with the expected positive sign. Here neither the size, concentration nor nominal protection variables are significant. The state ownership dummy is again non-significant and in this case has a positive sign. The foreign ownership dummy has a positive sign and is once more significant, this time at the 5 per cent level.

Finally, for growth of sales per unit of total assets the branch-average variable is strongly significant with a positive sign. In this case the concentration ratio is significant with the expected negative sign, so that firms in branches with higher concentration and, by implication, less internal competition, had below-average performance. The size variable (number of workers) is almost significant at the 10 per cent level, with the expected positive sign. Nominal protection is not significant. Here neither of the ownership dummy variables

Table 12.6 Regression results: performance indicator

Dependent variables	Constant	*L*	*TA*	*CR*	*CHNRP*	*CHAVSA*	*CHAVSA/L*	*CHAVSA/TA*	*DVS*	*DVF*	R^2	*n*
CHSA	0.35	−0.01		−0.01	−0.78	0.25				0.14	0.19	107
	(2.21)[b]	(−1.03)		(−0.52)	(−1.75)[c]	(2.62)[a]				(1.83)[c]		
CHSA	0.36		−0.01	−0.01	−0.95	(0.23)				0.12	0.18	111
	(2.23)[b]		(−0.97)	(−0.50)	(−2.10)[b]	(2.37)[b]				(1.66)[c]		
CHSA	0.37	−0.01		−0.01	−0.72	(0.28)			−0.17		0.16	107
	(2.35)[b]	(−0.58)		(−0.40)	(1.59)	(2.98)[a]			(−0.81)			
CHSA	0.38		−0.01	−0.01	−0.88	(0.26)			−0.16		6.16	111
	(2.39)[b]		(−0.58)	(−0.42)	(1.95)[c]	(2.71)[a]			(−0.75)			
CHSA/L	0.18		0.01	−0.01	−0.32		−0.38			0.18	0.07	104
	(1.02)		(0.59)	(−0.92)	(−0.68)		(2.71)[a]			(2.01)[b]		
CHSA/L	0.26		0.01	−0.01	−0.41		0.40		0.07		0.04	104
	(1.45)		(0.55)	(−0.99)	(−0.85)		(2.83)[a]		·(0.29)			
CHSA/TA	0.44	0.01		−0.01	−0.43			0.61		0.12	0.19	107
	(2.45)[b]	(1.37)		(−2.33)[b]	(0.93)			(4.92)[a]		(1.42)		
CHSA/TA	0.47	0.01		−0.01	−0.42			0.64	−0.26		0.18	107
	(2.64)[a]	(1.64)		(−2.31)[c]	(−0.91)			(5.15)[a]	(−1.02)			

Notes: *t* ratios are in brackets.
[a]denotes significant at 1% level.
[b]denotes significant at 5% level.
[c]denotes significant at 10% level.

are significant, although the state variable has a negative sign, and the foreign variable a positive sign.

12.6 Conclusion

The proposition that economic benefits follow from privatisations is currently a central part of the so-called Washington consensus on economic reform. Privatisations may induce economic benefits through the following factors:

1. Greater efficiency in private as opposed to public enterprise, due, for example, to greater managerial autonomy and incentives.
2. Reduction in budget deficits and thus in any inflationary and distortionary cost arising from these.
3. Creation of a more dynamic enabling environment as a result of a shrinking state sector.

This chapter addresses only the first of these mechanisms and from this perspective finds no support for privatisation on economic efficiency grounds.

It must be recognised that it is difficult to draw definite conclusions from this type of analysis. The performance indicators used are clearly not what is desired theoretically, although their rates of change may be more useful than their absolute values. Also the explanatory power of the cross-sectional regressions is relatively low. Nonetheless, there is evidence that firm performance is influenced strongly by branch-specific trends, with some influence from market structure, as measured by either concentration or nominal protection. In terms of the influence of ownership, which is the main focus of this analysis, there is no support for the view that state ownership *per se* implies poor performance. If state firms have a poor performance by any of the three indicators, this can be explained by other factors, not by the fact that they have some state equity. There is the possibility, however, that what may be affecting the results is that the less well-managed state enterprises were liquidated or privatised before 1985 and do not show up in the sample. In this case the state enterprises that are included may be more efficient and less likely to show any independent ownership effect. This is nevertheless unlikely, since few privatisations took place before 1985. What is clear, however, is that the results give no support for privatisation of the remaining enterprises on efficiency grounds.

On the question of foreign as opposed to national ownership the results do support the view that foreign-owned firms outperform national firms in the same branch, after size differences are allowed for. This superior performance is most significant for the sales-per-worker indicator. In terms of the two strands of ownership policy, there is support for part, but not all, of the official strategy.

This general conclusion may be surprising in that it conflicts with much recent policy thinking. Nonetheless it is consistent with an alternative interpretation of recent economic problems in Mexico and elsewhere in the region: that the key negative role of the state was in terms of creating a 'soft budget economic regime', with public investment undertaken for the benefit of sectional private groups (Bacha 1992: 19). A wide-ranging reform of the public sector, including privatisation, is needed in these circumstances, as a prerequisite for effective macrostabilisation and wider economic reform.[6] In this context privatisation is required less for its narrow efficiency effects and more for a hardening of the government budget constraint and a deregulation of the state sector and the economy in general. It is perhaps within this broader context that Mexican privatisation should be viewed.

Notes

1. Data on the financial position and number of state enterprises are given in Banco de Mexico *Informe Anual* Mexico DF various issues and Hacienda (1991).
2. Reported in *El Mercado de Valores* Mexico DF 1 April 1991.
3. $$\underset{(3.41)^a}{CR = 0.18} + \underset{(2.31)^b}{0.04\,VAG} + \underset{(1.33)}{0.13\,MS} + \underset{(1.48)}{0.33\,ES} + \underset{(0.26)}{0.02\,KO} + \underset{(2.13)^b}{0.21\,INT} + \underset{(4.04)^a}{0.24\,FFS}$$

   $R^2 = 0.16$
   $n = 185$

   $$\underset{(5.77)^a}{PCM = 0.13} + \underset{(2.53)^b}{0.16\,CR} + \underset{(0.64)}{0.29\,ADV} - \underset{(-0.19)}{0.006\,KO} + \underset{(0.69)}{0.02\,MS}$$

   $R^2 = -0.02$
   $n = 185$

   where:
   CR is 4-firm concentration ratio;
   VAG is growth of real value added 1975–80;
   MS is share of imports in internal demand;
   ES is share of exports in domestic production;
   KO is capital–output ratio;
   INT is an index of technology;
   FFS is share of foreign firms in branch production;
   ADV is share of advertising costs in output value;
   PCM is price–cost margin defined as revenue minus operating costs over revenue.

   All variables are explained in Weiss (1991).

   Note: *t* ratios are in brackets.
   [a] significant at 1% level.
   [b] significant at 5% level.
4. *Expansion* gives an allocation of firms between branches; however, there is a potential problem where multiproduct firms are involved, since they may operate in more than a single branch. Sales figures per firm at current prices are deflated by the output deflator for the branch concerned from the national accounts. For total

assets the capital stock branch deflator comes from the price series produced by the Banco de Mexico and available on disk.

5. The concentration ratios come from ILET-INEGI (1988) and the nominal protection data from Ten Kate and de Mateo (1989) and unpublished data supplied by Adriaan Ten Kate.
6. Since 1990, for example, proceeds from privatisation have been placed in a Contingency Fund and used to reduce the size of the public debt, thus contributing to a government budget surplus through lower interest payments.

References

Bacha, E. (1992), 'Comments', in V. Corbo, S. Fisher and S. Webb (eds), *Adjustment Lending Revisited: Policies to restore growth*, Washington, DC: World Bank.

Banco de Mexico (1990), *The Mexican Economy, 1990*, Mexico DF: Banco de Mexico.

Boardman, A and A. Vining (1989), 'Ownership and performance in competitive environments: a comparison of the performance of private, mixed and state-owned enterprises', *Journal of Law and Economics*, **32**, April.

Casar, J., C. Marquez Padilla, S. Marvan, G. Rodriguez and J. Ros (1990), *La Organización Industrial en México*, Mexico DF: Siglo Veinteuno.

Devine, P., N. Lee, R. Jones and W. Tyson (1986), *An Introduction to Industrial Economics*, London: Allen & Unwin.

Frischtak, C. (1989), 'Competition policies for industrializing countries', mimeo, Washington, DC: World Bank.

Hacienda (1991), *El Nuevo Perfil de la Economía Mexicana*. Mexico DF: Ministry of Finance.

ILET–INEGI (1988), *Estadísticas Industriales*, Mexico DF: Instituto Nacional de Estadística Geográfica e Informática.

Jenkins, R. (1984), *Transnational Corporations and Industrial Transformation in Latin America*, London: Macmillan.

Kirkpatrick, C., N. Lee and F. Nixson (1984), *Industrial Structure and Policy in Less Developed Countries*, London: Allen & Unwin.

Picot, A. and T. Kaufman (1989), 'Comparative performance of government-owned and privately-owned industrial corporations: empirical results from six countries', *Journal of Institutional and Theoretical Economics*, **145** (2).

Ten Kate, A. and F. de Mateo (1989), 'Apertura comercial y estructura de la protección en México: estimaciones cuantitivas de los ochenta', *Comercio Exterior*, **39** (4).

Weiss, J. (1991), 'Impact of trade policy reform on industrial performance: Mexico country study', mimeo, report to Overseas Development Administration, ESCOR Committee, Bradford.

Weiss, J. (1992), 'Trade policy reform and performance in manufacturing Mexico: 1975–88', *Journal of Development Studies*, **29**(1).

13

Malaysia's privatisation experience

K. S. Jomo

13.1 Introduction

In the 1980s, privatisation was strongly recommended in most developing countries where key sectors had been dominated by public enterprises. In the early and mid-1980s, external price shocks led to a marked deterioration in macroeconomic performance, precipitating fiscal and debt crises. In this context, loss-making public enterprises have been seen or portrayed as a particularly conspicuous drain on government resources. Privatisation has often been touted as the best answer to the many problems of these varied public enterprises.

The following discussion deals primarily with the implications of the privatisation of such utilities and public services, rather than statist capitalist activities without any public welfare pretensions whatsoever, which, in any case, have not been the main target of privatisation in Malaysia.

By the early 1980s, the generally lacklustre performance of the Malaysian public sector, including many public enterprises, required a policy response. The real question, however, has been whether such inefficiencies are necessarily characteristic of the public sector, and hence cannot be overcome except through privatisation. If the current record of the Malaysian public enterprises is primarily due to the nature, interests and abilities of those in charge, rather than to the fact of public ownership, then privatisation in itself cannot and will not overcome the root problem. Also, while privatisation may increase enterprise efficiency in order to increase profits for the private owners concerned, such changes may not necessarily benefit the public or consumers on balance.

Since a significant portion of such activities are monopolies, privatisation will hand over such monopoly powers to private interests who are likely to use them to maximise profits. The privatisation of public services tends to burden the people, especially if charges are raised for the privatised services. Obviously, private interests are only interested in profitable or potentially profitable activities and enterprises. This may mean that the government will be left with unprofitable and less profitable activities. And this will worsen overall public sector performance. Public sector inefficiencies and other problems need to be overcome, but privatisation in Malaysia has primarily enriched the few with strong political connections to secure many of these profitable opportunities, while the public interest increasingly becomes vulnerable to private capitalists' powers and interests.

While most affected public sector employees have felt threatened by privatisation, many other Malaysians, fed up with the waste, inefficiency and corruption usually associated with the public sector, have been indifferent to, if not supportive, of this policy. Many Malaysians also associate the growth of the public sector with increased state intervention and the ascendance of Malay hegemony under the New Economic Policy (NEP), and see privatisation as a desirable policy change that would reverse these trends, which have apparently discouraged private investment, and thus slowed down growth. Some others identify state intervention with socialism and support privatisation as a measure to restore capitalist hegemony. While statist capitalism is not socialism, undermining the public sector, especially public services, through privatisation has important welfare implications for the people, especially public sector employees, consumers and the poor.

13.2 Privatisation in Malaysia

The Malaysian government was among the first to climb on the privatisation bandwagon, enthusiastically endorsed and promoted by the Bretton Woods institutions, particularly the World Bank. Two years after becoming Prime Minister in 1981, Dr Mahathir Mohamad announced the Malaysian government's own commitment to privatisation in 1983. Unlike the 'Look East' policy and the 'Malaysia Incorporated' concept – also associated with Mahathir's administration – which seemed to fade in significance by the mid-1980s, privatisation achieved new vigour, especially after the appointment of Daim Zainuddin as finance minister in mid-1984 and the deepening economic crisis of 1985–86. To be sure, Mahathir's own commitment to private – rather than public – enterprise began much earlier, reflected in his *The Malay Dilemma* (1970) and especially his *Menghadapi Cabaran* (1976; published in English translation as *The Challenge* in the mid-1980s). This unwavering commitment is all the more remarkable because of his two predecessors' commitment to public enterprise as the main vehicle for furthering national, especially ethnic Malay communal business interests.

From 1971, the Malay elite-dominated Malaysian government's New Economic Policy was committed to reducing poverty and inter-ethnic economic disparity, ostensibly to achieve national unity, understood primarily in terms of reduced inter-ethnic resentment. New statutory bodies, government corporations, government-owned or controlled publicly listed companies as well as government-owned or controlled private companies, all became means to achieve government objectives, including the NEP's corporate wealth redistribution target of increasing indigenous (Bumiputera) share ownership to 30 per cent by 1990 from 2.4 per cent in 1970. The NEP's Outline Perspective Plan for 1971–90 also envisaged the creation of a Bumiputera commercial and industrial community (BCIC), while the Fourth Malaysia Plan for 1981–85 expected Bumiputera 'trust agencies' to account for 83 per cent of Bumiputera share capital in 1990 (i.e. only 17 per cent – or 5.2 per cent of total share capital – was to be held by Bumiputera individuals). By 1990, however, Bumiputera share capital had risen to 20.3 per cent of total share capital, with trust agencies accounting for 6.3 per cent and individuals for 14.0 per cent (i.e. 31 per cent and 69 per cent of the Bumiputera share respectively). However, it should also be pointed out that various criticisms have been made about official share distribution data. Besides the valuation problem raised by using nominal or par values – which, it is claimed, especially underestimates the market value of Bumiputera corporate wealth – and underestimation owing to the use of nominee companies, the Malaysian government has not explained how share capital owned directly by the government and other bodies – such as Bank Negara Malaysia (the central bank) or the Employees Provident Fund – is categorised.

In 1985, two years after the privatisation policy was announced, and possibly in response to public criticism, the Privatisation Section of the powerful Economic Planning Unit (EPU) of the Prime Minister's Department issued its *Guidelines on Privatisation* (Malaysia, 1985) which outlined policy aims, modes of privatisation and the means for implementation. Since then, various laws have been reformed to facilitate the incorporation of government departments and agencies as public limited companies and to facilitate privatisation more generally. The government also commissioned the drafting of a privatisation masterplan, the main elements of which were announced in various fora in 1989 (e.g. Sheriff, 1991). The EPU (Malaysia, 1991a) finally published the *Privatisation Masterplan* (*PMP*) document in February 1991, after the October 1990 general election and before announcing its post-NEP (or post-1990) policy in the form of three key documents:

1. Mahathir's (1991) inaugural paper to the National Business Council entitled *The Way Forward*, now more popularly referred to as the 'Vision 2020' speech, declaring the intention for Malaysia to achieve 'developed country' status by the year 2020 (i.e. after three decades).
2. The *Second Outline Perspective Plan* (*OPP2*) (Malaysia, 1991b) for 1991–2000 for the National Development Policy (NDP) replacing the NEP.
3. The *Sixth Malaysia Plan, 1991–1995* (Malaysia, 1991c).

Hence, the *PMP* is regarded as one of four major programmatic documents issued in 1991 outlining Malaysian economic development policy in the foreseeable future. Claiming success for its privatisation programme thus far, the *PMP* announced the government's intention to 'expand and accelerate further the pace of privatisation process' (sic).

Malaysia's privatisation experience is now critically reviewed here, after which the main features of the *Privatisation Masterplan* are summarised.

13.2.1 *Privatisation experience*

Privatisation – or denationalisation – refers to changing the status of a business, service or industry from state, government or public to private ownership or control. The term sometimes also refers to the use of private contractors to provide services previously rendered by the public sector.

In Malaysia and elsewhere, privatisation has been identified with a broad range of processes including those involving ownership transfer of enterprises from the public to the private sector. Privatisation can be strictly defined to include only cases of the sale of 100 per cent or at least a majority share of a public enterprise, or its assets, to private shareholders. However, in Malaysia, it is often understood to include cases where less than half of the assets or shares of public enterprises are sold to private shareholders, and even cases where public enterprises are allowed to undertake activities previously monopolised by the state.

In Malaysia, when a public enterprise, legally formed as a government department or statutory authority, is privatised, this necessarily first entails corporatisation, or the formation of a limited company incorporated under the Companies Act. On the other hand, the privatisation of a public enterprise which has been constituted as a limited company would merely entail a transfer in share ownership from the public to the private sector without any change in the legal form of the enterprise.

In contrast to privatisation, which essentially only involves property rights, the broader concept of marketisation is widely believed to entail not only denationalisation, but also market liberalisation, involving greater competition. Privatisation is then expected to be accompanied by the relaxation or abolition of monopolistic practices, including statutory monopoly powers, such as those usually conferred on and enjoyed by public utilities. Privatised entities are thus expected to find themselves in competitive markets or environments.

Competition generally encourages more efficient behaviour among private entities or companies, in order to achieve both productive and allocative efficiencies. Enhanced efficiency is therefore conceived of as the result of the interaction between private ownership and the competitive environment. Hence a privatisation exercise which merely involves selling a portion of the shares of a public enterprise to the public, but is not accompanied by greater exposure to market forces, may not bring about desired efficiency increases. Conversely, efficiency gains may be achieved through other changes – for example, management reforms – without any change in ownership. Even improvements in capital resource allocation may be achieved by eliminating a soft budget constraint and strengthening management accountability – for example, through greater organisational transparency.

In the case of Malaysia, therefore, desired increases in efficiency may not be achieved through privatisation, since there has been little evidence of increased competition associated with privatisation. Some of the selected enterprises already privatised or expected to be privatised are natural monopolies, such as airlines, toll roads, public utilities and telecommunications. Thus, if privatisation merely involves transforming a public monopoly into a private monopoly, consumer welfare may well be adversely affected. Improved enterprise efficiency may not enhance consumer welfare, but may simply increase the monopoly profits accruing to the privatised enterprise.

Full or complete privatisation means a complete transfer of ownership and control of a government enterprise or asset to the private sector. In Malaysia, such privatisations are not the norm, the most prominent cases involving the North-South Highway, Kumpulan Fima and Peremba.

In the case of Malaysian Airlines (MAS) and the Malaysian International Shipping Corporation (MISC), privatisation has actually only involved partial divestment, with majority ownership and hence ultimate control still in the hands of the government, which remains the majority shareholder. Even if the government share should decline to less than half, in preparing some enterprises for privatisation the government has created a 'golden share', allowing it to retain control even with considerably diminished minority ownership.

In Malaysia, privatisation has officially referred to:

1. Sale or divestment of state concerns. The public service concerned usually has to first be incorporated legally as a public limited company to facilitate such a sale: for example, the establishment of Syarikat Telekom Malaysia Berhad on 1 January 1987 to take over the activities of the Telecoms Department (Jabatan Telekom) or the incorporation of Tenaga Nasional Berhad, taking over the National Electricity Board (Lembaga Letrik Negara).
2. Public issue or sale of a minority or even a majority of shares in a state-owned public company: for example, Malaysian Airlines System (MAS) in 1985 and the Malaysian International Shipping Corporation (MISC) in 1987.
3. Placement of shares with institutional investors: for example, the sale of about 5 per cent of MAS stock to the Brunei government in 1986.
4. Sale or lease of physical assets: for example, the lease of the Lady Templer Hospital to Rampai Muda in 1984.
5. Joint public/private sector ventures: for example, the establishment of Perbadanan Otomobil Nasional (Proton) in 1983, with 70 per cent held by HICOM, the Heavy Industries Corporation of Malaysia, and 15 per cent

each by two Mitsubishi companies, the Mitsubishi Corporation and the Mitsubishi Motor Corporation.

6. Schemes to draw private financing into construction projects: for example, North Port Kelang toll road bypass, the Jalan Kuching toll flyover and the North-South Highway, as well as the low-cost housing scheme 'privatised' since the mid-1980s.
7. 'Contracting out' public services previously provided within the public sector: for example, the contracting out of various local government authorities' activities, such as parking services and garbage disposal, Telecoms $2.5 billion telecommunications development projects (Kennedy, 1991), Port Kelang's container terminal services.
8. Allowing private competition where the public sector previously enjoyed a monopoly: for example, the launching of a third television channel (TV3) in 1984 owned by Sistem Televisyen Malaysia Berhad, now controlled by the New Straits Press Berhad, and controlled in turn by the UMNO-owned Fleet Group, and now by the UMNO-controlled Renong Bhd.

The Malaysian government has summed up its argument for privatisation as follows in its *Guidelines on Privatisation*:

> Privatisation has a number of objectives. First, it is aimed at relieving the financial and administrative burden of the government in undertaking and maintaining a vast and constantly expanding network of services and investments in infrastructure. Second, privatisation is expected to promote competition, improve efficiency and increase the productivity of the services. Third, privatisation, by stimulating private entrepreneurship and investment, is expected to accelerate the rate of growth of the economy. Fourth, privatisation is expected to assist in reducing the presence and size of the public sector, with its monopolistic tendencies and bureaucratic support, in the economy. Fifth, privatisation is also expected to contribute towards meeting the objectives of the New Economic Policy (NEP), especially as Bumiputera entrepreneurship and presence have improved greatly since the early days of the NEP and they are therefore capable of taking up their share of the privatised services. (Malaysia, 1985)

These arguments in favour of privatisation have been refuted on the following grounds:

1. The public sector can be more efficiently run, as has been demonstrated by some other public sectors: for example, in Singapore (Rodan 1989), Taiwan (Wade 1990) and South Korea (Amsden, 1989). Also, privatisation is not going to provide a miracle cure for all the problems (especially the inefficiencies) associated with the public sector, nor can private enterprise guarantee that the public interest is most effectively served by private interests taking over public sector activities. Also, by diverting private sector capital from productive new investments to buying over public sector assets, economic growth would be retarded rather than encouraged.

2. Greater public accountability and a more transparent public sector would ensure greater efficiency in achieving the public and national interest while limiting public sector waste and borrowing.
3. The government would only be able to privatise profitable or potentially profitable enterprises and activities because the private sector would only be interested in these enterprises.
4. Privatisation may postpone a fiscal crisis by temporarily reducing fiscal deficits, but it would not necessarily resolve it because the public sector would lose income from the more profitable public sector activities, and would be stuck with financing the unprofitable ones, which would undermine the potential for cross-subsidisation within the public sector.
5. Privatisation tends to adversely affect the interests of the public sector employees and the public, especially poorer consumers, which the public sector is more sensitive to.
6. Privatisation would give priority to profit maximisation at the expense of social welfare and the public interest, except on the rare occasions when the former and the latter coincide; hence, for example, only profitable new services would be introduced, rather than services needed by the people, especially the poor and politically uninfluential.
7. Privatisation exercises in Malaysia may not even pretend to achieve their other alleged advantages and benefits by invoking NEP restructuring considerations, supposedly to increase Bumiputera wealth ownership and business opportunities. With increased Bumiputera competition, where prior collusion cannot be arranged, it seems that political influence and connections have become increasingly decisive.

In many cases of privatisation in Malaysia, it is popularly believed that there are strong influences from private interests who try to determine what is to be privatised, in what manner and to whom. For example, Sapura Holdings commissioned a consultancy report by Arthur D. Little of Boston entitled 'The advantages and feasibility of privatising Jabatan Telekom Malaysia' in 1983 for the attention of the Malaysian government; with the benefit of hindsight, it is generally acknowledged that Sapura is undoubtedly the main beneficiary of the privatisation of telecommunications in Malaysia (Kennedy 1991).

Often, privatisation in Malaysia does not even involve the formalities of an open tender system, as sanctioned by the official 'first come, first served' policy by which the government justifies awarding privatisation opportunities to those who have supposedly first proposed the privatisation of a government property or activity. Instead, many beneficiaries are believed to have been chosen on the basis of political and personal connections.

For example, in 1986, it was announced that M$1.4 billion worth of water supply projects involving 174 schemes had been awarded to Antah Biwater without open tender. Though hailed as the nation's first privatised water supply project, the government will remain responsible for the operation and maintenance of the schemes. Antah Biwater – which is 51 per cent owned by the Negeri Sembilan royal family's Antah Holdings Bhd and 49 per cent owned by the British water supply and treatment group, Biwater Ltd – had in fact secured a turnkey contract with a British government financing arrangement thrown in as an aid package. It is anticipated that all the design and engineering work will be handled by Biwater – since Antah has no relevant engineering track record – at the expense of Malaysian engineers and consultants who have long handled such projects.

In December 1986, the Malaysian parliament passed amendments to the Official Secrets Act (OSA) which extended the definition of official secrets to include, among other things, government tender documents (even after completion of the tender exercise) and any other documents or material which ministers and public officials may arbitrarily deem secret or confidential. The classification of a document or other material as an official secret cannot be challenged in any court of law, while the amendments impose a mandatory minimum one year jail sentence for any OSA offence. Such legislation, accompanying the privatisation drive, further limits the already limited scope for meaningful governmental transparency and public accountability.

Privatisation is also supposed to free market forces and encourage competition in the economy generally, especially in the sectors concerned. But this is negated by the fact that potential beneficiaries have a common interest in getting the public sector to privatise services, which can be far more important. Not surprisingly, with the limited experience of privatisation thus far, there is already widespread concern about and some evidence of:

- the existence of formal and informal collusion (e.g. cartel-like agreements);
- possible patterns in bidding for contracts, suggesting collusion among bidders; and
- some companies enjoying special influence and privileged information, thus being able consistently to bid successfully for profitable opportunities from privatisation.

Some other adverse consequences of privatisation to be considered include the following:

1. Increased 'costs' to the public of reduced, inferior or costlier services: for example, the unit charge for local telephone calls was increased by 30 per cent just before STMB was incorporated.
2. The implications of two sets of services: for example, one for those who can afford privatised services and the other for those who cannot, and hence have to continue to rely on public services (e.g. medical services and education).
3. The effects of minimal investments by private contractors concerned with short-term profits.

4. Increased costs of living and poorer services and utilities – especially in remote and rural areas – due to 'economic costing' of services (e.g. telephone, water supply and electricity).
5. Reduced jobs, overtime work and real wages for employees of privatised concerns.
6. The deflationary consequences of fewer jobs or lower wages, or both.

13.2.2 *Privatisation masterplan (PMP)*

As of the end of 1990, according to the *PMP*, 37 privatisations had taken place since the announcement of the policy, of which 27 involved private interests taking over existing government entities, while the other 10 involved the construction of new infrastructure. The government had also approved another 18 privatisations, of which 7 are new infrastructure projects. This did not include government divestments since 1981 to transfer government equity to Bumiputeras, involving some 30 companies transferred to Permodalan Nasional Berhad and another 120 or so to private Bumiputera interests – which remain to be systematically documented. Also, minor privatisations – such as contracting out of services (e.g. security, cleaning and laundry) – are not included. Of the 27 privatisations, 17 involved ownership divestment by sale of equity or assets to the public, or by way of private placement and management buy-out; 2 involved leasing arrangements, 5 involved management contracts and 2 more a combination of sale and lease; also the Lembaga Letrik Negara (LLN, or National Electricity Board) was corporatised as Tenaga Nasional Berhad (National Power Ltd.) as a step towards privatisation. Of the 10 new infrastructure projects, 8 involved 'build-operate-transfer' (BOT) (to government after some time), while the other 2 involved 'build-operate' (BO) (for perpetuity).

The *PMP* considers four main modes of implementing privatisation, namely: sale of assets or equity; lease of assets; management contract; and 'build-operate-transfer' (BOT) or 'build-operate' (BO) new infrastructure.

However, the document also cites other examples of privatisation which have nothing to do with any of these: for example, the so-called privatisation of TV3 through issue of a licence for a private television broadcasting company, and contracting-out services. The *PMP* also mentions broad alternative methods, considerations and criteria for the valuation of assets for sale or lease – net tangible assets (NTA), price–earning (PE) ratios, discounted cash flows (DCF) – emphasising that only the latter two take account of potential earnings, which the *PMP* favours. Yet, there is no evidence that any of these methods have been strictly adhered to in determining the actual price (or lease rate) of privatised government assets. On the contrary, very substantial discounts (in the case of sales) and premiums (in the case of privatised infrastructure projects) seem to have been the norm, with the proportion apparently not unrelated to the political influence of the beneficiary. It is believed that the predominance of the (politically most influential) Malays among public sector employees, the presence of relatively large unions in the big public utilities earmarked for privatisation, the virtual halt to public sector employee recruitment as a result of the post-election austerity drive since June 1982, and the virtual public sector wage freeze since 1980 (despite considerable inflation, especially in the early 1980s), encouraged the government to ensure employment security for five years and better service terms and conditions as inducements to workers not to resist privatisation. Hence, though workers can choose not to join the privatised entity, very few do so; the vast majority have yet another option – of continuing with the government's scheme of service or accepting the new company's scheme – which most tend to select.

The government has had to legislate many changes to existing laws to facilitate privatisation. The primary concern, however, has been with overcoming legal obstacles to privatisation. Little attention has been given to ensuring greater competition or public or consumer accountability, which are matters of considerable concern since many of the privatised entities remain virtual monopolies. Since the *PMP* acknowledges that there is not much scope for increasing competition with natural monopolies, it promises an appropriate regulatory framework to protect consumer interests, particularly in terms of price, quality and availability of services, as well as 'commercial freedom' for private monopolies. Implicit in this formulation is the acknowledgement that such regulation does not yet exist, and, if introduced, is unlikely to threaten enterprise autonomy. While privatisation undoubtedly exerts heavy demands on private sector financial resources to mobilise both debt and equity capital, it is not self-evident that deepening and broadening the Malaysian capital market are desirable in themselves. On the contrary, it has been suggested that with privatisation, capital resources – which might otherwise have been invested into expanding productive capacity – have instead been diverted into acquiring or transferring existing public sector assets. The *PMP* reiterates the government's intention to advance Bumiputera corporate participation through ethnically preferential privatisation. This is expected to include collaboration between Bumiputera institutional investors and others as well as management buy-outs (MBOs) and employee share ownership plans (ESOPs). The *PMP* also promises an institutional mechanism to ensure sustained Bumiputera participation after privatisation. Anticipating public objections, the *PMP* advocates minority (no more than 25 per cent) foreign investments in privatised entities where:

- foreign expertise is needed and local expertise is not available;
- foreign participation is crucial for export market access and promotion;
- international linkages and exposure are required by the business;
- the supply of local capital is not sufficient to buy up the shares offered.

An interesting innovation proposed by the *PMP* is the establishment of a special fund to finance related expenses such as feasibility studies, preparing candidates for privatisation and disbursing compensation related to privatisation.

To motivate staff, the *PMP* recommends employee share ownership as well as other incentives. However, it acknowledges that such schemes have not benefited poorer employees very much, while loyalty and commitment to the company have been undermined by the subsequent sale of shares. To overcome these problems, the *PMP* recommends Employee Share Ownership Plans (ESOPs) for future privatisations, involving the establishment of a trust to hold shares for employees who will only be able to sell them when they retire or resign. The *PMP* also recommends management as well as management-cum-employee buy-outs, i.e. MBOs and MEBOs. The *PMP* also proposes a Privatisation Action Plan (PAP) consisting of a two-year 'rolling plan' reviewed at the end of each year, identifying the targets for privatisation and for preparation for eventual privatisation in the following years. According to the *PMP*, 424 government-owned entities (GOEs) were studied by private consultants to determine the desirability and suitability of their privatisation. The consultants identified 246 as privatisable, with 69 to be privatised within two years, 107 in two to five years and the balance after five years; but the government has deemed some of this number not suitable for privatisation on various grounds.

The government also claims to be considering others not covered by the study for possible privatisation. Such government-initiated privatisations are supposed to be subject to competitive bidding. According to the *PMP*, however, the government is still prepared to consider private sector-initiated privatisation if it is convinced that no other private sector party can privatise a particular project, as in the following circumstances:

1. The proposer offers a unique cost-effective solution to an economic problem or potential savings to the government.
2. The proposer has unique possession of certain technical know-how or patent rights essential to the proposal.
3. The privatisation would not be viable on its own as its viability is dependent on another component possessed by the proposer.

Although still open to abuse, if strictly interpreted, these criteria represent a significant departure from the earlier 'first come, first served' policy, which has still not been unequivocally rejected.

The *PMP* claims to be influenced by both feasibility and desirability criteria in determining priorities for privatisation. Feasibility is, in turn, said to be determined by both ease of privatisation and attractiveness to the private sector, whereas desirability seems to be defined by the government's perception of private sector superiority. Using a 2×2 matrix, the *PMP* distinguishes the following four categories of candidates:

1. *Immediate privatisation* candidates will be the main focus in the early years of the PAP as they rank highly on the feasibility and desirability criteria.

2. *Priority restructuring* candidates are deemed to require preparation (e.g. restructuring) for privatisation despite the government's desire to privatise them.
3. *Back burner* candidates are deemed feasible for privatisation, though the benefits of privatisation are considered to be less than self-evident.
4. The *consider future* candidates rank poorly on both feasibility and desirability criteria.

The PAP also distinguishes six different categories of candidates for privatisation requiring different treatment, as follows:

1. *Flagships* – comprising GOEs of national importance, in terms of size and complexity, thus meriting special treatment (such as JTM and LLN) – are to be privatised over several years, usually at the rate of one per annum.
2. *Easily privatisable government majority-owned companies*, especially in manufacturing and agricultural production, are most likely to be given priority for privatisation.
3. *Restructuring candidates* mainly refers to unprofitable companies needing financial and operational restructuring; however, the government prefers to minimise pre-privatisation restructuring, which usually involves financial aspects.
4. *Services* previously protected from commercial competition are to be deregulated and privatised in the consumer interest.
5. *Listed and minority share holdings* are to be given low priority since the private sector is already quite involved.
6. *New projects* – usually involving infrastructural development – are to be privatised on a BOT basis.

To facilitate implementation, the PAP distinguishes those ready for privatisation from those requiring preparation (e.g. most flagships). The stages required for their preparation may include:

1. commercialisation (e.g. raising user charges, commercial accounting and commercial performance criteria); and
2. legal corporatisation;

and other changes at this stage before actual divestment may also include:

3. replacing bureaucratic administration with profit-oriented management;
4. replacing centralised production-oriented decision making with market-driven consumer preferences; and
5. introducing clear financial and operational performance criteria and commercial accounting.

While the *PMP* admits that 'it is still too early to make an assessment of the effectiveness of the privatisation programme', it nonetheless claims several significant achievements, as follows:

1. *Efficient gains* The *PMP* cites four examples:
   (a) reduction of average vessel turnaround time at the Kelang port container terminal from 11.7 hours to 8.9 hours two years after privatisation;
   (b) improvements in television broadcasting with greater competition after the licensing of a private third television channel, TV3;
   (c) improved telecommunication services since the corporatisation of STM in 1987;
   (d) completion of the Labuan water supply project ahead of schedule.

2. *Stimulus to growth* The *PMP* claims privatisation has stimulated economic growth by providing greater opportunities to (and thus motivating) the private sector, generating multiplier effects (e.g. TV3's stimulus to the domestic film making and advertising industries), compensating for the decline in public expenditure and encouraging private entrepreneurship.
3. *Reducing governmental responsibilities* The *PMP* claims a significant reduction in the government's administrative and financial burden due to privatisation, citing the reduction of the public sector workforce by 54,000, of whom 29,000 were Telecoms employees. One-off proceeds from the sale of government properties came to M$1.18 billion, while recurrent revenues are expected from taxation and leases (e.g. Kelang Container Terminal); meanwhile, the government's tax burden has been reduced as privatised companies take over loan refinancing. The *PMP* also claims that privatising new infrastructure projects has saved the government M$8.2 billion, while other capital spending (development expenditure) commitments have been significantly reduced.

4. *Redistribution* Since most privatisations have involved at least 30 per cent Bumiputera participation, the policy is said to have furthered the NEP's inter-ethnic wealth redistribution objectives. The *PMP* also claims that privatisation has enabled the government to spend more on poverty alleviation although there is no real evidence of this.

13.3 Concluding remarks

Despite the *PMP*'s claim that privatisation is 'premised on the superiority of market over administrative directives in governing economic activity to achieve efficiency' and that the 'Government's intervention in the economy will be minimal', actual deregulation efforts are well behind those of privatisation. While there has been a great deal of rhetoric about deregulation accompanying privatisation, such efforts have been quite limited and mainly oriented to inducing foreign investments. And in many instances, especially with public utilities, the government has retained effective control despite changes in ownership. Privatisation in itself only involves the transfer of property rights, and in many instances in Malaysia (e.g. the privatisation of large public utilities and management buy-outs), management personnel have not even been significantly changed.

Improvements in management generally reflect management initiatives encouraged by increased enterprise and administrative autonomy as well as new incentive systems – that is, changes which do not require privatisation as a prerequisite, but can alternatively be achieved by greater decentralisation, devolution or administrative authority. These changes have long been advocated by trade unions (e.g. see Mustapha Johan and Shamsulbahriah, 1987) and others in the public sector, which became increasingly centralised in the early 1980s with the Cabinet Committee Report on new salary structures for the public sector, chaired by then Deputy Prime Minister Mahathir, and the later centralisation of authority over the public sector, in the Prime Minister's Department under Mahathir, especially through the strengthening of the Public Services Department (JPA). Also, the so-called Non-Financial Public Enterprises (NFPEs), or Off-Budget Agencies (OBAs), were less subject to the Treasury's budgetary discipline, especially after then Finance Minister Tengku Razaleigh Hamzah challenged Mahathir's preferred candidate (Musa Hitam) for the ruling party's deputy leadership, and traditionally, the deputy prime ministership as well.

If one accepts the view that it is competition and enterprise reorganisation – rather than mere changes in ownership status – which are likely to induce greater enterprise efficiency, then it becomes difficult to conclude that economic efficiency has been improved because of privatisation in Malaysia. Some of the – often exaggerated – efficiency gains have been brought about by greater employee and managerial motivation with new incentive systems and greater scope for managerial initiatives with administrative autonomy and can hardly be attributed to privatisation *per se*. The advocates of privatisation in Malaysia have not been honest in presenting a full and balanced record of what has happened with privatisation. Instead, anecdotal claims have been selectively advanced to imply that the Malaysian experience has been an unqualified success, as in the *PMP*. The existence of mistakes or negative consequences and implications is not acknowledged, in order to avoid their recurrence. While the policy makers or those in charge presumably know better, the *PMP*'s failure publicly to consider the failings bears ominous implications about how the policy has been formulated, adopted and implemented.

While the *PMP* undoubtedly represents an advance, at least on paper, over some of the most blatant abuses of early Malaysian privatisation policy, especially the 'first come, first served' policy, it offers little ground for comfort about the future of privatisation in Malaysia, especially in light of what has taken place and seems likely to occur in the foreseeable future. While privatisation undoubtedly reduces the role of the public sector in the economy, it is not clear whether this is an end in itself or merely the means to an end. If the former, then the policy is essentially intended to aggrandise its politically influential beneficiaries, or is clearly ideological in inspiration, or is meant to please the ideologically motivated governments and powerful international economic institutions (such as the World Bank and the Asian Development Bank) the Malaysian government seeks to find favour with. There is evidence that all three factors may be operative in the Malaysian case.

Advocates of privatisation in Malaysia, including the *PMP*, also claim that it will reduce the government's financial and administrative burden. While there undoubtedly are one-off revenues for the government from the sale of public assets, it is not self-evident that the retention of such assets would not have been in the government's and the public's medium- and long-term interest for a variety of reasons mentioned above. Perhaps most importantly, the considerable evidence of heavy discounting in asset prices for sale or lease suggests otherwise. Also, the sale of the government's most valuable assets, while it is obliged to retain those less profitable activities and assets of little interest to the profit-seeking private sector, contributes to the self-fulfilling prophecy of the unprofitability of public sector economic activities. The diminution of the public sector also reduces the scope for government intervention, for example, for equity reasons or in support of industrial policy.

The *PMP*'s claim that privatisation contributes to growth is vague and even spurious. After the announcement of the policy in 1983, Malaysia went through a deep recession in 1985–86, before experiencing rapid manufacturing-led growth since the late 1980s. Although the mid-1980s recession was exacerbated by the deflationary consequences of public spending cuts, which can be analytically distinguished from privatisation *per se*, there is also no clear evidence that privatisation in particular has significantly contributed to recent economic growth. No claim has yet been made that privatisation is a necessary and indispensable ingredient for the broader economic liberalisation measures of the mid-1980s that probably induced the foreign investment increase associated with the recent boom. On the contrary, it may be argued that private acquisition of public assets has probably diverted potential investment funds, while it is now generally agreed that the stock market – undoubtedly expanded by privatisation – has not been important for corporate financing of the dynamic foreign-dominated manufacturing sector.

Privatisation in Malaysia might be said to have been most successful in contributing to the government's NEP objective, particularly Bumiputera wealth acquisition, though it should be emphasised that wealth concentration levels are very high and strongly related to political influence and access. One might even argue that the prioritisation of this objective has probably seriously undermined achievement of the other stated aims of its privatisation policy. However, it is unclear how the creation and distribution of substantial economic rents through ethnically-biased privatisation have been in the national interest, whether this is understood in developmentalist or equity terms. There is now official acknowledgement that most of these rents have not been efficiently deployed through productive investments to significantly accelerate industrialisation or to consolidate genuine Bumiputera entrepreneurship. Instead, much has been wasted on rent-seeking costs associated with political involvement in business, while the very source of such rents and the limited abilities of those who control them have contributed to their deployment in real property, construction, finance and other investments with a short-term time horizon, thus adversely affecting investment priorities and activities generally in an economy officially committed to sustained manufacturing-led growth. The foregoing analysis also implies that privatisation is unlikely to enhance the NEP's other equity objectives (e.g. inter-ethnic parity in occupational and employment distribution, poverty reduction), and may instead undermine public welfare as a result of the strengthening of private monopolistic interests.

In the increasingly authoritarian and centralised Malaysian polity, with public accountability and governmental transparency considerably diminished deliberately by those in power, the strengthening of private business interests, especially of those who are politically well connected, is very likely to transform, and even increase, rather than eliminate the opportunities for rent appropriation. Ironically, the remaining democratic features of the system in such a context may well serve to sustain rent-seeking behaviour and costs.

This is not intended to legitimise further authoritarianism to reduce such waste. Rather, it serves to emphasise that enhanced public accountability, governmental transparency and other democratic safeguards are crucial for reducing rents – which can still be productively deployed – and, more importantly, rent-seeking behaviour in the context of privatisation.

Instead of transferring or selling off activities and enterprises which have not been well run by the public sector, the government seems to be doing exactly the opposite. The better-run public sector activities and enterprises are being privatised, leaving the public sector with the poorly run loss-making remainder. The result will only further strain government revenues and appears to confirm the charges of public sector ineptitude, while enriching those well placed to gain from the privatisation exercises. This process has included and is expected to continue to involve the transfer of public monopolies into private hands, without adequate safeguards to protect and ensure the public interest after privatisation. Current policy also seems to fail to recognise that it is rarely privatisation *per se* that enhances efficiency, but rather competition. Also, the problems of poor management and inefficiency in the rest of the public sector have not been addressed by such a privatisation policy.

Instead, Malaysia's mixed economy can be reformed by other more equitable and desirable means. Public sector activities and enterprises directly competing with the private sector may be privatised, especially if they are poorly managed or draining public resources. To ensure that Bumiputera interests are not undermined in the process, privatisation could well involve management or leveraged buy-outs and other similar devices without incurring further loss of revenue, but without the huge 'subsidies' characterising earlier privatisations. In some cases, where little interest is shown, the enterprises involved may well have to be shut down as they were probably set up for dubious reasons in the first place.

However, where public sector enterprises and activities have been well run and properly managed, the government should not privatise for its own sake – that is, for ideological reasons – as this is not necessarily in the public interest. For the public monopolies and social services, particularly, privatisation should be avoided, though management reforms and greater competition are probably desirable, if not urgent. If such activities have been less than well run, organisational reforms should be instituted to enhance performance. In this regard, the public sector as a whole must be reorganised to allow for greater flexibility and variation than is permitted by current rules and regulations, as well as to reward initiative, productivity and performance.

Hence, this objection to privatisation does not recommend complacency or inaction with regards to problems of the public sector. Reforms are certainly urgently needed, and there is no single or simple solution to the varied problems of the public sector, as implied by some advocates of privatisation. The experience of some other countries, for example, neighbouring Singapore, has clearly demonstrated that the public sector can be run well and flexibly. Reforms towards this end are urgently required.

The current obsession with privatisation also has the unintended consequence of postponing or otherwise putting aside the urgent need for public sector reform. The privatisation of some public sector activities and enterprises will do little to improve the situation in the unaffected remainder of the public sector. Moreover it conveys the wrong impression that these problems can only be overcome by privatisation. The current eagerness to privatise also ignores the problems of market failure, better recognised in earlier times.

Malaysia's experience thus far suggests that the government-revenue-generating, government-deficit-reducing, private-sector-control-increasing, and capital-market-deepening official objectives of Malaysian privatisation have largely been subordinated to the ostensibly Malay-wealth-enhancing objective through rent redeployment, particularly to the politically well connected. The privatisation policy's multifarious objectives undoubtedly require various trade-offs, but the apparently consistent bias suggests serious abuse for the purposes of political patronage and personal aggrandisement at the expense of the other objectives of privatisation, ostensibly in the national interest.

There should instead be a comprehensive critical review of the public sector, including the statutory bodies and other public enterprises, with a view to reform in order to enhance efficiency and cost-effectiveness, as well as dynamic, equitable, balanced and sustainable national economic development. Such a critical review should consider the variety of modes of privatisation, marketisation and other reform measures as options in dealing with the public sector as it has evolved in Malaysia. In such an approach, privatisation becomes one among several options available to the government for dealing with the undoubted malaise of the Malaysian public sector. This flexible approach seems superior to the current, narrow and dogmatic approach which apparently views privatisation as the only – and presumably best – solution to a complex variety of problems faced by the Malaysian public sector.

This existing approach also tends to neglect the persistent problems faced by the rest of the public sector not targeted for privatisation, which may in fact require more urgent attention. Ironically, their problems are probably the most serious – and hence in greater need of remedy – which may explain the lack of private sector interest in privatising them. Furthermore, if successful on its own terms, the existing approach is likely to saddle the public sector with the most uneconomic, unprofitable and unattractive activities, thus only confirming prejudices and charges of public sector incompetence and inefficiency, besides worsening the public sector deficit with the loss of possibilities for cross-subsidisation.

Unfortunately, however, there does not seem to have been any significant progress in checking the various problems which have emerged from the privatisation process thus far, or in avoiding them with future privatisations. The entire privatisation process itself seems to be beyond accountability, and the lack of transparency hampers the few who might feel inclined towards, or rather would dare risk, speaking out against the present situation. The significant increases in consumer prices for privatised or soon to be privatised utilities, services and infrastructure have been reluctantly accepted by consumers without much public dissent, except in the case of the Cheras tolls just before the 1990 general election. The staggered nature of such price increases as well as of the privatisations themselves render mass protest against privatisation most unlikely.

However, when the cumulative effects of these privatisations are finally realised at the public level, it is quite possible that the political consequences may undermine the mandate to rule of those responsible.

References

Amsden, A. (1989), *Asia's Next Giant: South Korea and late industrialization*, New York: Oxford University Press.

Jomo K.S. (1990), *Growth and Structural Change in the Malaysian Economy*, London: Macmillan.

Kennedy, L. (1991), 'Liberalization, privatization and the politics of patronage in Malaysian telecommunications', paper presented at the 41st Annual Conference of the International Communications Association, Chicago, Ill., 24 May.

Mahathir, M. (1970), *The Malay Dilemma*, Singapore: Donald Moore.

Mahathir, M. (1976), *Menghadapi Cabaran*, Kuala Lumpur: Penerbit Utusan Melayu.

Mahathir, M. (1991), *The Way Forward*, Kuala Lumpur: ISIS.

Malaysia (1985), *Guidelines on Privatisation*, Kuala Lumpur: Economic Planning Unit.

Malaysia (1991a), *Privatisation Masterplan*, Kuala Lumpur: Economic Planning Unit.

Malaysia (1991b), *The Second Outline Perspective Plan, 1991–2000*, Kuala Lumpur: Economic Planning Unit.
Malaysia (1991c), *Sixth Malaysia Plan, 1991–1995*, Kuala Lumpur: Economic Planning Unit.
Mustapha Johan, A. and K. A. Shamsulbahriah (eds) (1987), *Penswastaan: Kebajikan pekerja atau untung kapitalis*, Kuala Lumpur: MBPBK.
Rodan, G. (1989), *The Political Economy of Singapore's Industrialization*, London: Macmillan.
Sheriff, M. K. (1991), 'Privatization: performance, problems and prospects', in L. K. Hock and S. Nagaraj (eds), *The Malaysian Economy Beyond 1990*, Kuala Lumpur: Malaysian Economic Association.
Wade, R. (1990), *Governing The Market: Economic theory and the role of government in East Asian industrialization*, Princeton, NJ: Princeton University Press.

14

Has privatisation improved profitability and performance of the public enterprises in Turkey?

Cevat Karatas*

14.1 Introduction

In Turkey, the initial impetus towards privatisation sprang from dissatisfaction with the performance of the public enterprises and the belief that transfer of state-owned enterprises to the private sector would improve their economic efficiency. In subsequent stages other policy aims, namely, raising finance for government expenditure, widening share ownership, and development of the capital markets in Turkey, became more prominent.

In particular, privatisation came to be seen as a policy instrument that was likely to be superior, in terms of the promotion of economic efficiency, to alternatives that were based upon the preservation of state ownership. The policy propounding sale of state assets rests on a belief that private ownership will lead to a more efficient use of those assets. However, it is difficult to establish the general validity of this proposition (Yarrow, 1988: 2). It is even claimed that privatisation may not be the proper policy option in order to raise extra revenue for the Treasury because it may be cheaper to raise additional revenue through taxation or sales of government bonds. Similarly, the experiences of some developing countries have shown that privatisation may not be the best available approach for encouraging wider share ownership. Therefore it becomes logical to argue that success of privatisation policies is likely to be judged in terms of their contribution to improvement of industrial performance.

In this context, this chapter will focus on the financial and economic performance of some of the privatised public enterprises in Turkey, namely, Teletas (switchboard equipment), USAS (airport service), Citosan (cement),

---

*The author is deeply indebted to Colin Kirkpatrick, Memet Kaytaz and Erdogan Özötün for clarifying some of the estimation problems in the chapter. The views expressed in this chapter are those of the author.

Petkim (petrochemicals), Erdemir (steel-iron), Tüpras (refinery) and other public participations in which the state is an important shareholder. Over the past three years there has been increasing public concern about quality and about the financial and economic performance of the above listed corporations. Therefore, the main objective of this chapter is to shed some light on the actual performance of the privatised public enterprises.

14.2 Privatisation practice in Turkey

14.2.1 *Background*

The privatisation programme which was completed by Morgan Guaranty Trust in 1986 has aimed to increase the industrial efficiency and growth in the economy, to develop the capital markets in Turkey, to reduce the financial support for the state economic enterprises (SEEs) by the Treasury, and to facilitate a wider distribution of share ownership. The lowest ranked objective of privatisation was to raise revenue for the Treasury (Morgan Guaranty, 1986: 16; Heper, 1987: 10).

In this section, the full list of activities whether completed or in progress are summarised and illustrated in successive tables in order to show the sequence of privatisation and the sales proceeds of public enterprises and public participations. Table 14.1 sets out the date of sale, proportion of shares sold and divestment mode applied in the course of privatisation.

Tables 14.1 and 14.2 illustrate the total proceeds from the sale of public assets in terms of domestic currency value. The total value of sales proceeds resulting from Teletas, Citosan, Petkim, Erdemir, THY, Migros, Tüpras, Petrol Ofisi, Gima and a number of other enterprises and subsidiaries has amounted to over TLt 1 trillion by 14 June 1991 (see Table 14.1). However, if proceeds from the block sales which reached TLt 458.7 billion are added, then total sale proceeds would increase to TLt 1.5 trillion ($211.8 million) by 13 March 1992 (see Table 14.2).

Table 14.3 is prepared in order to provide the necessary information related to products, turnover, gross profits and number employed in large privatised enterprises.

14.2.2 *Recent privatisations*

During the course of 1989 the government's privatisation programme was basically focused on the participation of foreign investors. Sumerbank and Petkim which are engaged in the manufacture of textiles and petrochemicals respectively were also identified as serious candidates for divestiture. However, it should be noted that the privatisation programme driven primarily by the

Table 14.1 Turkish central government: public sector divestment: 1988–92

Corporation or holding[a]	State share transferred to PPA (%)	Divestment date	Buyer or divestment mode	Shares offered for sale (%)	Proceeds (100 TLt)
Teletas (switchboard)	40.00	29.2.1988–2.3.1988	public offer	22.00	15,399,995
Erdemir (steel-iron)	51.53	9.4.1990–10.4.1990	public offer	2.93	132,392,537
Kepez Electric (electricity)	43.68	16.4.1990–17.4.1990	public offer	8.14	23,457,024
Cokurova electric (electricity)	25.45	16.4.1990–17.4.1990	public offer	5.45	96,995,475
Arcelik (electrical appliances)	15.00	30.4.1990–1.5.1990	public offer	5.83	50,162,080
Bolu cement	35.33	30.4.1990–1.5.1990	public offer	10.38	20,851,860
Celik-Halat (steel cables)	29.38	30.4.1990–1.5.1990	public offer	13.25	19,545,564
Petkim (petrochemicals)	99.97	18.6.1990–29.6.1990	public offer	7.83	384,462,812
Konya cement	39.87	24.10.1990–25.10.1990	public offer	31.13	48,619,750
Unye cement	49.21	1.11.1990–2.11.1990	public offer	2.86	2,570,500
Mardin cement	46.23	22.11.1990–23.11.1990	public offer	25.46	25,463,750
Turkish airlines (THY)	100.00	29.11.1990–7.12.1990	public offer	1.55	13,925,250
Adana cement (A)[b]	23.86	18.2.1991–19.2.1991	public offer	17.16	79,128,900
Adana cement (C)[b]	23.42	18.2.1991–19.2.1991	public offer	17.16	8,792,100
Migros (chain store)	42.22	25.2.1991–26.2.1991	public offer	36.40	18,199,200
Afyon cement[c]	99.59	25.3.1991–26.3.1991	block sale	39.87	29,899,650
Ditas (spare parts)	14.77	6.5.1991–7.5.1991	public offer	2.51	864,500
Nigde cements	99.83	13.5.1991–14.5.1991	block sale	12.72	10,494,000
TUPRAS (refinery)	100.00	27.5.1991–29.5.1991	public offer	1.64	24,278,800
Petrol ofisi	100.00	27.5.1991–29.5.1991	public offer	4.025	57,863,200
GIMA	49.81	3.6.1991–4.6.1991	public offer	4.15	1,660,900
TOFAS Turk Auto plant	23.13	13.6.1991–14.6.1991	public offer	0.85	25,809,600
TOFAS Auto Trade[c]	39.00	13.6.1991–14.6.1991	block sales	1.36	4,075,200
Total					1,094,912,647

Note: [a]Public share sold to the public is calculated on the basis of corporation's total capital.
[b]Adana cement (A) and (C) group shares were simultaneously sold by one-to-one basis.
[c]Some state shares in Afyon cement and TOFAS Auto Trade were previously sold by block sales.

Source: PPF (1992: 12), 1984–1992, p. 12.

Table 14.2 Privatised public corporations through block sales, 1989–92

Privatised corporation	Government share (%)	Sold share (%)	Buyer	Divestment dates	Sales proceeds (TLt m.)
USA	100.00	70.00	SAS service partner	9.2.1989	32,014.8[a]
Afyon cement	99.59	51.00	SCF[c]	9.5.1989	30,371.4[b]
Ankara cement	99.30	99.30	SCF	9.5.1989	77,097.0[b]
Balikesir cement	98.30	98.30	SCF	9.5.1989	53,733.7[b]
Pinarhisar cement	99.90	99.90	SCF	9.5.1989	58,406.8[b]
Soke cement	99.60	99.60	SCF	9.5.1989	25,699.3[b]
TOFAS Auto Trade	39.00	16.00	Fiat Auto SPA	22.2.1991	42,204.8
Nigde cement	99.83	87.10	OYAK-Sabanci	13.3.1992	139,216.5
Total					458,744.3

Note: [a] TLt 32.014.8 million which is worth $14.450 was received. Also, for 10 years, 21% of net profits (after tax) will be paid to Public Participation Authority (PPA).

[b] Sales revenue from privatisation of five cement plants was $105 million of which $85 million was paid in advance, and the remaining $20 million was paid a year after their sale. In the meantime, 40% of shares of Ankara, Balikesir, Pinarhisar and Soke cement plants will be sold to the public within 5 years.

[c] SCF: Société Ciment des Français.

Source: PPF (1992: 12).

Table 14.3 Major characteristics of privatised enterprises

Corporation	Sector	1989 (TLt bn.) Turnover	1989 Gross profits	1989 Number employed	1990 (TLt bn.) Turnover	1990 Gross profits	1990 Number employed
State economic enterprises and subsidiaries:							
USAS A.S.	Airport service/catering						
Petkim	Petrochemicals	582.0	80.7	3,470	2,577.8	348.6	7,297
Sumerbark	Textiles/banking	–	–	–	–	–	–
Erdemir	Iron–steel	1,937.2	699.6	8,349	2,236.6	603.4	8,595
Tüpras	Refinery	9,818.3	1.7	–	16,460.5	275.0	4,830
Citosan	Cement						
Afyon Cement		38.0	15.4	–	71.4	29.5	–
Ankara Cement		42.7	13.4	–	98.1	27.9	–
Balikesir cement							
Pinarhisar cement							
Soke cement							
Participations:							
Teletas	Telecommunications/ switchboard	182.4	37.0	1,479	432.5	53.7	1,718
Netas[a]	Telecommunications	198.3	2.9	1,779	503.8	42.1	1,733
Arcelik	Electrical appliances	1,268.0	83.6	3,426	2,375.1	286.5	3,434
Cokurova electric	Electricity	434.4	155.3	1,249	683.3	138.7	1,475
Celik-Halat	Steel cables	76.9	14.9	508	107.6	19.5	513
TOFAS Turc	Automotive	938.7	181.9	4,262	2,086.2	461.0	5,712

Note: [a]It was included in 1990's privatisation agenda. The state share in Netas is about 50%.
Source: ISO (Istanbul Chamber of Industry) 'Turkey's 500 large industrial establishments', in *Journal of Istanbul Chamber of Industry*, 22 August 1991, pp. 4–28; 22 August 1990, pp. 4–8. Also, Afyon Cement Co, accounts, 1992, and Ankara Cement Co, accounts, 1992.

participation of foreign investors, generated pronounced political opposition from both labour unions and private business.

In the second half of 1990, about 8 per cent of Petkim shares which had a nominal capital of TLt 2 billion, was offered for sale to the public through various local branches of Isbank in the country. The proceeds from the public sale of Petkim shares amounted to TLt 384.4 billion, while the number of domestic shareholders increased to 75,933 (*Yeni Ekonomi*, 1990: 8; Karatas, 1992: 9). It should be noted that, of this sale, shares worth TLt 22.5 billion were bought by the employees working at Petkim plants. Since August 1990, there have been some efforts to sell shares of Petkim on the Tokyo, London and New York stock markets.

Sumerbank, on the other hand, is considered to be one of the most efficient and profitable enterprises in the public sector, hence the benefits to be derived from privatisation has been questioned in various circles. Sumerbank (textiles, bank, retail outlets) has been converted into a 'bank holding' under PPF, but this has complicated its legal position. Consultant reports have almost been completed, but no positive decisions have yet been taken towards its privatisation (Kjellstrom, 1990: 14).

In May 1991, Turkish Petroleum Refinery (Tüpras) which provides almost 87 per cent of Turkey's petroleum requirements was nominated for partial privatisation. In May 1991, 1.64 per cent of Tüpras' shares and 4.02 per cent of Petrol Ofisi shares which controls 60 per cent of fuel marketed in Turkey were sold through offer to the public (*Yeni Ekonomi*, May 1991; PPF, 1992: 12). Privatisation proceeds amounted to TLt 24.2 billion in the case of Tüpras and TLt 57.8 billion in the case of Petrol Ofisi (see Table 14.1). Apparently, the employees and pensioners of both Tüpras and Petrol Ofisi were able to buy only the shares of the corporation they worked for or retired from.

Tüpras' turnover (at current prices) reached TLt 10.2 billion in 1990 and its net profits amounted to TLt 14 billion in 1988, TLt 1.7 billion in 1989 and showed an upward trend reaching TLt 207 billion in 1990 (*Yeni Ekonomi*, May 1991: 1–4). Petrol Ofisi recorded a spectacular financial performance over the same period. Its net profits showed a steady increase, reaching TLt 55.7 billion in 1988, TLt 139.9 billion in 1989 and TLt 199.4 billion in 1990 (*Yeni Ekonomi*, May 1991: 4). It should be noted that the remarkable performance attained by these monopolistic enterprises (Tüpras and Petrol Ofisi) can be largely attributed to higher prices charged by them for their products, and the accounting adjustments introduced in anticipation of later sales. It is often claimed that performance gains which were recorded cannot be attributed to improvement in their internal efficiency. On the contrary, a widely shared view is that both of these corporations are in need of radical changes in their management, production techniques and pricing policies.

Other public enterprises and public participations which were partially privatised are illustrated in Table 14.3.

During the second half of 1991, the Motherland Party (ANAP) which was then in power had continued to display a strong commitment in favour of its privatisation programme, despite severe objections raised and voiced by TUSIAD (corporate business association) and the Social Democratic Populist Party (SHP) particularly against direct sales to foreign investors (Onis, 1991: 247). It should be noted, however, that during the second half of 1991 the focus of divestiture of public assets was on sales via the capital market rather than to foreign investors through block sales.

Subsequent to the general election held in October 1991, the Suleyman Demirel government (a coalition between True Path Party and Social Democratic Populist Party) came to power. This new government has embarked upon a set of reforms aimed at a number of structural problems, such as unsatisfactory performance of state economic enterprises (SEEs) and the exceedingly high rate of inflation, which was primarily caused by public sector deficit financing. One of the chief aims of the newly elected government was to reduce both the level and scope of public expenditure. Therefore privatisation became an important item in the agenda of the new government and the new strategy was largely based on the norms of the free-market economy.

The privatised corporations and sale of state shares in the mixed corporations in the first three months of 1992 are illustrated in Table 14.4. Apparently, the total value of sales proceeds resulting from Tat Konserve (food/beverages), Camsan Agac (timber industry), Caybank (banking), Ipragaz (liquid gas) and Nigde Cimento (cement) is approximately TLt 553 billion. With the inclusion of this figure, total sales proceeds resulting from privatisation had reached almost TLt 2 trillion in April 1992 (PPF, 1992: 12).

14.3 Performance evaluation

In recent years, because of the wave of privatisation in developed and developing countries alike, a number of research works have concentrated on the analysis of performance of public and private enterprises using the criterion of productive efficiency (Millward, 1988). Yet there is an intractable difficulty in conducting

Table 14.4 Privatised enterprises and sales proceeds: first three months of 1992

Company	Public share sold (%)	Buyer	Total proceeds (TLt m.)
Tat Konserve	17.27	Koc Holding	41,440
Camsan Agac	26.83	Gokhan Poyraz	8,000
Caybank	49.00	Dervis Temel	13,500
Ipragaz	51.00	Primagaz	350,000
Nigde cement	87.10	Koc Holding + OYAK	140,000
Total			552,940

Source: *Hurriyet*, national newspaper, 27 March 1992, p. 5, also Sarsel (1992: 19).

comparisons between public and private sector enterprises due to the fact that an analyst is unable to isolate the effect of ownership on productive efficiency from factors such as scale of operation and product mix (Cook and Kirkpatrick, 1988: 5). It is therefore difficult to generalise that public enterprises' performance is inferior to similar enterprises in the private sector. In the Turkish case, it has been emphasised that the economic performance of public enterprises has been poor but, at the same time, they have been found to have the potential to achieve considerable improvements in efficiency.[1]

Evidence indicates that private enterprises are more subject to market discipline than public enterprises. In other words, competitive market conditions may force the management of private enterprises to be more efficient in both resource allocation and productivity than the management of public enterprises. It is often claimed that the management of private companies holds a relatively large degree of financial autonomy to undertake economic activities; while the public enterprise management is provided with limited financial autonomy and power.

In attempting to estimate performance one faces the difficult question of what criteria to use in the evaluation. Perhaps the best that can be done is to examine dimensions of performance that are of relevance to a more general evaluation, while recognising that no single measure is likely to be of decisive importance. For instance, profitability may be a key measure of success for a firm operating in a competitive market that is free of externalities, but it cannot be so regarded in cases where the firm enjoys an important monopoly power (Vickers and Yarrow, 1988: 143).

For performance evaluation of privatised enterprises in Turkey, it is necessary to study the performance of privatised corporations in terms of efficiency gains and improved productivity, and to test the claims that privatised enterprises have improved their profits because of freedom to pursue commercial objectives and to adjust themselves to a competitive environment. An attempt will be made in this chapter to shed some light on the actual performance of the privatised enterprises in the 1988–1991 period.

At the outset there are some immediate difficulties to be confronted in evaluating the effects of privatisation on the financial performance of these industries. First, it is a plain knowledge that only a few years have elapsed since the sale of public assets. Secondly, it may be argued that the pre-privatisation period to some extent involved laundering of figures by capital reconstructions, which may reduce the comparability of performance figures in the pre- and post-sale periods.

Two alternative profitability ratios are used to measure the financial returns to the new management of the privatised corporations. These are: rate of return on sales revenue (ROSR) (profit-to-sales ratio) and rate of return on total net assets (ROA). Owing to lack of data, rate of return on equity (ROE) has not been included in this analysis. The profits-to-sales ratio (ROSR) measures the rate of profit accruing per unit of sales revenue of privatised enterprises. On the other hand, ROA is the quotient of management profit to total assets. The ROA measures the rate of profits resulting from the use of funds in the purchase of both fixed and current assets (Sankar, Thak and Sal, 1988: 22–3).

However, it is important to note that all financial profitability ratios share the following shortcomings. First, they do not take into account the social objectives of public enterprises. Second, in non-competitive market conditions high financial profits may not genuinely reflect an efficient enterprise operation, but may simply result from 'above normal profits' being made because of the firm's monopoly powers. Third, financial profits fail to take into account the implicit subsidies like tariff concessions granted to the public enterprises. Therefore, while financial performance may be indicative of private enterprise efficiency, it should be used with some reservation in evaluating public enterprise performance.

14.3.1 Financial performance of the privatised enterprises

It is extremely difficult to measure improvements in performance as a result of corporatisation and privatisation. First, as already noted, only a short period of time has passed following the privatisation of public enterprises between February 1988 and June 1991. There is also the difficulty of separating out the effect of institutional change from other background factors. Second, it is a difficult task to obtain data on a consistent and comparable basis pre- and post-privatisation. Third, it is difficult to remove the financial effects of balance sheet restructuring and measure changes in quality of inputs and outputs (Bollard and Mayes, 1991: 23). Finally, differences in market outlook, competition and regulation are other factors which might affect performance. In view of all these difficulties, caution is needed in interpretation of turnover and profitability figures, listed in Table 14.3, for twelve large companies which have been partially or wholly privatised.

From Table 14.5 it can be seen that Teletas's turnover and profit-to-sales ratio (ROSR) showed a significant jump between 1989 and 1990, the former increasing from TLt 110.0 billion to TLt 169.0 billion and the latter (profit margins) from 2.95 per cent in 1986 to 20.29 per cent in 1989 and 12.42 per cent in 1990 (at constant prices). It is noticeable that Teletas's turnover continued to record a considerable growth in the post-privatisation period (1989–90); while its profitability (profit-to-sales ratio) registered a positive growth in 1989 (20.29 per cent) but slightly lower growth (12.42 per cent) in 1990. The 1986 figures for Teletas relate largely to a period where the company was still in the public sector. It is evident that a considerable improvement in profitability of Teletas has occurred in the post-privatisation period.

In fact a similar performance has also occurred in the case of Petkim (petrochemical) and Erdemir (iron-steel) where the profitability of the former increased from 4.38 per cent in 1983 to 7.23 per cent in 1986 (at constant prices),

Table 14.5 Real turnover (TLt bn) and profit margins (%) 1983–90 (at constant 1988 prices[a])

	Pre-privatisation		Post-privatisation	
	1983	1986	1989	1990
State economic enterprises				
Teletas				
Turnover	–	192,859,400	110,089,220	169,048,330
Profit margin (%)	–	2,9500	20.29	12.42
Netas				
Turnover	69,319,313	273,129,500	119,723,590	157,803,370
Profit margin (%)	34.38	8,3700	14.80	10.42
USAS				
Turnover	–	–	–	–
Profit margin (%)	–	–	–	–
Petkim				
Turnover	495,947,710	283,070,700	1,053,419,400	1,007,384,600
Profit margin (%)	4.38	7,2300	28.65	13.52
Yemsan				
Turnover	92,290,640	116,520.200	134,668,670	105,095,380
Profit margin (%)	5.05	4,2000	−6.73	−14.13
Citosan				
Turnover	–	–	–	–
Profit margin (%)	–	–	–	–
Erdemir				
Turnover	789,188,100	–	1,169,153,200	874,033,130
Profit margin (%)	4.98		36.11	26.97
Tüpras				
Turnover	–	–	5,925,378,900	6,432,401,300
Profit margin (%)	–	–	1.82	1.67
Participations				
Arcelik (electrical household)				
Turnover	–	–	751,465,900	928,148,880
Profit margin (%)	–	–	6.70	12.06
Cokurova Electric (electricity)				
Turnover	–	–	262,206,390	267,030,200
Profit margin (%)	–	–	35.75	20.30
Celik-Halat (steel-cables)				
Turnover	–	–	46,439,400	42,070,183
Profit margin (%)	–	–	19.38	18.12
Tofas Turc (automotive)				
Turnover	–	–	556,521,420	815,274,050
Profit margin (%)	–	–	19.73	22.09

Note: [a]Turnover and gross profit figures are converted to 1988 constant prices by use of GNP deflator.

Source: Calculated from data given in various tables in ISO (Istanbul Chamber of Industry), 'Turkey's 500 large industrial establisments' (1984, 1987, 1990 and 1991 issues).

while in the latter case profitability was 4.98 per cent in 1983 and rose to 36.11 per cent in 1989. It is, however, clear that in the post-privatisation period (1989–90) Petkim's turnover more or less remained at the same level while its profit margin had shown a remarkable increase (i.e. rate of profit rising to 28.65 per cent in 1989 and 13.52 per cent in 1990) (see Table 14.5). However, the same things cannot be said for Erdemir where turnover showed a considerable decline, but profitability recorded a significant increase both in 1989 and 1990 (rising to 36.11 per cent and 26.90 per cent respectively). Surprisingly, Yemsan (animal feed) has shown dramatically low and negative performance in the post-privatisation period. In the case of Petkim and Erdemir it is likely that profitability improvement was perhaps due to rehabilitation of these corporations rather than the partial privatisation which took place.

Reviewing the turnover and profit margin figures of Tüpras (petroleum refinery), we can observe that it has recorded relatively poor performance as compared to other enterprises.

The public participations (joint ventures) in which the state is an active shareholder have shown notable performance as compared to fully state-owned enterprises. For instance Arcelik (electrical household) represented financial profitability of 6.70 per cent in 1989 and 12.06 per cent in 1990, while Cokurova electric (electricity) which is a joint venture recorded an impressive profitability in 1989 (35.7 per cent) even though this dropped to 20.30 per cent in 1990 (see Table 14.5). In the meantime, Celik-Halat (steel cables) showed profit-to-sales ratio of 19.38 per cent in 1989, which more or less remained at the same level in 1990.

Perhaps the most striking financial performance was registered by Tofas-Turc-Auto (automotive), where turnover increased from TLt 556.5 billion to TLt 815.2 billion over the defined post-privatisation period. Meanwhile profitability of Tofas had shown a steady increase throughout (rising from 19.7 per cent to 22.0 per cent over the same period) (see Table 14.5).

Table 14.6 shows turnover and profitability figures for Citosan's five privatised cement plants which were bought in January 1989 by Société Ciment des Français, a French company.[2]

Citosan's five privatised cement plants had registered good performance in 1983 and 1986, with the exception of Ankara cement plant. All the remaining plants showed a near or above 20 per cent rate of profitability. More specifically, it can be inferred from Table 14.5, that in the post-privatisation period (1989–90), profitability of Ankara cement and Balikesir cement plants was negative, while profitability of Afyon cement had shown a steady increase throughout. The profit-to-sales ratio of Afyon cement plant increased from 15.4 per cent in 1989 to 16.09 per cent in 1990 (at constant prices). Negative profitability of Ankara cement and Balikesir cement was dramatically low both in 1989 and 1990.

In terms of the rate of return on net assets (ROA), the privatised cement plants, with the exception of the Ankara plant, showed an impressive profitability of over 50 per cent in 1986 during the pre-privatisation period. Hence, due to Citosan's observed high rate of profitability, privatisation of these plants was accomplished with great ease and as expected the bidding (block sales) attracted a large number of domestic and international firms, including Société Ciment des Français.

It is clear, however, that in the post-privatisation period (1989–90) the

Table 14.6 Financial performance of CITOSAN's privatised cement plants, 1983–90 (TLt m., at constant 1986 prices[a])

	Pre-privatisation		Post-privatisation	
Corporation	1983	1986	1989	1990
Ankara cement				
Turnover	10,943	18,190	133,334	19,261
Profit-margin (%)	−29.3	7.83	−15.80	−3.21
Profit-net assets ratio	−40.49	17.99	−30.41	−8.44
Balikesir				
Turnover	9,067	11,780	10,512	17,276
Profit-margin (%)	14.90	35.18	−12.59	−1.45
Profit-net assets ratio	18.75	53.45	−17.55	−4.06
Afyon cement				
Turnover	8,390	11,004	11,589	13,822
Profit-margin (%)	0.60	19.89	15.40	16.09
Profit-net assets ratio	1.70	54.48	46.94	49.29
Soke cement				
Turnover	5,993	6,579	–	–
Profit-margin (%)	1.50	21.60	–	–
Profit-net assets ratio	4.56	52.03	–	–
Pinarhisar cement				
Turnover	n.a.	n.a.	–	–
Profit-margin (%)	n.a.	n.a.	–	–
Profit-net assets ratio	n.a.	n.a.	–	–

Note: [a]All figures are converted into 1986 constant prices by use of GNP delfator.

Source: Calculated from data given in ISO (Istanbul Chamber of Industry), 'Turkey's 500 large industrial establishments', October 1987, pp. 4–32; special issue, 15 October 1984, pp. 4, 5, 6, 8; 22 August 1991, no. 306, pp. 4–28; 22 August 1990, no. 294, pp. 4–8.

turnover of Citosan's three cement plants had shown a significant increase, yet profits-to-net assets ratios (ROA) were dramatically negative both in 1989 and 1990, the only exception being Afyon cement which recorded net asset profitability of 46.9 per cent and 49.2 per cent respectively in the post-privatisation period (see Table 14.6). We are, however, unable to comment on the profitability of Soke and Pinarhisar cement plants due to lack of consistent statistical data.

It should be noted that the five privatised cement plants are already operating in competitive markets. Therefore an evaluation of performance was rather straightforward as internal efficiency changes can be traced by using some measure of financial profitability.

The Ozal and the subsequent ANAP (Motherland Party) governments were extremely liberal in attitude towards deregulation and their objectives were pro-competition. However, in the case of USAS which was sold to SAS (Scandinavian company), public monopoly power seems to have been transferred to a private monopoly without imposing pro-competitive measures.[3] Admittedly, for effective competition it is essential to have several airport service companies capable of competing with each other. Under the present circumstances, SAS faces little competition in airport and airline service and therefore seems to enjoy an advantage of privileged access to most airports in Turkey. In view of the weak competition from Celebi (a small airport service company), SAS does enjoy a strong market power and will have significant cost advantages.

It is often reported unofficially that SAS has been rather successful in promoting the quality of its airport services and increasing its operational profits since it took over in February 1989. SAS has also managed to reduce the size of its manpower in order to increase labour productivity. Data are not available on SAS; therefore, it is difficult to comment on its actual performance over the last three years. The government should promote competition in the airport service industry and introduce safeguards against anticompetitive behaviour by SAS which inherited an important monopoly power.

14.3.2 *Productivity performance*

In order to assess the internal efficiency of the privatised enterprises, it is necessary to base the analysis on one or more of a variety of productivity indices. The principal approaches have often been adopted in order to analyse labour productivity (output or value added per head) or total factor productivity.

In this section, attention will focus on the productivity of public enterprises which have been privatised during the last few years (1988–1991). It is important to note, however, that with respect to comparisons with privately owned industries, because of variations in markets and technologies it is obviously difficult to make efficiency judgements on the basis of observed productivity levels (Vickers and Yarrow, 1988: 148). It would be more plausible to assess changes in productivity over time; but this is only possible for some of the privatised enterprises, while statistical data for others are not available.

Table 14.7 sets out details relating to gross value added and the numbers of labour employed in these enterprises. Quite substantial improvements in labour productivity have been realised in the post-privatisation period (1989–90), particularly in the case of Netas, Petkim and Tüpras, while declining labour productivity was observed in Teletas and Erdemir and negative productivity in the case of Yemsan. The productivity of Petrol Ofisi, however, has remained more or less constant in the post-privatisation period. The improvements in the labour productivity of Netas, Petkim and Tüpras can be attributed to rising gross value added realised in the post-privatisation period.

Among the privatised public participations, the most significant productivity increase was exhibited by Arcelik and TOFAS (automotive) both in 1989 and 1990. Cokurova electric and Celik-Halat (steel cables) have shown declining labour productivity over the same period.

Note that in 1990, labour productivity in terms of GVA/employee ratio was TLt 18.7 million for Teletas, TLt 16.7 million for Netal, TLt 13.4 million for Petkim (Yarimca) and TLt 15.6 million for Erdemir. The most striking productivity

Table 14.7 Labour productivity in the privatised public enterprises, 1983–90[a]

Corporation	1983 GVA[b] (000 TLt)	1983 Average number employees	1983 GVA per employee (000 TLt)	1986 GVA[b] (000 TLt)	1986 Average number employees	1986 GVA per employee (000 TLt)	1989 GVA[b] (000 TLt)	1989 Average number employees	1989 GVA per employee (000 TLt)	1990 GVA[b] (000 TLt)	1990 Average number employees	1990 GVA per employee (000 TLt)
Public enterprises												
Teletas	–	–	–	41,441,600	1,715	24,164	34,917,973	1,479	23,609	32, 197,772	1,718	18,741
Netas[c]	21,740,546	1,974	11, 166	35,356,600	2,971	11,900	21, 339,394	1,779	11,995	29,041,309	1,733	16,757
USA$	n.a.	n.a.	n.a.	n.a.	n.a.	n.a.	n.a.	n.a.	n.a.	n.a.	n.a.	n.a.
Yemsan	5,116,396	1,384	3,696	5,592,800	1,580	3,539	1,792,053	–	–	4,991,397	1,676	2,978
Petkim (yarimca)	91,698, 104	6,086	15,067	28,871,400	3,628	7,957	56,608,789	3,470	16,313	97,991,139	7,297	13,428
Erdemir	99,494,169	7,909	12,579	–	–	–	232,757,710	8,349	27,878	134,593,530	8,595	15,659
Tüpras (refinery)	69,359,252	1,610	43,080	–	–	–	513,426,680	4,800	106,963	781,631,050	4,830	161,828
Petrol ofisi	–	–	–	–	–	–	81,931,315	7,877	10,401	93,136,020	8,000	11,642
Public participations												
Arcelik	26,395,600	2,887	9,142	–	–	–	65,049,815	3,426	18,987	89,949,948	3,434	26,913
Cokurova electric	10,486,464	798	13,193	–	–	–	47,420,684	1,249	37,966	38,172,074	1,475	25,879
Celik-Halat	5,792,946	322	17,990	–	–	–	8,272,071	508	16,283	7,723,020	513	15,054
TOFAS (auto plant)	23,796,538	1,744	13,644	–	–	–	80,537,842	4,262	18,896	126,664,280	5,712	22,175
Kepez electricity	–	–	–	–	–	–	8,081,645	354	22,829	n.a.	n.a.	–

Notes: [a]All figures are based on 1986 constant prices by using the GNP deflator.
[b]GVA = gross value added.
[c]Netas is included in the privatisation programme, but it has not been sold yet.

Source: Calculated from data given in ISO (Istanbul Chamber of Industry) Turkey's 500 large industrial establishments', 15 October 1984; 22 August 1990, pp. 4–8; 22 August 1991, pp. 4–28; and 15 October 1987, pp. 6–23.

improvement was recorded in the case of Tüpras (refinery) which enjoys a strong monopoly power. The labour productivity of Tüpras increased from TLt 106.9 million to TLt 161.8 million in the 1989–90 period (see Table 14.7). These findings reflect that privatised enterprises such as Teletas, Erdemir and Yemsan have not managed to adopt modern technologies in their production and that they have seemingly absorbed a larger labour force than required to achieve their production targets. In the case of Tüpras (refinery) and Petkim, favourable production performance was largely influenced by the monopoly power of these enterprises. These industries can easily meet stringent financial targets by raising prices to customers; therefore tighter financial controls are a weak instrument for promoting improvement in internal efficiency. It can be concluded that the privatisation programme has been most effective in the case of Netas, Tüpras, Arcelik and Tofas corporations.

A review of figures presented in Table 14.8 for Citosan's five cement plants indicates that prior to privatisation, especially in 1986, the highest labour productivity was recorded by Balikesir cement (TLt 14.2 million), followed by Ankara cement (TLt 12.2 million), and Afyon cement plant (TLt 10.6 million). Nevertheless, in the first year of post-privatisation period (1989), labour productivity (at constant prices) tended to decline significantly as compared to 1986 (base year), where the best productivity performance was attained by Afyon cement with TLt 9.8 million per employee followed by Ankara cement with TLt 7.3 million. It can be noted that labour productivity was not satisfactory in the first year of privatisation. However, marked improvement in labour productivity was registered by Ankara, Balikesir and Afyon cement plants in 1990 where the largest productivity was recorded by Afyon cement (TLt 18.1 million) and Ankara cement (TLt 16.8 million). The evidence presented above does suggest that privatisation has had a significant effect on the labour productivity of the privatised Citosan's plants. These findings may be largely due to reduction in the number of employees resulting from more plausible employment policy pursued under the new management.[4] Of course, an attempt should also be made to compare productivity of these enterprises with other privately owned cement plants or even with similar industries in foreign countries. Lack of data, however, does not enable us to carry out such a comparison.

14.4 Concluding remarks

Between 1988 and 1992 successive governments in Turkey have continued their efforts to carry out a series of privatisations mainly of state participations and, to a lesser degree, of state economic enterprises. A range of techniques has been used depending on the demand for the assets in the marketplace, the government's fiscal requirements and the political implications of different types of sales. In some cases, the intention to sell was enthusiastically announced and then retracted (e.g. Netas, BHT air cargo, Petkim, Erdemir).

Table 14.8 Labour productivity of CITOSAN's privatised cement plants, 1983–90[a]

Corporation	1983 GVA[b] (000 TLt)	1983 Average number employees	1983 GVA per employee (000 TLt)	1986 GVA[b] (000 TLt)	1986 Average number employees	1986 GVA per employee (000 TLt)	1989 GVA[b] (000 TLt)	1989 Average number employees	1989 GVA per employee (000 TLt)	1990 GVA[b] (000 TLt)	1990 Average number employees	1990 GVA per employee (000 TLt)
Ankara Cement	1,233,133	416	2,964	5,215,000	424	12,299	2,521,793	3,441	7,330	5,527,920	328	16,853
Balikesir cement	3,711,246	410	0,951	5,631,000	395	14,255	3,062,913	734	4,172	4,957,498	375	13,219
Afyon cement	2,277,444	412	5,527	4,157,900	390	10,661	3,400,594	344	9,885	5,910,756	325	18,186
Soke cement	780,560	300	2,601	2,113,200	296	7,139	n.a.	n.a.	n.a.	n.a.	n.a.	n.a.
Pinarhisar cement	n.a.	n.a.	n.a.	n.a.	n.a.	n.a.	n.a.	n.a.	n.a.	n.a.	n.a.	n.a.

Notes: [a]All figures are converted to 1986 constant prices by making use of the GNP deflator.
[b]GVA = gross value added.

Source: Calculated from data given in ISO (Istanbul Chamber of Industry) 'Turkey's 500 large industrial establishments', 15 October 1984; 22 August 1990, pp. 4–8; 22 August 1991, pp. 4–28; and 15 October 1987, pp. 6–32; see also Karatas (1990: 80).

Of the non-privatised state enterprises, some are already in the transitional phase where privatisation is possible, others could sell off all their assets over future years. Whether the state enterprises regard themselves as in a long-term operation mode or a transitional body preparing for future sell-off clearly affects their investment decisions and performance.

Partial privatisation of public participations (sale of state shares) proved relatively easy to carry out, being less contentious and more easily absorbed by the markets. The other mode of partial sale was to divest a small proportion of shares in the nominated state-owned enterprises either by floating on the stock market or by block sales to private buyers and companies.

Privatisation in Turkey was encouraged by the radical deregulation of the capital markets during the preceding years. The stock exchange grew rapidly between 1988 and 1991 (Kjellstrom, 1990). However, to date there have been no full market flotations such as the British government has used in the course of its privatisation programme. At present the Istanbul stock market for substantial assets has been regarded as thin, and this raised difficult problems about whether to proceed with the sales. The weak state of the Turkish stock market, particularly during the 1987 crash and 1990/91 Gulf War crisis, was the main constraint on the privatisation drive. In addition, investments in secure alternatives such as gold, government bonds and foreign exchange have become more attractive because they provide a significant hedge against rising inflation.

It is difficult to assess the overall impact of privatisation on enterprise performance when only a small proportion of shares in the SEEs has been transferred to private individuals. Nor is it easy to judge whether public participations (joint ventures) have improved productivity following the sale of some proportions of state shares. No doubt one has to be cautious in ascribing wholly the profitability and productivity improvement to privatisation alone.

Bearing in mind these limitations, however, from the foregoing analysis the following points can be made:

1. It is noticeable that a considerable improvement in profitability of Teletas has occurred in the post-privatisation period. Similar performance was observed in the case of Petkim and Erdemir, but this improvement may be partly attributable to the raising of prices of their products which was possible because they both enjoy significant market power. Yemsan (animal feed) has shown dramatically low and negative performance in the 1989–90 period. Turkish Petroleum refinery company (Tüpras) shows moderate performance compared to others.
2. The public participations (joint ventures) have shown better performance than fully state-owned enterprises in the post-privatisation period. For instance, Arcelik and Cokurova electric registered a remarkable increase in profitability in 1989 and 1990. A steady improvement in the financial

profitability of Tofas was also observed during the 1989–90 period.

3. As indicated earlier, among Citsan's five privatised cement plants in the post-privatisation period (1989–90), financial profitability of Ankara and Balikesir cement plants was negative, while profitability of Afyon cement registered a steady increase. In terms of profits-to-net assets ratios, the highest profitability was observed in the case of Afyon cement both in 1989 and 1990, while others showed negative performance.
4. Labour productivity was largely improved in the case of Netas, Petkim and Tüpras, while declining labour productivity was discovered in Teletas, Yemsan and Erdemir. In the latter group, the evidence does not suggest that privatisation has had a significant effect on their productivity. Marked improvement in labour productivity was noticed in Citosan's privatised cement plants in 1990, especially in the case of Afyon and Ankara cement plants.

Following the change of government in October 1991, the new Turkish coalition government has reviewed its privatisation strategy. The intention is to rehabilitate and restructure the SEEs before they are put on sale. It has committed itself to continuing with the sales of enterprises and participations that 'will perform better within the framework of market disciplines'. The process of privatisation, under Demirel's government is likely to continue, though the government has announced that in the future it will be guided by the ability of the market to absorb assets and sales of shares.

Notes

1. For a detailed account of productivity and total factor productivity in the private and public manufacturing sectors in Turkey for 1977–85 and 1973–85 periods, see Yildirim (1989) and Ozmucur and Karatas (1990: 34–6).
2. The French company made an offer of $105 million (TLt 195.8 million) for Citosan's five cement plants. The Société Ciment was also expected to undertake an investment of $75 million over the next 4 years. It would own 90 per cent of shares of Citosan's five plants, while the remaining 10 per cent was to be retained as a 'golden share', after three years, 39 per cent of the shares of Citosan's plants would be sold to individuals and, in particular, 10 per cent to the employees of the acquired plants. For details see Karatas, 1990: 46–8 and PPF, 1992: 1–14.
3. USAS was privatised by selling 70 per cent of its shares to the SAS (Scandinavian Airlines). According to the agreement concluded: (i) 70 per cent of USAS's TLt 10 billion nominal capital were transferred to the SAS service partner for $14 million; (ii) SAS guaranteed to pay 21 per cent of its net profits to the PPF for the 10-year period, 1989–99; and (iii) 30 per cent of the nominal capital after a certain period will be sold to private individuals, the first priority to be given to employees of USAS. For details see, Gultekin (1989: 1–4) and Karatas (1990: 48–9).
4. It is reported that under new management by SCF, Afyon and Ankara cement plants have reviewed staff requirements, and they have made some of their employees redundant. See Sarsel (1992: 43–55).

References

Bollard, A. and D. Mayes (1991), 'Corporatisation and privatisation in New Zealand', a paper presented at a Conference on International Privatisation, NZ Institute of Economic Research, St Andrews, NZ, 12–14 September.

Cook, P. and C. Kirkpatrick (eds) (1988), *Privatisation in Less-developed Countries*, Hemel Hempstead: Harvester Wheatsheaf.

Gultekin, B. (1989), 'Privatisation of USAS in PPF', *Restructuring Journal* (Yeniden Yapilanma), Public Participation Fund, 1 October, 1–5.

Heper, M. (1987), 'Recent developments towards privatisation of state economic enterprises in Turkey', mimeo, Manchester University.

ISO (Istanbul Chamber of Industry) (various dates), 'Turkey's 500 large industrial establishments', *Journal of the Istanbul Chamber of Industry*, various issues.

Karatas, C. (1990), 'Privatisation in Britain and Turkey', Istanbul Chamber of Industry, Research Department, November.

Karatas, C. (1992), 'Privatisation and regulation in Turkey: an assessment', *Journal of International Development*, **4**.

Kirkpatrick, C. (1987), 'The UK privatisation experience: is it transferable to LDCs?', Study No. 7, Oxford: Oxford Centre for Management Studies.

Kjellstrom, S. B. (1990), 'Privatisation in Turkey', *World Bank Working Papers*, Washington, DC: World Bank, November.

Millward, R. (1988), 'Measured sources of inefficiency in the performance of private and public enterprises in LDCs', in P. Cook and C. Kirkpatrick (eds), *Privatisation in Less Developed Countries*, Hemel Hempstead: Harvester Wheatsheaf.

Morgan Guaranty Bank (1986), *Privatisation Master Plan: SEEs recommended for sale, action plans*, Ankara: Morgan Guaranty Bank.

Onis, Z. (1991), 'Privatisation and the logic of coalition building: a comparative analysis of state divestiture in Turkey and UK', mimeo, Bogazici University, Istanbul.

Ozmucur, S. and C. Karatas (1990), 'Total factor productivity in Turkish manufacturing, 1973–1988', *Journal of Economics and Administrative Studies*, **4** (2), 289–322.

PPF (Prime Ministry – Public Participation Authority) (1992), 'Bazbakanlik Kamu Ortakligi Idaresi Baskankligi Faaliyetleri, 1984–1992', Istanbul: Prime Ministry, 1–15.

Sankar, T. I., M. B. G. Thak and S. S. T. Sal (1988), 'Relative profitability of public and private enterprises in India', paper from Conference on Privatisation: Diversification of Ownership of Public Enterprises, Institute of Public Enterprises and London Business School, 22–23 January, Hyderabad.

Sarsel, M. (1992), 'How to privatise public enterprises in Turkey: alternative methods of valuation', MA dissertation, Bogazici University, Istanbul, 20 July.

Vickers, J. and G. Yarrow (1988), *Privatisation: An economic analysis*, Cambridge, Mass.: MIT Press.

Yarrow, G. (1988), 'Privatisation and economic performance', *The Economic Review*, **6** (2), November, 2–6.

Yeni Ekonomi (1990, 1991), July, August, September 1990, May, 1991 and other issues.

Yildirim, E. (1989), 'Total factor productivity growth in Turkish manufacturing industry between 1963–1983: an analysis', *METU Studies in Development*, **16** (3–4), 65–83.

15

Transport regulation and privatisation in Indonesia

Tentative steps and looming constraints

A. J. Plumbe

15.1 Introduction

Traditionally the transport sector in Indonesia was subject to a comprehensive web of regulations. Licensing was and remains pervasive, yet each transport mode has taken steps towards greater private sector involvement. Those steps have so far left very differential imprints from one transport mode to another. Within each mode the extent and nature of the steps taken are variable.

Indonesia is full of contradictions. There are variants to any policy from one part of the country to another. Incremental and experimental approaches to change are often adopted, yet periodically very bold steps are enacted. Much decision making is centralised, yet there are many tiers of decentralised government and decision making.

Transport has always entailed interaction between private and public enterprise. Much transport, especially transport operations, has characteristically been in private hands. Yet it has operated usually within a regulatory framework of import, transfer, registration and fuel taxes, safety and speed regulations, operating licences and a supply of infrastructure controlled by the public sector. Private operations have usually been complemented by public provision of 'track'.

Comprising 13,000 islands scattered across over 3,000 miles of sea, Indonesia has placed great emphasis on transport. Expenditure of US$3.5 billion of official development monies on transport in the second Five Year Plan (Repelita 2) which ended in March 1979 was doubled to US$6.7 billions in Repelita 3. It was cut only to US$5.8 billions in Repelita 4. Since the decrease in the oil price in 1984/5 the shortfall in revenue has acted as a major stimulus to enhanced privatised sector involvement in transport. Over the 1980s, road transport expanded rapidly. The bus fleet expanded from 112,000 in 1981 to 434,903 by 1989; passenger cars from 722,400 to 1,182,253, and trucks from 590,500 to

952,391 over the same period (Biro Pusat Statistik, 1991a). In a country where rapid urbanisation is taking place, the bulk of the population still rely on public transport.

This chapter aims to record the nature of transport regulation in Indonesia, the steps taken to dismantle it and to privatise transport sector activities, and to draw conclusions on the nature and extent of the resulting privatised transport activities. Each transport mode is considered sequentially starting with road construction and operation.

15.2 Roads

Within the roads sector, the opportunity to privatise in Indonesia has been taken by pursuing two main avenues. In both cases the private sector has been harnessed in the provision of new capacity or facilities rather than by taking over existing roads or facilities. At the national level, private involvement in the construction of trunk expressways has been promoted. This is the focus of the rest of this section. In the next section, private involvement in the provision of smaller road transport facilities – more normally associated with local government – is explored.

Most interprovincial and trunk roads in Indonesia are developed by Bina Marga which is part of the Ministry of Public Works. These are all toll free. As long ago as 1978, the government established PT Jasa Marga to construct, operate and maintain toll roads and bridges. PT Jasa Marga is run on commercial business lines (a Persero) with paid-up share capital; it is not, however, isolated from government influence. PT Jasa Marga is intended to make a profit across its range of business activities, to support the implementation of government programmes and policies for economic development, to pioneer business activities that have not been undertaken by the private sector and co-operatives, and to undertake business activities complementary to private business activities (Jasa Marga, *c.*1988a). Hence, while Jasa Marga operates as a private company, it sometimes comes under pressure to develop toll routes like the Belmera (Belawan to Medan) which will remain unprofitable for many years to come. All its operating costs are covered from toll revenues which also contribute to capital investment in new toll roads. For the remainder of its capital expenditure, Jasa Marga issues interest-bearing bonds to which the public subscribe. Shares also exist and substantial dividends have been paid to private investors, but none to the government, which, however, is paid tax on profits.

Firms which parallel Jasa Marga, in that they are public sector firms but run on private sector commercial lines, are construction contractors (e.g. PT Waskita Karya). Hence one type of privatisation that occurred in Indonesia before privatisation was promoted in the 1980s was the creation of public sector firms structured and financed like any other private firm and expected to compete in the open market for work.

Toll road development is guided by certain principles. First, such roads have to be built as part of the development of the overall public roads network. Secondly, an alternative non-tolled road must always exist so that the public are not forced to use the toll road. Thirdly, toll roads tend to be in areas where the economy is more dynamic and the population wealthier, so levying a toll helps to meet the national policy of redistributing income. Fourthly, in the initial period of Jasa Marga's existence all toll roads were owned by the government, but that has changed with the recent thrust towards greater private sector involvement. Toll roads and bridges solely developed by PT Jasa Marga are given in Table 15.1.

With enhanced pressure on central government's revenue owing to the weakening of oil prices post-1983, and the high debt : equity ratio within Jasa Marga suggesting its capital structure was undesirable, joint operations or ventures between domestic and foreign private companies and Jasa Marga have been promoted since authorisation was given in Inpres 25/1987 in July 1987. In a joint operation no new company is created but the agreement determines the amount of capital investment, concession period and percentage share-out of revenues. PT Jasa Marga operate and maintain the road. The second option of joint venture has proved far more attractive. In a joint venture a new company is established between PT Jasa Marga and the private investor. If PT Jasa Marga are to operate and maintain the road (which is not a necessity) the new company negotiates a new agreement; the new company has the right to claim other income, say from service areas. Joint ventures are encouraged to use a BOT (build, operate, transfer) contract strategy. Since

Table 15.1 Toll roads and toll bridges constructed and operated solely by PT Jasa Marga

Location	Starting date of operation	Length (km)
Jakarta-Bogor-Ciawi (Jagorawi)	March 1978	53.0
Citarum Bridge	August 1979	–
Tallo Lama Bridge	August 1981	–
Kapuas Bridge (Pontianak)	January 1982	–
Wonokromo (Surabaya)	January 1982	–
Mojokerto Bridge	July 1982	–
Semarang Artery	July 1983	15.0
Pintas Ciujung and Serang by-pass	January 1984	12.0
Jakarta-Tangerang	November 1984	27.0
Prof. Dr. Ir. Sediyatmo (Pluit-Cengkareng – Jakarta Airport)	April 1985	14.0
Surabaya-Gempol	July 1986	39.4
Balmera (Belawan-Medan-Tanjung Morawa)	December 1986	34.6
Cawang-Semanggi (Jakarta)	April 1987	6.7
Jatingaleh-Krapyak (Semarang)	July 1987	8.0
Cawang-Cikampek	September 1988	71.4
Semanggi-Grogol (Jakarta)	1989	10.0
Padalarang-Cileunyi (Bandung)	1989	34.0

Source: PT Jasa Marga (*c*. 1988a, b).

completion of the Padalarang–Cileunyi toll road south of Bandung, Jasa Marga has only been able to develop further toll roads in joint ventures.

Many toll roads are for sale but those which are reported to be sold are recorded in Table 15.2. Private firms have generally been reticent in creating the joint ventures required. However, the first one, for the Cawang–Tanjung Priok link, comprises PT Citra Marga Nusaphala Persada (a consortium having connections with the President's daughter) and PT Jasa Marga. The 34.2 km Tangerang–Ciujung road is being built by PT Marga Mandalasakti, a consortium of PT Hanurata Coy Ltd, PT Humpass, PT Krakatau Steel & PT Jasa Marga – again a group with excellent political connections and able to entertain the risk of investing Rp.167.18 billions. One example of innovatory finance has been reported, namely Trafalgar House proposing to issue a revenue bond for the Cikampek–Padalarang road, which after seven years would entitle the holder to a share of toll revenues (EIU, 1990b).

The reticence of the private sector to enter into joint ventures and finance toll road construction is understandable in the light of the following factors which deter the privatisation process. First, land is appropriated and owned by government so it cannot be used as collateral against bank loans. Jasa Marga itself is not allowed to buy and sell land. Other collateral to satisfy a bank is difficult to find as roads are not saleable commodities. Further the toll road business is new to banks, so they lack experience on which to base their analysis and finance of such ventures. Secondly, private investors have to co-operate with PT Jasa Marga which has access to information on all other joint ventures: what if PT Jasa Marga proves an unsatisfactory partner in the long term? Thirdly, there is always an alternative road to the toll road so opportunities for local monopoly profits are curtailed. After the concession period, the private investor has to forfeit the asset to PT Jasa Marga.

The joint ventures are not free to set tariffs as they please. Rather, tariffs are set by government through presidential decrees. Nominally the decrees can be revised annually but in practice revisions are made only every three years, so investors are exposed to the dangers of rapid inflation. The tariffs set take

Table 15.2 Toll roads constructed or to be constructed by joint venture

Location	Starting date of operation	Length (km)
Cawang–Tanjung Priok	1991	14.0
Surabaya–Gresik	–	19.0
Jakarta Harbour Road	–	22.0
Cikampek–Padalarang	–	34.0
Grogol–Pluit (Jakarta)	–	7.0
Medan–Binjai	–	24.0
Cikampek–Cirebon	–	130.0
Tangerang–Ciujung	under construction	34.2
Surabaya–Mojokerto	–	98.0

Source: PT Jasa Marga (*c.* 1988b), *Investment Opportunities: Toll-roads in Indonesia.*

into account a number of factors including construction costs, vehicle operating costs and service quality but are not allowed to exceed 70 per cent of the vehicle operating cost savings inclusive of time savings achieved by using the toll road instead of the alternative untolled road. Hence estimates of revenue are acts of faith. Further, revenues will fluctuate according to traffic levels, and therefore forecasting the rate of traffic diversion to the toll road is an imprecise art, especially where, as in Indonesia, there are few past examples to guide one's judgement.

Loans raised abroad may be either attractive or undesirable. Private firms may be able to tap financial sources abroad that otherwise would be unaccessed, and that money may be available at interest rates below those charged domestically in Indonesia. Conversely, accessing overseas funds may increase the national debt burden and expose the joint venture investor to all the vicissitudes of fluctuating foreign exchange rates.

Returns on road investments are often long-term with positive contributions only being attained 10–15 years after the initial investment. Few private firms can afford to dilute their earnings for so long. Further, in Indonesia, there are many alternative investments that provide quicker yields, such as real estate development, supermarket development or office leasing.

The sheer size of the investments involved (US$100 million plus) is daunting to all but the largest conglomerate groups. In Indonesia this means that there are only a small number of diversified companies that can contemplate such ventures. Further, it means that private ownership of the toll road joint ventures will be confined to a select elite in society.

Offsetting these deterrents towards greater private involvement in road construction is the buoyancy of the Indonesian economy and rapid traffic growth – 24 per cent on toll roads in 1989 and 28 per cent in 1990.

An attraction of private toll road investment is that much more effective policing for overloading will occur. For example, PT Jasa Marga have flying teams that weigh axles of trucks before they enter the toll road. When overweight, such trucks are turned round to the detriment of the remainder of the public road network.

There is little evidence to date that private sector involvement in toll road construction has led to faster development of the network.

Before considering some particular issues raised by private sector investment in roads, those aspects that are common to all road construction and operation but which attract greater emphasis when private financing is involved, are discussed.

A private developer may be tempted to adopt compromised design standards which accord to the concession period rather than the normal design life of roads. Also different firms might use different design standards. Hence the public authority responsible for private financed developments needs to ensure standards and conformity of design are attained. The public authority is likely to have more confidence in their own design, whereas the private firm is likely to judge that there is less risk when the design is their own creation (Gupta,

1989). Underestimation of construction costs or traffic levels will be risks borne by the private investor but subject to greater rigour of prior analysis. The usual problem of design changes which become necessary during construction may pose greater difficulty because the private firm will need to renegotiate its financial package with its backers. A parallel situation will occur should there be unanticipated cost escalation during the construction period. Unlike government bodies, private firms usually cannot compulsorily purchase land. In Indonesia land acquisition can be a lengthy and convoluted process; most private firms will require a public body like Jasa Marga or the city administration to acquire and hand over the expropriated land. When construction is undertaken by joint ventures with foreign contractors, it is common for their plant to be imported duty free: private investors may seek similar dispensation. Governments generally do not insure themselves against structural failures of roads for which they are responsible, but public authorities are well advised to ensure private investors are insured against structural distress or failure during construction and subsequent operation, as well as against the private investor abandoning the investment before the end of the concession period. Bankruptcies amongst even large firms over concession periods of up to thirty years are real possibilities. The creation of joint ventures with PT Jasa Marga lessens this danger, and also reduces the possibility of takeovers.

The financial instruments used by private firms to raise their capital for such projects are varied. One advantage large private firms possess is their ability to tap international sources of money and thereby avoid paying domestic commercial rates, which are currently over 20 per cent in Indonesia. Few financiers, international or domestic, will offer fixed interest rates for long periods. This therefore renders private firms susceptible both to interest rate fluctuations and floating foreign exchange parities.

The privatisation of roads raises several general issues. The roads that will be most attractive to investors will be those with potentially high traffic levels and growth in traffic. Hence their investment will tend to polarise to the parts of the country that are wealthier and already most economically developed. For example, the 60 km Solo–Yogyakarta road in central Java currently has only about 16,000 vehicles a day on it and a diversion rate to a toll road estimated at only about 20 per cent owing to the low income levels of central Java: the upshot is that a toll road is considered to be viable only at some stage after 1995 despite it being between the two largest cities of central Java away from the coast. A further important implication is that in a country such as Indonesia possibilities for private financing of trunk roads will be confined to a small part of the total network, and the scope for further private involvement could be curtailed once the roads carrying the heaviest traffic have been developed.

A further requirement constraining the opportunity for private investment in the road network is that only links which can be isolated from the rest of the road network and have a limited number of access points are suitable for tolling and hence private investment. Roads that are fronted by commercial or residential premises, or are not expressway in urban centres, or are extensively connected along their length to other parts of the road network, will not offer the opportunity to collect tolls effectively. There is little scope for private investment in any part of the secondary road network.

The links that are proposed for private investment need to be fairly long, probably over 10 km in length. Otherwise the toll that can be exacted will be minimal. Likewise only a meagre toll can be levied if the differences in vehicle operating costs and time taken are minor between the tolled and untolled parallel roads. It will reward the private investor to pay the public authority to keep the alternative road in a poor state of repair. There is certainly no incentive to upgrade the non-tolled alternative road.

The final consequence of private investment in roads with its partial taxing away of the benefits enjoyed by users is that the multiplier effects of lowered transport costs stimulating other economic activity are largely foregone. This outcome is not being addressed in Indonesia.

Some conclusions are warranted on the entry of privatisation into the construction and operation of roads. A private sector style of operations has applied to all toll road construction and operation in Indonesia even though initially the sole agency involved was a publicly owned body. The regulatory framework under which private investment occurs means that its role will be confined to a small selection of routes that can be isolated as discrete links and offer the possibility of charging substantial tariffs. Just 1.9 per cent of the state road network and only 0.12 per cent of the total road network are tolled currently, though higher percentages would result if vehicle kms were the measurement unit. So far only 14 per cent of all the toll roads built or under construction have been financed by the private sector. The regulatory framework for private investments in roads offers many significant risks as managers can have little influence over revenues. Opportunities to enter into joint ventures are confined in practice to a very small group of large domestic conglomerates. Hence privatisation affects solely toll road development and a small group of potential companies. Privatisation's ability to mobilise much additional capital has yet to be proven.

15.3 Road transport facilities

There is much potential for private investment in road-related facilities like bus terminals, multistorey car parks and rest areas in Indonesia. A range of financial arrangements between the local government and the developer is possible. Many are of a 'value-capture' nature such that the private benefits are recouped by the state (Ministry of Communications, 1991). For example:

1. Central and/or local government can prepare a system to collect taxes from the indirect and direct beneficiaries of transport infrastructure development.
2. Costs of construction can be shared by transport operators and the communities benefiting.
3. A single entity can be established to operate both the transport facility and the surrounding land; once in operation, revenues from the land can be transferred to the loss-making transport facility.
4. When, in Jakarta at least, a developer intends to use land for residential purposes there is a requirement that 40 per cent of the land area should be allocated to community services and this can include transport services.
5. Again within Jakarta but also in other cities, the local government can levy a development fee on all developments involving areas of over 5,000 m^2: effectively this is a tax on development profits that can be reallocated to providing transport infrastructure.
6. Since DKI Decree No. 540 issued in 1989, developers of high-quality commercial and business property in Jakarta have been required to offer either 20 per cent of the saleable/leasable floor area or the equivalent sum of money to the local government with the specific requirement that the money or floor area is used to help lower income groups. Providing public transport facilities is seen to help such income groups.
7. Under the Ministry of Domestic Affairs Regulation No. 3 of 1986 local government assets such as land or buildings can be used by a third party under a variety of contracts, namely:

   (a) *management contracts*: the private third party manages a local government owned asset like a car-park;
   (b) *production contracts*: the third party provides working capital for operations as well as management expertise of a local government asset, takes all the risk of production failure, and pays a royalty;
   (c) *profit sharing contracts*: similar to a production contract but profit is shared between third party and local government on an agreed percentage basis;
   (d) *results/effect sharing contracts*: the third party provides all the development and start-up finance but the resulting business is managed through a local government agency; the results or effects of the goods or services produced are shared on agreed percentages between the third party and the local government;
   (e) *business location/space contracts*: the third party gets the right to construct on local government-owned land a building which it can then use for the duration stated in the permission to build, but at the end of the contract the building and land revert to the local government.

A version of this last type of contract is being used by the Directorate General of Land Transport to acquire its new offices in Jakarta! Other examples are as follows.

Within Jakarta, two large bus terminal redevelopments are being undertaken by private firms that will hold concessions to operate the resulting commercial development. The first is at Blok M, a bustling south Jakarta commercial centre. This involves a Rp 70 billions (*c*. US$ 40 millions) replacement terminal complete with 278 stores and 450 car-parking places below it. All the financing, construction and operation of this big development is being handled by P T Langgeng Ayom Lestari, which in turn gets a 30-year concession. The second development in Jakarta involves the replacement of the Cililitan bus station, which serves mostly intercity and commuter services to the east of Jakarta. Under a build-operate-transfer contract valued at Rp 8.6 billion, the private developer, P T Wahyu Permata Jaya, will build a replacement bus terminal, business and trade centre at Kampung Rambutan on the Jagorawi toll road. Part of the deal involves providing gratis kiosks, restaurants and offices for the police and bus station authority personnel at the new terminal, and the reconstruction of a transit terminal at Cililitan for inter-city buses and minibuses (*Jakarta Post*, 1–24 August 1991).

Recent development of off-street multistorey car parking has adopted a similar approach. To remove on-street parking on the busy Jalan Tunjungan in Surabaya, a developer was permitted in 1987 to build offices, shops and parking on a vacant plot of municipal-owned land in return for a concession to operate the building for 25 years. Given the particular mix of parking, shops and offices, P T Bismo estimated their Internal Rate of Return to be 20 per cent which compared to an opportunity cost of capital of 18 per cent, and the payback period was estimated to be fifteen years. Consequently a staged construction was adopted. On the same street in Surabaya, another firm had previously been induced to build a pedestrian bridge with shops at the upper level and the possibility of selling advertising billboard space in return for a 20-year concession.

These examples show that both modest and substantial investments can occur in road transport facilities which might often be considered to be provided solely by the public sector. Thus the hard-strapped budgets of local governments can be allocated to other causes. Opportunity to harness private sector capital and management skills in this fashion will only arise when discrete facilities can be identified and other non-transport commercial activities incorporated. What is also clear from the Indonesian context is that very flexible arrangements will be entertained by the public sector authorities.

15.4 Buses, paratransit and trucks

Trucks operating interprovincially in Java or between Java and Sumatra are required to have route licences. Such licences are fairly easily obtained. Elsewhere no route licences are required. Similarly, trucks are classified into those operating on 'own account' (white licences) and those offering their services for 'hire and reward' (yellow licences). In practice this is a distinction that has become blurred and not capable of policing. Bandung operates a 06.00–18.00 hours entry ban on heavy trucks. Building a back tailboard which exceeds the legal length of overhang beyond a truck's back axle or operating thoroughly overloaded are considered fair game by drivers. The government sets upper and lower tariff limits per tonne-km to apply throughout a province, and negotiation is supposed to occur between those limits. The limits do not take account of local variations in costs, are totally unenforceable and in practice the competitive market rules. Apart from the route licence, the regulation of truck operations is essentially benign. All the signs are that trucking is a competitive business.

Bus and paratransit regulation are completely different. Their regulation is extensive and enforced (often self-enforced). Regulation is by licensing. The licence is specific to a particular vehicle and allocates it to a specific route. This public transport licensing takes place at four administrative levels. Interprovincial buses and trucks are licensed by the central (national) Ministry of Communications, Directorate for Land Transportation (LLAJR). Intraprovincial bus operations are licensed by the applicable provincial government. Public transport operations within a town or city are licensed by the city government. Finally, for routes between *kabupaten* (regency or 'district') a separate law allows *kabupaten* administrations to issue licences. In so issuing licences, there is little to no communication between these separate bodies, such that all four types of public transport operations may spatially overlap. Commonly the officials at different administrative levels will be at loggerheads with one another.

Government is responsible for setting fares on all routes. Usually fares are fixed regardless of distance for urban and short rural routes, and vary directly in proportion to distance for intercity or longer rural routes (currently Rp.17/km in Java). This system of fare setting breaks down at times of peak demand (e.g. Id Fitr) or along very competitive routes such as between Jakarta and Cirebon. Differential fares are allowed for express (*Patas*) and air-conditioned (AC) services. Operators generally form associations or cartels to look after their interests. Operations along the route are usually demand responsive: buses depart when they are full at the terminii of their routes.

Most buses in Indonesia are owned privately, but there is a large and monopolistic public bus operator (PPD) in Jakarta which only faces competition on selected routes from private sector operators. Elsewhere in the larger cities, a public operator, Damri, runs fleets in competition with private operators. On a very limited scale Damri competes with private operators on intercity routes. Damri is intended to be run as a commercial company but it tends not to cover fully its bus replacement costs. This mix of private and public operators can lead to the private operator creaming off the lucrative market. There is some suggestion that the private operator, Mayasari Bakhti, was able to secure a disproportionate amount of the lucrative *Patas* services in north-east Jakarta.

Within the paratransit sector the same route licensing for each individual vehicle and fare setting is applied to midibuses, minibuses, mikrolets, and similar four-wheeled vehicles. This applies in both rural and urban contexts. Such vehicles tend to be allocated to feeder services with the size of the permitted vehicle type related to the width of the road. Vehicles such as three-wheeler autorickshaws (*bajaj*) and tricycles rickshaws (*becak*) which provide taxi-like services are licensed to operate anywhere or within certain zones of a city.

Regulatory control has been used in Jakarta to hound paratransit vehicles gradually out of business. Tricycle rickshaws provided a local cheap form of taxi service, but their slow speed and profuse numbers were adjudged to create congestion. As early as 1975, the Jakarta city administration confined their operations to one of four zones within the city and to feeder services along side roads leading to the arterial roads. By 1990 the authorities had banned tricycle rickshaws from within the administrative boundary of Jakarta, and mounted raids to confiscate any remaining such vehicles. Those found were dumped in the sea, an act that brought no protest owing to most of the owners being of Chinese descent or lower status Javanese, and many drivers being seasonal migrants to the city or able to survive by pursuing other informal sector activities. Other cities in Indonesia, such as Bandung, Surabaya and Medan have used licensing to confine the activities of tricycle rickshaws.

This system of regulation gives rise to a host of difficulties. The process of allocating licences offers ample opportunity for the extraction of supplementary payments. Applications from new entrants are played off against existing licence holders who may be forced to make additional payments to retain their licences. Indeed, it is said that new licences are sometimes offered to the highest bidder such that market forces may be claimed to be operative leading to optimal allocations of vehicles. Within Jakarta over the past decade, the private and co-operative transport groups known as Mayasari Bakhti, Metromini and Kopaja have been able to grow because they pay for licences in a way PPD cannot.

The specific allocation of vehicles to routes leads to inefficiencies as vehicles cannot be flexibly allocated over the day and throughout an area to the changing temporal and spatial patterns of demand. Further, fares are not related to route costs so some routes are far more profitable than others. Where many operators own only one vehicle, this leads to great variations in income amongst operators dependent upon the route to which their vehicle is allocated. To obviate this difficulty, minibus operators in Banjarmasin operate a route rotation system within their associations.

There is every incentive for officials to license every vehicle that wants to ply on a particular route. The result is that there is an oversupply of vehicles on many routes, despite the associations of existing operators trying to operate entry restrictions. Long queues of identical idle vehicles may be seen. This is paid for by the customers paying unnecessarily high fares, which are jacked up in agreement with the officials concerned to levels at which all operators can survive.

Regulation leads to buses operating routes that gravitate to bus terminii rather than meeting the pattern of travel demand. For example, in Jakarta 54 per cent of all bus trips entail a change of bus, suggesting an inefficient route structure.

Where cartels are strong, as amongst Jakarta's PPD, operators may withdraw buses from a route deliberately to ensure that those buses that operate do so with high load factors and so maximise their revenue per km. Again it is the customer who suffers from an uncomfortable trip.

Many of the licences are in fact obtained by officials within government organisations or the police themselves. This makes it very hard for any other official to take adverse decisions, or for bus management measures to be introduced. In East Jakarta the police own many of the minibuses. When the city administration instituted route restrictions and erected signs, the police removed all the signs and ignored the route restrictions thereby overruling the authority of the city administration to implement any traffic schemes.

A regulated bus network should be susceptible to area-wide planning and through ticketing, but the present licensing and fares system mitigate against these possibilities. Hence one of the claimed ills of deregulation already exists.

Along particular routes there is usually plenty of competition in terms of frequency of service, and indeed some of the reckless intercity driving suggests the competition is intense.

Deregulation of the bus operators is being considered in policy-making circles. This would probably be done first for intercity services and only later for intracity services. Given the constitutional objectives of promoting small businesses and equitable distribution of income, there is a valid fear that deregulation of buses would lead to the large firms squeezing the smaller firms out of the market. That additional vehicle-kms will result, thereby exacerbating congestion in the main cities, is also a tenable argument for retaining regulation. Certainly there is a possibility that the local governments will find one of their lucrative sources of income has evaporated. A final concern of officials is that buses will cease to make short detours for the convenience of small groups of passengers, but rather stay on the main line of haul.

The main deterrent to bus deregulation is, however, the very strong vested interest the bureaucracy has in maintaining the status quo.

15.5 Railways

The wind of privatisation and deregulation in the transport sector has affected the railways least. Since 1979 Perusahaan Jawatan Kereta Api (PJKA) has been a government department subject to civil service employment procedures. Between 1963–79 the railways had been a Perum, that is, a corporation with a profit motive but where the government provides capital funds and the corporation tries to cover its operating expenses. That had failed, though, as wages outstripped revenue.

In an effort to improve efficiency, parts of PJKA were stripped away. Its rolling stock manufacture and assembly operations were devolved to a new company, PT Inka, in 1981. This was followed in 1986 by the transfer of its interisland ferry services to a new Inland Waterway & Ferry Transport Public Corporation Perum (ASDP).

The Ministry of Communications retain a great deal of say in the running of PJKA. Personnel reductions and all decisions regarding lines and services operated have to be referred to the Ministry of Communications. Tariffs emanate from decrees made by the Minister of Communications. Until 1986 a published tariff for general freight existed, thereafter there were just two guideline rates, one for wagonload freight and one for packages. For basic bulk commodities, negotiated rates apply. Hence a traditional, inefficient, loss-making railway exists. Only in the case of negotiated tariffs and a few other initiatives mentioned below can one detect movement from a highly regulated environment.

Some railways have substantial private sector involvement through their main customers owning rolling stock and traction. While this occurs for rolling stock on PJKA, it is confined to freight cars, and then only a quarter of them, as shown in Table 15.3.

Fledging attempts to adopt a more commercial approach are apparent in recent years. For example, executive class carriages and faster services have been introduced between Jakarta and Bandung (the Parahyangan service) and between Jakarta and Bogor. In each case a premium fare is being charged to reflect the service's executive status and improved service quality. Concessional (free) travel by PJKA employees and government officials is not permitted on such trains, but its existence always poses a problem for privatised services.

In early July 1990, it was reported that the government was to allow private investment in train services (*Jakarta Post*, 9 July 1990). Owing to a lack of coaches and freight wagons, PJKA has low track utilisation; private operators can conclude joint operation or management contracts with PJKA to raise throughput. Almost immediately, on 16 July, an express cargo train service between Jakarta and Surabaya was inaugurated by PJKA in conjunction with the private firm, PT Banda Graha Reksa (EIU, 1990b). It operates three days a week to offer door-to-door delivery within 24 hours. The government was reported also to be keen to attract private sector participation in operating

Table 15.3 Railways: ownership of rolling stock on Java–Madura and Sumatra networks, 1989

	Owned by PJKA		Owned jointly with non-railway enterprise		Owned by non-railway enterprise	
	Total	%	Total	%	Total	%
Freight train cars	6,256	74.0	443	5.0	1,797	21.0
Passenger coaches	714	100.0	–	–	–	–

Source: Biro Pusat Statistik (1991b).

luxury tourist services on the Jakarta–Surabaya and Jakarta–Bandung routes. PJKA is believed also to be contemplating the offering of lines or services for lease as occurs on part of the State Railway of Thailand (Levy and Menendez, 1990).

Other moves towards commercialisation are thought to be in the offing. These include introducing advertising on stations and trains, and encouraging entrepreneurs to build and operate hotels and shopping centres adjacent to stations.

Railways remain essentially a regulated government department which, apart from tariff flexibility, are only just starting to explore the possible roles of private sector involvement, but could face enhanced competition resulting from deregulation in other transport modes.

15.6 Ports

Most Indonesian ports are owned and operated by public corporations. At the outset it should be noted that several specialised private ports have been developed and operated in Indonesia, sometimes for many years. These private ports include those operated by the US Freeport copper mining company in Irian Jaya, PT Barito's timber port at Mangole in North Maluku, and the coal terminal at Tanjung Bara operated by the joint venture PT Kaltim Prima Coal, Sanggata Holdings Ltd. and BP Coal Indonesia Ltd. Some ports already contain wharves owned by other public or private companies. For instance, of 26 piers at Cilacap, 18 are owned by the state oil company Pertamina, the private cement company PT Semen Nusantara and the private general mining company PT Aneka Tambang.

Deregulation initially affected ports in the period 1985–6, but it was an indirect effect resulting from the reorganisation of related port services and changes in macroeconomic management which stimulated export-oriented industrialisation.

In an attempt to improve government revenues, remove a plethora of paperwork and corruption, and hasten the movement of goods through Indonesian ports, the Société Générale de Surveillance (SGS) was appointed in May 1985 to inspect all Indonesian imports at their port of origin. Thereby the need for customs clearance on arrival was obviated. SGS acted as agent of a newly created state-owned inspection company, PT Sucofindo. This may be seen as a first attempt to circumvent domestic regulation and switch activities to private firms. The first three-year contract was extended for a further three years, but from May 1991 the SGS was gradually phased out as sole inspector: the function has reverted to the domestic Customs and Excise Tax Directorate General. Pre-shipment inspection was retained, however, with the establishment of PT Surveyor Indonesia, which initially for a year subcontracted the job to SGS (starting from August 1991).

National macroeconomic management reforms in 1986 led to substantial increases in port throughputs. The introduction of a flexible exchange rate, the

P4BM export facility, and the dismantling of non-tariff barriers by reclassifying items between tariff categories stimulated and diversified manufactured exports. This deregulation package also removed the shackles from the freight forwarding industry (see section 15.7 below). Further trade, banking and investment deregulation measures followed in 1988–89 to reinforce earlier initiatives.

The November 1988 package deregulated interisland shipping and simplified or relaxed licensing requirements, thereby again subjecting the ports to the impacts of deregulation.

The first steps towards the deregulation of the ports themselves came in the wake of these influences. Under the finance minister's Decree 740/1989, state port companies were permitted to reorganise or restructure. Taking advantage of this provision, the Petikemas Container Terminal at Tanjong Priok port was restructured in 1991 to detach it from its parent corporation (Perusahaan Umum Pelabuhan II) that runs the rest of the port. This was in preparation for joint ventures (see below).

By July 1990 the transport minister had announced that private investors were to be allowed to manage port facilities and port-related businesses under joint operations or management co-operation arrangements with the state port companies (Perusahaan Umum Pelabuhan I, II, III & IV). The minister further clarified that the government saw customs clearance, security arrangements, navigation and port administration as its exclusive preserve (*Jakarta Post*, 9 July 1990). This liberalisation of *modus operandi* means the private sector can build and manage a seaport or invest in individual port components such as tug boats, cargo handling equipment, wharves, warehouses, passenger terminals, shopping centres or offices within the port. Private firms can negotiate their own user charges for whatever they invest in. Hence there are many parallels to joint ventures negotiated with PT Jasa Marga, but smaller units of investment are possible in ports. The most notable response has been the almost immediate agreement between Perusahaan Umum Pelabuhan II and PT Samudera Reksabuana (a subsidiary of the Humpass group and hence with a direct connection with the President's youngest son) to build and operate two container terminals at Tanjong Priok at the immense cost of US$825 millions (*Jakarta Post*, 20 July 1990). Also, it has been reported that Bantem port in West Java which is intended to serve Cilegon and Serang will be developed with the help of private companies. Interestingly, disquiet has been expressed in the House of Representatives that the private involvement in ports will lead to their being controlled by conglomerates which will use them to enhance their own trading activities.

Overall, it may be concluded that ports, while moving rapidly to a position of partial liberation and to where a strong commercial sense guides decisions, also operate in a situation where the government acts as a watchdog and retains strategic activities for itself. As with toll roads, the private sector can only enter within a joint-venture marriage to a public body run on commercial lines.

15.7 Shipping

For the 25 years prior to 1989 the shipping industry was regulated by means of licensing. The aims of licensing promulgated in Regulation No. 5 of 1964 and reinforced in Regulation No. 2 of 1969 were (a) to divide the shipping industry into eight non-competing sectors, (b) within each sector, to control the entry and exit of firms so as to avoid overcapacity, reduce the number of operators and increase efficiency, and (c) for interisland (*nusantara*) shipping to exercise control over routes and the shipping of essential commodities (Dick, 1987). A further aim was to protect domestically owned small shipping companies. The eight sectors were deep-sea (liner), special carrier (overseas), special carrier (domestic), special carrier (industrial), interisland (*nusantara*), local (*lokal*), *prahu* (*rakyat*), and special carrier (offshore). Special carriers were those that conveyed homogeneous consignments, or, in the last mentioned sector, served the offshore oil industry. Firms could not hold more than one licence, so those wishing to trade in two or more sectors had to establish subsidiary firms. To operate in each sector minimum numbers of ships, tonnages and working capital needed to be possessed (see Table 15.4). Depending upon the sector, licences had validity of 5–10 years, but in practice interisland shipping firms were subject to periodic 'screening' by the Directorate General of Sea Communications. The 'screening' was selective, first applied in 1974 and still resulted in some firms with political connections not having their licences revoked when in breach of the licence regulations (Dick, 1987). In the mid-1960s and throughout the 1970s few new interisland licences were officially issued, but new entrants could buy their way into such shipping operations by taking over an existing firm or by placing their ships under the nominal management of a licensed interisland firm. Entry was easy but at an additional cost. Hence the market pressures for efficiency existed but were diluted by the extra entry costs.

In order to co-ordinate sailing schedules, to integrate cargo-handling and

Table 15.4 Licence categories and their minimum requirements

Category	Ships	Tonnage (dwt.)	Capital (Rp/b)	Validity years
Deep-sea (liner)	2	10,000	1.5	10
Special carrier (overseas)	2	10,000	1.5	7
Special carrier (domestic)	2	5,000	1.0	5
Special carrier (industrial)	1	5,000	n.a.[a]	5
Interisland (*nusantara*)	2	1,050	0.225	10
Local (*lokal*)	2	175	?	5
Prahu (*rakyat*)	2	175	?	5
Special carrier (offshore)	2 (barges)	1,000	0.1	5
	2 (tugs)	1,000 (hp)		

Note: [a] Minimum capital not specified but firm must hold a licence from the Department of Industry.

Source: Directorate General of Sea Communications (1979); Dick (1987).

ships' agencies, and to provide statistics to the government, interisland shipping firms were obliged to join groups from 1973 onwards. The advantage of such larger groups appears illusory, but was claimed to be the possibility to cross-subsidise between profitable and unprofitable routes.

During 1969 a new route system dubbed Regular Liner Service was instituted as part of the first Five Year Plan (Repelita I). Interisland ships were allocated to routes in one of four groups, namely, trunk routes, feeder routes (for smaller ships), 'Singapore' routes, and 'special' routes. These groups persisted throughout the 1970s, but recognising the arbitrary distinction between trunk and feeder routes, these were amalgamated as *nusantara* routes in 1980. The system was self-regulated by the shipowners themselves through the Badan Operasi Bersama Pelayaran Nusantara (BOPBERPAN or Interisland Shipping Combined Operations Board). The resultant flexibility meant most ships were allocated to the routes their owners preferred to ply. Allocations of ships were based on the previous year's cargo flows. Dick suggests that in practice this system was no more than a framework because about a fifth of all voyages were deviations made under some dispensation, principally because allocations were made on out-of-date information on trade flows and periodically instructions were issued to carry basic commodities like rice, flour, sugar, fertiliser and cement (Dick, 1987).

The Interisland Liner Services Team proposed a revision to the Regular Liner Service system in 1983. This entailed a four-level hierarchy of ports focused at the highest level on four gateway ports (Tanjung Priok, Tanjung Perak, Belawan and Ujung Pandang). In turn, these were served by 15 smaller 'collector ports'. Other ports were divided into 'trunk ports' and 'feeder ports'. A recommendation that *lokal* shipping should be allowed only to operate between feeder ports and the *adjacent* trunk, collector or gateway port meant double transhipment, so was not attractive to shipowners or consignors. It was envisaged the whole system could be modelled and ships allocated where there were mismatches of demand and supply. But this proposal meant much data had to be collected, shippers were not to decide on service frequency nor optimal vessel size and had little control over their profitability (Dick, 1987).

The existence of regulation enabled the government to insist basic commodities were carried by ships within the Regular Liner Service system and at freight rates that did not cover costs. The result has been a reluctance to use tramp market or chartered ships to cope with peaks of demand, and basic commodities are carried in smaller parcels and ships than would be optimal.

It may be concluded that regulation during the 1960s and 1970s diminished market forces in that some firms were able to survive when they would otherwise have ceased to trade while entry was made less easy. Regulation was not able to match demand with supply nor to foster larger shipping groups. Dick attributes the half-hearted implementation of the regulations to a desire to protect weak *pribumi* firms against non-national competition (Dick, 1987).

Technological evolution in shipping had long ago made the distinction blurred between interisland and local shipping. Inpres No. 5 of 1984 heralded further winds of change. This Inpres concerned the simplification and control of business licensing. The result for shipping was that the Department of Communications started to issue licences for an indefinite period without being subject to subsequent 'screening' and extended operating licences for specific routes to five years' duration.

Further intervention in the shipping market occurred in March 1984 when it was announced that all ships over thirty years of age in that year were to be scrapped in subsequent years (EIU, 1989). Replacement of the estimated 300 plus ships over thirty years of age was to be by 80 standardised domestically built vessels known as Caraka Jaya 1, 2 and 3 which respectively are 1,000 dwt, 2,000 dwt and 3,000 dwt in size. These are able to carry containers. If owners wished to replace their ships the normal choice would have been a second-hand vessel procured abroad, but only domestic purchases were permitted. Further, owners were forced to sell the scrap steel to the state-owned Krakatau steel company at prices half those offered in Singapore or Taiwan. Not surprisingly there was disquiet amongst shipowners. Gradually the government has backed away from this further form of regulation. With ship construction programmes running behind schedule, scrapping of vessels was deferred in 1987, concessional finance was offered and eventually the programme suspended in September 1988. The programme had resulted in a severe shortage of capacity as scrapped ships were not replaced, only to be overcome after liberalisation of the industry by leasing foreign ships.

Liberalisation of the shipping industry occurred in November 1988 as part of a wider policy reform package. Liberalisation meant reclassification of merchant ships into ocean-going or domestic/regional archipelago fleets, shipping companies needing to own only one instead of two ships to operate, thus allowing vessels to be chartered or leased. The first new entrants since 1976 and the first ever joint ventures with foreigners became possible, shippers could choose their own routes, and manufacturers or travel agencies could own their own ships (EIU, 1991). The International Commodities Exchange in Jakarta provided from January 1989 onwards a 'market' for information on sea cargoes and available cargo space. By October 1989, 682 vessels had been chartered by local shippers for interisland services.

This liberalisation has resulted in the restructuring of the market with larger operators containerising and smaller shipping companies developing market niches. Tariffs have not, however, been lowered.

The recent steps towards liberalisation have involved the opening of 164 ports to foreign ships and the granting of permission to international vessels that they sail through other straits than just the Malacca and Lombok straits. Inpres No. 3 of 1991 specifies that all freighters operated by foreign shipping lines already having agents in Indonesia can call at seaports handling international trade. Further, it freed ships of the obligation to file cargo reports, fiscal reports and tax clearance certificates, and allowed domestic shipping companies to become agents for foreign shipping lines.

Developments in liberalising shipping have been paralleled on-shore by changes in the regulations concerning cargo handling. Until the Presidential Instruction No. 4 of 1985, the holders of EMKL (Ekspedisi Muatan Kapal Laut) were able to operate a monopoly in the collection and delivery of cargoes to and from the shipping lines. This meant high commissions were charged to the consignors of goods but very low rates paid to hired transporters. Inpres 4/85 removed this monopoly power to the benefit of consignors and hauliers. Most significantly this Inpres enabled the introduction of through integrated transport.

Thus, in domestic interisland shipping there is a long history of intervention through licensing, but competitive pressures have always exerted influence below the surface and account for the partial offsetting of the intent of licensing. There has been a gradual but persistent move in recent years to relax regulations of earlier decades such that the shipping industry is now more open to market influences than ever before. The signs are that greater differentiation within the shipping industry is resulting. Recent moves question Rimmer's conclusion that the trend was to pursue privatisation without deregulation (Rimmer, 1990). Of all the transport subsectors, privatisation in shipping has been taken the furthest. One of its concomitants has been greater foreign ownership penetration of the Indonesian interisland shipping industry.

15.8 Air transport and airports

Air transport remains regulated internationally by the obligations of IATA membership by Garuda, the nationally owned airline. Indonesia also subscribes to the normal 'freedoms of the air' in all its bilateral negotiations with foreign airlines regarding landing and overflying rights.

Garuda, the main Indonesian-owned international carrier, is run as a commercial business. To improve its balance sheet it has in recent years switched from buying new aircraft outright to lease arrangements,

Domestic scheduled operations are provided by Garuda Indonesia Airways and its subsidiary Merpati Nusantara Airlines which are both state owned, and by five private airlines, namely Sempati Air Transport, Bouraq Airlines, Mandala Airlines, Seulawah Air Services and AQA Zemrud Aviation Corporation. All the private companies are small and serve primarily the domestic market. Sempati has only recently entered scheduled operations, having been a charter flight operator since 1968; this change coincides with a change in ownership from that of a wholly army company to being 40 per cent owned by Tri Usaha Bakti (the army company), 35 per cent by the Nusamba group and 25 per cent by Humpass. Its excellent political connections with the president and one of his sons have allowed it to flourish.

Private national airlines have been confined to serving domestic routes and international routes to immediately adjacent countries. The latter are termed 'border crossing' routes. For example, Merpati Nusantara Airlines serves the Kupang–Darwin route. Sempati Air has routes to Singapore and Malaysia, but when it wanted to start a service to Taipei it was refused and was offered instead the potentially far less lucrative route to Manila (*Jakarta Post*, 28 September 1991). A consequential strategy being pursued by the private airlines is to buy into other airlines serving overseas markets: an attempt to buy into Quantas was reported to be taking place with the negotiating assistance ironically provided by the state-owned airline, Garuda (*Jakarta Post*, 30 September 1991).

Rationalisation is taking place between Garuda and its subsidiary Merpati: their operations were reported to be fully integrated by September 1989, and it is expected that during 1992 Garuda will relinquish most of its remaining domestic routes. A further consequence of this rationalisation has been that Garuda has cast off a number of jets to Merpati. This led to some deregulation of air transport in July 1990 (*Jakarta Post*, 18 July 1990). Until that date, the smaller state-owned and private airlines plying domestic and some regional routes were prevented from operating jet aircraft or acquiring foreign-made planes. The policy had been adopted to protect the state-owned domestic aircraft manufacturer IPTN, but its range of aircraft was limited to a few small types and its output had lagged behind demand (EIU, 1989). So, now, private airlines are permitted to procure and operate jets on flights of more than two hours duration.

Fares remain partially controlled by government. Under present regulations, economy-class passenger fares are set by government for all operators, but companies are free to set their own fares for business- and first-class fares. This means fare changes are hesitant, but in practice discount markets operate to undermine the regulation and package deals are promoted.

All airport construction and operation, air traffic control, and navigation services are a public responsibility. This responsibility is diffuse with two public corporations Perum Angkasa Pura I & II responsible for the main civilian airports like Soekarno-Hatta (Jakarta), Ngurah Rai (Bali), Medan, Surabaya, Balikpapan and Ujung Pandang. Joint military and civilian airports like Halim are under the control of the armed forces. Other airports and airstrips are managed directly by the Directorate-General of Air Communications. This directorate sets all airport tariffs, which pay little regard to cost recovery. Hence most airports are run at a loss, sometimes with revenues not even covering operating and maintenance costs. Therefore airports are financially unattractive to the private sector, given the regulatory regime, and pose institutional constraints to their deregulation. The only involvement of the private sector is through concessions for shops and catering. Perum Angkasa Pura I & II are being encouraged to increase their revenues from concessions and advertising, but, as with the railways, commercial principles do not figure prominently in airport management.

15.9 Conclusions

The main motive for moving towards greater private sector involvement in transport sector investments has been to supplement the limited investment resources of the government itself and the government's ability to raise revenue. The propagation of a particular political philosophy has been far less a motive, though there are seen to be the additional benefits of furthering the process of democratisation of the economy and that of gaining more equitable distribution of growth.

The approach adopted in Indonesia has been mostly gradualist, though an occasional sudden change in policy has been announced. The extent to which private sector involvement or deregulation has been achieved is very variable across the transport subsectors. Deregulation is fully implemented in interisland shipping, joint ventures are the norm in toll road and port developments, but the railways and airports have seen few initiatives by the private sector or measures to reduce the impact of their regulatory environment.

Private sector involvement has always been introduced to new investments rather than to ongoing enterprises. Hence in its strictest sense of meaning a transfer of assets from public to private ownership, privatisation has not occurred. The pattern adopted most commonly has been incorporation of a private firm, usually a conglomerate, into a joint venture with a commercially run public sector body.

To date there are very few examples of transport activities where the government has completely removed all regulations; in most cases a guiding hand remains and this raises political uncertainty for private investors.

The sums of money involved are frequently huge. This has meant that only the largest Indonesian conglomerates have been able to become investors in transport developments. Only companies having connections with the social and economic elite of the country have entered the largest projects. Two interpretations may be placed on this. It could be that deregulation is being promoted because firms with such connections see it as being very much in their own interests of amassing greater wealth. Alternatively, such connections may be seen as a requirement to offset the political risks of such large investments and the residual regulatory roles of government such as in setting tariffs. So far the involvement of foreign private investors has lagged behind that of domestic groups.

The position will continue to evolve, but the momentum for deregulation within the transport sector has been generated. There are many forces within the public bureaucracies that will seek to dissipate that momentum.

References

Biro Pusat Statistik (1991a), *Statistik Kendaraan Bermotor dan Panjang Jalan 1989*, Jakarta: Biro Pusat Statistik.

Biro Pusat Statistik (1991b), *Statistik Angkutan Kereta Api 1989*, Jakarta: Biro Pusat Statistik.
Dick, H. W. (1987), *The Indonesian Interisland Shipping Industry: An analysis of competition and regulation*, Singapore: Institute of Southeast Asian Studies.
Directorate General of Sea Communications (1979), *Decrees*, 21 July, Jakarta: Ministry of Transport.
Economist Intelligence Unit (1989), *Indonesia*, EIU Country Profile 1988–89, London: Economist Intelligence Unit.
Economist Intelligence Unit (1990a), *Indonesia*, EIU Country Report No. 4, London: Economist Intelligence Unit.
Economist Intelligence Unit (1990b), *Indonesia*, EIU Country Report No. 3, London: Economist Intelligence Unit.
Economist Intelligence Unit (1991), *Indonesia*, EIU Country Profile 1990–91, London: Economist Intelligence Unit.
Gupta, D. P. (1989), 'Privatisation in the highway sector', *Journal of Indian Roads Congress*, **590** (3), 599–614.
Jasa Marga (*c*.1988a), *Laporan Tahunan* (*Annual Report 1987*), Jakarta: Jasa Marga.
Jasa Marga (*c*.1988b), *Investment Opportunities: Toll-roads in Indonesia*, Jakarta: Jasa Marga.
Levy, H. and A. Menendez (1990), 'Privatisation in transport: contracting out the provision of passenger railway services in Thailand', EDI Working Paper, Washington, DC: World Bank.
Ministry of Communications (1991), 'Assessment of existing land/transport development practice in Indonesia', Working Paper No. 4, Studies of Land and Public Transport Development in Jabotabek, Directorate General of Land Transport and Inland Waterways. Joint venture of JARTS/PCI in association with PT Intermatrix Bina Indonesia and PT Winapa Consultant.
Rimmer, P. J. (1990), 'Restructuring transport parastatals: case studies from South-East Asia', in P. Bell and P. Cloke (eds), *Deregulation and Transport: Market forces in the modernised world*, London: David Fulton.

Bibliography

Adam, C., W. Cavendish and P. S. Mistry (1992) *Adjusting Privatization: Case studies from developing countries*, London: Currey.
Akerlof, G. A., A. K. Rose, J. L. Yellen and H. Hessenius (1991), 'East Germany in from the cold: the economic aftermath of currency union', *Brookings Papers on Economic Activity*, **1**.
Alexander, M. (1986), 'L'Appui de la Banque Mondiale à la réforme des entreprises publiques en Afrique de l'Ouest', mimeo, World Bank.
Alexander, M. (1989), 'Privatisation in Africa', in V. V. Ramanadham (ed.), *Privatisation in Developing Countries*, London: Routledge.
Amsden, A. (1989), *Asia's Next Giant: South Korea and late industrialization*, New York: Oxford University Press.
Applebaum, A. (1992), 'Econophobia', *The Washington Post*, Washington, DC, 16 February 1992, C1–2.
Asian Development Bank (1985), *Privatization: Policies, methods and procedures*, Manila: ADB.
Babai, D. (1988), 'The World Bank and the IMF: rolling back the state or backing its role', in R. Vernon (ed.), *The Promise of Privatization: A challenge for US policy*, New York: Council on Foreign Relations.
Bacha, E. (1992), 'Comments', in V. Corbo, S. Fisher and S. Webb (eds), *Adjustment Lending Revisited: Policies to restore growth*, Washington, DC: World Bank.
Baklanoff, E. N. (1978), *The Economic Transformation of Spain and Portugal*, London: Praeger.
Banco de Mexico (1990), *The Mexican Economy, 1990*, Mexico DF: Banco de Mexico.
Banco de Portugal (annual), *Relatório do Conselho de Administração*, Lisboa: Banco de Portugal.
Bardhan, P. (1991), 'Risktaking, capital markets, and market socialism', paper presented to Conference on Perspectives on Market Socialism, University of California: Berkeley, Calif., 16–19 May.
Barzel, Y. (1989), *Economic Analysis of Property Rights*, Cambridge: Cambridge University Press.
Baum, D. (1989), 'The wayward siblings,' *Africa Report*, **34**, Jan.–Feb.
Benjamin, N. C. (1992), 'What happens to investment under structural adjustment: results from a simulation model', *World Development*, **20** (9).

Bennett, A. (1993), 'Regulatory framework for privatised monopolies', in *Methods and Practices of Privatisation*, UN Department for Development Support and Management Services. New York: UN.

Berg, E. and M. M. Shirley (1988), 'Divestiture in developing countries', Discussion Paper No. 11, Washington, DC: World Bank.

Bhaskar, V. (1992), 'Privatization and the developing countries: the issues and the evidence', Discussion Paper No. 47, Geneva: UNCTAD.

Biro Pusat Statistik (1991), *Statistik Kendaraan Bermotor dan Panjang Jalan 1989*, Jakarta: Biro Pusat Statistik.

Biro Pusat Statistik (1991), *Statistik Angkutan Kereta Api 1989*, Jakarta: Biro Pusat Statistik.

Bishop, M. R. and J. A. Kay (1989), 'Privatisation in the United Kingdom: lessons from experience', *World Development*, **17** (5).

Blanchard, O., R. Dornbusch, P. Krugman, R. Layard and L. Summers (1991), *Reform in Eastern Europe*, Cambridge, Mass.: MIT Press.

Blejer, M. and M. Khan (1984), 'Government policy and private investment in developing countries', *IMF Staff Papers*, **31** (2).

Blommestein, H. J. and M. Marrese (1991), 'Creating conditions for the development of competitive markets in economies in transition', revised draft of the paper prepared for the Conference on the Transition to a Market Economy in Central and Eastern Europe, OECD's Centre for Co-operation with the European Economies in Transition and the World Bank, Paris, 29–30 November, 1990.

Blommestein, H. J., M. Marrese and S. Zecchini (1991), 'Centrally planned economies in transition: an introductory overview of selected issues and strategies', in H. Blommestein and M. Marrese, (eds), *Transformation of Planned Economies: Property rights reform and macroeconomic stability*, Paris: OECD.

Boardman, A. and A. Vining (1989), 'Ownership and performance in competitive environments: a comparison of the performance of private, mixed and state-owned enterprises', *Journal of Law and Economics*, **32**, April.

Bohn, J. A. Jr and D. H. Levey (1991), 'Models of capital market development', in J. C. Brada and M. P. Claudon (eds), *The Emerging Russian Bear: Integrating the Soviet Union in to the world economy*, New York: New York University Press.

Bollard, A. and D. Mayes (1991), 'Corporatisation and privatisation in New Zealand', a paper presented at a Conference on International Privatisation, NZ Institute of Economic Research, St Andrews, NZ, 12–14 September.

Bolton, D. (1985), *Nationalisation: A road to socialism?*, London: Zed Press.

Borensztein, E. (1991), 'Comments on David Lipton and Jeffrey Sachs, "Privatization in Eastern Europe: the case of Poland", Roman Frydman and Andrzej Rapaczynski, "Markets and institutions in large-scale privatization: an approach to economic and social transformation in Eastern Europe", and Manuel Hinds, "A note on the privatization of socialized enterprises in Poland"', in V. Corbo, F. Coricelli and J. Bossek (eds), *Reforming Central and Eastern European Countries: Initial results and challenges*, Washington, DC: World Bank.

Borensztein, E. and M. S. Kumar (1991), 'Proposals for privatization in Eastern Europe', *IMF Staff Papers*, **2**.

Bös, D. (1991), *Privatisation: A theoretical treatment*, Oxford: Oxford University Press.

Bös, D. (1992), 'Privatisation in East Germany', Fiscal Affairs Department, Washington, DC: IMF.

Bouin, O. and C.-A. Michalet (1991), *Rebalancing the Public and Private Sectors: Developing country experience*, Paris: Development Centre, OECD.

Brabant, J. M. van (1989), 'Economic policy aims and their implementation: summary', in *Economic Reforms in the European Centrally Planned Economies*, New York: published by Adeco, Geneva, for the United Nations.

Brabant, J. M. van (1990), *Remaking Eastern Europe: On the political economy of transition*, Dordrecht: Kluwer Academic Publishers.
Brabant, J. M. van (1991), *Integrating Eastern Europe into the International Economy: Convertibility through a payments union*, Dordrecht: Kluwer Academic Publishers.
Brabant, J. M. van (1991), 'Property rights reform, macroeconomic performance and welfare', in H. Blommestein and M. Marrese (eds), *Transformation of Planned Economies: Property rights reform and macroeconomic stability*, Paris: OECD.
Brabant, J. M. van (1991), 'Economies in transition and privatization: the case of Eastern Europe', in W. Andraansen and J. van den Broeck (eds), *Changing Economic Order*, Dordrecht: Kluwer Academic Publishers.
Brabant, J. M. van (1991), 'Divestment of state capital in Eastern Europe and the Soviet Union', in K. Poznanski (ed.), *Great Transformation in Reverse*, Denver, Colo.: Westview Press.
Brabant, J. M. van (1991), 'The role of governments in Eastern Europe: a discussion', in G. Bertsch and S. Elliot-Gower (eds), *The Impact of Governments on East–West Economic Relations*, London: Macmillan.
Brabant, J. M. van (1991), 'Privatisation in post-communist societies: a comment', *Communist Economies and Economic Transformation*, **4**.
Brabant, J. M. van (1992), 'Privatizing Eastern Europe: the role of markets and ownership during the transition, manuscript, New York.
Brabant, J. M. van (1992), 'Privatization in economies in transition: an economic framework', in H. Genberg (ed.), *Privatization in Eastern Europe*, Geneva: Center for Monetary and Banking Studies.
Brainard, L. (1991), 'Strategies for economic transformation in central and eastern Europe: role of financial market reform', in H. Blommestein and M. Marrese (eds), *Transformation of Planned Economies: Property rights reform and macroeconomic stability*, Paris: OECD.
Bruno, M. (1992), 'Stabilization and reform in Eastern Europe: a preliminary evaluation', Washington, DC: IMF, 31 January.
Callaghy, T. M. and E. J. Wilson III (1988), 'Africa: policy, reality or ritual?', in R. Vernon (ed.), *The Promise of Privatization: A challenge for US policy*, New York: Council on Foreign Relations.
Calvo, G. and J. A. Frenkel (1991), 'From centrally planned to market economy: the road from CPE to PCPE', *IMF Staff Papers*, **2**.
Calvo, G. and J. A. Frenkel (1991), 'Obstacles to transforming centrally-planned economies: the role of capital markets', Working Paper No. WP/91/66, Washington, DC: IMF.
Candoy-Sekse, R. and A. R. Palmer (1988), *Techniques of Privatization of State-Owned Enterprises*, vol. 3, *Inventory of Country Experience and Reference Materials*, Technical Paper No.90, Washington, DC: World Bank.
Carlin, W. and C. Mayer (1992), 'The Treuhandanstalt: privatization by state and market', paper presented at the NBER conference on Transition in Eastern Europe, Cambridge, Mass.: 26–9 February.
Casar, J., C. Marquez Padilla, S. Marvan, G. Rodriguez and J. Ros (1990), *La Organización Industrial en México*, Mexico DF: Siglo Veinteuno.
Chang, H.-J. and A. Singh (1992), 'Public enterprises in developing countries and economic efficiency', Discussion Paper No. 48, Geneva: UNCTAD.
Chavagneux, C. (forthcoming), *Ghana, une révolution de bon sens, ou l'Afro-optimisme en marche, Paris.*
Chavagneux, C. and L. J. Grégoire (1992), 'Ghana: a promising future', *African Markets*, January, translated from *Marchés Tropicaux et Méditerranéens*, No. 2406, December 1991.

Chhibber, A. and S. Fischer (eds) (1991), *Economic Reform in Sub-Saharan Africa: A World Bank symposium*, Washington, DC: World Bank.
Christiansen, R. E. (1989), 'Editor's introduction to "Privatisation"', special issue of *World Development*, **17** (5).
Collins, P. and F. Nixson (with B. Evers and N.-A. Stewart) (eds) (1991), *Management Development and Economic Restructuring in the Mongolian Peoples' Republic*, Management Development Programme, New York: UNDP.
Comisso, E. (1989), 'Property rights in focus', *Acta Oeconomica*, **4**.
Comisso, E. (1991), 'Property rights, liberalism, and the transition from "actually existing" socialism', *East European Politics and Societies*, **1**.
Commander, S. (1992), 'Inflation and the transition to a market economy: an overview', *The World Bank Economic Review*, **6** (1).
Commander, S. and T. Killick (1988), 'Privatisation in developing countries: a survey of the issues', in P. Cook and C. Kirkpatrick (eds), *Privatisation in Less Developed Countries*, Hemel Hempstead: Harvester Wheatsheaf.
Cook, P. (1994), 'Privatisation and private sector development: the case of Myanmar', *South East Asia Research*, **2**(2).
Cook, P. and C. Kirkpatrick (eds) (1988), *Privatisation in Less Developed Countries*, Hemel Hempstead: Harvester Wheatsheaf.
Cook, P. and C. Kirkpatrick (1988), 'Privatisation in less developed countries: an overview', in P. Cook and C. Kirkpatrick (eds), *Privatisation in Less Developed Countries*, Hemel Hempstead: Wheatsheaf Books.
Cook P. and C. Kirkpatrick (1994), 'Privatisation and enterprise reform in transitional economies: a comparison of European and Asian experience', paper presented to UK Academy of International Business Annual Conference, Manchester, March.
Cook, P. and C. Kirkpatrick (1995), 'Privatisation in transition economics: East and Central European experience', in F. Burton, M. Yamin and S. Young (eds). *International Business and Europe in Transition*, London: Macmillan.
Cook. P. and M. Minogue (1990), 'Waiting for privatization in developing countries: towards the integration of economic and non-economic explanations,' *Public Administration and Development*, **10** (4).
Corbett, J. and C. Mayer (1991), 'Financial reform in Eastern Europe: progress with the wrong model', *Oxford Review of Economic Policy*, **7** (4).
Corbo, V., S. Fischer and S. Webb (eds) (1992), *Adjustment Lending Revisited: Policies to restore growth*, Washington, DC: World Bank.
Coulson, A. (1982), *Tanzania: A political economy*, London: Oxford University Press.
Dahrendorf, R. (1990), *Reflections on the Revolution in Europe: In a letter intended to have been sent to a gentleman in Warsaw*, New York: Times Books.
de Marques, A. H. (1981), *História de Portugal*, 6th edn, Lisboa: Palas Editores.
de Marques, A. H. (1988), *Política Econômica e Desenvolvimento em Portugal (1926–1959)*, Lisboa: Livros Horizonte.
Dembinski, P. H. (1990), 'Alternative financial approaches to privatisation', paper prepared for Conference on Transition in Eastern Europe, OECD, Paris, 29–30 November.
Dembinski, P. H. (1991), 'Alternative financial approaches to privatization of post-communist economies', paper prepared for conference on Privatization in Eastern Europe, International Center for Monetary and Banking Studies, Geneva, 20–21 September.
de Sousa, A. (1989), 'Reconfiguração do sector empresarial de Estado: uma abordagem de planeamento interactiva', *Economia*, **13** (3).
Devine, P., N. Lee, R. Jones and W. Tyson (1986), *An Introduction to Industrial Economics*, London: Allen & Unwin.

de Vylder, S. and A. Fford (1988), *Vietnam: An economy in transition*, Stockholm: Swedish International Development Authority.

Dhanji, F. and B. Milanovic (1990), 'Privatization in East and Central Europe: objectives, constraints and models of divestiture', paper presented at the Conference on Privatization and Ownership Changes in East and Central Europe, World Bank, Washington, DC, 13–14 June.

Dhanji, F. and B. Milanovic (1990), 'Privatization in East and Central Europe', paper prepared for the Conference on the Transition to a Market Economy in Central and Eastern Europe, OECD and the World Bank, Paris, 28–30 November.

Dick, H. W. (1987), *The Indonesian Interisland Shipping Industry: An analysis of competition and regulation*, Singapore: Institute of Southeast Asian Studies.

Directorate General of Sea Communications (1979), *Decrees*, 21 July, Jakarta: Ministry of Transport.

Djondo, K. (1988), 'Anatomy of a privatisation scheme: the Togo example', *African Business*, **114**, February.

Dornbusch, R. (1991), 'Comments and discussion', *Brookings Papers on Economic Activity*, **1**.

Dornbusch, R., R. S. Eckaus and L. Taylor (1979), 'Analysis and projection of macroeconomic conditions in Portugal', in L. S. Graham and H. M. Makler (eds), *Contemporary Portugal*.

Economist Intelligence Unit (1989), *Indonesia*, EIU Country Profile 1988–89, London: Economist Intelligence Unit.

Economist Intelligence Unit (1990), *Indonesia*, EIU Country Report No. 4, London: Economist Intelligence Unit.

Economist Intelligence Unit (1990), *Indonesia*, EIU Country Profile No. 3, London: Economist Intelligence Unit.

Economist Intelligence Unit (1991), *Indonesia*, EIU Country Profile 1990–91, London: Economist Intelligence Unit

Economist Intelligence Unit (1992), *Portugal 1991–92*, EIU Country Profile, London: Economist Intelligence Unit.

Elbadawi, I. (1992), 'Have World-Bank-supported adjustment programs improved economic performance in sub-Saharan Africa?', Policy Research Working Paper No. WPS 1001, Washington, DC: World Bank, October.

Elbadawi, I., D. Ghura and G. Uwujaren (1992), 'World Bank adjustment lending and economic performance in sub-Saharan Africa in the 1980s', Policy Research Working Paper No. WPS 1000, Washington, DC: World Bank.

Eliasson, G. (1991), 'The micro frustrations of privatizing Eastern Europe', paper prepared for Conference on Privatization in Eastern Europe, International Center for Monetary and Banking Studies, Geneva, 20–21 September.

Esseks, J. D. (1971), 'Government and indigenous private enterprise in Ghana', *Journal of Modern African Studies*, **9**, March.

Estrin, S. (1991), 'Some reflections on self-management, social choice, and reform in Eastern Europe', *Journal of Comparative Economics*, **2**.

European Bank for Reconstruction and Development (1993), *Annual Economic Outlook*, September, London: EBRD.

European Communities (1988), *The Public Enterprise in Portugal and Spain*, Brussels: EC Commission.

Falola, T. and J. Ihonubere (1985), *The Rise and Fall of Nigeria's Second Republic*, London: Zed Press..

Fanelli, J. M., R. Frenkel and G. Rozenwurcel (1992), 'Trade reform and growth resumption in Latin America', in J. M. Fontaine (ed.), *Foreign Trade Reforms and Development Strategy*, London: Routledge.

Fanelli, J. M., R. Frenkel and L. Taylor (1992), 'The World Development Report 1991:

a critical assessment', in *International Monetary and Financial Issues in the 90s*, vol. 1, Geneva: UNCTAD.

Feige, E. L. (1990), 'Perestroika and socialist privatization: what is to be done? and how?', *Comparative Economic Studies*, **3**.

Feige, E. L. (1990), 'Socialist privatization: response', *Comparative Economic Studies*, **3**.

Fershtman, C. (1990), 'The interdependence between ownership and market structure: the case of privatization', *Economica*, **3**.

Fford, A. (1989), 'The Socialist Republic of Vietnam since mid-1988: major policy changes and socio-economic developments', mimeo, report for SIDA, Hanoi, December.

First, R. (1970), *The Barrel of a Gun: Political power in Africa and the coup d'état*, Harmondsworth: Penguin.

Fischer, S. (1991), 'Privatization in East European transformation', Working Paper No. 3703, Cambridge, Mass.: NBER, May.

Flassbeck, H., G. Horn, W. Scheremet and R. Zwierer (1991), 'Subventionerung und Privatisierung durch die Treuhandanstalt: Kurswechsel erforderlich', *DIW Wochenbericht*, **41**.

Fontaine, J. M. (1992), 'Bias overkill? Removal of anti-export bias and manufacturing investment: Ghana 1983–89', in R. Adhikari, C. Kirkpatrick and J. Weiss (eds), *Industrial and Trade Policy Reforms in Developing Countries*, Manchester: Manchester University Press.

Fontaine, J. M. (1993), 'Reforming public enterprises and the public sector in sub-Saharan Africa', Discussion Paper No. 60, Geneva: UNCTAD.

Frischtak, C. (1989), 'Competition policies for industrializing countries', mimeo, Washington, DC: World Bank.

Frischtak, C., B. Hadjimichale and V. Zachau (1989), 'Competition policies for industrializing countries', Policy Planning and Research Paper No. 1, Washington, DC: World Bank.

Frydman, R. and A. Rapaczynski (1991), 'Markets and institutions in large-scale privatization: an approach to economic and social transformation in Eastern Europe', in V. Corbo, F. Coricelli and J. Bossek (eds), *Reforming Central and Eastern European Countries: Initial results and challenges*, Washington, DC: World Bank.

Frydman R. and A. Rapaczynski (1993), 'Privatisation in Eastern Europe: is the State withering away?', *Finance and Development* **30** (2).

Furubotn, E. G. and S. Pejovich (1972), 'Property rights and economic theory: a survey of recent literature', *The Journal of Economic Literature*, **2**.

Galal, A. (1991), 'Public enterprise reform', Discussion Paper No. 1119, Washington, DC: World Bank.

Galal, A., L. Jones, P. Tandon and I. Vogelsang (1992), 'Welfare consequences of selling public enterprises', Country Economics Department, Washington, DC: World Bank.

Garton, Ash, T. (1989), *The Uses of Adversity: On the fate of Central Europe*, New York: Random House.

Garton Ash, T. (1990), *We the People: The revolution of 89 witnessed in Warsaw, Budapest, Berlin & Prague*, Cambridge: Granta in association with Penguin Books.

Geourjon, A. M. (1992), 'Import liberalisation and the new industrial policy in Senegal', in J. M. Fontaine (ed.), *Foreign Trade Reforms and Development Strategy*, London: Routledge.

Geronimi V., S. Quiers Valette and E. Saint-Alary (1993), 'Les investissements directs étrangers en Afrique sub-Saharienne: du risque à l'incertitude', LAREA/CERED Working Paper, Nanterre Paris X University; forthcoming in P. Hugon, G. Pourcet and S. Quiers Valette (eds), *L'Afrique des Incertitudes*, Paris.

Gersovitz, M. and J. Waterbury (eds), *The Political Economy of Risk and Choice in Senegal*, London: Frank Cass.

Goldberg, V. P. (1974), 'Public choice: property rights', *Journal of Economic Issues*, **3**.

Gomez, E. T. (1990), *Politics in Business: UMNO's Corporate Investments*, Kuala Lumpur: Forum.

Gomez, E. T. (1991), *Money Politics in the Barisan Nasional*, Kuala Lumpur: Forum.

Gorbachov, M. (1987), *Perestroika*, London: Collins.

Graham, L. S. and H. M. Makler (eds) (1979), *Contemporary Portugal: The revolution and its antecedents*, Austin: University of Texas Press.

Gray, C. S. (1991), 'Antitrust as a component of policy reform: what relevance for economic development?', in D. Perkins and M. Roemer (eds), *Reforming Economic Systems in Developing Countries*, Boston: Harvard University Press.

Greenberg, S. (1991), 'Prague ministers are at odds over privatisation pace', *Guardian*, London, 16 November.

Greene, J. and D. Villanueva (1991), 'Private investment in developing countries: an empirical analysis', *IMF Staff Papers*, **38** (1).

Grindle, M. and J. Thomas (1991), *Public Choices and Policy Change: The political economy of reform in developing countries*, Baltimore: Johns Hopkins University Press.

Grosfeld, I. (1991), 'Privatization of state enterprises in Eastern Europe: the search for a market environment', *East European Politics and Societies*, **2**.

Grosh, B. (1992), *Public Enterprises in Kenya*, London: Lynn Reinner.

Gruszecki, T. and J. Winiecki (1991), 'Privatization in East-Central Europe: a comparative perspective', *Außenwirtschaft*, **46** (1).

Guillaumont, P., S. Guillaumont and P. Plane (1991), 'Comparison de l'efficacité des politiques d'ajustement structurel en Afrique, zone-franc et hors-zone franc', Notes et Etudes No. 41, Paris: Caisse Centrale de Coopération Économique.

Guitian, M. (1991), 'Comments and discussion', *Brookings Papers on Economic Activity*, **1**.

Gultekin, B. (1989), 'Privatisation of USAS in PPF', *Restructuring Journal* (Yeniden Yapilanma), Public Participation Fund, 1 October.

Gupta, D. P. (1989), 'Privatisation in the highway sector', *Journal of Indian Roads Congress*, **590** (3).

Hacienda (1991), *El Nuevo Perfil de la Economía Mexicana*, Mexico DF: Ministry of Finance.

Haile-Mariam, Y. and B. Mengistu (1988), 'Public enterprises and the privatisation thesis in the Third World', *Third World Quarterly*, **10**, October.

Hanke, S. (ed) (1987), *Privatization and Development*, San Francisco: Institute for Contemporary Studies.

Hankiss, E. (1990), *East European Alternatives*, Oxford: Clarendon Press.

Hare, P. G. (1991), 'The assessment: microeconomics of transition in Eastern Europe', *Oxford Review of Economic Policy*, **7** (4).

Hare, P. (1993), 'Privatisation in comparative perspective: an overview of the emerging issues', paper prepared for Workshop on Economic Transformation in Central and Eastern Europe, WZB, Berlin, May.

Hare, P. and I. Grosfeld (1991), 'Privatization in Hungary, Poland and Czechoslovakia', CEPR Discussion Paper No. 544, London: Centre for Economic Policy Research.

Härtel, H. H. *et al.* (1992), 'Unternehmenssanierung und Wettbewerb in den neuen Bundesländern', HWWA Report No. 103, Hamburg.

Härtel, H. H. *et al.* (1992), 'Der Einfluß nationaler und europäischer Institutionen auf den Wettbewerb in den neuen Bundesländern', HWWA Report No. 100, Hamburg.

Hartley, K. and A. F. Ott (eds) (1991), *Privatization and Economic Efficiency*, Aldershot: Edward Elgar.

Harvey, R. (1978), *Portugal: Birth of a democracy*, London: Macmillan.

Havel, V. (1989), *Interrogatoire à Distance: Entretien avec Karel Hvizd'ala*, Paris: Editions de l'Aube.

Havel, V. (1990), 'The future of Central Europe', *The New York Review of Books*, **5**.

Heald, D. (1990), 'The relevance of privatisation to developing countries', *Public Administration and Development*, **10**, (1).
Heald, D. (1992), 'How much privatisation should there be in developing countries?', *Annals of Public and Co-operative Economics*, **63** (2).
Hemming, R. (1992), 'Privatization of state enterprises', in V. Tanzi (ed.), *Fiscal Policies in Economies in Transition*, Washington, DC: IMF.
Hemming, R and A. M. Mansoor (1988), 'Is privatization the answer?', *Finance and Development*, **25**, September.
Hemming, R. and A. M. Mansoor (1988), 'Privatization and public enterprises', Occasional Paper No. 56, Washington, DC: IMF.
Hemming, R. and K. Miranda (1991), 'Privatization', in K. Chu and R. Hemming (eds), *Public Expenditure Handbook*, Washington, DC: IMF.
Heper, M. (1987), 'Recent developments towards privatisation of state economic enterprises in Turkey', mimeo, Manchester University.
Herrmann-Pillath, C. (1991), 'Systemic transformation as an economic problem', *Außenpolitik*, **2**.
Hinds, M. (1991), 'Issues in the introduction of market forces in Eastern European socialist economies', in S. Commander (ed.), *Managing Inflation in Socialist Economies in Transition*, Washington, DC: World Bank.
Hinds, M. (1991), 'A note on the privatization of socialized enterprises', in V. Corbo, F. Coricelli and J. Bossek (eds), *Reforming Central and Eastern European Countries: Initial results and challenges*, Washington, DC: World Bank.
Hume, I. and B. Pinto (1993), 'Prejudice and fact in Poland's industrial transformation', *Finance and Development*, **30** (2).
Hutchful, E. (ed) (1987), *The IMF and Ghana: The confidential record*, London: Zed Press.
IBRD (1983), *World Development Report 1983*, Washington, DC: World Bank.
Ickes, B. W. (1990), 'Obstacles to economic reform of socialism: an institutional-choice approach', *Annals of the American Academy of Political and Social Sciences*, **1**.
ILET–INEGI (1988), *Estadísticas Industriales*, Mexico DF: Instituto Nacional de Estadística Geografía e Informática.
IMF (1991), 'Ghana: adjustment and growth', mimeo, September.
IMF (1991), 'The Mongolian Peoples' Republic: toward a market economy', Occasional Paper No. 79, Washington, DC: IMF, April.
IMF (1993), *Economic Outlook*, Washington, DC: IMF, October.
ISO (Istanbul Chamber of Industry) (various dates), 'Turkey's 500 large industrial establishments', *Journal of the Istanbul Chamber of Industry*, various issues.
Israfil, C. (1987), 'The privatisation program in Turkey', *Turkish Review Quarterly Digest*, autumn.
Jasa Marga (*c.* 1988), *Laporan Tahunan* (*Annual Report 1987*), Jakarta: Jasa Marga.
Jasa Marga (*c.* 1988), *Investment Opportunities: Toll-roads in Indonesia*, Jakarta: Jasa Marga.
Jaycox, E. V. K. (1989), 'Structural adjustment in sub-Saharan Africa: the World Bank's perspective', *Issue*, **18** (1).
Jenkins, R. (1984), *Transnational Corporations and Industrial Transformation in Latin America*, London: Macmillan.
Jomo, K. S. (ed.) (1985), *The Sun Also Sets: Lessons in 'Looking East'*, 2nd edn, Kuala Lumpur: INSAN.
Jomo, K. S. (1986), *A Question of Class: Capital, the state and uneven development in Malaya*, Singapore: Oxford University Press.
Jomo, K. S. (1990), *Growth and Structural Change in the Malaysian Economy*, London: Macmillan.
Jomo, K. S. *et al.* (1989), *Mahathir's Economic Policies*, 2nd edn, Kuala Lumpur: INSAN.
Jones, L. P., P. Tandon and I. Vogelsang (1990), *Selling Public Enterprises*, Cambridge,

Mass.: MIT Press.
Jones, L. P., P. Tandon and I. Vogelsang (1991), 'Net benefits from privatization of public enterprises', in K. Hartley and A. F. Ott (eds), *Privatization and Economic Efficiency*, Aldershot: Edward Elgar.
Kagwe, S. (1987), 'Some organisational factors affecting the performance of public enterprises in Africa', in African Association for Public Administration and Management, *Public Enterprises Performance and the Privatization Debate: A review of options for Africa*, New Delhi: Vikas.
Kahama, G., T. L. Maliyamkono and G. Wells (1986), *The Challenge for Tanzania's Economy*, London: Currey and Heinemann.
Kanel, D. (1974), 'Property and economic power as issues in institutional economics', *Journal of Economic Issues*, **4**.
Karatas, C. (1990), 'Privatisation in Britain and Turkey', Istanbul Chamber of Industry, Research Department, November.
Karatas, C. (1992), 'Privatisation and regulation in Turkey: an assessment', *Journal of International Development*, **4**.
Keating, G. and J. Hoffman (1991), 'Privatisation theory: hold back for a swift advance', *Central European*, April.
Kemal, A. R. (1993), 'Retrenchment policies and labour shedding in Pakistan', Occasional Paper No. 17, Interdepartmental Project on Structural Adjustment, Geneva: ILO.
Kennedy, L. (1991), 'Liberalization, privatization and the politics of patronage in Malaysian telecommunications', paper presented at the 41st Annual Conference of the International Communications Association, Chicago, Ill., 24 May.
Kent, C. A. (1974), 'Privatization of public functions: promises and problems', in *idem* (ed.), *Entrepreneurship and the Privatizing of a Government*, New York: Quorum Books.
Khan, M. (1990), 'The macroeconomic effects of Fund-supported adjustment programs', *IMF Staff Papers*, **37** (2).
Khan, M. and C. Reinhart (1990), 'Private investment and economic growth in developing countries', *World Development*, **18** (1).
Kharas, H. J. (1991), 'Restructuring social industry: Poland's experience in 1990', World Bank Discussion Paper No. 142, Washington, DC: World Bank, December.
Killick, T. (1978), *Development Economics in Action: A study of economic policies in Ghana*, New York: St Martin's Press.
Killick, T. (1989), *A Reaction Too Far: Economic theory and the role of the state in developing countries*, London: ODI.
Killick, T. and S. Commander (1988), 'State divestiture as a policy instrument in developing countries', *World Development*, **16** (2).
Kirkpatrick, C. (1987), 'The UK privatisation experience: is it transferable to LDCs?', in V. V. Ramanadham (ed.), *Privatisation in the UK*, London: Routledge. Study No. 7, Oxford: Oxford Centre for Management Studies.
Kirkpatrick, C., N. Lee and F. Nixson (1984), *Industrial Structure and Policy in Less Developed Countries*, London: Allen & Unwin.
Kiss, J. (1992), 'All slaves to the past', *Guardian*, 21 February.
Kjellstrom, S. B. (1990), 'Privatisation in Turkey', *World Bank Working Papers*, Washington, DC: World Bank, November.
Kokalj, L. and W. Richter (1992), *Mittelstand und Mittelstandspolitik in den neuen Bundesländern: Privatisierung*, Stuttgart: Schaffer-Poeschel.
Konrad, G. (1984), *Antipolitics: An essay*, San Diego: Harcourt Brace Jovanovich.
Kopits, G. (1991), 'Fiscal reform in European economies in transition', Working Paper No. WP/91/43, Washington, DC: IMF, April.
Kornai, J. (1990), *The Road to a Free Economy – Shifting from a Socialist System: The*

example of Hungary, New York: Norton.

Kornai, J. (1990), *The Affinity between Ownership and Coordination Mechanisms: The common experience of reform in socialist countries*, Helsinki: World Institute for Development Economics Research.

Kornai, J. (1991), 'The principles of privatization in Eastern Europe', Harvard Institute of Economic Research Discussion Paper No. 1567, Cambridge, Mass.: Harvard University, September.

Kouassy, O. (1992), 'Etat et accumulation du capital en Afrique: les consquénces de la réforme du secteur public', unpublished Ph.D. thesis, Université Paris X, Nanterre.

Kupka, M. (1991), 'Transformation of ownership in Czechoslovakia', paper prepared for Conference on Privatization in Eastern Europe, International Center for Monetary and Banking Studies, Geneva, 20–21 September.

Lall, S. (1991), 'Explaining industrial success in the developing world', in V. N. Balasubramanyam and S. Lall (eds), *Current Issues in Development Economics*, London: Macmillan.

Landau, D. (1983), 'Government expenditure and economic growth: a cross-section study', *Southern Economic Journal*, **49** (3).

Lee, B. and J. Nellis (1990), 'Enterprise reform and privatization in socialist economies', World Bank Discussion Paper No. 104, Washington, DC: World Bank.

Leeds, R. (1989), 'Malaysia: genesis of a privatisation transaction', *World Development*, **17** (5).

Leenhardt, B. and M. F. L'Hériteau M.F. (1989), 'Situation macro économique et monétaire du Ghana', Notes et Etudes, No. 39, Paris: Caisse Centrale de Coopération Économique.

Leenhardt, B. and M. F. L'Hériteau (1991), 'Une décennie d'ajustement en Afrique: performances comparées de 28 pays africains, 1980–89', Notes et Etudes, No. 41, Paris: Caisse Centrale de Coopération Économique.

Leipold, H. (1983), 'Eigentumsrechte, Öffentlichkeitsgrad und Innovationsschwäche: Lehren aus dem Systemvergleich', in A. Schuller, H. Leipold and H. Hamel (eds), *Innovationsprobleme in Ost und West*, Stuttgart: Gustav Fischer Verlag.

Levy, B. and P. Spiller (1993), 'Regulation, institutions and commitment in telecommunications: a comparative analysis of five country studies', paper prepared for the Annual Conference on Development Economics, World Bank, Washington, DC, 3–4 May.

Levy, H. and A. Menendez (1990), 'Privatisation in transport: contracting out the provision of passenger railway services in Thailand', EDI Working Paper, Washington, DC: World Bank.

Lewis, J. P. (1987), 'Aid, structural adjustment, and Senegalese agriculture', in M. Gersovitz and J. Waterbury (eds), *The Political Economy of Risk and Choice in Senegal*, London: Frank Cass.

Lindblom, C. E. (1977), *Politics and Markets: The world's political-economic systems*, New York: Basic Books.

Lipton, D. and J. Sachs (1990), 'Privatization in Eastern Europe: the case of Poland', *Brookings Papers on Economic Activity*, **2**.

Lipton, D. and J. Sachs (1990), 'Creating a market economy in Eastern Europe: the case of Poland', *Brookings Papers on Economic Activity*, **1**.

Lipton, D. and J. Sachs (1991), 'Privatization in Eastern Europe: the case of Poland', in V. Corbo, F. Coricelli and J. Bossek (eds), *Reforming Central and Eastern European Countries: Initial results and challenges*, Washington, DC: World Bank.

Livermore, H. V. (1976), *A New History of Portugal*, Cambridge: Cambridge University Press.

MacArthur, J. D. (1988), *Appraisal of Projects in Developing Countries*, for H.M. Government, Overseas Development Administration, London: HMSO.

McKinnon, R. I. (1991), *The Order of Economic Liberalization*, Baltimore, Md.: Johns Hopkins University Press.
Madzar, L. (1990), 'The price of the turnaround', *Communist Economies*, **2**.
Mahathir, M. (1970), *The Malay Dilemma*, Singapore: Donald Moore.
Mahathir, M. (1976), *Menghadapi Cabaran*, Kuala Lumpur: Penerbit Utusan Melayu.
Mahathir M. (1991), *The Way Forward*, Kuala Lumpur: ISIS.
Malaysia (1985), *Guidelines on Privatisation*, Kuala Lumpur: Economic Planning Unit.
Malaysia (1991), *Privatisation Masterplan*, Kuala Lumpur: Economic Planning Unit.
Malaysia (1991), *The Second Outline Perspective Plan, 1991–2000*, Kuala Lumpur: Economic Planning Unit.
Malaysia (1991), *Sixth Malaysia Plan, 1991–1995*, Kuala Lumpur: Economic Planning Unit.
Mansoor, A. (1988), 'The fiscal impact of privatisation', in P. Cook and C. Kirkpatrick (eds), *Privatisation in Less Developed Countries*, Hemel Hempstead: Harvester Wheatsheaf.
Marsden, K. (1987), 'Private enterprise in Africa: creating a better environment', Discussion Paper No. 17, Washington, DC: World Bank.
Maurer, R., B. Sander and K.-D. Schmidt (1991), 'Privatisierung in Ostdeutschland – Zur Arbeit der Treuhandanstalt', *Weltwirtschaft*, **1**.
Mayhew, K. and P. Seabright (1993), 'Incentives and the management of enterprises in economic transition: capital markets are not enough', *Oxford Review of Economic Policy*, **8** (1).
Megginson, W. L., R. C. Nash and M. van Randenborgh (1993), 'The financial and operating performance of newly-privatized firms: an international empirical analysis', mimeo, University of Georgia; forthcoming, *Journal of Finance*, forthcoming.
Meller, P. (1992), 'Latin American adjustment and economic reforms: issues on recent experience', Discussion Paper No. 53, Geneva: UNCTAD, December.
Mello, A. and L. de Diogo (1987), mimeo, 'Política Econômica para as Privatizações em Portugal', Lisboa.
Milanovic, B. (1989), *Liberalization and Entrepreneurship*, New York: Sharpe.
Milanovic, B. (1991), 'Privatisation in post-communist societies', *Communist Economies and Economic Transformation*, **1**.
Millward, R. (1988), 'The comparative performance of public and private ownership', in J. Kay, C. Mayer and D. Thompson (eds), *Privatisation and Regulation: The UK experience*, London: Clarendon Press.
Millward, R. (1988), 'Measured sources of inefficiency in the performance of private and public enterprises in LDCs', in P. Cook and C. Kirkpatrick (eds), *Privatisation in Less Developed Countries*, Hemel Hempstead: Harvester Wheatsheaf.
Ministry of Communications (1991), 'Assessment of existing land/transport development practice in Indonesia', Working Paper No. 4, Studies of Land and Public Transport Development in Jabotabek, Directorate General of Land Transport and Inland Waterways. Joint venture of JARTS/PCI in association with PT Intermatrix Bina Indonesia and PT Winapa Consultant.
Ministry of Finance (CSFR) (1991), *Kupónová Privatizace* (Voucher Privatisation), Information booklet, Prague: Ministry of Finance.
Ministry of Privatization (Poland) (1991), *Guide to Foreign Investment in Poland*, Ministry of Privatization: Warsaw, Sept.–Dec.
Mitra, P. (1986), 'Adjustments to external shocks in selected semi-industrial countries', in G. Szego (ed.), *Studies in Banking and Finance*, Amsterdam: North Holland.
Mongolian Peoples' Republic (1991), 'Mongolia's economic situation: the government's reform programme and the role for external aid', mimeo, Donor Consultation Meeting, Ulaanbaatar, 9–10 October.
Morgan Guaranty Bank (1986), *Privatisation Master Plan: SEEs recommended for sale,*

action plans, Ankara: Morgan Guaranty Bank.
Morrison, R.J. (1981), *Portugal: Revolutionary change in an open economy*, Boston, Mass.: Auburn House Publishing.
Mosley, P. (1988), 'Privatisation, policy-based lending and World Bank behaviour', in P. Cook and C. Kirkpatrick (eds), *Privatisation in Less Developed Countries*, Hemel Hempstead: Harvester Wheatsheaf.
Mosley, P., J. Harrigan and J. Toye (1991), *Aid and Power*, 2 vols, London: Routledge.
Munzer, S. R. (1990), *A Theory of Property*, Cambridge: Cambridge University Press.
Murrell, P. (1990), '"Big bang" versus evolution: East European economic reforms in the light of recent economic history', PlanEcon Report, No. 26.
Murteira, M. (1975), 'Portugal: O problema da independência econômica', *Análise Social* (Lisboa), No. 44.
Murteira, M. (1979) 'The present economic situation: its origins and prospects', in L. S. Graham and H. M. Makler (eds), *Contemporary Portugal*.
Mustapha Johan, A. and K. A. Shamsulbahriah (eds) (1987), *Penswastaan: Kebajikan pekerja atau untung kapitalis*, Kuala Lumpur: MBPBK.
Myrdal, G. (1972), *Asian Drama*, London: Penguin Books (also Pelican edn 1977).
Nagy, A. (1991), '"Social choice" in Eastern Europe', *Journal of Comparative Economics*, **2**.
Nankani, H. (1988), *Techniques of Privatization of State-Owned Enterprises*, vol. 2, *Selected Country Case Studies*, Technical Paper No. 89, Washington, DC: World Bank.
Nankani, H. (1988), 'Malaysia', in *ibid.*, *Techniques of Privatization of State-owned Enterprises*, vol. 2, *Selected Country Case Studies*, Technical Paper No. 89, Washington, DC: World Bank.
Ndulu, B. (1991), 'Growth and adjustment in sub-Saharan Africa', in A. Chhibber and S. Fischer (eds), *Economic Reform in Sub-Saharan Africa: A World Bank symposium*, Washington, DC: World Bank.
Nellis, J. (1986), 'Public enterprises in sub-Saharan Africa', Discussion Paper No. 1, Washington, DC: World Bank.
Nellis, J. and S. Kikeri (1989), 'Public enterprise reform: privatization and the World Bank', *World Development*, **17**, May.
Newbery, D. M. (1991), 'Reform in Hungary: sequencing and privatisation', *European Economic Review*, **3**.
Ng, C. Y. and K. W. Toh (1992), 'Privatization in the Asian-Pacific region', *Asian-Pacific Economic Literature*, **6** (2).
Nixson, F. (1992), 'Economic reform and industrialisation in the Socialist Republic of Vietnam', in R. Adhikari, C. Kirkpatrick and J. Weiss (eds), *Industrial and Trade Policy Reform in Developing Countries*, Manchester: Manchester University Press.
Nixson, F. (1992), 'Economic reform in Asian socialist economies: a comparison of Vietnam, Mongolia and North Korea', mimeo, University of Manchester.
Nordhaus, W. D. (1990), 'Soviet economic reform: the longest road', *Brookings Papers on Economic Activity*, **1**.
North, D. C. (1989), 'Comments 2', in J. E. Stiglitz *et al.*, *The Economic Role of the State*, Oxford: Basil Blackwell in association with Bank Insinger de Beaufort.
North, D. C. (1990), *Institutions, Institutional Change and Economic Performance*, Cambridge: Cambridge University Press.
Nuti, D. M. (1991), 'Stabilization and sequencing in the reform of socialist economies', in S. Commander (ed.), *Managing Inflation in Socialist Economies in Transition*, Washington, DC: World Bank.
Nuti, D. M. (1991), 'Privatisation of socialist economies: general issues and the Polish case', in H. Blommestein and M. Marrese (eds), *Transformation of Planned Economies: Property rights reform and macroeconomic stability*, Paris: OECD.
Nyerere, J. (1968), *Freedom and Socialism*, London: Oxford University Press.

OECD (1992), *OECD Economic Surveys: Czech and Slovak Federal Republic, 1991*, Paris: OECD, January.

OECD (annual), *Economic Surveys: Portugal*, Paris: OECD.

Okokonko, I. C. (1986), 'Public vs. private investment in a mixed economy: an empirical investigation with Nigerian data', *Public Enterprise*, **7** (1).

Onis, Z. (1991), 'Privatisation and the logic of coalition building: a comparative analysis of state divestiture in Turkey and UK', mimeo, Bogazici University, Istanbul.

Oshikoya, T. W. (1992), 'Macroeconomic adjustment, uncertainty and private investment in Africa', Economic Research Paper No. 16, Abidjan: African Development Bank.

Ozmucur, S. and C. Karatas (1990), 'Total factor productivity in Turkish manufacturing, 1973–1988', *Journal of Economics and Administrative Studies*, **4** (2).

Pejovich, S. (1990), *The Economics of Property Rights: Towards a theory of comparative systems*, Dordrecht: Kluwer Academic Publishers.

Pfeffermann, G. P. and A. Madarassy (1993), 'Trends in private investment in developing countries, 1992 edition', International Finance Corporation, Discussion Paper No. 14, Washington, DC: World Bank.

Picot, A. and T. Kaufman (1989), 'Comparative performance of government-owned and privately-owned industrial corporations: empirical results from six countries', *Journal of Institutional and Theoretical Economics*, **145** (2).

Pinheiro, A. C. and B. R. Schneider (1994), 'The fiscal impact of privatisation in Latin America', mimeo, Federal University of Rio de Janeiro and Princeton University.

Pintado, C. (1984), *Economia portuguesa: Uma experiência, uma análise*, Lisboa, Caminho.

Pohl, G. (1991), 'Privatization in East Germany and Eastern Europe', paper prepared for Conference on Privatization in Eastern Europe, International Center for Monetary and Banking Studies, Geneva, 20–21 September.

Post, K. and P. Wright (1989), *Socialism and Underdevelopment*, London: Routledge.

Potts, D. J. (1991), 'Rehabilitation of export oriented estate agriculture in Tanzania', in C. Kirkpatrick (ed.), *Project Rehabilitation in Developing Countries*, London: Routledge.

Poznanski, K. (1991), 'Property rights perspective on changes in East European and Soviet economies', in *idem* (ed.), *Great Transformation in Reverse*, Denver, Colo.: Westview Press.

Poznanski, K. (1991), 'Privatization of the Polish economy: problems of transition' *Soviet Studies*, **44** (4).

PPF (Prime Ministry – Public Participation Authority) (1992), 'Bazbakanlik Kamu Ortakligi Idaresi Baskankligi Faaliyetleri, 1984–1992', Istanbul: Prime Ministry.

Prasnikar, J. and J. Svenjar (1991), 'Workers' participation in management vs. social ownership and government policies: Yugoslav lessons for transforming socialist economies', paper presented to the Conference on 'Perspectives on Market Socialism', Berkeley, Calif., 16–19 May.

Privatizações: Balanço e Reflexões Estratégicas (1991), seminar organised by the Research Centre for Financial Economics of ISEG with support from the Secretary of State for Finance.

Raikes, P. (1986), 'Eating the carrot and wielding the stick: the agricultural sector in Tanzania', in J. Boesen and K. J. Havnevik (eds), *Tanzania: Crisis and struggle for survival*, Uppsala: Scandinavian Institute of African Studies.

Ram, R. (1986), 'Government size and economic growth: a new framework and some evidence from cross-section and time-series data', *American Economic Review*, **76** (1).

Ramamurti, R. (1991), 'The search for remedies', in R. Ramamurti and R. Vernon (eds), *Privatisation and Control of State-owned Enterprises*, Washington, DC: World Bank.

Riddell, R. (ed.) (1990), *Manufacturing Africa: Performance and prospects of seven countries in sub-Saharan Africa*, London: Currey and Heinemann.

Rimmer, P. J. (1990), 'Restructuring transport parastatals: case studies from South-East Asia', in P. Bell and P. Cloke (eds), *Deregulation and Transport: Market forces in the modernised world*, London: David Fulton.

Rodan, G. (1989), *The Political Economy of Singapore's Industrialization*, London: Macmillan,

Rodriguez-Ulloa, R. A. (1990), 'Methodology to define Weltanschauungen', *Sistemica*, **1** (1), Lima: Instituto Andino de Sistemas.

Routh, G. (1989), *The Origin of Economic Ideas*, 2nd edn, London: Macmillan.

Ruthenberg, H. (1964), 'Agricultural development in Tanganyika', *IFO Afrika Studien*, No. 2, Munich: Springer Verlag.

Sachs, J. (1991), 'Privatization is top priority in Eastern Europe', *IMF Survey*, 27 May.

Sachs, J. (1991), 'Accelerating privatization in Eastern Europe', paper prepared for the World Bank Annual Conference on Development Economics 1991, World Bank, Washington, DC, 25–26 April.

Sachs, J. (1991), 'Crossing the valley of tears in East European reform', *Challenge*, Sept.–Oct.

Sader, F. (1993), 'The experience of privatization in the developing world: 1988–92', International Economics Department, WPS 1202, Washington, DC: World Bank, October.

Sadowski, Z. (1991), 'Privatization in Eastern Europe: goals, problems and implications', *Oxford Review of Economic Policy*, **7** (4).

Sandbrook, R. (1988), 'Patrimonialism and the failing of parastatals: Africa in comparative perspective', in P. Cook and C. Kirkpatrick (eds), *Privatisation in Less Developed Countries*, Hemel Hempstead: Harvester Wheatsheaf.

Sankar, T. I., M. B. G. Thak and S. S. T. Sal (1988), 'Relative profitability of public and private enterprises in India', paper from conference on Privatisation: Diversification of Ownership of Public Enterprises, Institute of Public Enterprises and London Business School, 22–23 January, Hyderabad.

Santos, A. (1989), 'Models of privatization and market structure', *Economia*, **13** (3).

Sarsel, M. (1992), 'How to privatise public enterprises in Turkey: alternative methods of valuation', MA dissertation, Bogazici University, Istanbul, 20 July.

Schroeder, G. E. (1988), 'Property rights issues in economic reforms in socialist countries', *Studies in Comparative Communism*, **2**.

Schwartz, G. (1991), 'Privatization: possible lessons from the Hungarian case', *World Development*, **19** (12).

Schwartz, G. and P. Lopes (1993), 'Privatization: expectation trade offs, and results', *Finance and Development*, **30** (2), June.

SEDES (Associação para o Desenvolvimento Econômico e Social) (1991), 'Privatizaçôes optar para o futuro', Lisbon: SEDES.

Serven, L. and A. Solimano (1992), 'Economic adjustment and investment performance in developing countries: the experience of the 1980s', in V. Corbo, S. Fischer and S. Webb (eds), *Adjustment Lending Revisited: Policies to restore growth*, Washington, DC: World Bank.

Sheriff, M. K. (1991), 'Privatization: performance, problems and prospects', in L. K. Hock and S. Nagaraj (eds), *The Malaysian Economy Beyond 1990*, Kuala Lumpur: Malaysian Economic Association.

Shirley, M. (1983), *Managing State-Owned Enterprises*, Washington, DC: IBRD.

Shirley, M. (1988), 'The experience with privatization', *Finance and Development*, **25**.

Shirley M. (1989), *The Reform of State-Owned Enterprises*, Policy and Research Series, Washington DC : World Bank .

Singer, H. W. and S. Roy (1993), *Economic Progress and Prospects in the Third World: Lessons of development experiences since 1945*, London: Edward Elgar.

Singh, A. (1990), 'The stock market in a socialist economy', in P. Nolan and D. Furen

(eds), *Economic Reform in Post-Mao China*, Cambridge: Polity Press.
Singh, A. (1992), 'The stock-market and economic development: should developing countries encourage stock markets?', Discussion Paper No. 49, Geneva: UNCTAD.
Sinn, G. and H. W. Sinn (1991), *Kaltstart: Volkswirtschaftliche Aspekte der deutschen Vereinigung*, Tübingen: Mohr (Siebeck). (*Jumpstart: The economic unification of Germany*, Cambridge: Mass.: MIT Press, 1992.)
Sklar, R. L. (1988), 'Beyond capitalism and socialism in Africa', *Journal of Modern African Studies*, **26**, March.
Song, D. (1993), 'Public enterprises in South Korea', paper presented to Third Asia Pacific Conference of Management, Brisbane, Australia, August.
Squire, L. and H. L. van der Tak (1975), *The Economic Analysis of Projects*, Washington, DC: Johns Hopkins for the World Bank.
State Property Agency (Hungary) (1991), *Privatization and Foreign Investment in Hungary*, Budapest: State Property Agency, March.
Stiglitz, J. E. (1991), 'Government, financial markets, and economic development', Working Paper No. 3669, Cambridge, Mass.: National Bureau of Economic Research, April.
Streeten, P. (1991), 'Markets and states', mimeo, Boston: Boston University.
Svejnar, J. (1991), 'Microeconomic issues in the transition to a market economy', *Journal of Economic Perspectives*, **5** (4).
Swanson, D. and T. Wolde-Semait (1989), 'Africa's public enterprise sector and evidence of reforms', Technical Paper No. 95, Washington, DC: World Bank.
Szalai, E. (1991), 'Integration of special interests in the Hungarian economy: the struggle between large companies and the Party and state bureaucracy', *Journal of Comparative Economics*, **2**.
Tangri, R. (1991), 'The politics of state divestiture in Ghana', *African Affairs*, **90**, October.
Tanoh, F. N. (1993), 'Structural adjustment in Africa: Ghana's experience in the 1980s', unpublished PhD thesis, University of Manchester.
Taylor, L. (1988), *Varieties of Stabilization Experiences: Towards sensible macroeconomics in the Third World*, Oxford: Clarendon Press
Ten Kate, A. and F. de Mateo (1989), 'Apertura comercial y estructura de la protección en México: estimaciones cuantitivas de los ochenta', *Comercio Exterior*, **39** (4).
Tomlinson, J. D. (1986), 'Ownership, organisation and efficiency', *The Royal Bank of Scotland Review*, **149**.
Toye, J. (1991), 'Ghana', in P. Mosley *et al.*, *Aid and Power*, vol. 2, ch. 14.
Ubeku, A. K., Chief (1990), 'Inability to manage: the bane of Nigeria', *The Bureaucrat*, **16** (1), Bendel State, Nigeria.
UNDP and World Bank (1989), *Adjustment and Growth in Sub-Saharan Countries in the 1980s*, Washington, DC: UNDP–World Bank.
UNECE (1991), *Economic Survey of Europe in 1990–1991*, Publication No. E91.II.1, New York: United Nations.
UNIDO (1986), 'Industry and external debt in Africa: a preliminary analysis', *Industry and Development*, **17**.
United Nations (1992), *World Investment Report, 1992*, Transnationals and Management Division, New York: UN.
United Nations Conference on Trade and Development (UNCTAD) (1993), 'Design, implementation and results of privatization programmes: a cross-country analysis of national experiences', Trade and Development Board, September.
United Nations Development Programme (1990), 'Report on the economy of Vietnam', report prepared for the Socialist Republic of Vietnam, State Planning Committee, Hanoi, December.
United Nations Industrial Development Organisation (1993), *Industry and Development*

Global Report, 1992–93, Vienna: UNIDO.
United Republic of Tanzania (1979), 'Annual review of the Tanzania sisal industry 1978', Dar es Salaam: Ministry of Agriculture, Marketing Development Bureau.
United Republic of Tanzania (1982), 'Structural adjustment programme', Dar es Salaam: Ministry of Economic Affairs and Planning.
United Republic of Tanzania (1983), 'Agricultural policy of Tanzania', Dar es Salaam: Ministry of Agriculture and Livestock Development.
United Republic of Tanzania (1984), 'Export crop packages: a framework for action', Dar es Salaam: Ministry of Agriculture and Livestock Development, Project Preparation and Monitoring Bureau.
UNWES (1988), *World Economic Survey 1988*, Publication No. E.88.IIC.1, New York: United Nations.
Utt, R. D. (1991), 'Privatization in the United States', in K. Hartley and A. F. Ott (eds), *Privatization and Economic Efficiency*, Aldershot: Edward Elgar.
Vickers, J. and V. Wright (1988), 'The politics of industrial privatization in Western Europe: an overview', *West European Politics*, **4**.
Vickers, J. and G. Yarrow (1988), *Privatization: An economic analysis*, Cambridge, Mass.: MIT Press.
Vickers, J. and G. Yarrow (1991), 'Economic perspectives on privatization', *Journal of Economic Perspectives*, **2**.
Vuylsteke, C. (1988), *Techniques of Privatization of State-Owned Enterprises*, vol. 1, *Methods and Implementation*, Technical Paper No. 88, Washington, DC: World Bank.
Vuylsteke, C. (1990), 'Privatization in emerging economies: constraints and practical responses', paper prepared for the Conference on Privatization and Ownership Changes in East and Central Europe, World Bank, Washington, DC, 13–14 June.
Wade, R. (1990), *Governing The Market: Economic theory and the role of government in East Asian industrialization*, Princeton, NJ: Princeton University Press.
Weiss, J. (1991), 'Impact of trade policy reform on industrial performance: Mexico country study', mimeo, report to Overseas Development Administration, ESCOR Committee, Bradford.
Weiss, J. (1992), 'Trade policy reform and performance in manufacturing Mexico: 1975–88', *Journal of Development Studies*, **29** (1).
Wellisz, C. (1991), 'Privatization in Poland: the problem of valuation', *Journal of International Affairs*, **465** (1).
Wellisz, S. (1991), 'Poland under "Solidarity" rule', *Journal of Economic Perspectives*, **5** (4).
Wiara, H. J. (1979), 'The corporatist tradition and the corporative system in Portugal: structure, evolving, transcended, persistent', in L. S. Graham and H. M. Makler, *Contemporary Portugal*, Austin: University of Texas Press.
Wilson III, E. J. (1984), 'Contested terrrain: a comparative and theoretical reassessment of state-owned enterprise in Africa', *Journal of Commonwealth and Comparative Politics*, **22**, March.
Wilson III, E. J. (1986), 'The public–private debate', *Africa Report*, **31**, July–Aug.
Wilson III, E. J. (1988), 'Privatization in Africa: domestic origins, current status and future scenarios', *Issue*, **16** (2).
Winiecki, J. (1991), *Resistance to Change in the Soviet Economic System: A property rights approach*, London: Routledge.
World Bank (1978), *Portugal: Current and Prospective Economic Trends*, Washington, DC: World Bank.
World Bank (1980), *Borrowing in International Capital Markets, 1979*, Washington, DC: World Bank.
World Bank (1983), *World Development Report*, Washington, DC: Oxford University

Press for the World Bank.
World Bank (1988), *Adjustment Lending: An evaluation of ten years of experience*, Policy & Research Series, No. 1, Washington, DC: World Bank.
World Bank (1989), *Sub-Saharan Africa from Crisis to Sustainable Growth*, Washington, DC: World Bank.
World Bank (1989), *The Reform of State Owned Enterprises: Lessons of World Bank lending*, Washington, DC: World Bank.
World Bank (1990), *Adjustment Lending: Policies for sustainable growth*, Policy & Research Series, No. 14, Washington, DC: World Bank.
World Bank (1991), *African Capacity Building Initiative*, Washington, DC: World Bank.
World Bank (1991), *Public Enterprise Reform: The lessons of experience*, EDI Development Studies, Washington, DC: World Bank.
World Bank (1991), 'Ghana: progress on adjustment', mimeo, April 16, Washington, DC: World Bank.
World Bank (1992), *Adjustment Lending and Mobilisation of Public and Private Resources for Growth*, Country Economics Department, Washington, DC: World Bank.
World Bank (1992), *Privatisation: The lessons of experience*, Country Economics Department, Washington, DC: World Bank.
World Bank (1993), *African Development Indicators*, 1992 issue, Washington, DC: World Bank.
World Bank (1993), *Global Economic Prospects and the Developing Countries, 1993*, Washington, DC: World Bank.
World Bank (1994), *Adjustment in Africa: Reforms, results and the road ahead*, World Bank Policy Research Report, Washington, DC: World Bank.
Yaffey, M. (1969), 'The effect of nationalisation on current external payments', ERB Paper No. 69.2, Economics Research Bureau, Dar es Salaam: University College.
Yaffey, M. (1975), 'Aspects of trade theory, with reference to Tanzanian experience', unpublished dissertation, University of Sussex.
Yarrow, G. (1986), 'Privatisation in theory and practice', *Economic Policy*, **2**.
Yarrow, G (1988), 'Privatisation and economic performance', *The Economic Review*, **6** (2), November
Yenal, O. (1990), 'Chinese reforms, inflation and the allocation of investment in a socialist economy', *World Development*, **18** (5), 1991.
Yeni Ekonomi (1990, 1991), July, August, September and other issues.
Yildirim, E. (1989), 'Total factor productivity growth in Turkish manufacturing industry between 1963–1983: an analysis', *METU Studies in Development*, **16** (3–4).
Young, P. (1988), *The Enterprise Imperative: Promoting growth in developing countries*, London: Adam Smith Institute.
Young, T. (1989), 'Restructuring the state in South Africa: new strategies of incorporation and control', *Political Studies*, **37**, March.
Zeckhauser, R. J. and M. Horn (1989), 'The control and performance of state-owned enterprises', in P. W. MacAvoy, W. T. Stanbury, G. Yarrow and R. J. Zeckhauser (eds), *Privatization and State-owned Enterprises: Lessons from the United States, Great Britain and Canada*, Dordrecht: Kluwer Academic Publishers.

Index

Note: Page numbers in italics indicate references in figures or tables only.